WILLIAM SAFFADY

Introduction
to
Automation
for
Librarians

FOURTH EDITION

AMERICAN LIBRARY ASSOCIATION
Chicago and London
1999

Project editor, Bradley Hannan

Cover and text design by Lesiak Design

Composition by the dotted i in Palatino and Helvetica Condensed using QuarkXPress 3.32 on a Macintosh G3

Printed on 50-pound white offset, a pH-neutral stock, and bound in 10-point cover stock by Data Reproductions

The paper used in this publication meets the minimum requirements of American National Standard for Information Sciences—Permanence of Paper for Printed Library Materials, ANSI Z39.48-1992. ∞

Library of Congress Cataloging-in-Publication Data

Saffady, William, 1944–
    Introduction to automation for librarians / William Saffady. — 4th ed.
        p.   cm.
    Includes bibliographical references and index.
    ISBN 0-8389-0764-4 (alk. paper)
    1. Libraries—United States—Automation.   2. Information technology—United States.   I. Title.
    Z678.9.A4U67   1999
    025'.00285—dc21   99-20936

03   02   01   00   99   5   4   3   2   1

Contents

Introduction

This book is intended for librarians, information specialists, library school students, and others who want a tutorial survey of those aspects of information technology that are most significant for library operations. Like its predecessors, this edition is divided into two parts, each consisting of four chapters.

Part 1 (chapters 1 through 4) discusses fundamental aspects of computing and related technologies, emphasizing terms and concepts that are essential for librarians who must communicate with data processing personnel, equipment vendors, software developers, telecommunications specialists, or others involved with the design and implementation of automated information systems.

• Chapter 1 provides a tutorial introduction to computer hardware. It has been completely updated to reflect recent developments and emerging trends in information processing equipment, including the proliferation of increasingly powerful microcomputers and the availability of high-capacity storage devices.

• Chapter 2 provides a tutorial treatment of computer software, emphasizing software development concepts and program characteristics. It includes an updated discussion of programming languages and prewritten software.

• Chapter 3 discusses various modes of data processing, including online computing and distributed processing. It also contains a survey of data communications terminology and concepts. The sections dealing with computer networks have been expanded and updated for this edition.

• Chapter 4 surveys recent developments and trends in automated office systems, including such non-computer technologies as micrographics, voice dictation, high-definition television, and facsimile transmission.

Part 2 (chapters 5 through 8) covers library automation concepts and discusses systems and services that automate specific library operations. Compared to previous editions, chapter topics and content have changed to reflect the latest developments in library automation.

• Chapter 5 discusses automated cataloging concepts and systems, including bibliographic utilities and CD-ROM cataloging support products.

• Chapter 6 deals with integrated library systems, modularized products that support online public access catalogs, circulation control, acquisitions, serials control, and other library operations.

• Chapter 7 discusses automated reference services, emphasizing online information services and CD-ROM reference databases.

• Chapter 8 deals with digital libraries, a rapidly emerging facet of library automation that provides online access to books, periodicals, and other library materials.

Throughout this book, specific products, systems, and services are discussed as examples of particular technologies or approaches to library automation. Mention of a particular product or service does not constitute endorsement, nor does the omission of a particular product imply lack of value in it.

Finally, this edition, like its predecessors, is a survey of technologies applicable to library operations. It intentionally omits some non-technological aspects of library automation—most notably, the interrelationship of automation and human resources and the implications of automated systems and services for staff development, utilization, and training. Readers interested in the personal, sociological, or cultural implications and consequences of information technology should consult the growing number of books and articles that deal with those subjects.

Fundamental Aspects of Computing and Related Technologies

1

Computer Hardware

A computer system consists of three major components: hardware, or equipment; software, or the programs that cause computers to perform specific operations; and data, or the information that hardware and software process, store, retrieve, or otherwise manipulate. From the hardware standpoint, a computer system may contain hundreds of thousands or millions of electronic components, the nature and functions of which need not be individually understood in order to effectively apply computers to library operations. For purposes of simplified description, a computer's hardware components are customarily divided into two broad groups:

1. The computer itself, variously called the central processor, the central processing unit, or simply the CPU; and

2. Peripheral devices, which are functionally associated with the central processor but are not a part of it.

Peripheral devices may, as their name suggests, be located around the central processor in a computer room or other installation site. If a given peripheral device is physically connected to a central processor—by a cable or wire, for example—it is said to be operating "online" to it. If a peripheral device is not so connected, it is described as "offline."

Most peripheral devices are designed to operate online. Information is transmitted electronically between computers and online peripherals. Offline operation is characteristic of some older peripheral devices, such as keypunch machines, that are now obsolete, although certain specialized offline peripherals, such as computerized typesetting devices and computer-output microfilm recorders, are operated by computer service bureaus. In such cases, the information to be processed by the offline peripheral must be physically transported to it. Offline peripherals play a limited but occasionally important role in library applications. Regardless of operating mode, the peripheral devices are designed to perform one or more of the specialized information processing tasks—input, output, and storage—discussed later in this chapter.

THE CENTRAL PROCESSOR

The term "computer" is widely and somewhat loosely used to denote a variety of information processing machines. The more descriptive phrases "central processor" or "central processing unit" better indicate the computer's role as the most important functional component in an information processing system. Paradoxically, the central processor is the hardware component that librarians need to know the least about. From the technical standpoint, computer operations are, and ought to be, transparent to the user; that is, the user should be aware of the purpose and results of particular operations rather than the manner in which the operations are performed.

In many library applications, such as searching subject-oriented databases offered by online information services or retrieval of cataloging records maintained by bibliographic utilities, the central processor is geographically remote from the user, who interacts with it through locally installed peripheral devices. In other cases, information such as a library's online catalog or a reference database resides on a computer that is located in an adjacent building or elsewhere on a college campus. Even when a computer is installed in the library itself or on a user's desk, detailed knowledge of the central processor's technical characteristics is unnecessary; librarians need to be able to apply computers, not build or repair them. Consequently, the discussion of central processors that follows is restricted to brief explanations of technical terms and concepts that are essential to an understanding of the application-oriented material presented in subsequent chapters. Emphasis is placed on the functional organization of the central processor, the characteristics of the computer industry, and the types and distinctive characteristics of computers encountered in library applications. Later sections of this chapter will describe the various types of peripheral devices and their significance for library operations.

Functional Components

In terms of its internal composition, or architecture, the typical central processor consists of three interrelated sections: a control section, an arithmetic/logic section, and a memory section. The first two sections, while important, are of limited interest to librarians. The control section, as its name implies, directs the operations of the other two sections, as well as the relationship of the central processor to its associated peripheral devices. A description of typical control tasks is presented in the discussion of operating systems in chapter 2.

The arithmetic/logic section contains the specialized electronic circuitry essential to computation. Computers were originally developed for scientific and technical applications requiring extensive mathematical calculations based on elaborate combinations of such simple arithmetic operations as addition, subtraction, multiplication, and division. Computers, however, are capable of more than mere calculation. Although scientific computing remains important, most computers today are used to process business information. Such applications are collectively described as electronic data processing (EDP) or, within U.S. government agencies, automated data processing (ADP). Their calculation requirements are often modest, but the central processor must perform repetitive logical operations involving the testing of specified conditions or the comparison of data. In most library-oriented information storage and retrieval applications, such logical operations are more important than arithmetic calculations.

The memory section provides storage for data and programs within the central processor itself. It is sometimes described as "main" or "primary" memory to distinguish it from the "auxiliary" or "secondary" storage peripherals and media described later in this chapter. Descriptive terminology aside, the memory section is reserved for programs and information that are being utilized by the central processor at a given moment; data and programs that will be used at some later time are relegated to the storage peripherals. Information stored in main memory is recorded in a specially coded form called "machine-readable" form. For purposes of this discussion, the terms "machine-readable" and "computer-processible" are synonymous. It should be noted, however, that the phrase "machine-readable" is applicable to other information technologies, such as audio and video systems, that also encode information for storage and retrieval. Thus, a videocassette contains machine-readable information. The machine that "reads" it is a videocassette recorder (VCR).

Machine-readable information is represented by a purposeful alteration of computer components—in this case, main memory circuits—in a manner that the central processor can detect. All modern computers use digital coding schemes to represent machine-readable information; analog computers, which were available in the 1960s, are now obsolete. The actual conversion of information to digitally coded form is accomplished by the input peripherals described later in this chapter. This section will describe the way in which information is stored in memory. To simplify the explanation, it is assumed that the information to be digitally coded consists of characters—that is, letters of the alphabet, numeric digits, punctuation marks, or other symbols that might be encountered in data or computer programs. A code is defined for each of the characters to be represented by a computer system. Although various coding schemes have been used since the inception of electronic information processing, most computer systems employ either the American Standard Code for Information Interchange—the so-called ASCII (pronounced "askey") code—or the Extended Binary Coded Decimal Interchange Code, typically abbreviated as EBCDIC. These codes are delineated in charts that use the symbols 1 and 0 to represent the code patterns for individual characters. This coding method is termed "binary" because it uses only two symbols to represent the various characters. Each symbol is termed a binary digit, or bit, and the accumulation of bits that encode a given character is called a byte. The number of bits per byte varies with the coding scheme employed. The EBCDIC code, for example, uses eight bits to represent each character, while the ASCII code uses seven. EBCDIC supports 256 different combinations of binary digits, which can encode 256 different characters. ASCII offers 128 binary combinations, but an extended version of the ASCII code, which uses eight bits per character, supports 256 combinations.

Regardless of the number of bits involved, the important equivalence is that between a byte and a character. The capacity of main memory, and of auxiliary storage media as well, is customarily measured in bytes. It is expressed as a number followed by an alphabetic abbreviation that denotes a specific quantity of bytes. The memory capacities of older computers were measured in kilobytes, abbreviated KB. A kilobyte is 1,024 bytes. A computer described as having 640KB of main memory could store 640 times 1,024 bytes or 655,360 characters. For convenience, the value of a KB is often rounded to 1,000, but that is technically incorrect.

Because the amount of available memory affects the types of programs a given computer system can use and the tasks it can effectively perform, main memory configurations have steadily expanded to meet the increasingly complex requirements of information processing applications. Main memories with kilobyte-level capacities are too small to run newer computer programs. Central processors with main memory capacities measured in millions of characters, or megabytes (MB), were once encountered only in the largest computer installations. Since the early 1990s, however, desktop computers have routinely supported megabyte-level memory capacities. (Technically, a megabyte equals 1,000 kilobytes or 1,000 times 1,024 bytes, but that amount is usually rounded down to a million.) Main memory capacities of larger computers are measured in billions of characters or gigabytes (GB). Future computers may have main memory capacities that are measured in trillions of characters or terabytes (TB). Gigabyte- and terabyte-level capacities are characteristic of certain auxiliary storage peripherals described later in this chapter.

With some older computers, memory sizes were occasionally measured in words. Today, however, the term "word" is used to describe a central processor's data manipulation capabilities. That usage bears no relationship to a word as a grammatical unit. As applied to computers, a word—also described as word size or word length—denotes the number of bits that can be processed—that is, retrieved from main memory or otherwise manipulated—in a single operation. Thus, a computer with an 8-bit word size can manipulate 8 bits, or one byte, of information at a time; a 16-bit computer can manipulate 16 bits of information at a time, and so on. Although 12-bit, 18-bit, and 24-bit word sizes have been employed by some computer systems, the word lengths of most central processors are fixed at a power of two. At the time of this writing, the most important word sizes were 32 bits and 64 bits. Older computers had smaller word sizes, but those devices have been discontinued. Word size has a direct impact on a computer's capabilities; other things being equal, the longer the word, the more powerful the central processor. Computers with longer word sizes can support greater amounts of main memory and a larger repertoire of program instructions.

The discussion to this point has focused on the concept of bits and bytes, and their symbolic representation by combinations of the binary digits 1 and 0. As previously noted, the actual storage of bits and bytes involves the physical alteration of memory components. Since the 1940s, computers have employed memory circuits that are capable of being altered in either of two ways for purposes of representing individual bits. The physical composition of main memory, however, has varied over time. Such variations are among the most important features that distinguish successive "generations" of computers.

In the earliest computers, for example, vacuum tubes were selectively turned on and off to represent the combinations of 1 and 0 bits that encode individual characters. The memory sections of central processors manufactured during the 1960s and 1970s consisted of small, circular-shaped metal cores that were capable of being magnetized in either of two directions. Individual characters were represented by the pattern of magnetization in a specified combination of cores. Through the mid-1980s, the phrase "core memory" was sometimes used as a synonym for main memory, but the memory sections of newer computers store information electronically rather than magnetically. They are composed of large numbers of highly miniaturized circuits that are consolidated or "integrated" on crystals or "chips" of semiconductor material.

Main memory circuits are typically categorized into two groups: random-access (RAM) and read-only memory (ROM). Random-access memory, the most widely encountered type of main memory circuit, is sometimes described as read/write memory. It is blank when purchased and blank when the computer that contains it is turned on. Random-access memory acquires its contents during a computer session. Information, in the form of data or programs, is entered into RAM circuits when required by the central processor. In many cases, the information is transferred from an auxiliary storage peripheral, such as a magnetic disk drive, on which it was previously recorded. Alternatively, it may be entered directly into random-access memory from keyboards or other input devices described later in this chapter. When their contents are no longer needed, RAM circuits are released for other uses.

The most common type of RAM circuit is termed Dynamic RAM (DRAM). It requires continuous rewriting or "refreshing" of its contents by the computer. This refreshing occurs many times per second. Static RAM (SRAM) circuits do not require refreshing and are faster than DRAM circuits, but they are more expensive and less compact. Consequently, they are used sparingly in computer configurations. As computers gain speed, however, memory circuits must keep up. In some cases, SRAM circuits are installed between the central processor and DRAM. Described as cache memory, their purpose is to speed computer access to information. Some new types of DRAM, such as Extended Data Output RAM (EDO RAM), Burst Extended Data Output RAM (BEDO RAM), and Synchronous DRAM (SDRAM), are likewise designed for rapid access to information by the central processor. Variety aside, all RAM circuits are volatile; that is, they lose their contents when their power supply is interrupted. Thus, information stored in RAM circuits is erased when a computer is turned off.

Read-only memory circuits are purchased with prerecorded information. As their name implies, the contents of ROM circuits can be read—that is, retrieved for use by the central processor—but not deleted, added to, or otherwise modified. ROM circuits are typically reserved for programs or occasionally data that must be immediately and continuously available to the central processor. Programs that start a computer up—so-called boot programs—are examples. Read-only memory is also used by other computing devices such as calculators and some peripherals. With computer printers, for example, definitions of type fonts are stored in ROM.

Unlike random-access memory, ROM circuits are nonvolatile. They do not require an uninterrupted power supply. The several forms of ROM circuits are variously described as programmable read-only memory (PROM), erasable programmable read-only memory (EPROM), and electrically erasable read-only memory (EEROM). While these names suggest recordability, their contents can only be altered by special mechanisms that are unavailable to most computer users. In computer configurations, read-only memory circuits are used much more sparingly than RAM circuits. They are more costly, and their contents cannot be easily updated. Computer manufacturers determine the amount of read-only memory to be utilized in a given central processor. Unlike random-access memory, read-only memory cannot be expanded by computer users. When undifferentiated main memory sizes and requirements are indicated for a given processor or computer program, they typically apply to random-access rather than read-only memory.

Random-access memory and read-only memory circuits are manufactured from highly miniaturized, integrated patterns that are photo-etched onto semiconductor material. Complementary metal oxide silicon (CMOS) is currently the most important and widely publicized semiconductor for that purpose. With semiconductor materials, individual memory circuits can assume one of two states—conducting electricity or not conducting electricity. One of the states represents the 1 bits in digitally coded information; the other represents the 0 bits. Individual characters are represented by the presence or absence of electrical current in a specified combination of circuits. The circuit capacities of silicon chips have increased steadily since the 1950s. The earliest models contained several hundred memory circuits. The manufacturing technology that produced such chips is today termed small-scale integration (SSI). During the 1960s, medium-scale integration (MSI) technology produced memory chips with several thousand circuits. By the early 1970s, large-scale integration (LSI) had produced chips containing tens of thousands of circuits. Its successor, very large-scale integration (VLSI), produced chips containing hundreds of thousands of circuits. Today, memory chips produced by ultra large-scale integration (ULSI) contain millions of circuits. Because many manufacturing and marketing costs are fixed, increased chip capacities and storage densities are an important factor in lowering the cost of memory components. Continuing improvements in circuit etching, pattern registration, line-width reduction, and other aspects of chip fabrication are expected to yield even higher densities.

Mainframe Computers

While available devices share the functional components described in the preceding section, central processors have traditionally been categorized as full-size computers, minicomputers, or microcomputers. Definitions of each category of computer, and differences among them, depend on such factors as physical size, processing power, the types of peripherals supported, intended applications, and costs. Because continuing advances in electronics technology and computer engineering have reduced the physical size and cost of all types of central processors, clear distinctions are increasingly difficult to delineate. The lack of precision inherent in these designations is further reflected in the development of such subcategories as mini-midi, midi-mini, and maxi-mini to represent gradations of processing power within a given product group. Even these descriptive labels make the various categories of computers appear inappropriately monolithic. Computer manufacturers increasingly emphasize scalability. Their product lines include a variety of models, which can be configured to satisfy a broad range of customer requirements. While some industry analysts contend that the terms used to denote the various categories of computers are more meaningful as advertising and marketing concepts than as informative product descriptions, a brief review of the historical development and current status of the various types of central processors may help to clarify their distinctive features.

Through the early 1970s, computer system designers emphasized the economies of scale inherent in large, powerful computing machinery that served many users from a centralized facility. Such large devices are often termed full-size computers. They are also described as "mainframes," although that term has no precise definition. During the 1960s, "mainframe" was used to distinguish the central processor as the most significant piece of hardware in a computer installation. At that time, computers were rarely differentiated by size. Today, the mainframe designation may be loosely applied to the largest computer at a given site. In that sense, it differentiates full-size and minicomputers from the smaller and presumably less powerful desktop and mobile computing devices described below. Throughout this book, however, mainframe will be used as a synonym for full-size computers.

Terminology aside, the historical, philosophical, and economic foundation for the centralized implementation of large-scale computing resources is derived from a principle called Grosch's Law, which, though never formally published, became a fundamental precept of computer engineering. Formulated in

Full-size computers, also known as "mainframes," serve a variety of computing needs in large organizations. This illustration depicts a "supercomputer," a special type of mainframe computer optimized for high-speed calculation. (Courtesy of Silicon Graphics Incorporated; used by permission)

the late 1940s by the computer scientist Herbert R. J. Grosch, it contended that larger, and consequently more expensive, computers provide significantly greater information processing power per dollar than small, less expensive machines. Assuming that considerable processing power is required, Grosch's Law implies that consolidation of an organization's computing capabilities in a single, relatively large computer rather than in multiple smaller ones reduces the unit cost of computing. By the mid-1960s, the development of time-sharing operating systems and telecommunication facilities for remote access made such consolidated computing resources possible and practical. Since that time, advances in electronics, combined with market demands, have resulted in the development of several subcategories of mainframe-class computers, each distinguished by such factors as operating speed, memory size, and cost.

At one end of this product group, the smallest mainframes resemble the largest minicomputers in their information processing capabilities. Installed in corporations, government agencies, and other organizations, including some libraries, such devices can support a variety of peripherals, including high-capacity disk drives and dozens or even hundreds of online terminals. Their operating speeds are measured in microseconds (millionths of a second), and their main memory capacities range from hundreds of megabytes to one gigabyte or more. At the other extreme, so-called supercomputers are powerful, special-purpose machines designed for scientific research, computer simulations, and other applications requiring rapid execution of high volumes of complex mathematical calculations. Their operating speeds are measured in fractions of a nanosecond (a billionth of a second), and their main memories have multi-gigabyte capacities. Supercomputers typically employ parallel processing techniques in which multiple calculations associated with a particular mathematical problem are performed simultaneously rather than sequentially. Supercomputers are not important for automated library operations or business data processing, since those activities do not involve extensive mathematical calculations.

Falling between the two extremes cited above, most mainframe computers are properly characterized as medium- or large-scale devices. Designed to perform commonly encountered business and scientific computing tasks, these machines are generally faster and have larger main memories than the small mainframes described above. Their operating speeds are measured in nanoseconds. Their main memories can exceed 10 gigabytes, and they can support hundreds or even thousands of online terminals as well as very high-capacity storage devices.

Measured by market share, IBM Corporation is the world's leading manufacturer of mainframe computers. Several other companies, including Amdahl and Hitachi Data Systems, manufacture full-size computers that can support the same peripheral devices and run the same software as IBM processors. Such computers are collectively described as plug-compatible mainframes (PCMs). Competing on price and performance, they are typically marketed as replacement products for IBM mainframe installations. Other mainframe-class computers are manufactured by companies such as Unisys and Tandem in the United States; Compagnie des Machines Bull, Siemens, and ICL in Europe; and Fujitsu and NEC in Japan. Such computer systems are based on proprietary technologies. They are not IBM-compatible. Supercomputer manufacturers include Cray Research, Fujitsu, Hitachi, IBM, and NEC.

As discussed in later chapters, mainframe computers are used by bibliographic utilities, online search services, and other organizations that provide automated reference and technical services to libraries. In addition, some library-oriented software products are designed for mainframe-class processors. A few large libraries and library systems have installed mainframes to run integrated systems of the type described in a later chapter. Many more libraries have access to mainframe-class computers operated by municipal, academic, corporate, or institutional data processing centers. Often libraries are encouraged to use centralized facilities to automate their applications. In such circumstances, computer resources are typically allocated to individual agencies according to a predefined set of priorities.

Minicomputers

As described above, mainframe computers are typically operated by centralized data processing departments, which provide shared computing services to other organizational units. For such centralized computing facilities, libraries can be demanding customers. Online catalog access, circulation control, and other library applications described in subsequent chapters require considerable input, output, and storage resources. They involve a high volume of transaction-processing activity and must be continuously available well beyond a typical eight-hour workday. Although centralized computer installations can provide good service, some libraries have expressed dissatisfaction with arrangements that force them to relinquish control over system resources and work scheduling. Such dissatisfaction, which is hardly unique to libraries, has a long history in data processing.

In the early 1970s, business users began complaining about the difficulties of dealing with seemingly unresponsive computing center personnel, indicating a strong preference for more direct control over computing resources that had become increasingly indispensable for mission-critical operations. Coincidentally, developments in electronics technology—specifically, improvements in the manufacturing of integrated circuitry—made such direct control possible through drastic reductions in the cost of smaller computers. Such machines were termed "minicomputers" because of their smaller physical dimensions when compared to mainframes. Minicomputers had been available since the 1950s, but high prices limited their use to specialized applications in such fields as aerospace and process control, where sharing of computing resources was impractical and the cost of a dedicated computer could be justified. By the mid-1970s, however, many businesses and government agencies were using minicomputers to decentralize or distribute their computing resources, thereby placing computers under the control of operating divisions or departments. Today, many minicomputers operate in office environments, close to the workers who use them. Others are installed in centralized computing facilities within medium-size organizations for which full-size computers are too powerful or too expensive. As discussed in chapter 3, minicomputers can also function as servers in computer networks. Many integrated library systems and other library automation products operate on minicomputer-class hardware.

As with mainframes, the term minicomputer encompasses products of diverse capabilities. Minicomputer manufacturers offer scalable product lines with a range of models suited to various customer requirements. The most powerful minicomputers offer information-processing capabilities that are equivalent to some mainframes. Their operating speeds are measured in nanoseconds. They have gigabyte-level memory capacities and may support hundreds or even thousands of online terminals. Reflecting their impressive performance characteristics and the imprecise nature of much data processing terminology, such high-end minicomputers are sometimes described as mainframes by their manufacturers and owners. Their categorization as minicomputers largely reflects the fact that they are manufactured by companies such as Digital Equipment Corporation and Hewlett-Packard that have historically been associated with the minicomputer segment of the data processing indus-

Minicomputer-class processors are available in a variety of sizes and configurations. (Courtesy of Hewlett-Packard; used by permission)

try. Less powerful minicomputers are measurably slower, have less memory capacity, and support fewer online terminals than mainframe-class processors. They are sometimes described as "midrange" machines because their position in the hierarchy of computer performance places them between the most powerful full-size machines and somewhat slower desktop systems. Most minicomputers have 32-bit word sizes, although 64-bit processors are increasingly common.

Industry analysts typically distinguish proprietary minicomputers, which employ manufacturer-supplied operating systems, from those models that utilize the Unix operating system, which is discussed in chapter 2. Examples of proprietary minicomputers include Digital Equipment's VAX and Alpha processors, which utilize the OpenVMS operating system; the IBM AS/400, which employs the OS/400 operating system; and Hewlett-Packard's HP-3000 product line, which utilizes the MPE operating system. Proprietary minicomputers have played an important role in library automation since the 1970s, but their greatest popularity is behind them. In recent years, libraries have increasingly preferred Unix-based processors, which offer excellent price/performance characteristics, convenient expandability, and superior scalability. Examples of Unix-based minicomputers include the IBM RS/6000 and the HP-9000 from Hewlett-Packard.

Most Unix-based minicomputers feature RISC processors. The acronym RISC stands for Reduced Instruction Set Computing. As their name suggests, RISC processors support a relatively small repertoire of program instructions, but they can execute them very quickly. For added speed, some models feature "pipelining" techniques in which the next instruction to be processed is retrieved from main memory and decoded while the current instruction is being executed. Others incorporate multiple processors and employ parallel processing techniques. RISC processors are not unique to minicomputers. They are also employed in some desktop devices, including Macintosh computers and so-called technical workstations. The latter devices, which utilize the Unix operating system, are intended for computer-aided design (CAD), image analysis, and other computationally intensive applications in the sciences and engineering. They are also used for desktop publishing, computer animation, and multimedia applications.

Microcomputers

Like minicomputers, microcomputers defy precise categorization. The historical definition, now a quarter of a century old, describes a microcomputer as a computer that incorporates a microprocessor as its central processor. The most dramatic end product of the VLSI and ULSI manufacturing techniques described earlier in this chapter, a microprocessor is a single-chip integrated circuit device that is capable of performing the operations typically associated with the control and arithmetic/logic sections of a central processor. The mere incorporation of a microprocessor does not make a device a microcomputer, however. Mainframes and minicomputers also utilize microprocessors, usually multiple devices, as central processors. Thus, the historical definition presented above, while accurate, does not differentiate microcomputers from other computing devices. Further, microprocessors are widely incorporated into calculators, photocopiers, fax machines, and many consumer products including automobiles, television receivers, audio systems, kitchen appliances, thermostats, and digital watches. While they make extensive use of integrated electronic circuitry, such devices are designed by their manufacturers to perform specific tasks. Unlike the computer systems discussed in this book, they are not programmable.

Internal architecture aside, microcomputers' intended applications and implementation patterns distinguish them from larger central processors. For the most part, mainframes are installed in computer centers that are operated by corporations, government agencies, universities, hospitals, or other large organizations. Minicomputers are widely installed in centralized data processing facilities operated by medium-size organizations. They are also decentralized at the division or department level in larger organizations. Microcomputers permit a further decentralization of computing power at the desk level, where their entire information processing capabilities are at the complete disposal of individual workers—a role that is reflected in the widespread use of the phrase "personal computer" as a synonym for microcomputer. Portable microcomputers—including notebook computers, handheld computers, and other mobile computing devices—provide self-contained information processing capabilities outside traditional work environments.

The foregoing description of microcomputers as personal information processing machines is accurate but potentially misleading. As will be described in chapter 3, microcomputers are increasingly linked in networked configurations that promote electronic communication and resource sharing. In a startling and widely publicized reversal of Grosch's Law, many industry analysts, product developers, and information professionals view networked microcomputers as cost-effective replacements for minicomputers or even mainframes. The most powerful microcomputers feature multiple microprocessors, offer powerful information processing capabilities, and are much less expensive than larger computers. As discussed in subsequent chapters, they are designed as servers for computer networks. Since the early 1990s, a number of corporations, government agencies, and organizations have converted important applications to networked microcomputers from larger processors. Some minicomputer-based library automation products have similarly been redeveloped for microcomputers. This substitution of small computers for larger ones is variously termed "downsizing" or, more optimistically, "right-sizing" by its proponents. More philosophically, some sociologists and futurists view the advent of powerful microcomputers as the basis for an information processing revolution that will drastically alter the character of our society and economy. Certainly, the development of microcomputers has made computing power available to many libraries that otherwise could not afford it.

At the time of this writing, microcomputers employ microprocessors with 32-bit word sizes, although 64-bit microprocessors are in development. Older microcomputers, equipped with 8-bit or 16-bit microprocessors, are no longer manufactured. The vast majority of newly installed microcomputers are char-

Desktop systems bring significant computing power to libraries, offices, laboratories, schools, and homes. (Courtesy of Apple Computer; used by permission)

acterized as "Wintel" machines because they utilize the Microsoft Windows operating environment, in any of its several versions, and they incorporate microprocessors manufactured by Intel Corporation. Alternatively, some Wintel microcomputers contain Intel-compatible microprocessors manufactured by such companies as Advanced Micro Devices, IBM, and National Semiconductor. Wintel machines are available from dozens of manufacturers. Examples include Compaq Computer, Dell Computer, Gateway 2000, Hewlett-Packard, Hitachi, Micron, IBM, Packard Bell, Sony, and Toshiba. They offer Wintel products, including desktop systems, network servers, and mobile computing devices, in a variety of configurations including desktop systems, network servers, and mobile computing devices. Worldwide sales of such products range from 70 million to 100 million units annually. Their processor speeds and main memory capacities have increased steadily and significantly since the late 1970s. Faster microprocessors are being introduced at very short intervals. Desktop computers with 64 megabytes or more of random-access memory are now commonplace. In the early 1990s, such memory capacities were characteristic of larger minicomputers.

Macintosh systems are the only remaining alternative to Wintel machines for most microcomputer users. Manufactured by Apple Computer and others, Macintosh computers incorporate RISC-type microprocessors and have their own operating systems. While Macintosh products have experienced reduced sales and a shrinking installed base since the mid-1990s, they continue to be widely utilized in certain business applications such as graphic arts and desktop publishing. Macintosh computers are also installed in many educational institutions. Some library automation products are available for Macintosh computers, but they are outnumbered by their Wintel counterparts. Other non-Wintel microcomputers have been discontinued in the United States, although they remain available in other countries.

A handheld personal computer (HPC) is a very compact information processing device that offers a low cost, lightweight alternative to conventional notebook computers for straightforward applications. Compared to notebook computers, handheld personal computers are smaller and less capable. They have lower power microprocessors for extended battery operation, less random-access memory, and much smaller video displays. For input, handheld personal computers have small, typewriter-style keyboards, but they lack hard drives or other auxiliary storage peripherals. Most handheld personal computers are configured with simple programs for word processing, appointment scheduling, and contact management. These programs usually reside in read-only memory circuits.

Handheld personal computers are intended as companions rather than replacements for conventional microcomputers. In effect, they are personal organizers with enhanced capabilities. For information transfer, they can be connected to desktop computers. They are also equipped with modems. A handheld personal computer should not be confused with a personal digital assistant (PDA). The latter is a compact portable computing device that uses a pen, rather than a keyboard, for input. Compared to handheld personal computers, personal digital assistants have less powerful microprocessors, smaller amounts of random-access memory, and more limited communication capabilities.

Portable computers like this notebook model provide self-contained information processing capabilities outside traditional work environments. (Courtesy of NEC; used by permission)

INPUT PERIPHERALS

As noted earlier, a computer system, as opposed to merely a computer, consists of a central processor and its associated peripheral devices. The peripherals are dedicated to one or more of the following specialized information processing tasks: input, output, or storage. The function of the input peripherals is to convert human-readable information to the machine-readable form required by the central processor. The information to be converted is usually contained in type-written or handwritten documents, which are called source documents. The input process is also known as data entry or data conversion.

Available input peripherals are customarily categorized by the conversion methods they employ. In library applications and business data processing, two methods account for the majority of input activity: key-entry (typing) and optical scanning. Other, more specialized input methods such as speech recognition are currently limited in capabilities and consequently in application, although that situation may change in the future. Historically, speech recognition systems have had limited vocabularies and required measurable pauses between spoken words. During the late 1990s, several companies introduced improved speech recognition products for microcomputer installations, where they offer an alternative to typing for word processing and similar applications. Words spoken into a microphone are converted by speech recognition software to the equivalent of typed text or data values, which can then be edited or otherwise manipulated by specific computer programs. Lengthy setup procedures and some practice may be required for accurate speech recognition, but the best products have large vocabularies and permit normal speaking rates. They are a viable

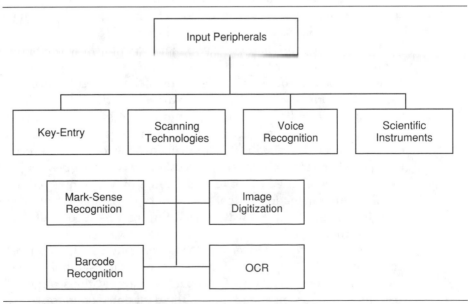

Customarily categorized by the conversion method employed, the input peripherals convert information to the machine-readable form required for computer processing.

alternative to typing for some applications. They are particularly appealing for slow typists or for frequent computer users seeking relief from carpal tunnel syndrome or other repetitive motion injuries associated with typing. Continuing performance improvements are expected as the technology develops.

A simpler group of speech recognition products supports voice entry of commands rather than text or data. When used with specific computer programs, they permit voice activation of menu options, cursor movements, and other controls. Input peripherals also include pointing devices, such as mice, trackballs, and touch-sensitive pads. Those devices are principally used for selection of menu options or for cursor positioning. Other input devices, such as graphic tablets and scientific instrumentation, are intended for special applications and have limited significance for libraries.

Key-Entry Devices and Methods

As their name suggests, key-entry devices feature a typewriter-like keyboard at which the information to be converted is typed, character by character. Used in this context, the term "character" denotes a letter of the alphabet, numeric digit, punctuation mark, or other symbol encountered in books, journal articles, technical reports, business correspondence, or other textual documents. The first generation of key-entry equipment recorded typed characters in machine-readable form on paper media such as cards or tapes. Keypunch machines, which were widely used in business and library applications through the 1970s, converted individually typed characters to a specified pattern of holes punched in successive columns of a tabulating card. The punched cards were then taken to a card reader, a peripheral device that operated online to a computer. The card reader detected the pattern of holes punched in successive columns of each card and converted it to computer-processable form for immediate processing or transfer to other media such as magnetic disks or tapes.

While isolated installations may remain, keypunching is an obsolete input methodology. Key-entry now relies on video display devices with keyboards that are connected to computers on which the entered information will be processed. Information typed at a video display device is transmitted to a computer, where it is initially captured in random-access memory, then transferred to a hard disk drive for storage pending later processing. This input methodology is variously described as key-to-disk, key-to-storage, or direct data entry. The typed characters are converted to computer codes. Depending on the computer installation, the ASCII or EBCDIC codes may be employed. Key-to-tape, a similar input methodology that recorded typed characters on magnetic tape rather than magnetic disks, was utilized through the 1980s, but it is rarely encountered today.

As noted above, key-entered information may contain alphabetic characters, numeric digits, punctuation marks, or other symbols. The key-entry process itself is controlled by software. In most applications, a specially formatted input screen prompts and guides the data-entry operator. The screen is a key-entry template with labeled areas and accompanying blank spaces into which specific information is to be typed. The operator "fills in the blanks," using the tab or enter key to advance from one labeled area to the next. As discussed in chapter 6, bibliographic utilities and CD-ROM products use such for-matted screens to simplify the entry and editing of cataloging records. Labels, consisting of words or special numeric codes, identify the screen areas where the author, title, and other bibliographic information is to be typed.

Key-entry rates are affected by operator skill, input procedures, source docu-ment characteristics, and other factors. Full-time, experienced data entry person-nel may average 10,000 to 11,000 keystrokes (characters) per hour, sustained throughout an eight-hour workday. That key-entry rate is equivalent to typing about 30 words per minute. Less experienced operators, however, may average just 6,000 to 8,000 keystrokes per hour. As in word processing, typing errors can be corrected by backspacing and overtyping with the correct character or charac-ters. Depending on the system, software for direct data entry may also perform error-detection and entry validation routines. It can check names, subject head-ings, or other alphabetic entries to be sure that they do not contain numeric dig-its, for example. It can determine whether numeric values fall within a specified range of acceptable values and ensure that entries are complete prior to transfer to disk storage.

Compared to older keypunch technologies, direct data entry is much faster and more convenient, but typing is an error-prone activity. Depending on oper-ator skill, as much as 5 percent of typed characters may be incorrect. While this percentage may seem relatively low, it is considered unacceptable in most li-brary applications. Even a small quantity of data entry errors can have a nega-tive impact on system performance. In the case of bibliographic data, for example, an erroneous character in an author's name, title, or subject heading will affect sorting operations. Where searches are based on exact matches of specified character strings, typing errors can render information unretrievable. In acquisitions and serials control, key-entry errors can generate incorrect pay-ments or pose other problems for book orders and periodical subscriptions. For libraries making a long-term investment in machine-readable information to support online catalog access, circulation control, and other applications dis-cussed in later chapters, it is important that incorrectly typed characters be de-tected and corrected.

The process of detecting and correcting errors in entered data is termed data verification. In key-entry applications, the most accurate method of data verifi-cation is double-keying, also known as keystroke verification. The information to be converted to computer-processible form is typed twice. The second typing may occur immediately after initial key-entry or at some later time; it may be performed by the key-entry operator or by a different person. Under software control, the second set of keystrokes is compared to the first, and the verifying operator is alerted to any discrepancies. An error may have occurred in the ini-tial typing, in the second typing, or in both sets of keystrokes. The suspect char-acters must be examined to determine the error and corrective action taken.

As an obvious disadvantage, keystroke verification increases the already substantial time and labor required for data entry. The work effort is more than doubled, since all information must be typed twice and detected errors must be examined and corrected. Taken together, these steps will increase the time and labor requirement by a factor of about 2.3 when compared to initial key-entry. Consider, as an example, a library application involving the conversion of borrower identification data to machine-readable form for use in a computerized circulation control system. Assuming that the library has 30,000 registered borrowers and will record 125 characters of information about each of them, the data entry effort will involve 3.75 million keystrokes. At a typing rate of 10,000 keystrokes per hour, 375 hours will be required for initial data entry. Data verification by double-keying will increase that requirement by about 2.3 times to 863 hours, including error correction. At an operator wage of $10 per hour, the labor cost for this data entry application will be $8,630.

As an alternative to keystroke verification, some data entry applications employ sight verification (proofreading) for error detection. An operator examines key-entered information on a video monitor or in a printed listing, comparing it to source documents as necessary. As its principal advantage, sight verification requires less time and labor than double-keying. The combination of proofreading and error correction typically increases data entry time by a factor of about 1.6. Thus an application that requires 375 hours for initial data entry will require 600 hours when proofreading and error correction are included. At an operator wage of $10 per hour, the labor cost will be $6,000—which is approximately 30 percent less than the double-keying cost estimated above.

Proofreading, however, demands a high level of sustained operator attentiveness. As a verification method, it may not detect all incorrect characters in entered data; the presence of typographical errors in books and other publications attests to the unreliability of proofreading. Double-keying, in contrast, is a highly reliable method of error detection. Its failure rate is limited to those cases where exactly the same mistake is made during both the initial and second typing. It has been suggested that proofreading can be augmented by spell-checking software, but such programs have notable limitations as data verification tools. They cannot detect keystroking errors in personal names, numeric values, or non-alphabetic symbols such as punctuation marks. Their effectiveness is further limited by the contents of their spelling dictionaries, which may not include specialized terminology associated with certain subject disciplines. While spelling dictionaries can be customized to include such terminology, that process is laborious. Finally, spell-checking programs do not detect typing errors that create an inappropriate but correctly spelled word.

Optical Scanning Technologies

The cost of data entry and verification should not be underestimated. Library systems analysts and others responsible for planning and implementing computer-based information systems must calculate such costs and include them in their project budgets. In some applications, the labor cost for data entry and verification will exceed the cost of computer hardware and software. This is often the case in retrospective conversion projects that involve large numbers of bibliographic records. In such situations, data entry costs can be significantly reduced by purchasing or otherwise obtaining existing machine-readable data from bibliographic utilities or other sources discussed in later chapters. Where local conversion of data is required, however, optical scanning technologies can minimize data entry labor by reducing or eliminating keystroking requirements.

Broadly defined, optical scanning technologies use light to convert information from source documents to computer-processible form. Specifically, these technologies measure the amount of light reflected by all or part of a document. In so doing, they determine the light and dark patterns that the document contains. Those patterns are then interpreted to identify alphabetic characters, numeric digits, punctuation marks, or other symbols. Once identified, the information is encoded and transferred to a computer, where it is typically recorded on magnetic disks in the manner of the key-entry methods described above.

Several types of optical scanning technologies have been developed for special situations. Mark-sense recognition, for example, relies on specially designed input documents that contain demarcated spaces to be filled in by pencil. Completed documents are scanned by a machine that determines the meanings of individual marks by their locations. Because source document characteristics are tightly controlled and the marking instrument—a no. 2 pencil, for example—is specified, mark-sense recognition is a highly reliable input method, but its applicability is limited to a narrow range of information processing problems. Mark-sense recognition is most widely employed in educational testing and survey applications where the source document is a specially designed answer sheet or questionnaire. Dark marks placed in the demarcated spaces correspond to answers to multiple-choice test questions or to responses to survey questions.

In barcode recognition, a data value is encoded by predetermined patterns of vertical lines that vary in width and spacing. In most cases, the encoded value is a numeric identifier such as a book number or a borrower number in circulation control applications. Barcodes are pervasive in retailing, where they encode product numbers. Barcodes can also represent alphabetic characters, but that is rarely done. Barcodes may be printed directly on objects such as books or borrower identification cards. More commonly in library applications, barcodes are printed on adhesive labels that are affixed to objects. A typical barcode label measures one and one-half to two inches wide by one-half to three-quarters of an inch high. In addition to the barcode itself, the label may contain the numeric identifier in human-readable form and other printed information such as a library name. The meanings of specific barcodes are defined by the symbology, or symbol patterns, employed in a particular system. Examples of barcode symbologies include Code 39, CODABAR, Code 128, and Interleaved 2 of 5.

Barcodes are read by specially designed scanners that interpret the numbers they encode and transmit them to a computer in lieu of key-entry. The least expensive barcode scanner is a handheld light pen, sometimes described as a "barwand." Other equipment configurations include a CCD scanner, a handheld device that resembles a hair dryer, and a laser scanner, which is a desktop unit. While barcode recognition is a reliable alternative to key-entry for certain types of information, its accuracy is affected by the clarity of vertical line patterns in a given barcode, as well as by the contrast between lines and spaces. Compared to light pens, CCD and laser scanners permit faster operation as well as more reliable reading of barcodes of marginal quality. As an additional advantage, laser scanners can read barcodes without contact, thereby preventing scratches or other damage to the barcodes themselves. Barcode scanners may be configured with a calculator-style keyboard that is used to activate commands and to enter numbers from unreadable barcodes.

An increasingly important group of optical scanning devices converts documents to electronic images for computer processing and storage. These devices are variously described as "document scanners," "page scanners," "document digitizers," or "image digitizers." The documents may be handwritten, typed, or printed. They may contain textual or graphic information in black-and-white or color. Unlike key-entry devices, document scanners can convert non-textual information to computer-processable form. The scanning process is properly termed "document digitization," and the resulting electronic images are described as "digitized images."

Document scanners are available in floor-standing and desktop configurations. Floor-standing scanners are intended for high-volume applications requiring high-speed equipment operation. Desktop scanners, the more common configuration, can be subdivided by mode of operation into flatbed and sheetfed varieties. Flatbed models, as their name indicates, feature a flat surface on which pages are individually positioned for scanning. Because they can accommodate books, periodicals, technical reports, and other bound volumes, flatbed scanners are particularly well suited to library applications. Flatbed scanners resemble photocopiers. A source document is positioned face down on a glass surface. An optical head assembly and light source move across the glass beneath the document, illuminating successive picture elements and measuring their reflectance characteristics. Sheetfed models, by contrast, are sometimes described as "pass-through" or "pull-through" scanners. Individual pages, inserted into a narrow

Document scanners like this desktop model generate digitized images suitable for computer processing and storage. (Courtesy of Hewlett-Packard; used by permission)

opening, are transported by rollers across a stationary optical head assembly and light source. Compared to flatbed models, sheetfed scanners are faster. For that reason, they are preferred for business applications, where bound volumes are seldom encountered. An automatic page feeder may be a standard or optional feature. Depending on equipment design, scanned pages are ejected at the back or bottom of the machine.

Regardless of equipment design, a document scanner creates a digitized image by converting a page's tonal values into digital bit patterns. The scanner divides a page into a grid of small scannable units that are variously called "picture elements," "pixels," or "dots." Using photosensitive components, the scanner measures the amount of light reflected by successively encountered dots within a page. In the case of black-and-white documents, dots that reflect light in excess of a predetermined threshold amount are considered white and are each encoded as 0 bits. Where light reflectance values are lower than the predetermined threshold amount, the corresponding dots are considered black and are each encoded as 1 bits. Various combinations of 1 and 0 bits are used to encode gray tones or colors. By using 8 bits to encode each dot, a scanner can differentiate among 256 shades of gray. Most color scanners employ 24 bits to encode each dot. Such devices can represent over 16.7 million different colors.

Scanning resolution is defined by the number of dots that are analyzed per horizontal and vertical inch within a page. Possibilities range from fewer than 75 dots per inch (dpi) to more than 1,000 dots per inch, although not all scanners support that broad range. The scanning resolution selected for a particular application determines the sharpness of digitized images. As resolution increases, the size of each dot decreases, and the amount of detail captured by the scanner increases. While scanning resolutions of 75 to 100 dots per inch are often adequate for graphic documents, 200 dots per inch is the minimum resolution required for consistently legible digitization of typewritten documents and typeset publications. Some library materials with small typefaces may require higher scanning resolutions.

Document scanners are used in several applications of interest to libraries. In desktop publishing, for example, they can digitize photographs and other illustrations for resizing, cropping, or other manipulation by image editing or page composition software. The images can then be inserted into page layouts for printing. Alternatively, electronic images created by document scanners can be inserted into Web pages or other electronic publications. In the digital library implementations discussed in chapter 8, electronic images of books, journal articles, technical reports, and other library documents can be recorded on hard drives, optical disks, or other computer media for online access. Assuming an appropriate equipment configuration, electronic images generated by document scanners can be transmitted to facsimile machines, which are themselves examples of special purpose document digitizers.

Optical character recognition (OCR) combines optical scanning and image analysis components to identify characters contained in document images and convert them to the machine-readable form required for computer storage and processing. In a typical OCR implementation, a scanner converts paper documents to electronic images in the manner described above. An OCR program

ABCDEFGHIJKLMNOPQRSTUVWXYZ
abcdefghijklmnopqrstuvwxyz
1234567890!?/.⌐$%&*()_+=;:

OCR-A is an example of a type font designed specifically for optical character recognition. Many OCR programs, however, can recognize a variety of fonts.

analyzes the digitized images and attempts to identify the characters they contain. The recognized characters are then converted to predetermined combinations of bits, just as if they had been key-entered. The encoded characters are typically recorded on hard drives or other computer storage media.

Because document scanning is an essential preliminary to optical character recognition, the terms OCR and scanning are often used interchangeably, but that usage is imprecise and misleading. Document scanning is merely one work step in an OCR implementation; the digitized images generated by document scanners must be analyzed by OCR programs and the recognized characters converted to computer-processible codes. An OCR program may be built into a document scanner, which stores it in read-only memory circuits. Such scanners are sometimes described as "OCR readers." More commonly, OCR software operates on a computer to which the scanner is attached. Since the late 1980s, the availability of relatively inexpensive document scanners and microcomputer-based OCR software packages has made optical character recognition an attractive data-entry option for many computer users. Compared to key-entry, optical character recognition is faster and requires less labor. OCR affects only initial data entry, however; error detection, via proofreading of recognized characters, is still required.

Optical character recognition's potential for library applications is obvious: it offers a faster, more automated, and presumably less costly alternative to the key-entry methods described above. In theory, an OCR system should be able to accept a library's existing source documents—catalog cards, bibliographic lists, borrower rosters, even books and journal articles—and convert their contents to machine-readable form for computer storage and processing. In actual practice, however, OCR's suitability for library applications depends on its ability to accurately recognize characters. Over the years, the technology has improved steadily and significantly. Older OCR products could only recognize characters printed in a limited selection of typewritten or typeset fonts, including certain fonts—such as OCR-A and OCR-B—that were optimized for machine recognition. Today, the most flexible and capable products offer omnifont recognition capabilities based on feature extraction concepts, which identify characters by their distinctive attributes. An uppercase letter "A," for example, is recognized as a character with two diagonal lines joined at the top and bisected by a horizontal crossbar. Similarly, an uppercase "D" is recognized as having one vertical line joined at the ends by a loop. As their principal advantage, feature extraction methodologies transcend ornamental differences associated with particular type fonts, sizes, and styles; presumably, the letter "O" will be recognizable as a continuous loop whether it is printed in the Courier or Times Roman font, boldface or italicized, large or small.

The most powerful OCR programs, sometimes described as Intelligent Character Recognition (ICR) products, incorporate special pre- and post-recognition features to improve accuracy. Pre-recognition features include deskewing, image lightening or darkening, line sharpening, and removal of speckles and background patterns to produce clearer, more easily recognizable images. When processing business forms, some ICR programs can remove horizontal and vertical lines that overlap textual information. They can also detect areas within pages that contain charts, illustrations, or other graphic information and will automatically exclude those areas from recognition processing. Post-recognition processing includes contextual analysis, dictionary searches, frequency counts, and other techniques that increase the likelihood of accurate character identification.

OUTPUT PERIPHERALS

The function of the output peripherals is to convert machine-readable information to human-readable form. They present the results of computer processing to users. As with input peripherals, there are a number of available output options, but some are inappropriate for library applications. Indicator lights and

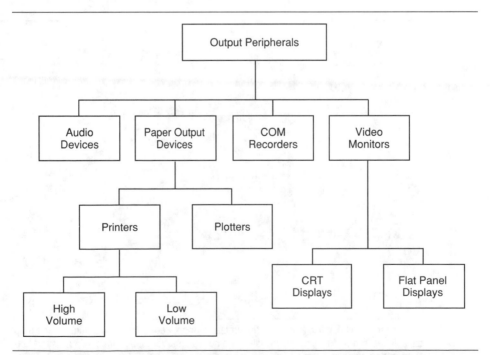

Categorized by the medium produced, output peripherals convert the machine-readable results of computer processing to human-readable form.

audio alarms, for example, are widely used as output mechanisms for computer-controlled instrumentation, in computer-assisted aviation, and in many automobiles, but they have no utility for bibliographic applications. Similarly, synthesized voice output has little significance for libraries. Instead, library automation relies on those output peripherals that print information onto paper, record it on microfilm, or display it on a screen.

Paper Output Devices

Although the use of computers to implement "paperless" information systems has been widely discussed, paper printers remain indispensable output devices. Even applications that are heavily oriented toward screen displays rely on paper output for reference copies of selected information, for backup, or for the production of supplemental reports. As with other types of peripheral devices, paper printers vary considerably in technology, output characteristics, operating speeds, and suitability for specific applications. As might be expected, mainframes, centralized minicomputers, and network servers support fast, high-volume printing devices. High-speed laser printers, often described as page printers, dominate such installations.

Page printers use a combination of laser and xerographic technologies. Based on definitions stored in electronic memory circuits, latent (invisible) images of alphabetic characters or other information are generated as dot patterns on a photosensitive surface inside the page printer. The latent images, which consist of closely spaced electrical charges, are developed by applying finely

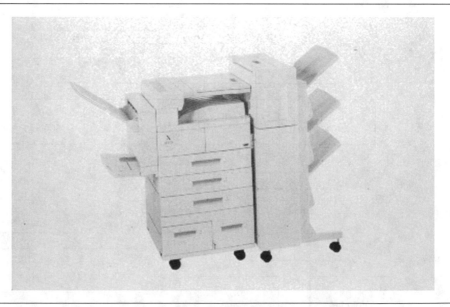

Page printers, which use a combination of lasers and xerography, provide high-speed output capabilities in mainframe, minicomputer, and network server installations. (Courtesy of Xerox Corporation; used by permission)

powdered, oppositely charged ink particles called toner. The resulting visible images are then transferred to paper at speeds ranging from three seconds per page to three pages per second, depending on the model; the fastest devices are intended for large mainframe installations with very high volume printing requirements. In addition to fast operation, page printers provide extensive typographical and document formatting capabilities. They print onto single sheets of letter-size (8.5-by-11-inch) paper rather than the larger (11-by-14-inch), fanfolded paper stock used by older computer printers. The most versatile devices can print on both sides of a sheet of paper. With some models, printed output can be reduced to fit four or even eight pages on a single two-sided sheet. Page printers support multiple type fonts and styles, which can be printed in various sizes. In a book catalog, for example, the body and tracings portion of a catalog record can be printed in one size and the collation and notes in another. Specific information, such as the main entry, can be emphasized by boldface printing, shading, or italics. Vertical and horizontal spacing can be adjusted to meet special application requirements. Because multiple copies are created by successive printer runs rather than carbon paper, quality is uniform from copy to copy. Images of business forms are stored by computer programs and superimposed on data at printing time, thereby eliminating the need to maintain inventories of preprinted blank forms for special applications.

Older high-speed printers, often described as line printers, remain in use in some mainframe and minicomputer installations. Characterized as "impact" devices, they print information by forcing metal type slugs into an inked ribbon, in the manner of typewriters. (By contrast, the page printers described above are "non-impact" devices; they are based on photocopier rather than typewriter technology.) One type of line printer features a printing chain with characters represented on embossed metal slugs that are linked in an endless loop. The simplest devices can print the uppercase roman alphabet, numeric digits, and the most widely used punctuation symbols. Special print chains, with diacritics and special symbols, have been developed for applications involving bibliographic data. Typographic characteristics aside, most line printers accept continuous, fanfolded paper stock, with the bottom of one page connected to the top of the next. Each page measures 11 by 14 inches and can contain up to 64 lines with as many as 132 characters or print positions per line. The line printer operates online to a computer that transmits information indicating the print positions for specified characters. The print chain rotates at high speed. When characters on the chain reach their designated print positions, small hammers strike the paper, driving it against an inked ribbon and the embossed type slugs. Because multiple hammers may be activated simultaneously, the device appears to print entire lines at one time, hence its name. Other line printers utilize belts, bands, or drums rather than print chains, but their output characteristics are similar to those of chain-type printers.

Line printers are slower and less versatile than page printers. Their output speeds range from several hundred to more than 1,000 lines per minute, depending on equipment characteristics, line lengths, page lengths, and the size of the printable character set. Page printers, by contrast, routinely generate 3,000 or more lines per minute. One page printer can consequently replace several line printers in mainframe or minicomputer installations. The quality of line printer output—which depends on ribbon condition, mechanical adjustments, and other factors—is fair at best. Carbon-interleaved paper is used to produce multiple copies, with resulting variations in quality from copy to copy. As an additional disadvantage, many users find 11-by-14-inch paper cumbersome to handle, even when the pages are separated and bound.

Slower printers are intended for desktop computer installations where workloads are lighter and speed requirements are less stringent. High-volume printers are engineered for reliable, multishift operation; in large mainframe installations, page printers operate all day, every day with only brief interruptions for job setup, paper replacement, and preventive maintenance. In desktop computer installations, by contrast, printers are characteristically idle during much of the workday. In word processing applications, for example, most work time is spent typing and editing documents; printing occurs only when those tasks are completed.

Operating speeds for low-volume printers are typically measured in characters per second or pages per minute. Among the low-volume impact printers, the most common device is a dot matrix printer, so-called because it prints individual characters from predetermined patterns of closely spaced dots. The dots are formed by selectively driving a set of needles, sometimes described as pins, into an inked ribbon. Depending on the model, output speeds range from less than 50 to more than 400 characters per second. Output quality varies with the number of dots used to shape individual characters. Documents produced by 24-pin dot matrix printers are often described as "near letter quality," meaning they approach but do not quite equal the quality of documents produced by

Desktop laser and inkjet printers provide excellent output quality and typographic versatility. (Courtesy of Hewlett-Packard; used by permission)

typewriters. Nine-pin dot matrix printers produce "draft quality" documents that are typically legible but unsuitable for many business purposes.

Since the late 1980s, desktop computer users have increasingly relied on non-impact laser and inkjet printers as higher-quality alternatives to impact-type dot matrix devices. Desktop laser printers are the low-volume counterparts of the page printers described above. They employ electrostatic printing technology based on a combination of lasers and xerography. Typical operating speeds range from 4 to 20 pages per minute. The fastest devices are intended for network installations in which several desktop computers share a printer. Inkjet printers, which create characters by spraying microscopic ink pellets at a sheet of paper, are less expensive than laser printers. Output speeds of three to six pages per minute are typical. Most newer inkjet printers have color output capabilities. As a group, inkjet and laser printers are well suited to microcomputer-based word processing and desktop publishing installations. They offer typewriter like quality and excellent typographic versatility. While individual characters are formed from dot matrix patterns, the dots are so closely spaced that the characters appear to be fully formed.

The paper output devices discussed to this point were originally developed for textual documents that contain alphanumeric characters, punctuation marks, and perhaps some special symbols. Inkjet printers, laser printers, and dot matrix printers can also generate bar charts, line graphs, pie charts, and other diagrammatic information, including graphic images associated with computer programs and Web pages. Such devices are sometimes described as "graphic printers." They offer acceptable quality and performance for business and library applications that involve relatively straightforward graphic presentations. Digital plotters are a special class of paper output devices designed for scientific, engineering, and other applications with complex graphic output requirements. Plotters are most often encountered in computer-aided design (CAD) installations, where they produce engineering drawings, circuit diagrams, architectural renderings, and other technical documents in a variety of sizes and formats. Plotters are also used to print maps and land surveys in geographic information systems. Compared to most printers, plotters can print information on larger sheets of paper. Many engineering drawings, for example, measure three-by-four feet.

Computer-Output Microfilm Recorders

Computer-output microfilm (COM) is a variant form of non-impact output technology in which textual or graphic information is recorded on microfilm rather than printed on paper. The information is miniaturized but human-readable with appropriate magnification. Actually, a computer-output microfilmer—often described as a COM recorder—is both a computer peripheral device and a high-speed microfilm production unit. As a computer peripheral, a COM recorder can be configured for either online or offline operation. In the latter case, information generated by a computer must be brought to the COM recorder on magnetic tape or other media. In either operating mode, COM recorders—like page printers—can produce documents at high speed. Like high-volume printers, COM recorders are designed for centralized operation in a large mainframe or minicomputer installation.

COM technology makes it appear that computer-generated information was first printed onto paper and then microfilmed, but paper documents are not produced at any stage in the process. With some COM recorders, pages of computer-processible information are displayed on a video monitor that is built into the recorder itself. The displayed pages are then microfilmed by a specially designed camera that uses silver-gelatin photographic film as its recording medium. Other devices use lasers to write information onto a thermally sensitive microfilm. With either method, document images are recorded in greatly reduced size on microfiche or, less commonly, on rolls of 16 mm or 35 mm microfilm. As with all photographic processes, the microfiche or roll film must be developed following exposure. Some COM recorders include a microfilm processor as an integral component. In other cases, a separate microfilm processor is required.

In the typical application, a COM recorder produces a master microfiche or microfilm roll from which multiple working copies will be produced, using a microform duplicator. The working copies are distributed for use in display devices called readers. Where paper enlargement of microfilm images is required, combination units called reader/printers are available. Once a master microfiche or microfilm roll is created, its information content cannot be updated or otherwise changed. For updating, a replacement microform must be produced.

Image capacities vary with the type of microform and amount of photographic reduction employed. A single microfiche, for example, measures 105 by 148 millimeters. It can contain the equivalent of 270 computer-printout-size (11-by-14-inch) pages or 420 letter-size (8.5-by-11-inch) pages reduced 48 to 1. The capacity of a 100-foot roll of 16 mm microfilm ranges from 1,800 to 7,200 computer-printout-size pages, depending on reduction. With some COM recorders, page boundaries can be eliminated altogether, so that information is recorded as a series of continuous lines on microfiche or roll film. The typographic characteristics of COM recorders vary from model to model. The most versatile devices can print information in different type fonts, sizes, and styles.

The earliest COM recorders were introduced in the late 1950s as the high-speed alternatives to mechanical plotters in scientific and technical applications requiring the high-volume production of engineering drawings and other computer-generated graphics. Alphanumeric COM recorders, designed for business data processing, became available shortly thereafter, but they were not widely utilized until the early 1970s. Initial, limited library interest in COM accompanied the introduction of machine-readable bibliographic databases in the mid-1960s. The first library application, a computer-produced microfilm catalog, was reported in 1967 by the Lockheed Technical Information Center. Similar applications were commonplace during the late 1970s and early 1980s, although they have since been supplanted by other technologies discussed elsewhere in this book. In addition to library catalogs, COM has been successfully utilized for serials holding lists, various technical services reports, and popular micropublications. Most library applications rely on COM recorders that are operated by computer or microfilm service bureaus. Several vendors offer specialized COM services to libraries.

Video Display Devices

Rather than printing human-readable information on paper or microfilm, a third class of output peripherals displays the result of computer processing on a screen. Such devices are collectively called video monitors or video display units (VDUs). Most video display units feature a television-like cathode-ray tube (CRT) that is mounted in a plastic or metal case. Screen sizes range from less than nine inches to more than twenty-one inches, measured diagonally, with fourteen to fifteen inches being a typical size for video monitors intended for desktop computers and interactive terminals. Larger video display units are expensive and occupy considerable desk space. They are usually reserved for special situations, such as computer-aided design or computer-based page composition, where large documents or complicated graphics must be displayed in their entirety. Screen size aside, a cathode ray tube employs a rapidly deflected electron beam to write information on a phosphorescent faceplate. The electronic beam scans the faceplate in a series of horizontal lines composed of illuminatable picture elements (pixels). The energized pixels glow briefly. In most cases the displayed image lasts only a fraction of a second, and the phosphorescent picture must be repeatedly reilluminated or "refreshed."

While it has been criticized for bulkiness, high power consumption, and health hazards associated with radiation, CRT technology is well developed, readily available, competitively priced, and suitable for a broad range of computer applications, including those requiring varied visual attributes and color

Most video display units employ CRT technology, which is well suited to a broad range of computing applications. (Courtesy of ViewSonic; used by permission)

display capabilities. The simplest, least expensive CRT-based video monitors are monochrome devices that display light characters on a dark background, a screen presentation described as standard video. Depending on the particular screen phosphor employed, the displayed characters may be white, green, or amber. For flexibility in application development, most devices give the user the option of displaying dark characters on a light background, a screen presentation described as reverse video. Many computer programs rely on reverse video for emphasis, although some applications, such as desktop publishing and electronic document imaging, utilize it as the normal display mode. Color video monitors, while rarely encountered with conventional terminals that interact with mainframes and minicomputers, are the norm in microcomputer installations.

Depending on the model, a CRT-based video monitor may offer alphanumeric or bit-mapped display capabilities. Alphanumeric video monitors, as their name indicates, can display textual information, including letters of the alphabet, numeric digits, and punctuation marks. Some models can display accented characters, a potentially useful capability for certain library applications. Conforming to a de facto industry standard, most alphanumeric video monitors display twenty-four or twenty-five lines of textual information with eighty columns or character positions per line. Bit-mapped CRTs offer both textual and graphic display capabilities. They generate graphic images by illuminating a screen's picture elements (pixels) in a specified pattern. A bit-mapped video monitor's display resolution is determined by the number of pixels it can illuminate. Low-resolution bit-mapped monitors are commonly encountered in microcomputer installations. VGA displays, with 480 (vertical) by 640 (horizontal) pixels, and Super VGA displays, with 768 (vertical) by 1,024 (horizontal) pixels, are the most common examples. Higher-resolution bit-mapped video monitors can display several thousand pixels horizontally and vertically. They are designed for desktop publishing, electronic document imaging, computer-aided design, and other special applications. Whether alphanumeric or bit-mapped, most CRT-based video monitors are landscape-oriented, meaning that screen width exceeds screen height.

Despite the relative economy, excellent visual attributes, and other significant advantages of CRT-based video monitors, alternative display technologies have attracted considerable attention among peripheral equipment manufacturers and prospective customers. Collectively called "flat panel displays," the alternative technologies have characteristics and capabilities that CRTs lack. As their name suggests, flat panel displays offer a compact alternative to bulky cathode-ray tubes. Depth is their smallest dimension, and their light weight and low power consumption are particularly appropriate for portable computer configurations. As additional advantages, flat panel displays can withstand considerable vibration and shock. They can operate reliably under a wider range of environmental conditions than CRT devices, are less susceptible to magnetic or electrical interference, and emit no radiation. On the other hand, flat panel displays are more expensive than their CRT counterparts and, while their display attributes have improved, they seldom match the quality, brightness, and versatility of CRT devices.

Flat panel displays, like this LCD model, are increasingly available in desktop configurations. (Courtesy of Silicon Graphics Incorporated; used by permission)

Commonplace in portable computers, handheld calculators, digital watches, and various other devices, liquid crystal displays (LCDs) are the most widely utilized and least expensive flat panel technology. LCDs use electricity to alter the light reflectance properties of liquid crystal compounds that are trapped between two sheets of polarizing material. When an electrical current passes through the liquid, the crystals align to block the transmission of light, thereby displaying information. Because they consume relatively little power, liquid crystal displays are well suited to battery-operated equipment configurations. Display quality has improved steadily and significantly since the mid-1980s. The newest models provide highly legible, bit-mapped color displays with good brightness and contrast. Several companies offer LCD monitors for desktop computers. They are attractively compact but much more expensive than CRT-based displays with comparable or even superior visual attributes.

Among other flat panel technologies, electroluminescent (EL) displays feature a thin polycrystalline film that glows when energized at specific points. The resulting images are bright and pleasing, with sufficient contrast for textual information plus gray scale capabilities for straightforward graphics applications. Several significant limitations, including high power consumption and cost, have impeded their market acceptance, however. Gas-plasma displays activate electric currents to energize gas that is trapped between glass plates. The energized gas glows to illuminate points on a video monitor. Alternating current (AC) and direct current (DC) gas-plasma displays have been commercially available for many years, but they offer few advantages over CRTs in desktop computer installations. Gas-plasma displays are reliable and have good visual attributes, but high power consumption renders them unsuitable for portable computing devices.

AUXILIARY STORAGE PERIPHERALS AND MEDIA

Auxiliary storage peripherals and media are designed to retain information in machine-readable form, pending computer processing. As such, they supplement the necessarily limited capacity of main memory, the latter being reserved for the storage of programs and information that the computer is processing at a given moment. Consequently, auxiliary storage is sometimes described as "secondary" storage to differentiate it from the "primary" storage provided by main memory. If auxiliary storage peripherals and media did not exist, data would have to be reentered before each incident of computer processing, and applications involving large amounts of information could not be computerized successfully.

Although early computer systems used paper media, such as punched cards or punched tape, for storage of machine-readable data, magnetic recording devices and media have dominated auxiliary storage technology since the early 1970s. Magnetic storage peripherals record digitally coded information by altering the magnetizable properties of a given medium. To retrieve information, a magnetic storage peripheral detects the alterations, interpreting them as 1 bits or 0 bits. Of the several types of magnetic storage media, magnetic disks offer the highest performance, while magnetic tapes are the most economical. Optical storage devices and media, which became available in the 1980s, use lasers to record and retrieve information. As discussed later in this chapter, they are most notable for their high capacities.

Magnetic Disks

A magnetic disk is a platter-shaped medium coated with a magnetizable metallic recording material. The disk's recording surface is divided into concentric rings or tracks. The individual bits that represent text, quantitative values, images, or other computer-processible information are usually recorded linearly within each track. A movable electromagnetic mechanism called a read/write head is used for recording and playback (retrieval) of information. On instructions received from a host computer, a magnetic disk drive positions the read/write head above a designated track while the rotating platter brings the desired disk segment under the electromagnetic mechanism. Reading or recording occurs at very high speed as the indicated segment passes by. To record information, the read/write head aligns the disk's magnetizable material in predetermined directions. Alignment toward the north pole of a magnetic field, for example, may record the 1 bits in digitally coded information, while alignment toward the south pole records the 0 bits. Playback of recorded bits involves the detection of alignment patterns.

Magnetic disk platters may be rigid (aluminum or occasionally glass) or flexible (polyester). The former are termed hard disks, the latter floppy disks.

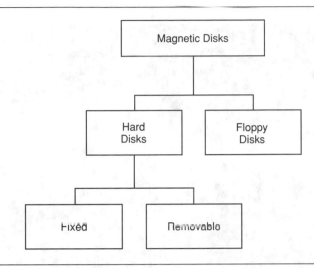

Magnetic disks include fixed hard disks, removable hard disks, and floppy disks.

Since their introduction in the 1950s, hard disk drives have been the principal storage devices for digitally coded information and programs that need to be immediately and continuously available to computer users. With the most widely encountered hard disk configuration, one or more platters are built into a drive mechanism that records and retrieves information. Because the platters cannot be removed, the resulting computer storage device is properly characterized as a fixed, rigid magnetic disk drive, although it is popularly described as a hard drive. In such peripheral equipment configurations, the storage device (the drive) and recording medium (the hard disk) are inseparable.

Storage capacities of most hard drives are measured in gigabytes, or billions of bytes. Multiple platters within a given drive are treated as a unit for capacity measurement. The principal determinants of hard disk capacity are the number of platters per drive and the recording density within each platter. In mainframe and minicomputer configurations, hard disk drives are often described as Direct Access Storage Devices or DASD (pronounced "dazdee"). Since the 1950s, the number and sizes of platters in DASD configurations have decreased steadily, while technological innovation and improved product designs have dramatically enhanced recording densities and storage capacities per platter. DASD configurations with six-to-fourteen-inch platters, which dominated mainframe and minicomputer installations through the early 1990s, have been replaced by hard disk arrays, which contain multiple drives with 3.5-inch platters. Such smaller drives require less floor space, consume less electrical power, and are much less expensive to purchase, install, operate, and maintain than larger drives. Further, they are more reliable, can be more easily scaled to address varied storage requirements, and support faster access times for reading and recording. A computer treats the multiple physical drives in a hard disk array as a single logical drive for recording and retrieval purposes. Multidrive arrays are usually supplied in RAID configurations, which incorporate redundant recording and storage procedures for fault-tolerant operation and data protection. The RAID

Hard disk drives, shown here in a cutaway view, provide rapid, convenient access to computer-processible information. (Courtesy of Seagate Technology; used by permission)

acronym stands for Redundant Array of Independent Disks. Using special techniques, a RAID system can reconstruct data files for uninterrupted operation in the event of a drive failure within a hard disk array.

While the DASD designation is typically reserved for mainframe and mini-computer configurations, small computers have relied on hard drives for online storage of information and programs since the early 1980s. The much-publicized complexity of newer computer programs, combined with the growing volume and variety of computer-processible information generated by such programs, has led to dramatically increased hard disk storage requirements in desktop and portable computer installations. Newer microcomputer operating systems and application programs, for example, can require 50 megabytes or more of hard disk space for installation and operation. As organizations downsize mainframe and minicomputer applications, networked microcomputers must store large databases and text files. Multimedia computing involves unprecedented quantities of information: One minute of stereo audio requires 10 megabytes of hard disk space, while one minute of full-motion color video will occupy 100 to 200 megabytes, even when compression is utilized.

Like their mainframe and minicomputer counterparts, small computers can be equipped with RAID products for high storage capacity and fault-tolerant operation. Such multidrive arrays are increasingly utilized by microcomputers that function as network servers. Conventional single-drive configurations are more common in desktop and portable computer configurations. Now 3.5-inch hard drives dominate desktop installations, while 2.5-inch and smaller hard drives are available for portable computing devices. Since the early 1990s, technical advances have raised the recording densities and storage capacities of these hard drives to extraordinary levels. Multigigabyte storage configurations, once reserved for mainframe and large minicomputer installations, have become standard equipment with entry-level microcomputers. With hard drive capacities doubling at intervals of twelve to eighteen months, continuing improvements can be expected. Given the rapid pace of technological development, new models are announced soon after their predecessors become readily available.

Even with multigigabyte capacities, fixed magnetic disks can become full, necessitating their replacement with higher capacity models or the purchase of additional drives. Alternatively, space must be recaptured by deleting information or transferring some data to magnetic tapes or other media for offline storage. Hard drives with removable disks address this problem. With such devices, a single hard drive can support an infinite number of media, any of which can be inserted into the drive for recording or retrieval of information as needed. If greater storage capacity is required, the user merely purchases additional recording media rather than upgrading or replacing an entire drive. When not in use, the removable disks are housed in cabinets or on shelves. Hard drives with removable media consequently offer unlimited recording capacity, provided that offline storage is acceptable for some information.

In most computer installations, removable hard drives serve as supplements or complements, rather than replacements, for conventional hard drives. Because removable hard disks must be retrieved from their storage locations and mounted in a drive when required, they are not suitable for information that must be immediately and continuously accessible online. As an important consideration for corporate and government libraries that store proprietary technical or business data, removable hard disks can be kept in locked containers, vaults, or other secure locations to protect sensitive or valuable information against unauthorized access. As an additional advantage, removable hard disks provide a convenient method of moving files between computer systems that are equipped with compatible drives. They can consequently be used for physical exchange of machine-readable information. Removable hard drives also offer a measure of fault-tolerance. If a removable hard disk drive associated with a given computer system fails, a compatible replacement can be substituted without loss of information.

Introduced in the 1960s, the earliest removable hard disk drives were intended for computer installations that could not afford enough fixed magnetic disk capacity to satisfy their data storage requirements. At that time, hard disk storage was very expensive. Removable hard disk drives were widely encountered in mainframe and minicomputer installations through the early 1980s, but they have since been discontinued. Removable hard disk technology remains a viable contemporary storage option for small computer configurations, however. Several manufacturers offer removable hard disk products that separate a drive's read/write head assembly from its platter-shaped recording medium. The latter is enclosed in a removable plastic cartridge. Such devices are often described as hard disk cartridge drives. They are widely used for information, such as computer-aided design or desktop publishing files, that do not need to be immediately and continuously available online. Other uses include the transporting or exchange of databases, typesetter files, or other information; grouping of project-related information by type or activity on individual cartridges; and recording of music, compressed video, or multimedia programs that require considerable storage space. Like their fixed counterparts, hard disk cartridge capacities have improved steadily and significantly since the 1980s. The newest hard disk cartridge drives support gigabyte-level media.

Whether fixed or removable media are involved, a hard drive's read/write head is suspended aerodynamically above the surface of a rapidly spinning disk. Should the drive become contaminated by dust or pollutants, or should its power supply be momentarily interrupted, the read/write head will make contact with the disk's surface, damaging some or all of the recorded information. While the reliability of hard drives has improved dramatically in recent years, this malfunction, commonly known as a "head crash," is an ever-present threat and an inevitability for hard drives that remain in service for long periods of time. Protective measures are consequently required. The usual protection method, called hard disk backup, involves periodic copying of information onto magnetic tape or other media for offline storage. Depending on the frequency with which new information is generated, this copying procedure may be performed daily or at longer or shorter intervals. In some cases, the backup copies are limited to information that has changed since the last copying interval; alternatively, the entire contents of a hard drive may be duplicated periodically. In the event of a hard disk failure, information can be recovered up to the point of last copying, thereby limiting the adverse impact of a system malfunction.

Floppy disks, also called diskettes, are the most widely encountered type of removable magnetic disk. Floppy disks have circular polyester substrates that are coated with a magnetizable recording layer. The earliest examples, introduced in 1971, measured eight inches in diameter. They were supplanted by 5.25-inch diskettes in the mid-1970s. Encapsulated in plastic cartridges, 3.5-inch diskettes have been the dominant size since the mid-1980s. Now 3.5-inch floppy disk drives are standard equipment with desktop and portable computers. Double-sided, high-density diskettes, the most common 3.5-inch format, can store 1.44 megabytes.

Floppy disks are widely used for software distribution and selective backup of information stored on hard drives. They can also be used for data archiving—the transfer of inactive information from hard drives for offline retention. Because a floppy disk drive's read/write head is in contact with the diskette's surface, crashes are not a problem, although duplicate copies of important diskettes should be made for security purposes. As a potentially significant disadvantage, floppy disk drives operate much more slowly than hard drives, and their limited storage capacity renders them unsuitable for some applications; most computer programs and many data files contain more than 1.44 megabytes. Addressing this problem, several peripheral equipment manufacturers have developed higher capacity floppy disk systems that employ innovative recording technologies. Depending on the model, such products can store more than 100 megabytes per 3.5-inch diskette.

Magnetic Tape

Broadly defined, a magnetic tape is a ribbon of polyester film coated with a magnetizable recording layer. Magnetic tape devices and media have a long history in information storage. Audiotapes for voice dictation and music date from the 1920s. Videotape recorders were introduced in the 1950s. Magnetic tape drives, which predated hard drives, were the principal auxiliary storage devices in early computer installations, and successor models have been in continuous use since that time. Today, magnetic tapes enjoy a well-established position in computer applications: They are the most widely utilized media for data backup (the

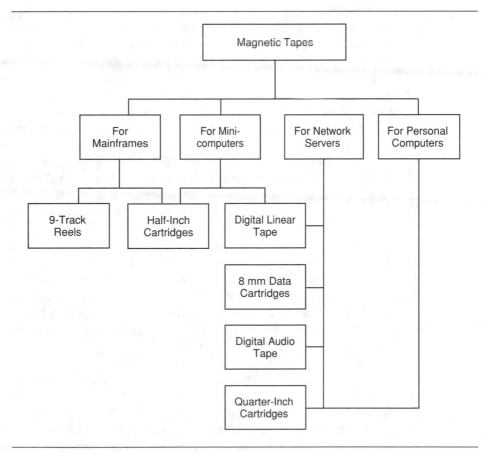

Magnetic tapes are available in various formats for use with mainframes, minicomputers, network servers, and personal computers.

periodic copying of information from hard drives for disaster recovery) and data archiving (the transfer of inactive information from hard drives for offline storage). As such, magnetic tapes complement rather than compete with the magnetic disk technologies described above. Magnetic tapes are also used for distribution and exchange of information and software, particularly in mainframe and minicomputer installations. As described in later chapters, many libraries acquire cataloging records and reference databases on magnetic tapes from bibliographic utilities and information publishers.

Magnetic tapes offer high recording capacities at reasonable costs relative to other computer storage media. As removable media, magnetic tapes are stored offline, in cabinets or on shelves, when not in use. When required for recording or playback of information, a magnetic tape must be manually retrieved from its storage location and mounted on a tape drive. Magnetic tapes are consequently unsuitable for information that must be immediately and continuously accessible online. Robotic tape libraries, which automatically fetch and mount tapes as instructed by a computer, are available, but they are rarely encountered in library applications. As a further limitation, the recording or reading of information onto or from a particular portion of a magnetic tape requires that the preceding portions be moved past the tape drive's read/write head. Because this process is time-consuming, magnetic tape is unsuitable for interactive computing applications that require rapid, often unpredictable access to information. Such applications must utilize platter-shaped media, which have direct-access capabilities. With a hard drive, for example, the read/write head moves directly to the track location where information will be recorded or read. It does not spiral through the preceding tracks to reach the desired location.

Data backup, data archiving, software distribution, and information exchange are supported by a diverse group of magnetic tape formats, some of which have multiple varieties. Magnetic tapes may be packaged on open reels, in cartridges, or in cassettes. Tape widths range from four millimeters to one-half inch. Tape lengths vary from format to format and, within a given format, from model to model. Half-inch tape on plastic reels is the oldest magnetic tape format for computer applications. It has been used for data storage since the 1950s. The most widely encountered reels measure 10.5 inches in diameter and contain 2,400 feet of tape. Such media are typically described as nine-track tapes because individual bits are recorded across the tape in nine parallel tracks. The storage capacity per reel varies with the recording density, which is measured in bits per inch (bpi). The highest density models, which operate at 6,250 bpi, store approximately 160 megabytes per 2,400-foot reel. Older, lower-capacity tapes are recorded at 800 or 1,600 bpi.

Half-inch data cartridges offer a compact, convenient, higher-capacity alternative to nine-track tape drives and media. The first half-inch data cartridge drive, the IBM 3480 Magnetic Tape Cartridge Subsystem, was introduced in 1984 for mainframe computer installations. It recorded information on a half-inch magnetic tape packaged in a plastic cartridge measuring four inches by five inches by one inch in size. The 3480 cartridge's storage capacity is 200 megabytes. Other manufacturers of auxiliary storage peripherals soon added 3480-type tape drives to their product lines. An improved version, the 3490 data cartridge, was introduced in 1989. Using data compression techniques, it tripled the capacity of a 3480-type cartridge. The 3490E format, introduced in 1991, increased cartridge capacity to 800 megabytes or 2.4 gigabytes with compression. The 3590 format, introduced in 1995, can store 10 gigabytes per cartridge, or three times that amount when data compression is utilized. All of these formats remain in use. Since the 1980s, half-inch data cartridges have steadily supplanted nine-track reels in mainframe and minicomputer installations. Compared to nine-track magnetic tapes, half-inch data cartridges require less shelf space for a given quantity of computer-processable information. Their space saving advantages are particularly significant where large numbers of magnetic tapes must be stored in environmentally controlled vaults, computer rooms, or other expensive facilities.

Digital Linear Tape (DLT), another half-inch data cartridge technology, was introduced in the early 1990s. Principally intended for hard disk backup and data archiving in minicomputer and network server installations, DLT cartridges can store over 35 gigabytes of computer-processable information. They can consequently back up the entire contents of most hard drives. Several computer tape technologies introduced in the late 1980s are based on products that were developed originally for video or audio recording. Eight-millimeter data cartridges, for example, are based on 8 mm videotape technology. They can store over 20 gigabytes of computer-processable information. Digital Audio Tape (DAT), as its name indicates, is an audio-derivative technology adapted for data recording. DAT cartridges can store over 12 gigabytes. Like DLT, 8 mm data cartridges and DAT cartridges are intended for hard drive backup and data archiving in minicomputer and network server installations. Quarter-inch cartridge (QIC) tapes were introduced in the early 1970s for small computer installations. Widely available and competitively priced, they are used for hard disk backup and data archiving by desktop computers and network servers. QIC cartridges are available in two sizes and more than a dozen recording formats. Storage capacities of the various QIC formats range from less than 100 megabytes to several gigabytes. Like hard drives, the storage capacities of all magnetic tape formats are subject to continuous improvement.

Optical Disks

Optical disks use light—specifically, light generated by lasers—to record and retrieve information. The magnetic storage products described above record information by detectably altering the magnetizable properties of a disk or tape. In a conceptually similar but technically different manner, optical disks record information by altering the way in which a platter-shaped medium reflects light. Such alteration may be accomplished in various ways: by forming microscopic bits or bubbles in the medium's surface (ablative recording), by irradiating an organic dye material (dye-based recording), by changing the direction of light reflected from a magnetizable surface (magneto-optical recording), by inducing crystalline-to-amorphous transitions (phase change recording), or by other means. Regardless of method, a "playback" laser detects the alterations and decodes or "reads" the recorded information. The playback laser typically

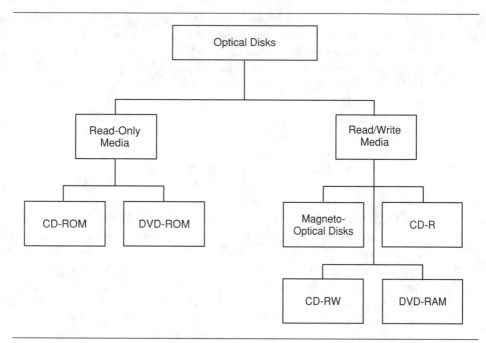

Optical disks are available in read-only and read/write versions. Each type has several varieties.

operates at a lower power or at a different wavelength than the laser that is used for recording. As its most attractive and significant characteristic, optical storage supports very high areal recording densities, which yield correspondingly high media capacities. Optical disks can consequently accommodate huge quantities of character-coded text, quantitative data, and graphic images, as well as video and audio information.

All optical disks are removable storage media. They are available in read-only and read/write configurations. Read-only optical disks contain prerecorded information that is produced by a mastering and replication process. Premastering procedures organize, index, and otherwise prepare information for recording on read-only optical disks. The formatted information is then sent to an optical disk factory, where a master disk is produced. The master disk's surface contours, which represent information encoded as combinations of microscopic holes and spaces, are impressed on plastic copies, which are then distributed or sold to libraries, businesses, government agencies, consumers, or other end users. The copies themselves have no recordable properties; they are designed to be read in playback devices (read-only optical disk drives) that have no recording mechanisms.

Compact discs are the most important group of read-only optical disks. Compact disc (CD) is the collective designation for a group of interrelated optical storage formats that are based on technology developed during the 1970s and 1980s by Sony and Philips. Introduced in 1980, the most widely encountered type of compact disc is a rigid plastic platter that measures 4.75 inches (120 millimeters) in diameter. Compact discs have a reflective metal layer covered with a protective coating.

Various compact disc formats have been developed for specific types of information. Compact Disc–Read-Only Memory (CD-ROM) is the compact disc format for computer-processable data. CD-ROM is an electronic publishing technology. It is intended for applications that require multiple copies of databases, graphic images, software, or other computer-processable information for sale to the public or distribution to closed user groups. A 4.75-inch CD-ROM can store approximately 540 megabytes. It is particularly well suited to the distribution of large databases or other voluminous information. Recorded information is read by specially designed drives that are standard equipment with most desktop computers. Multidrive CD-ROM towers and multidisc CD-ROM autochangers are available for network server installations. In library applications, CD-ROM technology is utilized for database searching, copy cataloging, and preparation of union catalogs. Examples are discussed in chapters 6 and 7.

DVD, originally known as the Digital Video Disk and later as the Digital Versatile Disk, is the compatible successor to compact discs. DVD media are the same size as compact discs, but they offer higher storage capacities. DVD-ROM, a read-only optical disk format for computer-processable information, can store 4.7 gigabytes, which is approximately eight times the capacity of a CD-ROM. Introduced in 1997, DVD is attractive for large reference databases and library catalogs that occupy multiple CD-ROMs. DVD-ROM drives can read CD-ROM media.

While read-only optical disks contain prerecorded information, read/write optical media permit direct recording of machine-readable information. Such media are blank when purchased, and their drives have recording as well as playback capabilities. In computer storage applications, read/write optical media can record machine-readable information generated by keyboards, scanners, scientific instrumentation, or other input devices. They can also store data files, word processing documents, electronic images, or other information transferred from magnetic disks, magnetic tapes, or other optical disks. Read/right optical media are commonly divided into rewritable and write-once (WORM) varieties. Rewritable optical disks are erasable and reusable. The contents of previously recorded media segments can be deleted and/or overwritten with new information. Write-once optical disks, in contrast, are not erasable. Once information is recorded in a given area of a write-once optical disk, that area cannot be reused.

A popular type of read/write optical disk uses magneto-optical (MO) recording, a hybrid technology that combines lasers and magnetism. Encapsulated in plastic cartridges, magneto-optical media are available in rewritable and write-once versions. The 5.25-inch magneto-optical disks can store over 5 gigabytes of computer-processable information. The 3.5-inch magneto-optical disks can store over 600 megabytes. Media capacities are doubling at 18-to-24-month intervals. Compact Disc-Recordable (CD-R) is a write-once optical disk in the compact disc product family. Compact Disc-Rewritable (CD-RW) is its erasable counterpart. Both technologies can record over 600 megabytes on a 4.75-inch compact disc. DVD-RAM is a recordable DVD product that can store over 2 gigabytes of computer-processable information. At the time of this writing, DVD-RAM systems were demonstrated in prototype versions only.

Optical disk autochangers provide unattended access to large quantities of computer-processible information. (Courtesy of Hewlett-Packard; used by permission)

Read/write optical disk drives are available for computers of all types and sizes. As removable media, optical disks must be manually inserted into compatible drives for recording or retrieval of information. Alternatively, optical disk autochangers, sometimes described as jukebox units, can provide unattended access to large quantities of information recorded on multiple optical disks. The disks, which are stored on shelves or bins inside the autochanger, are fetched by a robotic mechanism and mounted in an optical disk drive when required by a particular computer program. The robotic mechanism also removes disks when they are no longer needed and returns them to their shelf locations. Autochanger capacities range from 10 gigabytes for desktop units to more than one terabyte for large-scale devices intended for storage-intensive applications. While optical disk autochangers operate as online peripheral devices, individual optical disks are not brought online until they are requested by a computer program. Consequently, autochangers are characterized as "nearline" peripherals. Their access times are measured in seconds rather than the fractions of a second associated with true online devices.

SUMMARY

A computer hardware system consists of a central processor and its associated peripheral devices. The central processor, which performs the actual work of computation, contains interrelated arithmetic/logic, control, and memory circuitry. The last of these stores programs and information with which a computer is working at a given moment. Computer-processible information is encoded in machine-readable binary form, each character being represented by a predetermined pattern of bits. Newer computers feature semiconductor memories in which individual characters are represented by the presence or absence of electrical current in a specified combination of circuits.

Historically, central processors have been categorized as mainframes, minicomputers, or microcomputers, depending on such factors as physical size, processing power, intended application, and price. Recent advances in electronic technology, however, have blurred whatever clear distinctions previously existed among these categories. Smaller mainframe computers, for example, are indistinguishable from the most powerful minicomputers, while the most powerful microcomputers offer capabilities that equal or exceed those of certain minicomputers. While generalizations are necessarily subject to exceptions, mainframe computers are usually operated by centralized data processing departments within large organizations, while minicomputers may be installed in decentralized departments or as centralized processors in medium-sized organizations. In libraries, minicomputers are often dedicated to a specific task, such as online catalog access or circulation control. While most microcomputers function as desktop workstations or portable computing devices, there has been much interest in the implementation of microcomputer networks as less expensive alternatives to larger computer systems for complex information processing tasks.

While central processors perform the actual work of computation, the peripheral devices provide specialized input, output, or auxiliary storage capabilities. The input peripherals convert human-readable information to the machine-readable form required for computer processing. In library applications, most input operations rely on key-entry (typing) of information. Alternatively, optical recognition technologies scan documents, converting their content to machine-readable form automatically. Barcode label recognition, a limited form of optical recognition, is used in many library circulation control applications. Optical character recognition (OCR), which analyzes reflected light to identify the individual characters contained in documents, supports a broader range of applications. Document digitizers convert textual or graphic documents to electronic pictures for computer processing and storage. They are encountered in desktop publishing and image storage and retrieval systems, among other applications.

The output peripherals convert the machine-readable results of computer processing to human-readable form. In library applications, computer-processed information may be printed on paper, recorded on microfilm, or displayed on a screen. Paper printers range from very expensive devices with operating speeds measured in pages per second to relatively inexpensive desktop printers designed for decentralized installations. The latter product group is dominated by laser and inkjet printers with versatile typographic capabilities. Digital plotters, a special class of paper printers, are designed for graphic output, principally in scientific and engineering applications. A COM recorder is a variant form of computer printer that transfers machine-readable data to human-readable information on microfilm or microfiche rather than paper. The resulting miniaturized document images can be enlarged for display on a microform reader or copied onto paper using a reader/printer. Video display units likewise present the results of computer processing on a screen. Most models incorporate a television-like cathode ray tube (CRT) as their display mechanism. Among flat panel alternatives to CRT technology, liquid crystal displays (LCDs) are widely used in portable computers.

Auxiliary storage peripherals and media are designed to retain information in machine-readable form, pending computer processing or reprocessing. They thus serve as extensions to the central processor's necessarily limited memory section. While early computer systems used paper storage media, magnetic disk and tapes have dominated auxiliary storage for decades. Magnetic disk drives, particularly hard drives, are the preferred storage devices in applications where data must be continuously available for rapid access in an unpredictable manner. Floppy disks, a type of removable magnetic disk, are used for software distribution and other applications in small computer installations. Magnetic tapes are the storage media of choice for data backup and data archiving. Available in various formats and storage capacities, they are also used for software and information distribution in mainframe and minicomputer installations. Optical disks, in read-only and read/write varieties, are notable for their high capacities. Among read-only optical disks, CD-ROM has been used for database publishing and other library-related applications.

2

Computer
Software

The term hardware, as defined in the preceding chapter, denotes the equipment components in a computer system. The term software denotes the programs, or predefined sequences of instructions, that a computer executes to accomplish information processing tasks. The software concepts discussed in this chapter are normally applicable only to the central processor in a computer system. Most peripheral devices operate under the control of the central processor and are not programmable by computer users in the conventional sense, although some peripherals, such as printers, are controlled by prewritten, internally stored programs of a type described below.

The hardware components in a computer system are visible, tangible, and readily comprehensible; software, on the other hand, is an intellectual product. It does have a tangible manifestation: The individual instructions that make up a computer program may be written or printed on paper in the more or less human-readable form described later in this chapter. Such human-readable instructions, however, must be converted to machine-readable form for computer execution. As with data, this conversion is typically accomplished by typing the instructions, character by character, at a computer input device. The resulting machine-readable program is typically maintained on a magnetic or optical storage medium, from which it is loaded into the central processor's random-access memory for execution. This is most obviously the case with prewritten software packages for small computers, most of which are distributed on floppy disks or CD-ROMs. Prewritten programs for mainframes and minicomputers, by contrast, are typically distributed on magnetic tape.

In some computer configurations, frequently executed programs—and, occasionally, frequently referenced information—may be permanently recorded in the read-only memory circuits described in chapter 1. This approach to software implementation is typically used for programs that must be immediately and continuously available to the central processor. It is also used for programs that control peripheral devices. Programs stored in this manner are termed "firmware" to reflect their embodiment in hardware components and to distinguish them from conventional software, which is maintained on auxiliary storage media for transfer to the central processor's random-access memory when required. Among the most important uses of firmware are "bootstrap" programs that start a computer system and instruct it to load additional programs located on a hard drive. Firmware is also used for diagnostic programs that check the operating status of specific hardware components when a computer is first turned on. In most computer configurations, however, firmware is used sparingly, principally because read-only memory circuits are relatively expensive storage media. As an additional constraint, programs stored in firmware must be updated by replacement of hardware components. Conventional software, in contrast, is easily updated by issuing replacement diskettes, tapes, or CD-ROMs.

It is possible to build computing equipment with fixed electronic circuitry designed to perform one or more specific operations; certain calculators and electronic typewriters are examples of such products. The power and versatility of computers, however, are largely derived from their general-purpose, programmable nature. However, at a time when a varied and flexible range of hardware components is readily available and increasingly affordable, problems of software development constitute the most significant impediment to the implementation of computer systems in both library and non-library installations. This chapter discusses the characteristics and problems of computer software, beginning with a description of the two basic types of software and the role of system software and programming languages in computer systems. Later sections deal with application software, the software development process, and prewritten software packages. Throughout the chapter, emphasis is placed on concepts and terminology that are essential for librarians who must purchase programs from software developers or communicate software requirements to computer specialists.

SYSTEM SOFTWARE

Historically, the computer industry has differentiated system software (programs that enable a computer to function and control its own operations) from application software (programs that perform user-specified tasks, records such as printing purchase orders in acquisitions applications, programs that calculate fines for overdue library materials or generate bibliographic lists). Until recently, the computing industry viewed the development of application software as the user's responsibility. As discussed later in this chapter, many mainframe and minicomputer installations continue to rely heavily on customized programming for specific applications. Since the 1950s, however, most computer manufacturers have provided prewritten system software for use with their equipment. In addition, some software development companies specialize in system programs for specific types of computers.

Operating Systems

The most important category of system software is a group of multifunctional supervisory programs variously called an operating system, an executive system, or a system monitor. At the most fundamental level, an operating system identifies users and determines whether, and to what extent, they are to be given access to particular computer resources. It responds to user-entered commands that initiate the execution of specific programs, allocates required hardware and software resources to those programs, and controls their progress and termination. An operating system must also act on exceptional conditions that arise during the execution of a computer program and alert the user with appropriate messages.

As software products, operating systems are typically given initialed or acronym names. Historically, operating systems have been developed and sold by computer manufacturers for use with their equipment. Well-known examples that may be encountered in library installations include the MVS and VM operating systems for IBM mainframes; the VMS and OpenVMS operating systems for Digital Equipment's VAX and Alpha product lines; OS/400 operating system for IBM AS/400 minicomputers; the MPE operating system developed by Hewlett-Packard for its HP 3000 series minicomputers; the OS/2 operating system developed by IBM for desktop microcomputers and network servers; and the Mac OS, developed by Apple Computer for Macintosh installations.

As a supplement or alternative to manufacturer-supplied products, several popular operating systems have been developed by companies or other organizations that specialize in system software. Rather than being limited to a specific manufacturer's hardware, such third-party operating systems are often designed for computers that share certain hardware components or other characteristics. The best-known and most widely installed examples are the MS-DOS and Windows operating systems, which were developed by Microsoft Corporation. MS-DOS was introduced in the early 1980s for the IBM Personal Computer and compatible devices. It was the dominant operating system for desktop and portable computers through the late 1980s. While no longer state-of-the-art, MS-DOS continues to be used for some business and library applications. Microsoft Windows is a family of operating systems for small computers and related devices. The original Windows program, introduced in the mid-1980s as an enhancement for MS-DOS, has been replaced by Windows 95 and its successor, Windows 98. Designed for machines equipped with Intel or compatible microprocessors, those operating systems have dominated desktop computing since the late 1990s. Windows NT, the most powerful operating system in the Windows product line, is available in versions for desktop computers and network servers. Windows NT Workstation provides an alternative to Windows 95 and Windows 98 for desktop and certain portable computers. Compared to Windows 95 and Windows 98, it requires a more powerful computer system and greater amounts of random-access memory. The Windows NT Server is principally intended for local area networks, which are discussed in chapter 3. Featuring integrated networking and communications capabilities, it can run on Intel-based computers or on Alpha processors from Digital

Equipment. Windows CE is an operating system for handheld personal computers and related devices.

The Unix operating system has attracted considerable attention in a broad range of information processing applications, including library automation. An outgrowth of software research conducted at Bell Telephone Laboratories during the 1960s and 1970s, versions of Unix are available for hardware configurations ranging from portable computers to supercomputers, but Unix most often serves as the operating system for minicomputers and network servers. Versions of Unix are marketed by many companies under a variety of names. Examples include Unix System V, AT&T's own implementation; AIX, a Unix implementation for IBM RS/6000 computers; HP-UX, which was developed by Hewlett-Packard for HP 9000 computers; and Solaris, a version of Unix developed by Sun Microsystems. Several versions of the Unix operating system are available for microcomputers. Examples include Linux and SCO Unix.

The simplest operating systems are designed for stand-alone microcomputers. They serve one user and can execute one computer program at a time. Thus, if a user is doing word processing and wants to switch to a spreadsheet program, the word processing program must be terminated before the spreadsheet program can be activated. MS-DOS is the most widely encountered example of such a single-user, single-tasking operating system. Microsoft Windows added multitasking capabilities, among other functionality, to the MS-DOS operating system. Windows 95 and Windows 98 are single-user operating systems, but they permit simultaneous execution of multiple programs. A word processing program can remain open while a spreadsheet program is activated. Tasks such as printing that do not require continuous computer-user interaction can be performed in an unattended "background" mode. Other examples of single-user, multitasking operating systems include OS/2 and the Mac OS.

Operating systems for mainframes and minicomputers must support multiple users and multiple programs simultaneously. Such multiuser operating systems are described as time-sharing operating systems. As discussed in the next chapter, they support multiple terminals. Some multiuser, multitasking operating systems also support multiprocessing capabilities in which a given program can run on two or more central processors.

Specific processing modes aside, a successful operating system must perform its work in a manner that is largely transparent to the computer user, giving the impression that its capabilities are inherent in the computer hardware itself. A successful time-sharing operating system must further sustain the illusion that a computer's processing resources are at the complete disposal of each simultaneous user. Among their most important tasks, operating systems provide an interface between computers and users. In the most primitive implementations, an operating system accepts and responds to commands that are submitted by the user in a special job control language (JCL). Since the inception of computing, conventional operating systems have relied on an often cryptic repertoire of terse textual messages combined with uninformative prompts that indicate a computer's readiness to receive a command. The MS-DOS operating system, for example, displays "C:/>" or a similar prompt with no explanation of the commands available to the computer user at a given moment. The user must understand the prompt's significance and know the responses required to initiate desired operations.

As a further complication, the commands that make up a specific operating system's job control language may have many variations and can prove difficult to memorize. This poses few problems in mainframe and minicomputer installations where system functions are initiated by trained operators and end-users have little or no direct contact with system software. Microcomputer users, however, must learn the operating system commands necessary to activate programs, store and load data, format disks, and perform other routine tasks. To better serve such users, some software developers offer special interfaces that rely on menus and other features to activate specific functions, thereby minimizing or eliminating the memorization of commands. Designed as operating system extensions, such interfaces are often described as "user-friendly" because they simplify the learning requirements associated with particular work routines.

Based on ideas originally developed at the Xerox Palo Alto Research Center (PARC), the Macintosh interface was the first commercially successful example of a graphical user interface (GUI). The Windows product line offers similar capabilities, as does IBM's Presentation Manager for the OS/2 operating system and MOTIF for the Unix operating system. While specific characteristics vary from program to program, a graphical user interface treats a user's video display as a "desktop." It combines menus of commands with small graphics symbols called icons that represent the programs and data files normally listed in disk directories. The graphical user interface supports "point and click" initiation of computer operations. A mechanical/optical device called a mouse is

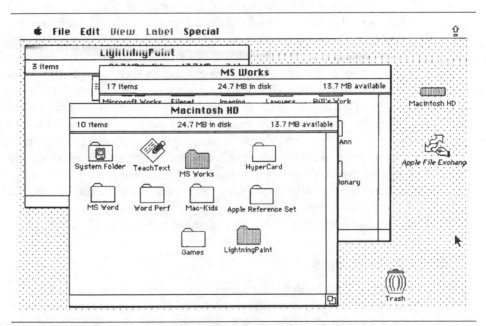

Graphical user interfaces rely on symbols to represent programs and data.

used to activate menus and icons by positioning a displayed arrow or other marker over them and pressing a designated button on the mouse itself. Mouse alternatives, such as trackballs or touchpads, may also be employed. Some menu selections lead to submenus. Others activate dialog boxes with additional lists of options or blank spaces for the entry of specific values. Individual application programs are displayed in one or more windows that can be scrolled, moved, enlarged, reduced, or otherwise manipulated. Some programs also display toolbars with icons for the most frequently executed commands and operations.

Utility Programs

As their name suggests, utility programs perform tasks that are routinely required by, and are generally useful to, computer users. As with other types of system software, utility programs may be obtained from computer equipment manufacturers or from companies that specialize in system software development. Some utility programs are implemented as operating system extensions. Microcomputer operating systems, for example, routinely include utility programs to format disks, selectively copy files between disks, and perform other commonly encountered tasks. Alternatively, utility programs may be custom-developed by local programmers in a manner discussed later in this chapter.

Among the most important types of utility programs are those that copy information from one medium to another, such as from magnetic disks to magnetic tape, in order to remove inactive data from online storage or to create backup copies of important information. Other common utility programs are designed to recover information in the event of a system failure, determine the remaining storage capacity of a given medium, scan hard drives for damaged areas, consolidate unused areas within a hard drive for more efficient operation, remove programs that are no longer needed, detect and remove computer viruses, sort lists of data into a predefined sequence, or merge two or more files of previously stored information. Some utility programs can compress files for more efficient storage or encrypt them for security. File viewer utilities will display or print the contents of a file, even if the program that created the file is not available.

Several types of utility programs are specifically designed to facilitate the software development process by simplifying the work of programmers. Editor programs, for example, allow other programs to be conveniently entered into online storage and modified as required. Other utility programs assist in the detection and correction of errors or "bugs" encountered during program testing. The most important category of software development tools, however, consists of the assemblers, compilers, and interpreters discussed in the following section.

Programming Languages

A program is a predefined sequence of commands or instructions that a computer executes to accomplish one or more tasks. All computers are built to respond to a predetermined set of instructions that initiate the execution of arithmetic calculations, logical comparisons, or other data manipulations, as well as the transfer of information between various system components. For a given information processing task, the number and nature of required instructions will vary with the size and power of the central processor and, for computers of a given type, from model to model. As noted in chapter 1, some processors employ Reduced Instruction Set Computing (RISC) technology, which supports a relatively small repertoire of instructions that are optimized for rapid execution. The central processors encountered in conventional computer systems are sometimes described as Complex Instruction Set Computing (CISC) devices. Compared to RISC processors, they support a much larger repertoire of executable instructions.

Regardless of the number of instructions supported by a given computer configuration, programming is that activity in which executable instructions are selected and combined in an appropriate sequence. The term properly denotes the development of either system software or application software, although it most often denotes the latter—that is, those programs that perform user-defined tasks. A programming language is a set of syntactical and semantic rules that specify the manner in which particular instructions are to be used and combined. The syntactical rules specify the format for instructions, while the semantic rules indicate the meanings of specific commands.

Computers can only process instructions that are encoded in machine-readable, binary form. Programs coded in binary form are said to be written in machine-level language, the only type of programming language that is immediately executable by computer. In machine-level programming, binary-coded instructions may be initially written in handprinted form on ordinary paper or specially designed programmers' worksheets. The instructions, which consist of the human-readable symbols "1" and "0," must then be converted to the machine-readable form required for computer processing. This is usually accomplished by typing them, line by line, at an input device. An editing utility or word processing program is typically used to simplify the entry, insertion, modification, and deletion of instructions. Manuals prepared by the computer's manufacturer provide syntactical guidelines and tell the programmer which binary codes represent particular information processing operations.

Within a machine-level program, instructions consist of two parts: A code for an arithmetic, logical, or other operation to be performed is followed by the binary-coded address within main memory of the intended operand—that is, the object of a specific operation. Thus, a machine-level program instruction of the form

$$01000001110$$

might cause the information stored in memory location number 14 to be brought into an accumulator register within the central processor's arithmetic/logic unit, while the following instruction sequence:

$$01100001111$$
$$00110010000$$

may cause the contents of memory location number 15 to be added to it, and the results stored in memory location number 16.

Historically, there has been an unfortunate disparity between the computer industry's ability to manufacture sophisticated hardware and the customer's ability to produce or otherwise obtain effective software to address specific information processing requirements. As the foregoing example suggests, programming in machine-level language is a time-consuming, error-prone activity. Machine-level language is difficult to learn and produces programs that can prove very difficult to proofread, test, and modify. As a result, machine-level language is rarely used, even by experienced programmers. Instead, the software development process is better served by simpler methodologies that enable programmers to accomplish more work in a shorter amount of time. These simpler methodologies are based on the following model: Programs written in a simpler format are translated by other, specially designed programs into the machine-level language required for computer execution.

In assembler language programming, for example, mnemonic commands and symbolic operands are substituted for binary codes. Thus, the three-instruction sequence

MOV 14
ADD 15
STO 16

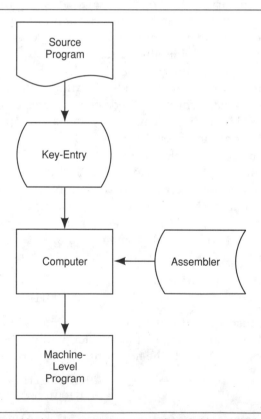

Programs written in assembler language must be converted to machine-readable form, then translated into the machine-level language required for computer execution. The translation is performed by a special program called an assembler.

is the assembler language equivalent of the binary-coded, machine-level instructions presented above. From the standpoint of programmers' productivity, mnemonic assembler language commands are much easier to remember than their machine-level counterparts, and the resulting programs are obviously easier to proofread and correct. In most cases, assembler language programming can be further simplified by substituting mnemonic names for numeric memory locations and combining frequently used sequences of instructions into programmer-designed "macro" instructions that can be invoked with a single command.

While they are easier to write, the individual instructions that comprise an assembler language program must eventually be translated into machine-level language for computer execution. This translation is performed automatically by the computer itself, using a special program called an assembler—an example of system software. The assembler program, which is often obtained from the manufacturer of the central processor on which the program will execute, may itself be written in machine-level language. All available computers support an assembler program of some type, although assemblers designed for different machines are typically incompatible with one another.

Assembler language is most often used when a programmer requires very close control over the internal operation of the central processor, in order, for example, to optimize the allocation of memory space or the speed with which a given program is executed. Consequently, assembler language programming is a useful methodology for writing operating systems, sort/merge programs, and other system software. Its general-purpose character, combined with the efficient utilization of computing resources, makes assembler language highly suitable for writing application programs as well. In many cases, however, speed of software development is more important than efficient program execution; programming labor costs are increasing, while the cost of computer processing power continues to fall dramatically. As a result, application software is often written in one of the higher-level programming languages to reduce programming time and its associated labor costs. Further, because computerization often saves money when compared to the labor-intensive manual procedures it replaces, speed of implementation is important. The faster an application is computerized, the sooner the resulting savings will begin.

While they differ in ease of use, machine-level and assembler languages are collectively categorized as lower-level languages because a programmer must pay close attention to the specific central processor components used in a given operation. The higher-level languages, by contrast, allow a programmer to encode successive instructions in a comparatively abstract notation with little concern for details of machine design. Thus, a sequence of three instructions designed to add numeric values contained in two specified memory locations and store the result in a third location may be simply expressed in the algebraic form

$$C = A + B$$

When higher-level languages are used, a programmer can devote full attention to the problem to be solved, rather than to the computer on which a given program will be executed. As a further advantage, each instruction written in a higher-level language is typically the equivalent of several machine-level language instructions. In short, higher-level language programs are easier, faster, and less expensive to develop than those written in assembler languages.

The resulting programs, however, must be translated into machine-level language prior to execution. As with assembler language programs, this translation is performed by the computer itself, using a special program called a compiler. Before its initial execution, a higher-level language program (sometimes called a source program) is translated by a compiler into a machine-level object program. A variant form of compiler called an interpreter does not generate a formal object program. Instead, it translates individual instructions into

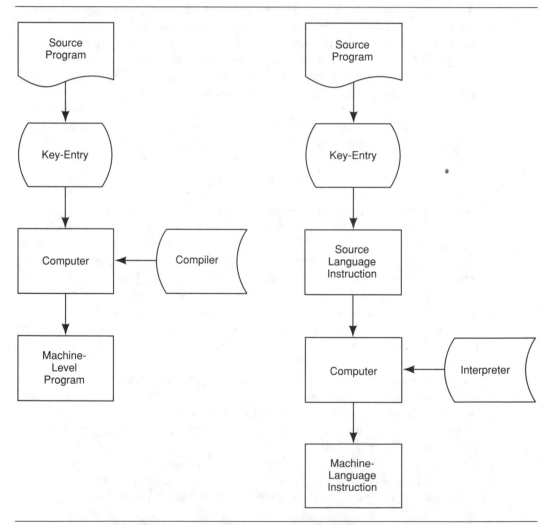

Compilers and interpreters translate programs written in higher-level languages to the machine-level language required for computer execution. A compiler translates the entire source program before execution. Interpreters translate individual program instructions and execute them immediately. In either case, the program must be first converted to machine-readable form, usually by key-entry.

their machine-level equivalents as they are encountered during the execution of a higher-level language program. As a rule, programs written in higher-level languages that use interpreters execute more slowly than those written in languages that use compilers because instructions that initiate repetitive operations must be retranslated each time they are encountered.

Compilers and interpreters are examples of system software. Like assemblers, they translate programs into the machine-level language required for computer execution. Compilers and interpreters may be obtained from computer equipment manufacturers or from software development companies. They have also been developed by research laboratories and universities. Compilers and interpreters of the latter type often incorporate special features to assist student programmers.

Regardless of source, the nature and number of higher-level programming languages available in a particular situation vary with the type of central processor utilized and the mission of the computing facility that operates it. Although hundreds of higher-level languages have been developed, only a small percentage are significant. Some early programming languages were intended for a narrow range of applications or for computers that no longer exist. Others offered useful capabilities but failed to attract a sizable user base. The most famous higher-level languages of the past—FORTRAN, COBOL, and PL/1, for example—dominated software development for a quarter of a century, but they are no longer the preferred programming tools for new projects. They receive little attention in computer science curricula, and few younger programmers are familiar with them. Older programming languages cannot be ignored, however. They were used to create tens of thousands of programs for businesses, government agencies, and other organizations, including some libraries. Running on mainframes and minicomputers, many of those programs continue to automate mission-critical accounting and transaction-processing operations. Eventually, such programs will be rewritten in newer languages or the applications they automate will be reconceptualized. Until that occurs, knowledge of older higher-level languages will be required for repair of defects, enhancements, or other maintenance operations. The following discussion provides a historical survey of selected older and recent higher-level languages, emphasizing their most important uses, notable characteristics, and current status.

From the late 1950s through the mid-1970s, higher-level languages were typically categorized by the type of computer applications for which they were originally developed, although programming languages that are principally intended for a specific purpose, such as business data processing, may also be used for other types of tasks. Paralleling the development of computer hardware, the earliest higher-level languages were designed for technical applications. FORTRAN (an acronym coined from the phrase "formula translator") is the most important example. FORTRAN instructions are written in an algebraic notation that is well suited to the mathematical problems encountered in the sciences and engineering. FORTRAN has also been used for social science and business applications involving statistical analysis. Beneficially affected by more than two decades of enhancement, FORTRAN compilers are available for computers of all types and sizes, including microcomputers. But FORTRAN is principally a programming language for mainframes and minicomputers. FORTRAN programs written for execution on a given computer system will not necessarily execute on other hardware configurations. In fact, a given mainframe or minicomputer installation may maintain several different FORTRAN compilers, each supporting a different version or dialect of the language. Although FORTRAN standards have been developed by the American National Standards Institute (ANSI), most compilers deviate from the standards and offer additional features that are designed to both enhance the language's utility and bolster a given compiler's competitive position.

COBOL (the Common Business-Oriented Language) has long been the most widely utilized higher-level programming language for business data processing in mainframe and minicomputer installations. Unlike scientific computing, with its complex mathematical calculations, business applications are typically characterized by the repetitive performance of fairly simple computations involving large amounts of information. As a result, COBOL instructions emphasize data handling and report production. The language's mathematical capabilities are generally limited to the straightforward arithmetic operations required in such applications as general ledger maintenance or the writing of payment orders. COBOL instructions themselves are written in an English-like notation designed for simplified readability. As originally developed by a committee of computer manufacturers and users, COBOL was intended to be as machine-independent as possible. While COBOL compilers are available for virtually all mainframes and most smaller hardware configurations, a COBOL program written for a particular computer cannot usually be executed on different processors without modification. COBOL standards have been adopted by the American National Standards Institute, but most COBOL compilers offer enhancements that are not included in the standard version. COBOL's historical and continuing importance as a programming language for business applications is underscored by the so-called Year 2000 problem, which necessitates the modification of certain computer programs to avoid misinterpretation of dates after 1999. Many of the affected programs are written in COBOL.

While circulation control, book ordering, and other aspects of library work share many characteristics of business data processing, applications involving information retrieval or the production of indexes and bibliographies require the ability to perform complex operations on character strings (finite, ordered sequences of alphabet characters, numeric digits, punctuation marks, or other symbols) without regard to the numeric values. Programs written in conventional higher-level languages, such as FORTRAN or COBOL, can do little more than store such character strings for later printing as headings or identifying lines in tables or reports that are otherwise heavily numeric.

Where more complex manipulations are required, a group of string processing programming languages features special instructions that permit such operations as the concatenation, or joining, of two character strings to form a third; the bifurcation of character strings into their component parts (sentences into words or words into characters, for example); and pattern matching, or the examination of a character string for the occurrence of a specified substring. SNOBOL, the most important example of a string processing programming language, was originally developed by Bell Telephone Laboratories for the manipulation of formal algebraic expressions and writing of compilers. During the 1970s, SNOBOL received considerable attention from library educators and automation specialists for the development of information retrieval and text analysis programs. Intended principally for IBM mainframe computers, SNOBOL interpreters and compilers are rarely encountered today. LISP, another string processing language, has been used in artificial intelligence applications and "expert" simulation projects in which computer programs attempt to emulate human thought processes.

Several well-known higher-level languages have played an important role in the development of computing activities, but their limited significance for library applications places them beyond the scope of this discussion. Examples include ALGOL, which was seldom used for practical applications in the United States but had a significant impact on the development of other programming languages; JOVIAL, an ALGOL-like language developed for the United States Air Force; MUMPS, which was developed specifically for data processing and clinical applications in hospitals and other medical environments; RPG, a specialized language for report production; Prolog, which has been used for expert system development; LOGO and PILOT, two programming languages designed for educational applications; and Dynamo, GPSS, Simula, and Simscript, which are scripting languages for computer-based simulations.

While the higher-level programming languages were developed for specific types of applications, the PL/1 programming language was designed with generality in mind. Introduced in the 1960s, it combines FORTRAN-like mathematical capabilities with COBOL-like data handling features. Some string processing facilities are also included. The resulting broad applicability proved conceptually attractive to computer center managers interested in simplifying their staffing and training requirements. PL/1 is principally a programming language for IBM mainframe computers. It enjoyed its greatest popularity during the 1960s and 1970s, when computing activities were dominated by mainframe systems. Although compilers have been developed for other hardware configurations, including microcomputers, PL/1 was never widely adopted in such installations.

Programming languages developed during the 1950s and 1960s were designed for work environments in which the individual instructions that make up a program were punched on cards and submitted to a computing facility for execution. The programmer or user returned to the computing facility at some later time to obtain a paper printout containing the results. With the development and rapid spread of online computer systems during the 1970s, programmers and users began working at terminals, and programming languages were introduced that returned results immediately. BASIC (the Beginners All-Purpose Symbolic Instruction Code) was the best known and most widely used of such "online" languages. BASIC was developed at Dartmouth College in the mid-1960s as a pedagogical device rather than a practical programming language. It has since been implemented on a wide range of computers, including most microcomputers. Although it employs a FORTRAN-like algebraic notation, BASIC can be used for both scientific computing and business data processing.

Easy to learn and widely taught in entry-level computer science courses, BASIC is generally viewed as a language for so-called user programmers—that is, persons who write programs for their own use, as opposed to professional programmers who write programs for use by others. BASIC is available in so many different versions that programs developed for one computer configuration cannot usually be executed on others without modification. Most versions of BASIC have been steadily augmented by their developers to incorporate new capabilities and take advantage of the latest developments in computing technology. Visual BASIC, introduced by Microsoft in 1990, facilitates the development of programs with windows, pulldown menus, dialog boxes, and other graphical user interface components.

Since the mid-1970s, managers responsible for computer operations have been increasingly concerned about the maintainability of programs. Used in this context, maintainability denotes the ease with which programs written by one person can be corrected, enhanced, or otherwise modified by others. As organizations computerize greater numbers of applications, such "maintenance" programming accounts for an increasingly large percentage of the software development workload. Given the changing requirements of users and the high programmer turnover rate that characterizes many computer operations, the availability of readily maintainable programs is of great importance.

From the standpoint of maintainability, the rather abstract notation employed by higher-level languages represents a significant improvement over the machine-specific, very detailed code employed in assembler-language programming. COBOL programs, as previously noted, feature a readable English-like notation in which individual instructions take the form of imperative sentences. Critics of conventional higher-level languages, however, contend that their procedures for sequencing instructions greatly increase the potential for error and result in programs that can prove very difficult to maintain. These critics advocate the use of "structured" programming techniques that simplify and clarify the development of programs. Specifically, structured programming replaces the most troublesome logical constructs found in conventional programming methodologies with simple sequences of instructions that are claimed to produce more accurate, readable, and maintainable programs.

While FORTRAN, COBOL, BASIC, and other conventional languages can be modified or otherwise adapted to the requirements of these improved programming techniques, several higher-level languages were specifically developed for structured programming. The best known of these, Pascal, organizes programs into self-contained blocks that facilitate the development of software for complicated applications and simplify the detection and correction of errors. Pascal forces programmers to proceed methodologically. Popularized in the early 1970s as a language for teaching computer programming as a systematic discipline, Pascal quickly replaced BASIC as the language of first instruction in many college-level computer science courses. It can also be used for practical programming, although it is seldom used by professional software developers. Strongly influenced by the ALGOL programming language, Pascal has been implemented on computers of all types and sizes. Although Pascal was originally designed to produce "portable" programs that could be executed on different computers with very little modification, most Pascal compilers, like their counterparts in other programming languages, incorporate special features that promote incompatibility and complicate portability.

Other structured programming languages, such as MODULA-2 and MODULA-3, were directly influenced by Pascal and, through it, ALGOL. The C language, which was developed at Bell Telephone Laboratories in the mid-1970s, is a structured programming language that combines the attributes of higher-level and assembler languages. As a higher-level language, C is relatively easy to learn and use. Like assembler language, however, C gives programmers considerable control over machine operations, memory allocations, and the speed of program execution. C is widely regarded as an effective programming language for operating systems and other system software; the Unix operating system, for example, is largely written in C. It can also be used to create application software and is preferred by many professional software developers for its ability to produce fast, compact, efficient programs that are highly portable. C compilers are widely available for microcomputers and Unix-based systems. ADA, another structured programming language, was developed by the United States Department of Defense as a standard software development tool. ADA compilers are available for various types of computers. The Perl programming language, which resembles C, is easy to learn and useful for a broad range of applications. Perl interpreters are available for several types of computers.

Since the late 1980s, software developers have given considerable attention to object-oriented programming (OOP) languages and methodologies. Object-oriented programs describe arithmetic calculations, logical comparisons, and other computing operations as self-contained data structures called objects, which can be combined and reused by programmers. An object consists of information accompanied by directions for manipulating it. The information might be a number, for example, and the directions might tell how to multiply or divide it by other numbers. The manipulation of objects is facilitated by a graphical user interface of the type described above. Advocates of object-oriented methodologies claim that they simplify programming procedures and produce compact, accurate, readily maintainable programs. As an additional advantage, object-oriented languages and methods are designed to produce reusable program segments, called class libraries, that can be incorporated into other programs. Examples of object-oriented programming languages include Smalltalk and such derivatives as Visual Smalltalk, VisualWorks, and VisualAge; C++, the object-oriented version of the C programming language described above; EIFFEL; Object Pascal; and IRIS.

Java, an object-oriented language introduced in the early 1990s by Sun Microsystems, is one of the most widely publicized programming languages. Java gained considerable notoriety for its Internet applications, but it can be used to create programs for a broad range of computers and computer-like devices, including personal organizers, television set-top boxes, and microprocessor-controlled appliances. Java interpreters, known as Java Virtual Machines, have been developed for many types of computers, including Intel-based microcomputers, Macintosh systems, and Unix-based computers. As one of their principal advantages, Java programs created for one computer can be easily transported to other brands of computers. Like other object-oriented languages, Java is designed to produce reusable program segments, called JavaBeans, that can be combined to build complex applications. Java programming is particularly notable for its small programs, called applets, which are encountered at many Internet sites. Designed to operate with the Web browser programs discussed later in this book, Java applets typically animate pages on the World Wide Web.

Some database management systems, described later in this chapter, feature programming languages that support the development of highly customized computer applications. Such programming languages extend the range of database management products. They are often characterized as fourth-generation languages, or 4GLs, a designation that reflects their developmental relationship to higher-level programming languages (the third generation), assembler language (the second generation), and machine-level language (the first generation). As a group, fourth-generation languages are non-procedural; 4GL programs tell a computer what to do, rather than how to do it. Other programming languages, by contrast, are procedural. They provide step-by-step instructions for the completion of specific operations. Compared to other programming methodologies, fourth-generation languages are easier to learn and use.

APPLICATION SOFTWARE

The assemblers, compilers, and interpreters described above support the development of application software, which consists of programs that perform one or more user-specified tasks. For most users, including librarians who want to automate particular operations, such application software is the most important computer system component.

Unlike system software, which is customarily obtained from computer manufacturers or other sources, the development of application software has historically been viewed as the user's responsibility. While an increasing amount of application software is purchased prewritten, custom-developed programs continue to play an important role in many computer installations. Although the automated library systems described in later chapters make extensive use of prewritten software, customized enhancements to such programs may be developed for specific situations. This section describes the software development process, emphasizing those aspects that are most important for librarians who must explain their application requirements to computer professionals. Even where a library installation relies completely on prewritten software, familiarity with software development methodologies and procedures can facilitate an understanding of a given program's operating characteristics and limitations.

Systems Analysis

In most applications, the software development process begins with a detailed study of the existing operations or combination of operations that accomplish the task or tasks to be computerized. This study is called a systems analysis. In the broadest sense, its purpose is to gather and evaluate the information necessary to improve the existing system or replace it with a new one. Over the past several decades, systems analyses have emphasized the evaluation of manual operations for possible improvement through automation. After three decades of pervasive computerization, however, increasing attention is being given to the analysis of automated applications. This is the case, for example, in those libraries that are considering the replacement of previously implemented computer systems, particularly those that incorporate older technologies.

Whether its subject is manual or automated, a systems analysis is typically performed by an information professional, aptly called a systems analyst, who determines what is being done in an existing system; whether, and to what extent, it is deficient; and what alternative for improvement exists. The process of developing a modified or alternative system, sometimes called systems design, is discussed later in this chapter. Although it is the customary first step in the development of an automated system, a systems analysis need not invariably result in the recommendation of a computerized alternative. Systems analysts trained in industrial engineering, for example, often recommend the simplification of manual work steps or the routinization of procedures previously performed in a discretionary manner. Some systems analysts specialize in the application of technologies other than computers. Examples include micrographics, facsimile transmission, printing, or voice communication systems. Computer systems analysts, while necessarily predisposed to computer-oriented solutions, are presumably alert to problems that computers cannot effectively address and situations for which other technologies or procedural approaches will prove more useful.

Although some large academic and public libraries employ one or more computer systems analysts, most librarians interested in automating a given activity will hire a consultant or work with a systems analyst employed by their organization's computing center or an external service bureau. Some systems analyses are of sufficiently narrow scope to be conducted by a single person. Complex problems typically require a team approach, with multiple analysts working under the direction of a project leader or principal investigator. Such teams customarily include one or more entry-level analysts who are assigned to various information-gathering tasks. More experienced senior analysts assume responsibility for project planning, system evaluation, the formulation of recommendations, report writing, and oral presentations. In some applications, an analytical team may employ consultants with special expertise relevant to specific aspects of a project.

While formal training and work experience will vary among analysts, the typical systems analysis is based on rather straightforward investigative and evaluative techniques. A series of preliminary meetings defines the scope of work, establishing major objectives and specifying constraints within which the analyst must work. These early meetings also provide useful opportunities for "preanalysis familiarization," in which the analysts can examine background documents and ask questions about the organization's mission and structure. The formal analysis begins with an intensive information-gathering phase that is designed to reveal the characteristics of the system under study and the requirements for a replacement system. Potentially useful information is generally obtained from a combination of sources.

1. Systems analysts will invariably inspect any available handbooks, manuals, policy and procedural statements, organization charts, and other written documents pertinent to the existing system and its users. Standardized forms, such as catalogers' worksheets or purchase requisitions, are particularly important classes of documents that reveal both the type of information collected in a given activity and the flow of information through a given system. In addition, some libraries have collected data or compiled statistics pertinent to circulation control, acquisitions, or other activities. Such information can prove useful to the systems analyst, as can previously prepared reports or studies.

2. In most systems analyses, the data-gathering effort relies heavily on personal interviews as a means of identifying application requirements and user ex-

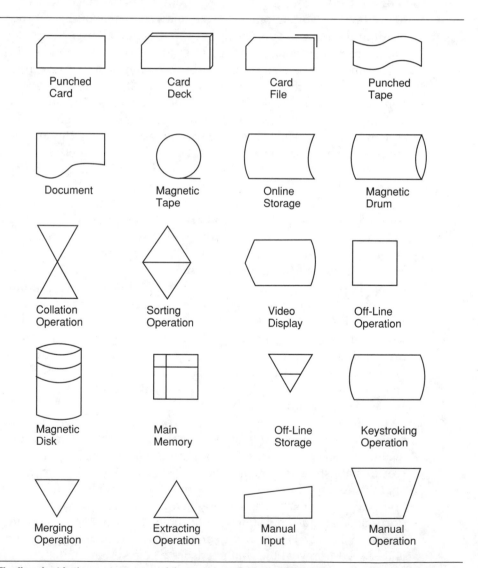

The flowchart is the most common of the graphic tools employed by systems analysts. Standard flowcharting templates contain a wide range of symbols that can be used to represent the work steps or equipment components in a given system.

pectations, as well as eliciting opinions about the strength and problems of an existing system. In a well-planned system study, interviews will involve a representative cross-section of workers, including professional and clerical personnel. In some library applications, users may be interviewed as well. In studies of large systems or where personnel are geographically scattered, questionnaires often serve as a supplement or alternative to personal interviews.

3. Most systems analysts agree that personal observation is essential to verify data collected from the study of existing documents, interviews, and questionnaires. Personal observation may take several forms, including site visits; equipment inventories; desk audits, in which the work of one or more persons is closely monitored; transaction walk-throughs, in which the flow of business forms or other paperwork involved in transactions is traced; and work-volume measurements, in which work is sampled for selected time periods.

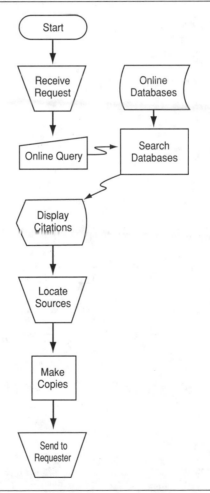

Task-oriented flowcharts depict flow of data in terms of a given activity. In the above example, requests for library materials on a given subject are received. Online databases are searched for relevant citations, the appropriate sources located, and copies made for distribution to the requester.

The systems analyst uses information gathered by the above methods to prepare a narrative description of the tasks performed within the system being studied. This narrative description, which may be embodied in a formal report or in informal working documents, is often supplemented by tabular or graphic presentations. Tables are usually the preferred format for summaries of such system features as equipment and file characteristics, transaction frequencies, or resources allocated to particular tasks. Organization charts are commonly used to depict interrelationships among human resources in the system. Similarly, the movement of documents or other information is usually depicted in charts consisting of interconnected, labeled symbols that represent various system components or work steps.

The flowchart is the most firmly established and widely encountered type of graphic tool for business process analysis. Program flowcharts, as described later in this chapter, are essentially logic diagrams used by programmers to prepare problems for computer solution. System flowcharts, the subject of this discussion, are of two types: task-oriented flowcharts, which depict the flow of

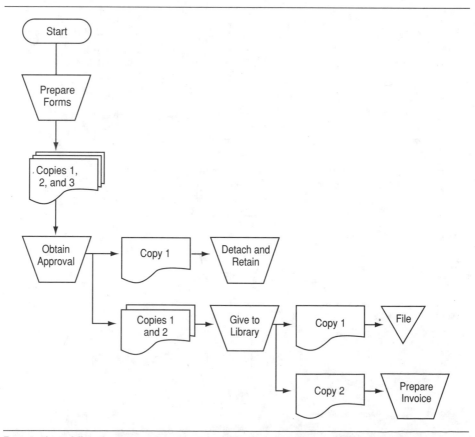

Forms-oriented flowcharts trace the movement of forms or other documents through a given system. In the above example, requests for book orders initiated by a library user are prepared in triplicate. The required approvals are obtained. The requester retains the first copy and submits the other two to the library, which uses one to prepare an invoice and retains the other for its files.

information in a given activity, and forms-oriented flowcharts, which trace the movement of forms or other documents through a system. With both types, a plastic template may be used to draw the symbols that represent various activities and components. Alternatively, flowcharting programs can generate appropriate symbols for display or printing. In either case, most flowcharts employ a subset of the available symbols to depict such basic operations as input, output, processing, and storage.

As alternatives or supplements to flowcharts, some systems analysts employ graphic representations that are variously known as data flow diagrams, data flow graphs, Petri networks, or bubble charts. Rather than concentrating on tasks or documents, as in conventional flowcharting, data flow diagrams trace the movement and transformation of information through a system. These diagrams use combinations of interconnected circles, boxes, lines, and arrows to represent various systems operations. They are often preferred by computer personnel who employ a variant form of systems analysis called structured analysis. Proponents of structured analysis contend that data flow diagrams and related techniques clarify and facilitate the design and development of computer applications when compared to conventional analytical methodologies.

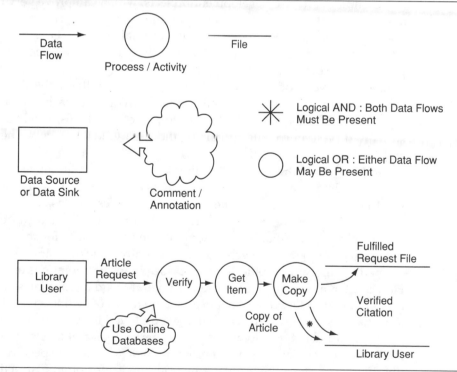

As an alternative to conventional system flowcharts, some analysts employ data flow diagrams that use combinations of interconnected circles, boxes, lines, and arrows to represent various system operations. In the above example, typical data flow symbols are depicted and their combined use indicated in an application involving the fulfillment of user requests for journal articles.

Program Development

While some systems analyses confirm the appropriateness of an organization's existing work procedures, most culminate in a series of oral presentations and written reports that present recommendations for improvement or replacement of the system under study. If the existing system is to be replaced, a design is presented as an alternative. If the proposed alternative involves computers, the design includes specifications that describe the hardware components to be used and the required application programs. The amount of detail presented in the software descriptions varies but usually includes a discussion of the purpose of each required program, accompanied by system flowcharts and brief descriptions of specific program operations. The analyst also describes data characteristics and input procedures, the screen displays and reports to be produced as output, and computer storage requirements.

Assuming that management accepts the systems analyst's recommendations, this information will be given to programmers who will expand the software specification by defining the application's requirements in greater detail and converting them into coded programs. In some cases, especially those involving small applications, the systems analyst is also responsible for program writing. Such information professionals are often described as analyst/programmers or programmer/analysts.

Complex software development projects, which can prove very difficult to manage, usually rely on teams of programmers and support personnel. The application's software requirements are conceptualized as a series of hierarchical, interrelated modules, each of which is assigned to a team headed by a chief programmer. Using a "top-down" development approach to facilitate integration, lower-level modules are not programmed until the higher-level modules that invoke them have been coded and tested. This approach to software engineering, which has been widely adopted since the 1980s, produces logically structured programs while optimizing the deployment of computing resources and personnel.

Regardless of the specific developmental approach employed, a programmer must define the algorithms, or sequences of work steps, that a computer must perform to accomplish the information processing tasks specified by the systems analyst. Like systems analysts, programmers have historically relied on a combination of narrative description and flowcharts for this purpose. As noted earlier, program flowcharts are essentially logic diagrams. They use predefined symbols to graphically depict a sequence of operations and decisions. Flowchart symbols may be hand-drawn with the aid of templates or generated by software developed for that purpose. The range of symbols used in program flowcharts is usually narrower than that employed in systems flowcharts.

Programmers typically prepare flowcharts in several levels of detail, ranging from an overview of general program logic to detailed specifications of individual work steps that can later be translated into coded instructions. Some computer specialists, however, question the value of conventional program flowcharts. They advocate the use of alternative graphic presentations, such as Hierarchical Input-Process-Output (HIPO) charts, which depict the hierarchical

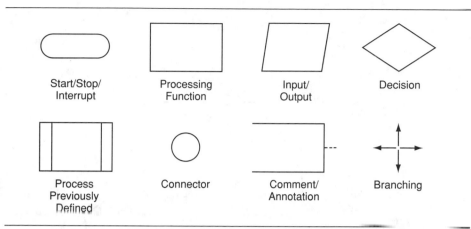

Program flowcharts are logic diagrams that graphically depict a sequence of operations and decisions. Special symbols, different from those employed in system flowcharts, are used in program flowcharts.

interrelationship of input, processing, and output functions in a given system. Some software specialists reject all graphic presentations in favor of outline-like narrative descriptions that use indentions to reflect the hierarchical interrelationships among program operations. To formalize the preparation of software specifications for complex projects, computer systems analysts and programmers may use specially developed specification languages, such as PSL/PSA (Problem Statement Language/Problem Specification Analyzer) or RSL (Requirements Specification Language). Such languages produce software specifications that resemble hierarchically structured programs, but they replace actual programming language instructions with English statements that describe the operations to be performed by specific program segments.

Once the algorithms that specify the operations necessary to accomplish particular tasks have been developed, the programmer uses an appropriate programming language to represent them as coded sequences of instructions for computer execution. In the past, the selection of a programming language for a particular application depended heavily on the nature of the operations to be performed. Some old higher-level programming languages, as previously noted, were designed for specific types of applications. Newer programming languages, however, are generally suitable for a broad range of information processing problems. In all cases, language selection is constrained by the programmer's knowledge and the availability of appropriate compilers and interpreters. Speed of program execution and efficiency of computer performance are the critical considerations in a programmer's decision to use assembler language in preference to one of the higher-level languages. Because the automatic translation inherent in compilation and interpretation can introduce inefficiencies into the resulting machine-level object code, a program written in a higher-level language will usually execute more slowly than its assembler language counterpart.

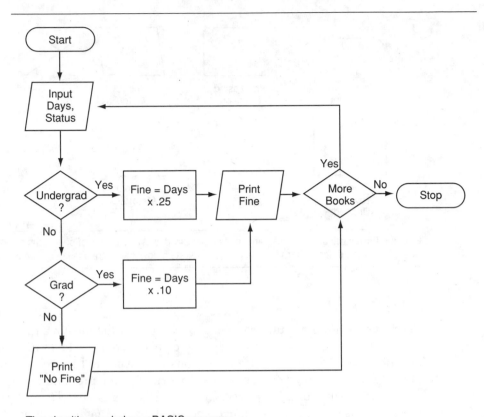

The algorithm coded as a BASIC program:

```
 5   DIM RESPONSE$ (1), STATUS$ (1)
10   PRINT "ENTER NUMBER OF DAYS OVERDUE:"
15   INPUT DAYS
20   PRINT "ENTER BORROWER'S STATUS -- UNDERGRAD, GRAD, FACULTY:"
25   INPUT STATUS$
30   IF STATUS$="U" THEN GOTO 50
35   IF STATUS$="G" THEN GOTO 60
40   PRINT "NO FINE"
45   GOTO 70
50   FINE = DAYS * .25
55   GOTO 65
60   FINE = DAYS * .10
65   PRINT "THE FINE IS $";FINE
70   PRINT "ARE THERE MORE BOOKS? TYPE YES OR NO:"
75   INPUT RESPONSE$
80   IF RESPONSE$="Y" THEN GOTO 10
85   END
```

Computer programming essentially consists of the formulation of algorithms and their encoding as sequences of instructions or computer execution. In the above example, a program flowchart is used to depict the algorithm that computes fines for overdue books in an academic library. The algorithm is then encoded as a BASIC program.

The extent of assembler language's speed advantage is subject to debate and varies with the particular compiler or interpreter with which comparisons are made. Because a single program instruction written in a higher-level language is often the equivalent of several assembler language instructions, the higher-level languages permit a significant reduction in software development time. As previously noted, the cost of computer hardware is falling, but programmers' salaries are rising. Savings in software development costs attributable to the use of higher-level languages will often outweigh the disadvantages of less efficient processing for all but the most complex and frequently executed programs. In addition, rapid software development is highly valued in applications where a newly programmed computer system will replace a more costly manual or automated system. As a further advantage, programs written in higher-level languages are typically easier to maintain—that is, to correct or modify—than those written in assembler language.

The foregoing discussion gives the misleading impression that higher-level language and assembler language programming are mutually exclusive software development options that cannot coexist in a given application. If requirements warrant, the two methodologies can be combined in a single program. Most computer programs are composed of interrelated modules, called subroutines, that perform sequences of operations associated with particular program activities such as input or output. While the bulk of an application program may be written in a higher-level language, certain frequently executed subroutines may be coded in assembler language for faster execution.

Maintenance and Documentation

Once the instructions that perform desired information processing tasks are coded in assembler or a higher-level language, the resulting programs are tested and any detected errors or "bugs" are corrected. While this testing or "debugging" procedure attempts to confirm that a given program will function in the intended manner, the length and complexity of most programs, combined with budget and schedule constraints, make it impossible to verify the correctness of all facets of program execution. Programmers cannot foresee every contingency or fully test every instruction. The reliability of the typical computer program is consequently uncertain. While a given program may operate correctly for a period of time following its initial implementation, most programs eventually fail when some previously unanticipated situation is encountered. When a failure occurs, the program must be reexamined, the problem diagnosed, and the incorrect instructions rewritten. This "repair" activity is commonly described as "maintenance programming."

Because the characteristics of most information processing applications are dynamic rather than static, a second important type of maintenance programming involves the modification of previously written programs to incorporate enhancements or to accommodate changes in application requirements. These modifications may occur months or even years after the program was originally written. In some computing installations, especially long-established ones, such maintenance programming may account for 80 percent or more of total programming activity. It is the most common type of work assignment for entry-level programmers, who seldom do original programming. In recent years, many organizations have undertaken business process reengineering (BPR) projects that involve significant modification or complete rewriting of application programs. Such projects are based on an in-depth examination of specific business processes and a reevaluation of the objectives of computerization. Reengineering projects often focus on so-called legacy systems—that is, mainframe and minicomputer programs that were developed in the 1960s and 1970s. Over the years, such programs may have been modified, in patchwork fashion, on multiple occasions.

Whatever the reasons for maintenance programming, the successively corrected or otherwise altered versions of a given program are termed "releases." The counterparts of revised editions of a printed book, successive software releases are usually identified by number. The initial operating version of a program is numbered 1.0. Test versions are typically assigned numbers lower than one; a final test release, sometimes described as a "beta" version, may be numbered 0.90 or higher. Minor revisions of an operational program are identified by decimal increments, such as 1.1 or 1.2. Small adjustments to such modified releases are often identified by incrementing the hundredths decimal position to 1.15 or 1.25, for example. Such minor revisions usually involve the correction of specific errors reported by users or discovered by software developers. Major program revisions are typically assigned the next whole number—2.0 in the case of the first major revision—to indicate the new version offers significant enhancements when compared to its predecessor. Vendors of prewritten software for general-purpose and library-specific applications use major revisions to keep their products competitive and broaden their market appeal. Release numbers greater than 3.0 usually indicate programs that have been in use for some time and that have undergone successive, substantial improvement and augmentation.

Because maintenance programming requires an understanding of the purpose, structure, logic, and operation of previously written programs, the availability of adequate documentation is critical to its successful completion. Documentation is the written information recorded during the development of a computer system that explains pertinent aspects of that system. Its purpose is to ensure that the details of a system are understood by those persons who have a need to know about it. Such documentation may address either the hardware or the software characteristics of a given system. This discussion is primarily concerned with software documentation, which is typically divided into three categories: analytical, developmental, and operational.

As its name suggests, analytical documentation is prepared at the systems analysis stage of program development. As previously discussed, it provides narrative and graphic descriptions of the characteristics, advantages, and disadvantages of an existing manual system. It delineates and analyzes the information processing requirements of a given application, evaluates alternative courses of action, and presents recommendations for the improvement of an existing system or the development of a new one. For maintenance programming, analytical documentation is useful in determining the rationale for particular features of the system to be maintained.

The actual work of program modification relies more heavily, however, on developmental documentation. Such documentation consists of detailed narrative and graphic descriptions of the programs that implement a particular computer application. It includes, but is not necessarily limited to, a general statement of purpose of a given program or set of programs; a discussion of the algorithms employed, with flowcharts or other graphic presentations of program logic; a listing of program statements (the source code) as written in assembler or higher-level languages; a description of the hardware configuration for which the program was developed, including memory requirements, online and offline storage media, and input/output peripherals; a listing of required system software and related support programs, including operating systems, assemblers, compilers, interpreters, utility programs, and prewritten subroutines; and a discussion of the program's input and data requirements.

The third category, operational documentation, includes installation and operating instructions. User manuals, an extremely important class of documentation, are included in this category. The best user manuals include tutorial material, which provides a step-by-step discussion of all program operations, and a reference section, which contains alphabetically arranged descriptions of specific program commands. Illustrations of typical screen displays can be used to clarify and supplement narrative explanations. To further facilitate learning and operation of a given program, a user manual may be accompanied by summary command tables, wall charts, or similar reference aids. Recognizing that users may not read printed manuals carefully, if at all, many programs include an online "help" feature that provides access to information about specific operations from within the program itself. A typical online help module displays excerpts from printed program manuals. In most cases, the user selects the desired information from a list of topics displayed when the help module is invoked. A "content sensitive" help system automatically displays information appropriate to the task being performed at the time a help command is activated.

The preparation of appropriate analytical and developmental documentation is normally the responsibility of the systems analysts and programmers involved in a given software development effort. For best results, operational documentation should be prepared by technical writers. While most computer professionals recognize the value of complete documentation, programmers working under the pressure of a tight schedule may neglect to document software development activities fully. When the actual cost of software creation threatens to exceed the budgeted amount, as it often does, the reduction or limitation of documentation-related activities is too often viewed as a means of achieving greater economy in program writing. Unfortunately, any reduction in documentation typically proves to be a false economy that results in significant increases in the time and costs associated with program maintenance and utilization.

Prewritten Software

The discussion to this point has dealt with software that is custom-developed for a specific situation. As noted above, the cost of such customized software development accounts for an increasingly large percentage of total computer system costs and can be a significant impediment to the automation of library operations. This is particularly the case in small computer installations where the procurement of customized programming services on a contract basis, whether from independent consultants or from computer service companies that specialize in contract programming, can cost several times the purchase price of the computer equipment itself.

Even if cost were not an issue, many librarians do not have convenient access to programming expertise. Because of large software development backlogs and the increasingly significant burden of maintenance programming, most institutional and corporate data processing centers limit their customized programming activities to high-priority tasks. As a further constraint, customized software development projects are rarely completed on schedule. They often exceed budget allocations, partly because customers routinely augment their original program specifications to incorporate additions and enhancements after software development has begun. Success is never assured; customized programming can result in a disappointing end product that does not meet all application requirements.

For computer applications with relatively straightforward requirements, prewritten software packages are invariably more economical than custom-developed programs, and they offer the significant advantage of faster implementation. As the name implies, a prewritten software package is a program or group of programs that is marketed as a finished product. Such packages can be divided into two broad categories: general-purpose programs and industry-specific programs. General-purpose programs are designed to automate accounting, word processing, database management, and other commonly encountered computer applications in a broad range of work environments. Industry-specific programs, by contrast, are designed to automate one or more operations in a specific work environment, such as a school, engineering consulting firm, hospital, or law office. Software packages for library automation fall into the industry-specific category.

As an alternative to custom-developed programs, well-designed prewritten software packages can effectively address the applications for which they are intended. The best examples are intelligently conceived and attractively implemented. Newer products typically incorporate the latest advances in software development. It is important to note, however, that prewritten software packages are intended for a class of applications, of which any given user's application is just one example. In many applications, information processing requirements vary little among users who must perform the same tasks; circulation control, for instance, is performed in a similar manner by libraries of different types and sizes. By studying the way in which specific activities are performed in various work environments, software developers can write broadly useful programs to automate them.

While some variations in local practice may be accommodated, prewritten software packages necessarily address the operations and work requirements that many users share. Custom-developed programs, in contrast, are designed for a specific installation, to the exclusion of other environments where similar operations may be performed. They are tailored to the requirements of a particular work environment and to the stated preferences of users who ordered the programs to be written. If properly developed, they will address those requirements and preferences exactly—albeit at a penalty in cost and time when compared to prewritten packages.

Regardless of type, prewritten software packages, like all computer programs, are designed for use with specific hardware configurations. As previously noted, computer manufacturers routinely supply operating systems and other system software for use with their equipment. Most mainframe and minicomputer manufacturers also offer consulting services and contract programming to support their hardware installations. Since the 1960s, they have marketed some prewritten programs, principally for such common business applications as general ledger maintenance, accounts payable, payroll, accounts receivable, inventory management, human resources, and project scheduling. They may also offer one or more data management programs suitable for information retrieval, document indexing, and other applications that are directly relevant to professional library activities.

A large percentage of prewritten software for mainframes and minicomputers is developed by third parties—that is, by organizations other than the computer system manufacturer or the customer. In most cases, such packages are developed by independent software companies—so-called software houses—or by computer service bureaus. As might be expected, their products are usually designed for widely installed central processors. Most software developers specialize in a particular computer configuration, such as IBM mainframes or Unix-based processors. Some software development companies offer general accounting and administrative programs; many, however, emphasize products for specific "vertical" markets such as banking, insurance, manufacturing, pharmaceuticals, utility companies, and transportation. As described in later chapters, a number of companies offer library automation programs for mainframes and minicomputers. Such programs are often implemented on computers operated by a university, municipality, corporation, or other organization with which a library is affiliated.

To further simplify implementation, some software developers offer complete "turnkey" systems that consist of preselected combinations of hardware and software designed to automate specific operations. In most cases, the hardware configuration includes a minicomputer or microcomputer as its central processor. The turnkey system provider rarely manufactures computer hardware components; typically, it has a business relationship with one or more hardware manufacturers from whom it obtains equipment appropriate to a customer's application requirements. The turnkey designation suggests that a customer need only add the information associated with a given application to begin immediately realizing the benefits of automation, without worrying about hardware/software compatibility and without the involvement of programmers or other computer professionals. Although such effortless implementations are rarely encountered in actual installations, the turnkey approach is appealing to customers interested in a complete, single-source solution to a particular information processing problem. In libraries, turnkey systems have been widely and successfully implemented for circulation control, online public access catalogs, and other operations.

To some extent, an emphasis on customized software development is inherent in mainframe and minicomputer installations. As noted in chapter 1, such systems are operated by centralized computing facilities that employ professional programmers. Historically, they have preferred to write application software rather than purchase it, although that situation is changing. Rather than trying to modernize programs written in the 1960s and 1970s, a number of corporations, government agencies, and other organizations have acquired prewritten software packages for accounting, human resources, payroll, order processing, and other mission-critical applications that operate on mainframes and minicomputers. Hundreds of software companies offer such prewritten programs. Examples include Computer Associates, Information Builders, Oracle Corporation, Peoplesoft, and SAP AG. A growing selection of prewritten mainframe and minicomputer programs is also available for specific vertical markets such as hospital management, law office management, court docket management, land records management, and geographical information systems. Mainframe and minicomputer manufacturers have established business alliances with software developers, allowing them to offer prospective customers complete solutions to information processing problems. Many prewritten programs for mainframes and minicomputers are complex products, however. They often require programmer involvement for installation and ongoing operation. Alternatively, software developers and consulting firms offer fee-based support services for program installation and customized adaptations.

Small computer installations are typically controlled by end-users rather than by computer professionals. Lacking programming knowledge or access to programming talent, microcomputer users have historically relied on prewritten software packages for rapid, economical implementation of information processing applications. Tens of thousands of prewritten programs are available for Intel-based microcomputers, for example. A smaller but still impressive selection is available for Macintosh systems. Like their mainframe and minicomputer counterparts, microcomputer software packages can be divided into general-purpose and industry-specific categories. Library-specific microcomputer software packages will be discussed in later chapters. General-purpose microcomputer programs, which are of considerable interest to libraries, address commonly encountered business applications.

1. Word processing software packages support the preparation of typewritten documents. Available for more than fifteen years, these widely used products provide a large and flexible repertoire of text editing and document formatting capabilities, supplemented by such special features as spelling verification, an online thesaurus for simplified identification of synonyms, grammar checking, production of customized form letters from mailing lists, table of contents preparation, document indexing, and document outlining. Examples of microcomputer-based word processing programs include Microsoft Word, WordPerfect from Corel, and Word Pro from IBM.

2. A related group of prewritten software packages is designed for desktop publishing. These programs can compose text into pages for printing in multiple fonts, sizes, styles, and columns. In most cases, text is created by a word processing program and transferred into the desktop publishing package,

although some desktop publishing programs incorporate straightforward editing capabilities. Textual information can be merged with graphics to produce attractively formatted documents. Examples of desktop publishing programs for microcomputer systems include FrameMaker, PageMaker, and Photoshop from Adobe Systems; Microsoft Publisher; and QuarkXPress from Quark Incorporated. As recent enhancements, desktop publishing programs have added the ability to produce pages for the World Wide Web.

3. Spreadsheet programs are designed for administrative and analytical workers with complex planning and decision-making responsibilities. They take their name from the large sheets of paper that accountants have traditionally used to present financial information in a tabular format. Spreadsheet programs permit the creation and subsequent manipulation of financial and statistical models represented as matrices of intersecting rows and columns. They can simplify the preparation of budgets, cost estimates, cost justification statements, income projections, statistical tabulations, and similar planning documents. Spreadsheet programs are particularly useful for applications in which a variety of interrelated variables must be considered and many recalculations are required. The most widely used spreadsheet programs, such as Excel from Microsoft and Lotus 1-2-3 from IBM, support an extensive repertoire of predefined functions that can quickly perform a variety of mathematical, statistical, financial, and logical computations. Results may be displayed or printed in tabular or graphics formats.

4. Data management software packages permit the creation and manipulation of machine-readable records stored in data files. They are useful in a variety of applications involving information retrieval and report generation. As explained in chapter 3, the majority of data management programs operate on records that are organized into user-defined data elements called fields. The simplest data management software packages, sometimes described as "flat file" programs, can only process information contained in a single data file. More sophisticated products, which can process several data files simultaneously, permit the implementation of complex applications. Widely encountered examples include the Access and FoxPro programs from Microsoft, FileMaker Pro from FileMaker, DataFlex from Data Access Corporation, Oracle from Oracle Corporation, Progress from Progress Software, Paradox from Corel, and the dBASE product line from Borland International. As noted above, some database management packages support a proprietary programming language, which can address application requirements that exceed the package's preprogrammed scope. While conventional database management programs operate on structured records that are organized into fields, an interesting group of microcomputer software packages can manipulate unstructured segments. Such programs are variously known as text storage and retrieval systems, text-based data management systems, text information systems, or full-text retrieval systems. The text segments may consist of complete documents or shorter document representations, such as abstracts or annotations. In most cases, text is imported from a word processing software package, although optical character recognition can be used to convert paper documents to character-coded text files. Regardless of input source, the text storage and retrieval program creates indexes to every significant word on every page within the stored documents. The indexes permit full text searches for rapid identification of text segments that contain specified character strings. The text segments, or the complete documents that contain them, can be displayed or printed to satisfy specified retrieval requirements. This technology is described more fully in chapter 3. Examples of microcomputer-based text storage and retrieval programs include askSAM Professional from askSAM Systems, Fulcrum SearchServer from Fulcrum Technologies, Sonar Professional from Virginia Systems, dtSearch from DT Software, and DB/Text product line from Inmagic Incorporated.

5. Presentation graphics programs facilitate the creation of reports, slides, overhead transparencies, promotional materials, and other business documents that contain charts, line graphs, diagrams, and other graphic components. Such programs can generate very attractive graphic output in a broad range of styles and colors. In most cases, numeric data can be entered directly, and a straightforward text-editing module permits typing of word charts. Alternatively, textual or numeric information on which graphic presentations are to be based may be transferred from word processing programs, spreadsheet programs, data management programs, or other sources. Graphic images can also be imported from collections of clip art, some of which are distributed on CD-ROM. Most products provide drawing and annotation tools for editing and enhancing presentations. Graphic images can be cropped, resized, rotated, or otherwise manipulated. Notes, labels, and legends can be appended to them. Headings can be changed or repositioned. Presentations can be displayed on bit-mapped video monitors as selected images or in a slide show format. Hard copy output can be generated by color printers. Examples of microcomputer-based presentation graphics programs include PowerPoint for Microsoft, Freelance from IBM, and Corel Presentations from Corel.

6. Communications software packages enable a personal computer to function as a terminal for purposes of communicating with a remote device. As described more fully in chapter 3, a communications program interacts with a modem and other hardware components. Examples of communication software packages for microcomputers include Hyperterm, which is supplied with many Windows-based systems; SmartCom from Hayes Microcomputer Products; and Procomm Plus from Quarterdeck. Web browsers, a special type of communications software package, are designed to access the World Wide Web portion of the Internet. The two most widely used examples are Microsoft Internet Explorer and Netscape Navigator.

7. Integrated software packages (not to be confused with the integrated libraries systems discussed in later chapters) combine word processing, spreadsheet processing, data management, and communications capabilities in a single, modularized product. A presentation graphics component may be included as well. Examples of microcomputer-based integrated software packages include Microsoft Works and Claris Works. Integrated software packages have proven especially popular with students and novice computer users. Compared to an equivalent number of stand-alone programs, they usually cost less, are easier to learn, and simplify the exchange of information between program modules. They are particularly effective in applications where information manipulated by spreadsheet or data management modules must be incorporated into word processing documents. As a potential disadvantage, integrated software packages seldom offer the broad range of features supported by the best stand-alone software packages. Integrated software packages should not be confused with so-called office suites, which combine several stand-alone programs for sale as a unit. Examples include Microsoft Office, Lotus SmartSuite from IBM, and WordPerfect Suite from Corel. In most cases, office suites feature tightly integrated programs that facilitate the exchange of information between applications.

While tens of thousands of prewritten software packages are available for computers of all types and sizes, it can prove difficult to identify products suitable for a specific application. There is, unfortunately, no single authoritative directory of such programs comparable to the directories available for books, periodicals, and related bibliographic materials. Problems inherent in the preparation of such a directory are formidable. Unlike book publishing, which requires a significant capital investment in production facilities, software can be created by anyone with access to a computer. While some software packages are widely advertised, most are not. As additional complications, software packages are frequently revised, often retitled, and sometimes discontinued. Software companies merge, change names, and go out of business. As a result, it is virtually impossible to produce a comprehensive, up-to-date list of available prewritten programs, although certain publications can identify software developers and resellers who can be contacted for current information about their products.

Increasingly, mainframe and minicomputer manufacturers publish catalogs of prewritten programs for use with their equipment. Informative as they are, such catalogs are not comprehensive. They are typically limited to products sold by the computer manufacturer and its affiliated companies, often described as "business partners." They often omit interesting programs developed by independent software companies, user groups, talented individuals, and other third parties. Printed directories of microcomputer software are so numerous that a detailed survey is beyond the scope of this discussion. Some publications list programs for all types of microcomputers and many kinds of applications. Others are limited to a specific type of microcomputer; dozens of directories list software packages for Windows-based systems, for example. Some computer-specific directories are further limited to particular applications, such as accounting or office automation. Several directories list public domain and user-supported programs that are available at nominal cost. Sometimes described as "shareware," most user-supported programs can be duplicated for distribution to others, provided that the distributing party does not profit from the transaction. Recipients who find a shareware program useful are asked to make a modest payment to its developers, in return for which they usually receive documentation, technical support, and access to future enhancements.

Software product profiles, reviews, and availability reports are included in journals, newsletters, and other periodicals that deal with computers and information management. Microcomputer magazines and user-group publications, in particular, contain software descriptions and reviews as regular features. Software information and reviews are likewise available through online information services and Internet sites.

SUMMARY

Software is a program, or predefined sequence of instructions, that a computer executes to perform information processing operations. The computer industry typically distinguishes between system software (those programs that enable a computer to function and control its own operations) and application software (those programs that perform user-specified tasks). Examples of system software include the group of supervisory programs called the operating system; various utility programs that perform housekeeping operations, sorting, or other tasks routinely required by computer users; and assemblers, compilers, and interpreters that support programming activities.

A computer can only execute programs that are presented to it in a binary-coded form called machine-level language. Because writing such programs is a time-consuming, error-prone task, the computer industry has developed various programming languages that employ non-binary instructions, thereby facilitating the software development process. In assembler language programming, mnemonic commands and symbolic operands are substituted for binary codes. The resulting program is then translated into machine-level language by a special program called an assembler. The higher-level languages use a more abstract notation that greatly simplifies the programming task. The resulting programs must be translated into the machine-level language by compilers or interpreters.

The earliest higher-level programming languages were often categorized by the type of information processing applications that they were designed to support. FORTRAN, one of the oldest higher-level languages, continues to be used in scientific and engineering applications. COBOL has long been the most important programming language for business applications that run on mainframes and minicomputers. While they are interesting for libraries, string-processing languages such as SNOBOL were never widely used and are rarely encountered today. PL/1 was designed as a general-purpose, higher-level language that combined scientific, business, and string-processing attributes. BASIC was one of the first programming languages for online computing environments. Easy to learn, it is widely available for microcomputers. Since the 1980s, designers of programming languages have emphasized structured methodologies that foster improved programming practice and the creation of more reliable and easily maintainable programs. Pascal and C are examples of such structured programming languages. The C programming language, which combines the attributes of assembler and higher-level languages, is particularly popular with professional software developers. Much recent attention has been given to object-oriented programming methodologies that produce reusable code. Examples of object-oriented programming languages include C++ and SmallTalk.

While system software is often bundled for sale with computer hardware, the development of application software has historically been considered the customer's responsibility. Properly undertaken, the software development process begins with a study by a systems analyst of application characteristics and requirements. The result is a report that presents recommendations for the improvement or replacement of the system under study, including specifications for any required computer equipment and application programs. These specifications are then given to one or more programmers who will formulate the required algorithms, select an appropriate programming language, and write and test the necessary programs.

Because most computer programs are not fully tested prior to implementation, the likelihood of future operational failures is high. When such failures occur, the program must be reexamined and any incorrect instructions rewritten. This activity, called maintenance programming, is greatly facilitated by the availability of thorough documentation.

As an alternative to the time and expense required for customized software development, prewritten application software packages are increasingly available for computers of all types and sizes. In mainframe and minicomputer installations, where data processing professionals have traditionally preferred custom-developed programs, software packages offer an increasingly popular approach to the implementation of commonly encountered administrative and accounting operations. Most microcomputer installations rely heavily on prewritten software packages, and an excellent selection of programs is available for word processing, spreadsheet analysis, data management, presentation graphics, communications, and various industry-specific tasks.

3 ◆ ◆ ◆ ◆ ◆ ◆ ◆ ◆ ◆ ◆ ◆ ◆ ◆

Data Management and
Data Communications Concepts

The preceding chapters described the most common hardware and software components in a computer system. This chapter examines the ways in which those components interact to produce, manage, and distribute data. In doing so, it presents descriptions of some additional hardware and software concepts and products. The chapter begins with a discussion of basic modes of data processing, emphasizing the significance and pervasiveness of online, real-time, interactive computing in new information management applications. Later sections will discuss the organization and management of machine-readable data, fundamental data communications terminology, and the characteristics of computer networks. As with preceding chapters, the discussion is selective rather than comprehensive. It emphasizes facets of these topics that are of greatest importance for library automation.

MODES OF DATA PROCESSING

The terms "online" and "offline" indicate, respectively, the presence or absence of electrical or other connections between computing devices. As noted in chapter 1, the terms most often describe the presence or absence of connections between the central processor and its associated peripherals. Thus, an online peripheral, such as a printer, is physically connected to the computer on which the information to be printed is processed, while an offline peripheral, such as a computer-output microfilm recorder operated by a service bureau, is not so connected. In addition, the two terms are sometimes used to describe particular computer system configurations. In an online system, information is stored on direct-access devices and media, usually fixed magnetic disk drives connected to a mainframe, minicomputer, or network server. Terminals, desktop microcomputers, or portable computing devices are used to access the computer system for information retrieval, transaction processing, or other purposes. An offline system, in contrast, typically relies on magnetic tape or other removable media for information storage, while printed reports communicate the results of computer processing.

When used to describe particular computer configurations, the adjectives online and offline are sometimes confused with two other terms: "real time" and "batch." The two pairs of terms are not, however, interchangeable. Rather than referring to the presence or absence of electrical connections between computing devices, batch and real time denote modes of data processing. Specifically, they refer to the relationship between transactions or other events and computer processing of information about those events. The essential characteristics of batch and real-time processing implementations are described below.

Real-Time vs. Batch Processing

Batch processing systems, sometimes described as "batch-oriented systems," dominated data processing implementations through the early 1970s. While no longer the preferred approach to computing, some batch processing systems developed several decades ago for mainframes or large minicomputers remain in use. The essential characteristics and inherent limitations of batch processing systems can be introduced through an example involving computerized circulation control. As implemented by various public and academic libraries during the 1960s and 1970s, a typical batch-oriented circulation control system used keypunch or key-to-tape technology to record information in the machine-readable, computer-processable form required for automated charging and discharging of library materials. With some systems, specially prepared decks of tabulating cards—prepunched with such information as an accession number or other item identifier, an abbreviated author's name, and a truncated title—were stored in pockets affixed to books or other circulating materials. The additional information required to charge or discharge an item—a borrower identification number, date, and transaction code, for example—was punched into predefined portions of one of the cards as individual transactions took place. In other systems, blank cards were punched in their entirety in a predetermined format by circulation clerks as each transaction occurred. Alternatively, key-to-tape devices were sometimes used to record machine-readable data pertaining to successive circulation transactions on reels or cassettes of magnetic tape. During the early to mid-1970s, several companies marketed key-to-tape data collection equipment specifically for library circulation control applications.

Regardless of the input method employed, machine-readable records pertaining to successive circulation transactions (charges and discharges) were accumulated at the circulation point on punched cards or magnetic tapes. At predetermined intervals, the cards or tapes were taken to an institutional computing center or computer service bureau for processing in a batch. The computer processing typically involved updating a master circulation file that contained one machine-readable record for each circulating item in the library's collection. The file was usually stored on magnetic tape, the records being arranged by accession number or in some other sequence. (Characteristics of such circulation files are described in chapter 6.) After being sorted into the same sequence as the master file, records representing circulation transactions were read by the computer, and their corresponding master records located on tape. If a transaction reflected a charge, the borrower's number and other identifying information were added to the master record for the indicated item; if the transaction reflected the return of an item, the previously recorded charge-out information was erased.

When all circulation transactions had been processed, one or more lists were printed. These lists, which were printed on paper or microfilm, contained information about items in circulation. Abbreviated lists, arranged by call number, included short titles and due dates for items in circulation. Such lists were customarily made available for reference by library users, enabling them to determine whether a given item was in circulation and when it was due to be returned. More detailed lists, which included borrower information, were usually produced for circulation department personnel. At predetermined intervals, the master circulation file was further processed to identify overdue items, produce recall notices, derive and report circulation statistics, or print special lists of delinquent borrowers or circulating items placed on hold.

The foregoing description reflects the operating characteristics of a typical batch processing system. In summary:

1. Machine-readable information is collected offline for subsequent processing at predetermined intervals.

2. In some cases, batches of data are physically transported to a centralized computing facility. Alternatively, information may be submitted to that facility electronically. During the 1960s and 1970s, specially designed remote job entry (RJE) stations were used for that purpose.

3. The frequency with which batches are submitted for processing depends on several factors, including the user's information processing requirements, the data accumulation rate, and the availability of computing resources.

4. Machine-readable information, organized in files as explained later in this chapter, is recorded on one or more magnetic tapes.

5. The tapes are maintained offline until the prescheduled processing time. When a tape is needed, it is removed from its offline location and mounted on an online tape drive.

6. To accommodate the serial access requirements of magnetic tape, data about new transactions are customarily sorted prior to processing into the sequence in which information is recorded on tape.

Variations in the above pattern are widely encountered. Online terminals may be used for data collection, for example. In such configurations, information about circulation transactions is key-entered at a terminal for direct transmission to a central processor and online disk storage. The information is not processed immediately, however; it is merely collected in a temporary file on a hard drive, awaiting processing against a master file at predetermined intervals. Similarly, data access by online terminals can be used as an output alternative to paper or microfilm listings. In such an approach, the master circulation file is maintained online on a hard drive rather than offline on magnetic tapes. Using a terminal and specially designed application programs, the file is queried to determine the circulation status of an item or to retrieve other information. The file's contents, however, are still updated in the batch mode.

Since the 1960s, the batch processing methodology described above has been widely utilized in transaction-oriented computer applications such as accounts payable and receivable, general ledger maintenance, payroll, and sales and order processing. When magnetic tape is used for the storage of data files and printed reports are generated, batch systems are relatively simple and economical to implement and operate. The use of online terminals for input and output, however, can raise batch processing costs to levels approaching those of real-time systems, although the cost associated with online terminals and disk storage has declined steadily and significantly over the past two decades.

Regardless of the particular equipment configuration employed, batch processing systems have an unavoidable and potentially significant disadvantage: Because information is accumulated for processing at predetermined intervals, there is a gap in time between the occurrence of a transaction or other event and a computer's processing of information about that event. Thus, in the circulation control example described above, the printed lists that report the results of computer processing reflect the status of the library's circulating collection at the time when the latest batch of transaction records was taken from the library to the computing center for processing. If the library remains open, some information contained in the printed lists will necessarily be invalidated by circulation transactions occurring after a batch was removed for processing.

As an example, a batch-oriented implementation may process records pertaining to circulation transactions at 5 P.M. each day, with updated lists being delivered to the library by 9 A.M. the following morning. Information about a given charge or discharge occurring at 5:01 P.M. on a Monday will not be reflected in a computer-generated listing until 9 A.M. the following Wednesday. In a transaction-based application of this type, some of the items that appear in a printed list of materials in circulation may have been returned, while other items not included in the list will have been checked out. Thus, unless a supplemental file is maintained manually, it is impossible to determine accurately the circulating status of a given item—but maintenance of such a manual file would obviously defeat the purpose of automating the circulation activity. The potential for inaccuracy inherent in batch processing systems can be minimized, of course, by processing batches and printing lists more frequently, but inaccuracy can only be eliminated entirely by real-time data processing.

In computer implementations, the phrase "real-time" can have several meanings. It is sometimes used to denote a type of computer system in which information is made available to the operator of an online terminal within a few seconds of the entry of a command or the submission of a task. As an example of such usage, computer-based information services that provide online access to machine-readable databases of bibliographic citations can be said to operate in a real-time mode because the computer provides an immediate or extremely rapid response to entered search commands. For purposes of this discussion of modes of data processing, however, real-time is used in a somewhat different sense: It denotes a type of computer system in which information about transactions or other events is processed immediately after the transactions or events are initiated. Machine-readable data files are usually updated as an integral and essential step in the completion of a transaction or event. As a result, real-time computer systems maintain information that reflects the current status of a specific application or situation. Batch processing systems, in contrast, reflect the status of an application or situation at some point in the past.

In a real-time circulation control system, for example, charges, discharges, or other transactions are transmitted to and processed by a computer as they occur. The hardware and software characteristics of such systems differ from those required for batch processing. The information to be processed by real-time systems is entered at online terminals and stored on hard drives. Unlike magnetic tapes, which must be retrieved from offline storage locations and mounted before use, hard drives are continuously resident online. As an alternative to the printed lists employed in batch processing implementations, terminals are used for online retrieval of information, such as the circulation status and due date of a given item.

Real-time computer systems were originally developed in the late 1960s for processing airline reservations. They have since been utilized in a wide variety of applications where access to up-to-date information is essential. (Examples of real-time systems for library applications are described in later chapters.) Although the cost differential is narrowing, real-time systems have historically been more expensive to develop and implement than batch processing systems. Areas of potential higher cost include the following:

1. The online terminals and support equipment required in real-time implementations have no counterpart in typical batch processing systems. They consequently represent an added cost. Terminal equipment cost may be partially defrayed, however, by the elimination of costs associated with the production of paper or microform lists.

2. The hard drives required for online storage of information in real-time systems are more expensive than the magnetic tapes used in batch processing applications. While hard drive costs are falling, they remain higher than magnetic tape costs. Information stored on hard drives must be replicated on magnetic tape or other media for backup attention, thus further increasing the expense associated with real-time systems.

3. Telecommunication facilities are required to link terminals and related local-site equipment with the computers on which information is maintained and processed. No such costs are incurred in the typical batch processing installation, although there is a labor cost associated with physical transportation of batches from a remote data entry site to a computer facility.

4. With many real-time systems, a batch processing component is retained to produce printed reports as a backup information resource in the event of system failure, telecommunication outage, or other unavailability. In addition, certain tasks related to real-time operations may be performed in the batch mode. In circulation control applications, for example, charging and discharging of library materials may occur in real-time, but overdue notices, hold notices, and other borrower communications are typically processed and printed in batches.

Higher costs aside, however, real-time systems are preferred for their greater accuracy and consequently higher value. Where reliable, up-to-date information is essential, batch processing is unacceptable.

The introduction to this chapter noted that the two pairs of terms—online and real-time, offline and batch—are sometimes used interchangeably, even though they denote different concepts. The relationship between these terms requires further clarification. As described above, real-time systems are invariably online systems, but batch processing systems may use online terminals to enter information. Similarly, information that is processed in batches may be maintained on hard drives for online retrieval through terminals. This is the case, for example, with most online library catalogs as well as with the databases maintained by online information services. Such information is typically updated in batches at predetermined intervals. As described in later chapters, library catalogs are usually updated at the end of each workday or at weekly intervals, depending on the method used to create new bibliographic records. Databases maintained by online information services may be updated daily, weekly, monthly, or at other intervals, depending on the receipt of new information from publishers or other sources. As a generalization, all real-time systems are online systems, but online systems may employ batch or real-time processing methods. Computer systems that use offline components are necessarily batch processing systems. It should further be noted that the two modes of data processing are not mutually exclusive, since most real-time systems have one or more batch processing components.

Interactive Computing

Whether information is processed in the batch or real-time mode, most mainframe and minicomputer applications involve online systems in which users, working at terminals, are prompted or otherwise guided by the computer in the performance of various information processing tasks. Such online systems are characterized as interactive because user commands and computer responses alternate in a more or less conversational manner. An interactive computer program provides immediate information or instructions that may cause the user to modify work patterns. Such computer/user interaction is an obvious and indispensable component in online searching of library catalogs and other bibliographic databases. A computer responds to a user's search command with an indication of the number of potential relevant citations or with a partial listing of bibliographic information. Depending on the computer's response, the user may decide to proceed with the search, modify the retrieval parameters to obtain more appropriate results, or take other action.

Although the advent of desktop computers permits the development of interactive applications in which a computer's entire resources are dedicated to a single user, interactive computing has historically been implemented in a time-sharing environment. As the term suggests, time-sharing is a method of computing that allows two or more users to submit work for immediate processing. The computer's operating system employs a predetermined method to schedule and execute each job. Some time-sharing operating systems use a straightforward first-in/first-out method of scheduling. Others employ a round-robin or "time slicing" approach in which the central processor begins, interrupts, and later returns to individual jobs, devoting some predetermined amount of time—usually a fraction of a second—to them at each processing interval. In still another method, a time-sharing operating system prioritizes jobs on the basis of their predetermined importance, estimated completion time, the status of the user submitting the work, or other factors.

Regardless of the particular job scheduling method employed, the operating system attempts to minimize the user's perception of the time-sharing process, giving the impression that the computer's resources are entirely at each user's disposal. Because powerful mainframes and large minicomputers can perform many operations per second, a user might not perceive a delay in the execution of even a low-priority or complex task. The illusion that all computing resources are dedicated to one user becomes extremely difficult to sustain, however, during peak work periods when many terminals are submitting jobs simultaneously or when an underpowered computer must serve multiple users. In such situations, the computer's response to a user's commands may be measured in minutes rather than seconds. The degraded response times sometimes experienced by librarians who use online information services and bibliographic utilities during mid-afternoon hours are often attributable to the high demand associated with peak periods of terminal activity. Similarly, a computer upgrade is often necessary to maintain acceptable response time when public access terminals are added to an online catalog installation.

Appropriate response time, measured from the time a command is entered until information is displayed at a user's workstation, is one of several factors that ultimately influence a user's acceptance of online, interactive computing as an effective and comfortable alternative to other work methods. In any information processing system, user resistance can arise whenever established work habits must be changed. While it offers the substantial advantage of rapid response for retrieval or other information processing tasks, interactive computing may require significant user reorientation and retraining. In recent years, software developers and other computer specialists have given considerable attention to the design of interactive programs that minimize problems associated with user adjustment. Such programs are often described as "user-friendly." The computing industry's acknowledgment of their importance contrasts sharply with the previous data processing practice in which users were too often required to have extensive familiarity with computer operations and technical concepts.

Simplicity and clarity are increasingly viewed as essential attributes of interactive computer programs. The best examples provide relatively few but powerful commands that enable users to perform significant amounts of work quickly and easily. A new user may be prompted or otherwise guided by one or more menus of alternatives or by unambiguous questions requiring the entry of straightforward responses. Microcomputer software packages, many of which are designed for first-time computer users, have done much to popularize such menu-driven interfaces. The graphical user interfaces described in chapter 2 are

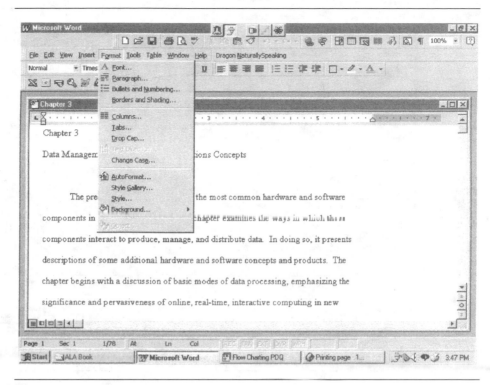

Modern software makes effective use of "pull-down" menus to facilitate command selection.

particularly noteworthy for their reliance on pull-down menu bars—horizontal lines of menu titles that expand to display lists of available commands when selected by the user. Menu titles and commands that do not apply to a particular program operation are usually displayed in a light shade and cannot be activated. Some menu selections lead to more detailed submenus. Others activate dialog boxes with blank spaces for the entry of specific values or lists of options for operator selection. To maintain a consistent user interface and facilitate learning, software packages intended for a particular graphical user environment, such as Microsoft Windows or Macintosh systems, may employ similar menus and dialog boxes for such commonly encountered tasks as file creation, page setup, and printing.

As noted in chapter 2, online documentation can often be consulted at any point in computer/user interaction without exiting from a given program or invalidating work previously performed. Shortcuts or abbreviated commands are usually provided for experienced users who may be intolerant of the delays inherent in menu selections or computer prompting. Well-designed interactive programs are forgiving of operator error and provide users with every opportunity to correct their own mistakes. When errors do occur, the best programs respond with clear explanations of the mistakes and their correction procedures. Above all, a well-designed computer program makes users feel that they are in control of, rather than being controlled by, the interaction.

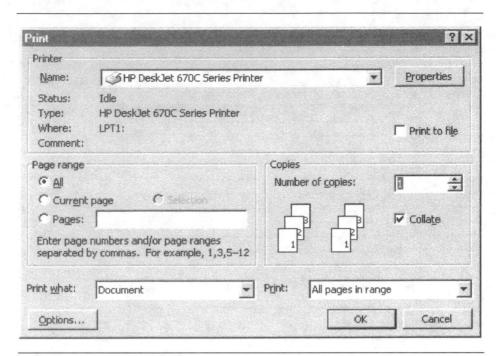

Dialog boxes solicit specific values or list options for operator selection.

Online Terminals

While well-written programs offer an effective intellectual interface between a computer and the user of an interactive system, online terminals provide the required physical interface. For many librarians and library users, online terminals are the most important computer system components. In mainframe and minicomputer installations, in particular, they are the points of interaction between users and remote computing devices. When used in conjunction with appropriate telecommunication facilities, online terminals can access a wide variety of computers and information processing services on a time-sharing basis. Chapter 1 contained brief references to the hardware characteristics of online terminals. This section presents a more detailed discussion of their role in interactive computer systems, emphasizing those features and capabilities that are of greatest significance for library installations. It also provides an introduction to some fundamental telecommunication terminology and concepts.

Broadly defined, an online terminal allows users to transmit information to, and receive information from, a computer by means of electronic digital pulses transmitted over connecting wires or other telecommunication facilities. The terminal and computer may be installed in the same room or, more commonly, in different locations. This definition encompasses a wide range of data communication devices and must be refined to be meaningful. During the 1970s and 1980s, terminals were subdivided by mode of operation into batch

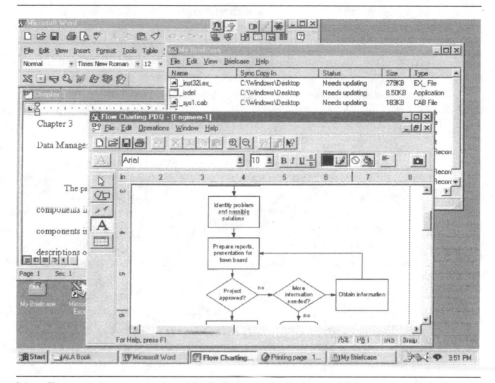

Interactive computer programs increasingly rely on special display capabilities, such as windowing.

and interactive varieties. Those subdivisions are no longer meaningful; batch terminals, which were intended for remote input and output operations where interaction between a terminal operator and computer was not required, play little role in modern computer installations. Interactive terminals, the subject of this discussion, are designed for time-sharing applications in which a user interacts with a computer in a more or less conversational manner. As a product group, interactive online terminals can be categorized in four ways: (1) by their innate information processing capabilities, (2) by their output technologies, (3) by their hardware components, and (4) by their communication codes.

In terms of innate information processing capabilities, interactive terminals may be categorized as dumb, smart, or intelligent. Dumb terminals are the oldest and simplest interactive terminals. As the name suggests, a dumb terminal derives all of its information processing capabilities from the computer with which it is communicating. It is not programmable, has no self-contained functionality, and can perform no work unless it is operating online to a computer. Commonly encountered in mainframe and minicomputer installations, dumb terminals are the least expensive terminals. They are consequently preferred for straightforward computer operations in which a large number of interactive terminals is needed and special functionality is not required. Dumb terminals are widely and successfully used in a variety of library applications, including online public access catalogs, circulation control, and automated acquisitions.

More a marketing concept than a precisely definable product group, smart terminals are essentially advanced dumb terminals. They lack self-contained information processing capabilities, but they do incorporate some special features that set them apart from the simplest dumb terminals. Such features include operator-selectable display attributes, internal memory for offline preparation of information or temporary storage of received data, and the ability to define or redefine the functions of specified keys to address special application requirements. Many newer interactive terminals are properly categorized as smart devices, although conventional dumb terminals remain available.

As information processing devices assume an increasingly important role in business and library operations, online terminals must compete with microcomputers for available desk space. While dumb and smart terminals are readily available and attractively priced, they do not offer the stand-alone functionality—especially the ability to execute prewritten software packages—that many computer users want or need. Where such flexibility is required, an intelligent terminal is actually a microcomputer that can operate as a terminal for purposes of communicating with another computer. To function as a terminal, a microcomputer must be equipped with communications software, as described briefly in chapter 2. In most cases, special hardware components are also required. Intelligent terminals can access remote computers to obtain information or programs for local processing. They can also be used in data entry applications to perform certain preparation and validation routines prior to transmission of information to other computers.

As a microcomputer, an intelligent terminal is a programmable device with self-contained information processing capabilities. It can consequently execute prewritten software packages. When not interacting with a remote computer, it can be used for word processing, statistical analysis, database management, or other tasks. In some installations, stand-alone computing is the device's primary application, and its ability to function as a terminal is reserved for occasional or supplemental communication requirements. As microcomputer prices have declined, however, intelligent terminals are increasingly the online devices of choice for computer users in businesses, government agencies, and other organizations.

As a significant performance advantage over conventional terminals, microcomputers equipped with appropriate communications software can exchange data and program files with other computing devices. If a communications software package is used to transmit one or more files to a remote device, the process is termed "uploading." Thus, a document prepared by a word processing program can be uploaded, via electronic mail, to a designated recipient. Similarly, an intelligent terminal installed in a bookmobile can collect information about circulation transactions for uploading to a computer in the library at predetermined intervals. When a microcomputer captures incoming information on a hard drive or other local storage media for later use, the process is termed "downloading." In the most common library application of downloading, bibliographic citations or other results of an online information search are recorded on a hard drive for editing and printing by a word processing program following termination of the online session. Depending on the application, the downloaded information may also serve as input to database management or spreadsheet programs.

With respect to output technologies, interactive terminals are commonly divided into printing and display varieties. Printing terminals, sometimes described as teleprinters, produce paper output as a record of computer/user interaction. They dominated interactive computing during the 1970s but have since been supplanted by video display terminals (VDTs). Most video display terminals feature cathode-ray tubes (CRTs) as their display mechanisms. Most CRT-based terminals provide a 12-to-14-inch (diagonally measured) screen, although larger and smaller models are available. Small-screen models, which are designed for portability, utilize the flat panel display technologies described in chapter 1. Screen size aside, a video display terminal is considered a "soft copy" output device, but it can be connected to an auxiliary printer if paper output ("hard copy") is desired.

The simplest video display terminals are alphanumeric devices. Usually dumb or smart terminals, they can display the letters of the alphabet, numeric digits, punctuation marks, and other symbols contained in textual documents. Depending on the model, the displayable repertoire will range from less than 100 to more than 250 different characters and symbols. Most alphanumeric terminals employ dot matrix display technologies. They form individual characters by illuminating points on a video screen in a predetermined pattern. Such terminals are equipped with character-generation tables stored in read-only memory. On receipt of an incoming character code, the terminal looks up the appropriate dot matrix pattern for display. Of particular interest for bibliographic applications, some models are equipped with multiple character generation tables for foreign character sets, scientific character sets, or other special symbols.

Typographic capabilities aside, the most common alphanumeric display format provides twenty-four lines with up to eighty character positions in each line for a total of 1,920 characters per screen. Some video terminals provide one or two additional lines for prompts, menus, or operating status information. Regardless of the display format, a cursor—a special character in the shape of a rectangular block, vertical line, or underscore—marks the position where the next character will be displayed. With most alphanumeric terminals, entered or received information is displayed in successive lines that begin at the top or bottom of the screen. As the screen fills up, the display typically scrolls upward to make room for additional lines. Normally, information is lost as lines disappear from the top of the screen. Some smart video display terminals, however, feature internal memories that can store the contents of several screens. In such cases, the video display serves as a kind of "window" into memory. Special controls and scrolling commands allow the operator to recall previously displayed lines from memory to the screen. With intelligent terminals, communications software offers similar capabilities. With dumb terminals, in contrast, a user must request retransmission of the previously displayed lines from the remote computer.

Some smart and intelligent terminals feature split-screen capabilities that allow ongoing computer interaction to be combined with the continuous display of information from one or more segments of memory. Thus, in a bibliographic searching application, the top portion of the screen might be dedicated to the continuous display of a search strategy, while retrieved citations are displayed in the bottom portion. Certain video terminals permit the simultaneous display of interaction with two or more application programs operating on one or more computers. Interaction with the different programs is displayed in separate windows.

The typical dumb or smart alphanumeric video terminal displays light characters on a dark background, although most models allow an operator to select a reverse video presentation with dark characters on a light background. Many computer programs use reverse video for headings, data labels, and instructions that require special emphasis. Some alphanumeric video terminals allow an operator to selectively adjust the intensity and polarity of portions of the display in order, for example, to highlight certain information. This highlighting effect can be enhanced by causing specified information to blink or by displaying selected characters in larger or smaller sizes. Color alphanumeric display terminals are available for applications where a multicolor presentation can effectively highlight important information and clarify relationships among displayed information, but intelligent terminals are typically preferred where color is required.

As their principal shortcoming, alphanumeric video terminals cannot display graphic information, an increasingly important component of many computer applications. Once reserved for scientific and engineering installations, bit-mapped video display terminals are now commonplace, particularly where microcomputers are used as terminals; most desktop and portable computing devices feature bit-mapped displays as standard equipment. As described in chapter 1, bit-mapped video monitors provide graphic as well as alphanumeric display capabilities. Sometimes described as "raster" displays, they draw graphic presentations as patterns of picture elements on a video screen. They can display line graphs, bar charts, pie charts, and other business-type graphics generated by spreadsheets, statistical analysis programs, and accounting software. Bit-mapped video terminals can also display graphic images generated by desktop publishing software, electronic document imaging systems, multimedia information products, and Web pages. A special type of graphics terminal employs vector rather than bit-mapped display technology. Principally intended for computer-aided design and other engineering applications, such devices display geometric shapes by drawing lines between specific points.

Categorized by the combinations of hardware components they include, interactive computer terminals may be keyboard send-receive (KSR), receive-only (RO), or automatic send-receive (ASR) devices. A KSR terminal, the most widely encountered variety in mainframe and minicomputer installations, can both transmit and receive information. Its distinguishing hardware component is a keyboard that is used for the entry of information or commands. Most KSR terminals are dumb or smart video display devices; KSR teleprinters, popular in the 1970s, are obsolete. The KSR terminal's keyboard may be built into the terminal's chassis or connected to it by a cord. The latter design is preferred from the human engineering standpoint because it allows the operator to position the keyboard for maximum comfort during prolonged terminal use. It also permits convenient replacement of a malfunctioning keyboard. Whether integral or detached, the KSR terminal's keyboard typically features a typewriter-like layout with additional keys to manipulate the cursor, simplify the entry of numeric values, activate functions associated with specific programs, and initiate and control the transmission of information.

As its name indicates, a receive-only terminal is capable of displaying or printing information received from a computer, but it cannot itself transmit information. Physically, an RO terminal is distinguished from a KSR device by the absence of a keyboard. Receive-only video display terminals are widely used for information dissemination in public locations. At airports, for example, such devices display the identifying numbers, gate locations, and status of arriving and departing flights. Hotels and convention centers likewise rely on RO video terminals to display times and room assignments for meetings and other events. Receive-only teleprinters are most commonly attached to KSR display terminals in applications that require selective paper output of computer/user interaction. At a circulation desk, for example, dumb or smart KSR display terminals are customarily used for charging and discharging library materials, while an RO teleprinter generates date-due slips and receipts on demand.

Automatic send-receive terminals include local storage components for preparation of information in advance of transmission (uploading) or capture of incoming information (downloading), as described above. Dumb and smart ASR terminals were manufactured through the early 1980s, but they are no longer available. They were essentially KSR terminals with peripheral storage attachments, such as magnetic tape recorders. They have been replaced by microcomputers operating as intelligent terminals, which provide ASR functionality through hard drives or other storage peripherals.

Regardless of configuration, output method, or innate information processing capabilities, interactive terminals transmit and receive digitally coded information. Two coding schemes are widely utilized for terminal-to-computer interaction: the American Standard Code for Information Interchange (ASCII) and the Extended Binary Coded Decimal Interchange Code (EBCDIC). Both were described briefly in chapter 1.

The majority of interactive terminals transmit the ASCII code. Many computer programs are designed to operate with the simplest ASCII terminals, sometimes described as TTY terminals. Most online information services, for example, support TTY terminals. (The abbreviation originally stood for the Teletype Corporation, one of the earliest manufacturers of ASCII teleprinters; the first video display terminals were widely described as "glass teletypes.") Other computer programs require a specific type of ASCII terminal, such as a VT52 or VT100 terminal. The VT series of interactive terminals was originally developed by Digital Equipment Corporation; compatible devices have since been introduced by other manufacturers. A VT100-compatible terminal is typically required to access library catalogs over the Internet. Where microcomputers are used as intelligent terminals, most communication software can emulate, or behave like, TTY and VT100 terminals. The operator selects the emulation appropriate to the task at hand. Special communication programs are available for applications that require other ASCII terminal emulations.

Regardless of type, ASCII terminals employ asynchronous transmission methods, in which the individual bits that represent a given character are framed (preceded and followed) by additional bits that separate successively transmitted characters from one another. The framing bits are required because such terminals are not synchronized with the computers with which they are communicating. In most cases, ASCII asynchronous terminals transmit an additional error-detection bit, called a parity bit, with each character. Thus, each character is represented by ten bits: seven character bits, two framing bits, and one parity bit.

ASCII terminals are supported by computers of all types and sizes. For the most part, EBCDIC terminals communicate with the IBM and plug-compatible mainframes described in chapter 1. Terminals that transmit the EBCDIC code are sometimes described as 3270-compatible terminals. That designation refers to an early EBCDIC video terminal, the IBM 3270 Display Station, that was widely installed in the 1970s and 1980s. EBCDIC terminals operate in the synchronous transmission mode, sometimes described as the bisynchronous mode. Eight bits are used to encode each character, and framing bits are not required.

Whether asynchronous or synchronous transmission is employed, data communication speeds are variously measured in bauds or bits per second (bps). While the two measures are sometimes used interchangeably, they are not identical. Terminals and computers transmit data by altering the amplitude, phase, or other characteristics of a telephone line or other communication facility. Successive alterations in line conditions represent the bits that encode digital data. Bits per second, sometimes termed the "bit rate," is the most accurate and reflective expression of communication speed. It measures the number of bits transmitted by a terminal or computer in a specified time period. Bauds, in contrast, measure the number of changes per second in the condition of a telephone line or other communication facility. In the simplest case, successive telephone line fluctuations occur as the pulses that represent individual bits are transmitted. In such situations, the bit rate and baud rate are identical. At transmission rates above 600 bits per second, however, special coding schemes transmit multiple bits per telephone line fluctuation. In such cases, the bit rate exceeds the baud rate, although some product descriptions and library literature often fail to observe this distinction. To avoid confusion, the bit rate should be cited exclusively. Where the baud rate is cited, it should be interpreted as identical to the bit rate, although that is technically incorrect.

In ASCII asynchronous communications, as described above, each character is composed of 10 bits. Thus a bit rate of 28,800 bits per second is equivalent to 2,880 characters per second. Interactive terminals can transmit and receive information at speeds ranging from less than 100 bits per second (10 characters per second) to more than 50,000 bits per second (5,000 characters per second). The transmission speed employed in a particular situation depends on various factors, including application requirements and available telecommunication facilities. Bit rates below 2,400 bits per second (240 characters per second) were commonplace in the 1980s, but are rarely encountered today. High bit rates are most useful for file transfers or other applications, such as access to Web pages with extensive graphics, that involve large quantities of information.

Transmission speed aside, most terminals can operate in either of two line modes: half-duplex and full-duplex. In the half-duplex mode, information entered at a terminal keyboard is both displayed locally and transmitted to a remote computer. Reception and transmission of information cannot occur simultaneously, however, and it is not possible to interrupt the reception and display or printing of information once they have begun. In the full-duplex line mode, information entered at a terminal keyboard is transmitted to a remote computer, which echoes it back for display and verification of accurate reception. This usually happens instantaneously, giving the impression that the typed characters are being transferred directly to the terminal's screen, just as they are in the half-duplex mode. Occasionally, however, there are noticeable delays between typing and display of information. Unlike the half-duplex mode, full-duplex operation permits simultaneous transmission and reception.

The decision to operate in the half- or full-duplex mode is determined by the requirements of the computer system with which a given terminal is interacting. The user must know the mode required for communication with a particular computer and set the appropriate terminal controls, typically by positioning a switch on the terminal's chassis or selecting a command from a menu displayed by communications software. Selection of the incorrect line mode is the source of a common but easily corrected problem in terminal-to-computer interaction: If characters typed at the terminal's keyboard are not displayed on the screen or if each character is displayed twice, the wrong line mode has been activated.

Modems

Interactive terminals communicate information in the form of electrical signals that consist of discrete digital pulses. If a terminal is located in close proximity—typically, less than 1,000 feet—to the computer with which it must communicate, the digital signals can be transmitted over direct cable connections or other customer-owned wires. In such situations, successive bits are represented by the presence or absence of electrical current. This is the case, for example, where public access terminals are connected to a minicomputer installed in a library building. For longer distance terminal-to-computer communications, however, the public telephone network is often utilized.

While it has been routinely employed for data transmission for several decades, the public telephone network was originally designed to transmit the continuously varying analog signals that are characteristic of the human voice. The discrete, digitally coded signals generated by interactive terminals and other computing devices must consequently be converted to analog form prior to transmission over voice-grade telephone lines. The resulting analog signals must be converted back to digital form at the reception point. This conversion process is termed "modulation" and "demodulation." It is performed by modems. A modem—the term is actually a contraction of modulator/demodulator—is an electronic device that converts digital signals to and from the analog form required for transmission over telephone lines. In terminal-to-computer interaction over analog telephone lines, both devices must be equipped with compatible modems.

Conventional "industrial" modems are designed for use with dumb and smart terminals. While some terminals are equipped with internal modems, most are not. In such cases, an external modem and connector cable must be purchased separately. So-called smart modems are designed specifically for installations where microcomputers will operate as intelligent terminals. They make extensive use of microprocessors and prewritten programs stored in read-only memory circuits to control operations, enhance flexibility, diagnose equipment malfunctions, simplify repair, and reduce the number of component parts, with resulting improvements in reliability. As their distinguishing characteristic, smart modems can respond to commands entered at a microcomputer's keyboard or generated by communications software. These commands specify transmission parameters and initiate operations that would otherwise have to be performed manually or by the microcomputer itself. Most smart modems include automatic dialers, and they support unattended reception. Some smart modems can even transmit and receive data when the microcomputer is turned off. Like their industrial counterparts, smart modems are available in internal and external configurations. As their principal advantages, internal modems are less expensive than external modems; they occupy no desk space and draw power from the computer in which they are installed, eliminating the need for an additional electrical outlet. Internal modems for portable computers often consist of PCMCIA (Personal Computer Memory Card International Association) cards. Whether internal or external, most modems establish a direct electrical connection to the public telephone network via modular jacks and cords.

Modem protocols specify the procedures that modems observe when communicating with one another. Historically, modem protocols have been established through a combination of industry practice and standard-setting organizations, such as the International Telecommunications Union (ITU). Standard protocols provide the compatibility that is essential to effective communication between modems of different manufacturers. Older modem protocols intended for low-speed data transmission are now obsolete. Since the mid-1990s, the most popular modem protocols have supported speeds of 28,800 bits per second or higher, although such fast transmission rates are not attained in every case. Depending on telephone line conditions, these modems will automatically adjust their signaling rates downward to counteract the effects of line noise or other interference. Some modem protocols use data compression to effectively increase the communication rate. The results obtained in a particular situation depend on the characteristics of the information being transmitted; databases, spreadsheets, and graphic files typically yield higher compression ratios than word processing documents.

ORGANIZATION AND MANAGEMENT OF DATA

Whether it is accessed through online terminals for real-time updating or submitted in batches for offline processing, computer-processable information is usually organized in a structured format for storage, retrieval, and processing.

Chapter 1 discussed the various auxiliary storage devices and media on which machine-readable information can be stored while awaiting or following processing. The first part of this chapter briefly described the role of magnetic disks and tapes in real-time and batch processing implementations. In considering the organization of information recorded on such media, it is necessary to distinguish between physical and logical storage structures.

Physical and Logical Data Structures

As defined in chapter 1, computer-processable information consists of a sequence of bits recorded on magnetic or optical media. For a computer to update, retrieve, or otherwise process specified information, the physical location of the information—that is, its position within a magnetic disk, magnetic tape, or other machine-readable storage medium—must be known. Once the information has been located by the central processor, its logical structure—that is, the method by which recorded bits are combined to represent numbers, characters, words, or other information—must be understood. With both physical location and logical data structure, a hierarchy of organizational concepts is recognized. Certain terms are widely used to denote the various levels in the hierarchy. Some data management concepts and terminology are most meaningful to programmers or other computer specialists. The following discussion concentrates on those concepts and terms that are significant for library automation.

While specific physical storage structures are largely determined by the types of auxiliary storage devices and machine-readable media employed, a hierarchy of structural levels can be delineated in a general way. At the highest level, for example, information is stored on a particular magnetic disk drive, magnetic tape unit, optical disk drive, or other hardware device. One level lower in the hierarchy, the physical medium on which machine-readable information is recorded is called the volume. Examples of volumes include hard disks, floppy disks, magnetic tape reels or cartridges, and optical disks. In some hardware configurations, the physical storage device and volume are identical; this is usually the case, for example, with hard drives. With removable media, however, the one-to-one correspondence between a device and a volume is temporary.

In either case, a given storage volume is further partitioned in a manner that varies with the type of auxiliary storage peripheral employed. With multiple-platter magnetic disk cartridges (removable hard disks), for example, the volume is divided into cylinders, which are, in turned, subdivided into tracks. Within individual tracks, information is recorded sequentially, bit by bit. The unit of stored information that can be read into, or written from, main memory in a single operation is called a physical record. Each physical record is composed of a sequence of bits. With floppy disks, optical disks, and magnetic tapes, this structure hierarchy is abbreviated; each physical volume is subdivided into records and the cylinder concept is eliminated.

While these physical storage structures denote the locations of computer-maintained information, logical storage structures are concerned with its content. Earlier in this chapter, the term "file" was used to denote a collection of machine-readable information to be processed by a given application. The term is derived from the manual information systems that computers typically replace. It is often preceded by a descriptor that denotes the storage medium on which information is recorded—hence such expressions as "disk file" and "tape file." Alternatively and more meaningfully, a given file may be described in terms of its information content and the application it serves. Computerization of circulation control, for example, typically requires a bibliographic file that contains information about a library's holdings, an item file that contains information about individual circulating copies, and a patron file that contains information about registered borrowers. Similarly, computerization of library acquisitions activities requires machine-readable files that contain information about vendors and items on order. Often additional adjectives, such as "master," "update," "temporary," or "backup," are used to reflect a file's relationship to other files. Computer files may be further categorized as text files, data files, or image files, depending on the type of information they contain.

Text files are widely associated with word processing programs. They are also created by desktop publishing and computerized typesetting programs, electronic messaging systems, workgroup software, optical character recognition (OCR) products, and text editors of the type furnished as utility programs with some operating systems. As their name suggests, text files contain machine-readable information in character-coded form. The symbolic content of text files is determined by the language in which documents or other textual information is created and the character-generating capabilities of specific computer systems and programs. To address international markets, most new computers support multiple languages. Windows-based computers sold in North America, for example, support European character sets, including Cyrillic and Greek. Characters that are not represented on a keyboard can be generated by specified key-combinations or selected from displayed lists.

The bit sequences that represent individual characters in text files are determined by the digital coding scheme employed in a particular application. Since the 1960s, most text files have utilized the American Standard Code for Information Interchange (ASCII), as previously described. The original ASCII implementation, which dates from 1963, specified a 7-bit code capable of representing 128 different characters. Several enhanced versions, or supersets, of the ASCII coding scheme have since been introduced. An 8-bit implementation, capable of representing 256 different characters, is described as the extended ASCII character set. It includes accented characters associated with European languages, additional mathematical and logical symbols, and special shapes for drawing pictures. The extended ASCII character set is used by the MS-DOS operating system. The ANSI character set, another superset of ASCII, likewise includes accented characters, as well as special punctuation marks—bullets, em and en dashes, and ellipses, for example—plus useful business symbols such as the trademark and copyright symbols and fractions for one-quarter, one-half, and three-quarters. The ANSI character set is used by Microsoft Windows 3.x, Windows 95, and Windows 98. It omits some symbols contained in the extended ASCII character set. The ISO Latin-1 character set is an ASCII superset that is similar but not identical to the ANSI character set. Unicode, which uses 16 bits to encode 65,000 different characters, was developed to support the increasingly global nature of the computer industry. Supported by the Windows

NT operating system and some library automation products, Unicode may ultimately supplant ASCII and its variants.

Regardless of coding scheme, text files store information in a relatively unstructured manner. In most word processing applications, for example, a text file usually consists of a single record—the machine-readable equivalent of a typewritten document containing one or more pages. Alternatively, text files may contain several or many documents. In such cases, individual records may be separated by page break commands or other delimiting characters. Their physical sequence within a text file may be based on their order of creation or logical interrelationships. Word processing and other text-oriented computer programs typically place few significant restrictions on the lengths of text files or the records they contain, although limits may be imposed by available memory or other hardware characteristics.

Within text files, numeric digits are simply stored as characters, without regard to their quantitative significance. Data files, in contrast, store numbers as quantitative values. They can also store character-coded textual information, but they differ from text files in their more structured format. Data files contain records that are subdivided into one or more data elements, called fields, that store particular categories of information. As an example, a data file designed for bibliographic control of technical reports maintained by a scientific library will contain one record for each technical report in the library's collection. Within each record, designated fields may store such information as a report number, author, title, date the report was prepared, originating department, and subjects. Fields are sometimes divided into subfields. Within bibliographic records, for example, an imprint field may include subfields for publisher, place of publication, and date of publication. Similarly, the home address field in a borrower data file may be subdivided into street number and name, city, state, and zip code.

In the hierarchy of logical storage structures, a field is a component of a logical record used for a particular category of information. Fields may be fixed or variable in length. In the former case, a predetermined amount of storage space—sufficient to accommodate a specified number of alphanumeric characters, for example—is allocated for each field value. Long field values are truncated to fit the predetermined allocation; short field values are padded with blanks to attain the desired length. In contrast, space allocated to variable-length fields is dynamically adjusted to accommodate specific values. Fixed- and variable-length fields may be intermingled within records. This is often the case in library applications. As described in chapter 6, the MARC format for bibliographic records incorporates both fixed- and variable-length fields.

Within data files, records may be arranged in various sequences. Commonly encountered possibilities include sequential files, indexed-sequential files, direct data files, and indexed data files. Sequential arrangements are the simplest; records are ordered, or sorted, by values contained in a designated field, which is variously described as the "sort field," "key field," or "sort key." Records in a borrower data file, for example, may be arranged in alphabetical order by borrower name, while records in an acquisitions file may be arranged in ascending or descending sequence by order number. In some cases, a secondary sort field must be used to differentiate records that contain identical values in the primary sort field. Borrower records for persons with the same name, for example, may be sorted by zip code or borrower number. Sequential arrangements are typically employed in applications with straightforward processing characteristics and infrequent updating requirements. Sequential data files are updated by reorganization at scheduled intervals. In some applications, several versions of sequential data files, arranged by different sort fields, may be created for specific purposes.

In the indexed-sequential approach to data file arrangement, records are ordered sequentially as described above, but indexes indicate the physical locations—typically, the block numbers—of records that contain particular values in one or more designated fields. To process a given record, the appropriate index is first consulted to determine its block number. Individual records within that block are then examined sequentially until the desired record is located. Availability of an index improves access time by eliminating the time-consuming examination of all records, as is the case with conventional sequential files. In some implementations, multilayer indexes are created to improve access time.

With direct data files, the arrangement of records is determined by arithmetic calculations performed on designated field values. Typically, a computer program transforms specific field values—such as a borrower's social security number or a book's accession number—into physical storage locations on magnetic disks or other direct-access media. As an example, a field value may be divided by a specified number and the quotient utilized as the record's disk location. Such computational procedures are sometimes termed "hashing." Direct data files permit rapid access, but records can only be retrieved by the field values from which their storage locations were derived.

Where rapid retrieval by multiple parameters is required, indexed data files provide access to records through one or more indexes that contain pointers to records having specified values in designated fields. The indexes are stored in separate files sometimes described as inverted files. They may be created for all or selected fields. In the latter case, the fields selected for indexing are termed "key fields." Index data files are invariably stored on hard drives or other direct-access storage devices. Unlike the indexed-sequential method described above, the physical arrangement of records within indexed files is insignificant, since all access is based on index lookups.

The Database Approach

In many data processing applications, individual data files—based on the physical and logical structures outlined in the preceding section—are specifically designed to meet the requirements of particular application programs. Thus, a library that has computerized both circulation control and acquisition activities may have separate bibliographic data files, each with record formats suited to the requirements of programs written to support those applications. That approach, which dominated data processing through the 1970s, poses several problems, the most obvious being data redundancy with resulting wasted storage space and higher storage costs. It is likely, for example, that much of the same bibliographic data will be contained in both circulation and acquisition files. As an additional difficulty, the potential for inconsistencies and inaccuracy is increased when identical information is stored in multiple, unrelated files, since a change made in one file will not necessarily be replicated in other files.

As a further limitation, the maintenance of separate data files limits flexibility. Because existing file arrangements and record formats are optimized for processing by particular application programs, writing of new programs requires creation of additional data files formatted to address the new programs' requirements. Similarly, modifications to existing application programs often require changes in file structure, while changes in file structure—the addition of a new field, for example—may necessitate extensive program modifications.

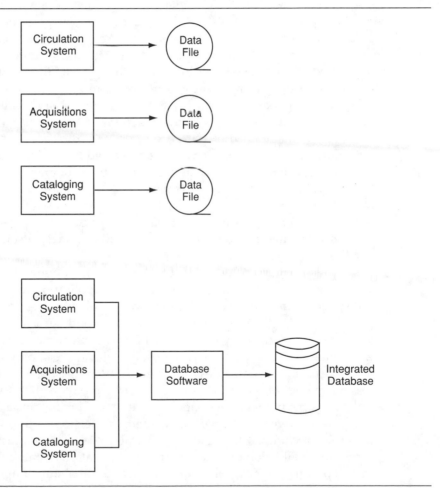

In older approaches to data management, individual but related applications were served by separate data files tailored to the requirements of specific application programs (top). The resulting problems of data redundancy and integrity have led many computer users to establish integrated databases that can be used by several applications (bottom). Database management systems, an example of systems software, provide the necessary interface between the database and individual application programs.

Finally, and perhaps most significant for library automation, the separate data file approach ignores relationships among applications and activities. If files are integrated, information captured by a computerized acquisition system at the time an item is ordered can later be used and enhanced by computerized cataloging and circulation activities. Similarly, the same bibliographic records that support computerized circulation control can serve as the basis for an online catalog, and information about the circulation status of particular items can be incorporated into bibliographic records. This integrated approach is a major focus of library automation products described in chapter 6.

While separate data files are still used, particularly in older applications developed for mainframes and minicomputers, system developers emphasize the advantages of the database approach for organizing and managing machine-readable information. Because terminology dealing with this facet of information processing is subject to considerable variation, it is important to distinguish databases from the data files described above. For purposes of this discussion, a database is an integrated accumulation of computer-processible information organized for use in various applications. Database information may be numeric, textual, or even graphic in nature. Unlike a data file, a database is not established for use by any one computer program. Instead, it is designed to be program-independent. It provides a common repository of information organized in a manner that various application programs can use. While databases are typically maintained on hard drives or other direct-access storage devices for online availability, they can also be processed by programs operating in the batch mode. Many librarians are familiar with bibliographic databases maintained by integrated library systems and with database services that provide online access to various types of bibliographic and non-bibliographic information. The importance of those systems and services for library automation are discussed in later chapters. This section will summarize some fundamental database concepts.

A given database's organization and contents are initially determined by systems analysts following a careful study of application requirements, users' expectations, and the types of information maintained in existing files. Once a database is established, continuing additions to and refinement of its structure and contents are typically the responsibility of a database administrator (DBA) who maintains close working relationships with application programmers and database users. The database administrator, often assisted by a staff of data processing specialists and an advisory committee, monitors database performance, supervises the preparation of documentation, and maintains a data dictionary. The data dictionary is a machine-readable collection of information about a database, including its content, physical storage structures, authorization checks and validation procedures, and the utilization of particular data by specific departments. Such collections of information about computer-processible data are often described as "metadata." In addition to these duties, database administrators develop strategies for backup and recovery of information in the event of a computer system failure.

Properly applied, the database approach addresses the previously discussed problems associated with data files. The integration of separate files in a single database eliminates redundancy, reduces storage requirements, and improves data integrity. Because an integrated database is program-independent, changes can be made in its organization and contents without requiring corresponding modifications in application programs. Similarly, changes in existing programs will not necessarily be accompanied by database modifications.

The implementation of an integrated database offering these advantages is accomplished through a database management system (DBMS), a complex set of programs designed to facilitate the creation and utilization of databases. This definition and the discussion that follows apply mainly to database management systems for mainframes, minicomputers, and network servers. As discussed in chapter 2, database management software packages are also available for microcomputer installations, but such products may not offer all of the characteristics and capabilities of their larger counterparts. As the most significant difference, some microcomputer products maintain information in separate but linked data files rather than in a unified database.

Database management systems for mainframes, minicomputers, and network servers customarily include programs that organize and load a user's information onto hard drives or other direct-access storage devices, while establishing and maintaining various indexes to the stored information. Such database management systems are properly categorized as examples of system software. While they can be custom developed to meet the requirements of a specific computer installation, they are usually purchased as prewritten software packages. Examples include Oracle from Oracle Corporation, the Adaptive Server product line from Sybase Incorporated, Informix Dynamic Server from Informix, IMS and DB2 from IBM, IDMS and Ingres II from Computer Associates, ADABAS from Software AG, Model 204 and System 1032 from Computer Corporation of America, and SUPRA from Cincom Systems.

Available database management programs differ in the methods, or models, they employ to organize stored information. Some systems use a treelike hierarchy or network storage structure that reflects logical relationships among records. In that model, a field within each record contains a reference, or pointer, to the location(s) of a subordinate record(s) elsewhere in the database. Such database management systems are sometimes described as physically linked because their pointers provide pathways along which the system seeks desired information. As an alternative to physical linkage, some database management systems establish indexes to storage records. This approach, sometimes called the "inverted access method," is especially useful in applications that require the retrieval of information by multiple parameters. A third method, which is based on the theories derived from relational mathematics, uses a series of relatively simple tables to reflect relationships among stored records. This relational database management system (RDMS) model is employed by some of the most widely publicized and popular database programs for mainframes, minicomputers, and network servers. It is also used by certain database management software packages for microcomputer installations.

Regardless of the particular organizational model employed, a database serves as a common repository for computer-processible information. As described above, it replaces separate files that address the specific needs of individual application programs. Database records must consequently be accessible to programs written in assembler or higher-level languages, and each program must be able to access those parts of a database that are appropriate to its purpose. From the programmer's standpoint, processing of database records is accomplished through procedural statements that can be embedded in application programs. Beyond the fact of its existence, this interface between computer programs and database management systems is of little interest to librarians or other database users.

More significant is the incorporation of fourth-generation programming languages (4GLs) into database management systems. As noted briefly in chapter 2, this nomenclature reflects the position of database management systems in a chain of software development that began with first-generation machine-level languages and includes assembler languages as the second generation and higher-level languages as the third generation. Presumably, a fifth-generation approach to software development will emphasize natural language programming involving simple English-language instructions with few or no syntactic or semantic restrictions.

Unlike conventional programming languages, which require the specification of detailed instructions that a computer must follow to identify and retrieve information, fourth-generation languages permit rapid application development. Further, fourth-generation query languages allow non-programmers to initiate searches and produce reports by entering a series of commands accompanied by specified retrieval parameters. A query language does not require the training in algorithmic thought and memorization of elaborate sets of rules that characterize the use of most conventional programming languages. In applications involving a bibliographic database, for example, the entry of a specified sequence of commands might result in the rapid retrieval of books and articles indexed with a particular subject heading or written by a particular author. Some database management systems support proprietary query languages. Others utilize the structured query language (SQL), which is covered by an American national standard. In either case, query languages function at a higher level of abstraction than conventional programming languages. They are important features in the information retrieval capabilities offered by various online information services discussed in chapter 7. Support for query languages that can initiate complex searches involving the logical coordination of several or many retrieval parameters is an important feature of database management systems. It enables such systems to satisfy information retrieval requirements that either cannot be anticipated or occur too infrequently to justify customized programming.

Since the mid-1990s, system developers in businesses and government agencies have emphasized the creation of subject-oriented repositories containing information extracted from databases and conventional data files. The resulting repositories, called data warehouses, are designed to support decision making rather than transaction processing, information retrieval, or other application-oriented tasks. Typically associated with mainframe or large minicomputer installations, data warehouses are enterprise-wide information resources. They are designed to serve an entire corporation, government agency, or other large organization. Their contents span multiple business units. Smaller versions, called data marts, may be implemented by individual departments. Compared to a data warehouse, a data mart has a narrower purpose and scope. A growing number of software developers offer tools for designing, populating, updating, and managing data warehouses and data marts. Data mining programs process the information contained in data warehouses and data marts, seeking meaningful patterns and statistically significant correlations. To date, data mining concepts have attracted little library attention, but they may play an important future role in library decision making.

Text Storage and Retrieval Systems

The characteristics of text storage and retrieval programs as a special category of database management systems were briefly discussed in chapter 2. Like conventional database management systems, such programs create, maintain, and manipulate files of computer-processible records, but the records contain the unstructured textual contents of complete documents. The documents, which are stored in character-coded form, may be generated by word processing programs, electronic messaging systems, or other computer applications capable of creating text files of the type described earlier in this chapter. Alternatively, existing paper documents may be converted to character-coded text by optical character recognition or, as a last resort, key entry. In any case, text storage and retrieval programs permit full-text retrieval by creating indexes to every significant word in stored documents. The indexes can rapidly identify and retrieve text segments that contain specified character strings. Some text storage and retrieval programs also support field-oriented records in the manner of conventional database management systems. In a library application involving technical reports, for example, each bibliographic record might contain fields for such data elements as author, title, originating department, release date, and subject headings, plus an additional long field that contains the complete text of a report.

Experimental text storage and retrieval implementations date from the mid-1960s. Typically conceived as demonstration projects designed to test the efficacy of particular indexing and retrieval methodologies, they involved small numbers of documents, narrowly circumscribed applications, and tightly controlled user groups. Operational systems intended for library reference and research applications were implemented in the early 1970s when online information services introduced full-text storage and retrieval capabilities. Such implementations were initially limited to relatively short bibliographic records, some of which contained abstracts. The LEXIS information service, which is discussed more fully in chapter 7, was the first operational system to provide online access to the complete text of large document collections. Prewritten software packages suitable for in-house implementation of text storage and retrieval capabilities became available during the 1960s. The earliest examples were designed for mainframe installations. Product availability for minicomputers and subsequently microcomputers increased significantly during the 1970s and 1980s.

Libraries, archives, and related organizations have utilized text storage and retrieval programs to manage a variety of documents, including proprietary scientific, technical, and managerial reports; laboratory notebooks; patent case files; material safety data sheets; standard operating procedures; and conference presentations, preprints, and reprints. Most implementations have been in industrial, technical, medical, and law libraries, where complex retrieval operations require powerful search capabilities. Text storage and retrieval programs can search the complete contents of documents for specific words or, in most cases, root words. Boolean operators can be used to broaden or narrow retrieval specifications. Most text storage and retrieval programs also support commands that can locate documents containing two or more words in a specified proximity relationship. Depending on the program, such commands may be able to retrieve documents containing two or more words in the same paragraph, in the same sentence, or within a specified number of words of one another. An increasing number of text storage and retrieval programs offer hypertext capabilities, which link interrelated documents and allow words in previously retrieved text segments to be used as search terms.

Depending on the program utilized and the operator's preferences, documents identified by a full-text search may be displayed or printed in their entirety. Alternatively, retrieval may be limited to sentences, paragraphs, or other text segments that contain specified search terms. Some text storage and retrieval programs rank documents or document segments by their presumed relevance and will display them in ranked sequence. Such rankings are usually based on the frequency and proximity of the search terms the documents contain.

As an unusual alternative to conventional text storage and retrieval programs, several vendors offer products that are described as associative processors or text array processors. Rather than consulting indexes to determine the text file locations of records meeting specified retrieval requirements, an associative processor examines specified text files sequentially, seeking a match for specified words or phrases. In some respects, associated processors represent a reversion to older retrieval methodologies. Early information retrieval systems that employed sequential searching of magnetic tape files were ultimately replaced by high-performance software that relied on direct-access storage devices and indexes. In returning to sequential searching, such processors rely on the increasing speed of new computers to attain very rapid search rates. They can effectively address certain information retrieval requirements for which indexed access is impractical. As an example, associative processors are utilized by corporations and government agencies to continuously monitor newswire feeds or similar incoming data streams for records that contain specific subject terms, personal names, company names, or other text segments.

DISTRIBUTED COMPUTING

Centralized computing facilities that serve entire corporations, government agencies, or other organizations have often been criticized for failure to respond satisfactorily to users' information processing requirements. Decentralized computing configurations can give individual departments or offices greater control over those information processing activities that affect their operations directly.

Decentralization of computing resources gained considerable popularity during the early to mid-1970s. At that time, interest in decentralized computing was stimulated by the emerging availability of relatively inexpensive minicomputers, as discussed in chapter 1. Interest intensified with the availability of business-oriented microcomputers in the 1980s. Over the last two decades, many corporations, government agencies, and other organizations have implemented departmental minicomputer and microcomputer installations to supplement centralized mainframes. Typically, these departmental installations operated under the control of individual business units rather than centralized data processing staff. Presumably, they are more responsive to the business units' information processing priorities and requirements. Autonomous decentralized systems can, however, create coordination problems in organizations where related activities must have access to identical information. Properly implemented, distributed computer systems can effectively address such coordination problems.

Distributed System Concepts

Distributed processing is a method of managing computing resources in which information processing capabilities are placed closer to the user while preserving the overall coordination of resources. In distributed processing, two or more computers are combined to perform the work associated with a particular application. An integrated configuration of computers functioning in this manner is described as a distributed system. If the computers that constitute a distributed system are geographically dispersed, the system may be described as a computer network. The technology and organization of computer networks are discussed later in this section.

While the phrase "distributed system" was first used in the mid-1970s, the division of functions among multiple computers has been a familiar data processing practice since the 1960s. Mainframes and minicomputers, for example, can be configured for multiprocessing operations, in which portions of a given program are simultaneously executed by two or more processors. Similarly, in multiprogramming configurations, two or more programs are simultaneously executed on two or more computers that share main memory. Historically, however, the widespread implementation of distributed systems has been linked to the development of small, relatively inexpensive computers. While the earliest minicomputers were most often configured as decentralized, self-sufficient computing devices dedicated to particular applications, the early 1970s saw their increased use as special purpose processors operating online to large computers. This practice continues today. As an example, centralized data processing facilities and commercial information services often use front-end minicomputers to control online terminal systems in time-sharing installations, thereby freeing mainframes or larger minicomputers for more complex information processing operations. Similarly, a minicomputer may be used as a back-end processor dedicated to database management or other specialized tasks.

While ideas about the interrelationships of distributed system components are still evolving, two different structures—horizontal and hierarchical—are

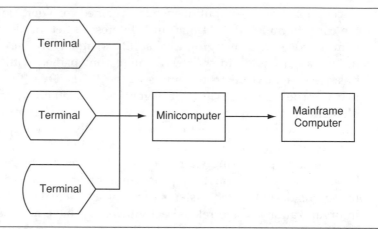

In a simple and commonly found example of distributed processing, a front-end minicomputer performs the time-consuming tasks associated with the control of online terminals in a time-sharing system, thereby allowing the resources of the system's mainframe computer to be used more effectively.

widely implemented. In a horizontal distributed system, two or more computers are interconnected for purposes of information or resource sharing. By supporting computer-to-computer file transfers, such horizontal distributed configurations can minimize or eliminate the use of magnetic tape or other removable media for high-volume data exchange. They also allow specialized or expensive peripheral devices located at one computer site to be accessed by other computers with an occasional need for them. Often, horizontal distributed systems are used to spread an information processing workload over multiple machines. In a system composed of two computers, for example, one of the central processors may be used primarily for online computing; the other may perform batch processing while being prepared to shift to online work in the event the first computer fails or becomes overloaded. Regardless of purpose, the computers employed in a horizontal distributed system are considered peers, although they may be of different brands and vary somewhat in computing power. The horizontal distributed model applies to automated library networks in which one library's computer accesses the computers of other libraries in search of bibliographic records or other information that is not available locally.

Client/server computing is perhaps the most widely publicized form of horizontal distributed processing. In a client/server system, the information processing operations associated with specific applications are divided between relatively powerful computers called servers and desktop computing devices called clients. Typically, servers perform database management, information retrieval, and transaction processing tasks, while clients handle the user interface and input/output operations. In a public catalog access application, for example, a library's bibliographic database may be maintained on hard drives connected to a server, while client devices provide a graphical user interface, with pulldown menus and dialog boxes that simplify the entry of cata-

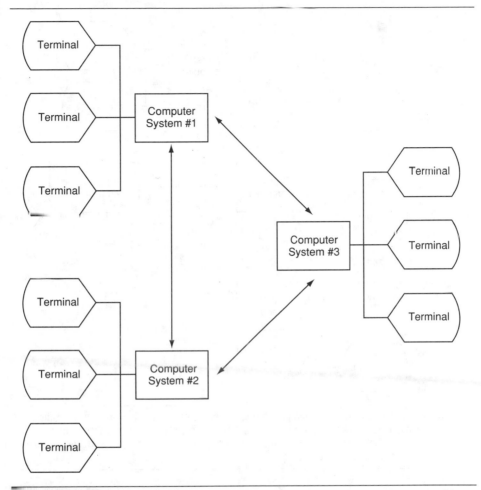

In a horizontal distributed processing system, two or more central processors are interconnected for purposes of sharing data or hardware resources. The central processors are considered peers, although they may vary in computing power.

log search instructions. When a retrieval request is formulated, the client device converts it to a form required by the server. The server then retrieves the specified bibliographic records and sends them to the client, which displays them in a format specified by the system developer or user. As an example, the client may initially display a list of brief records, containing an author, truncated title, and publication date. The user can select additional information for any of the listed works, in which case the client will present a more complete record with labeled fields, call number, and circulation status. Unencumbered by these input/output responsibilities, the server can perform other tasks.

Clients and servers are each computing devices, but their specific characteristics vary from implementation to implementation. As noted above, a server is typically more powerful than the clients with which it cooperates. Depend-

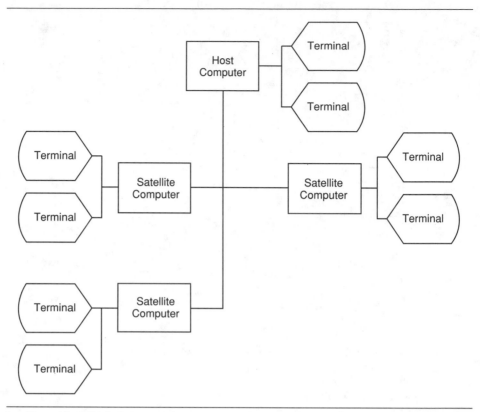

In a hierarchical distributed processing system, certain computers are logically subordinated to other computers. The subordinated computers are considered satellite processors, and they support the vertical distribution of work. Note that the host computer may support some terminals directly as well as through satellite processors.

ing on application requirements, a server may be a Unix-based minicomputer-class machine, a high-end microcomputer running the Windows NT operating system, or, less commonly, a mainframe or proprietary minicomputer of the type discussed in chapter 1. Client devices are usually Windows-based micro-computers or, occasionally, Macintosh systems. Many client/server imple-mentations are designed to replace or downsize conventional time-shared applications that run on expensive mainframes or proprietary minicomputers. While cost saving is the principal motive for downsizing, client/server systems can prove expensive to implement and operate; microcomputer-based clients are more expensive to purchase and maintain than the dumb terminals em-ployed in time-shared computer systems, for example. To reduce costs, some client/server implementations employ "thin" clients, so-called because they lack the hardware components and/or information processing capabilities of full-fledged microcomputers and are not suitable for stand-alone operation. Ex-amples of thin clients include Network Personal Computers (Net PCs), mini-mally configured Windows-based microcomputers that lack local storage peripherals; Network Computers (NCs), which can execute programs written in Java but are not Windows-based; and Windows Terminals, a type of dumb terminal that operates with a Windows NT server and displays a Windows interface. Advocates of thin clients claim that they reduce the total cost of ownership (TCO)—that is, the purchase price plus the cost of installation, hardware and software upgrades, maintenance, technical support, and training—when compared to conventional Windows-based clients.

In hierarchical distributed systems, certain computers are logically subordinated to other computers as application functions are subdivided in vertical fashion. The most common hierarchical systems feature a treelike structure in which information flows from and to the top. The computer at the apex of the hierarchy is often termed the "host." It is often, but not necessarily, a mainframe or large minicomputer. Computers that are subordinate to the host are described as "satellite processors." They may be microcomputers or minicomputers. Rather than enhancing the host's processing power in the manner of the multiple processors used in horizontal systems, the satellite processors in hierarchical distributed systems may be used to simplify the interface between the user and the host computer. As an example, microcomputer-based intelligent terminals may store and display various screen formats for data entry. They may prompt the operator for the entry of data in specific fields and check the entries for such obvious errors as alphabetic characters in an exclusively numeric field or numeric values that fall outside a specified range. Detected errors are reported to the operator for correction prior to transmission of data to the host computer.

In another example, users working at online terminals may enter a few sentences or a paragraph summarizing their information retrieval requirements. This input might then be analyzed by a minicomputer- or microcomputer-based artificial intelligence program that determines appropriate search terms, initiates information retrieval operations, and returns the results to the user. In a simpler application, a microcomputer-based program can be used to translate the search commands required by one information retrieval system into those employed by others, thereby simplifying training requirements in libraries where one system is searched frequently but the others are accessed too occasionally to warrant detailed study of their search procedures. As a more commonly encountered application, a microcomputer operating as an intelligent terminal may be used to retrieve bibliographic citations or other information from databases stored on one or more mainframes or minicomputers. Using local software packages, the retrieved citations may be combined with information from other sources or reformatted for input to databases maintained by other computers.

While they differ in design, horizontal and hierarchical systems are not mutually exclusive distributed processing options. Some distributed systems feature a hybrid structure in which two or more hierarchical systems are linked horizontally at the host processor level. Alternatively, a given hierarchical system may have multiple host processors. Whether based on horizontal, hierarchical, or hybrid models, distributed data processing systems may employ distributed databases that place required information close to the hardware and software that will process it. As the name suggests, a distributed database is one that is partly or entirely stored in multiple locations. Databases can be distributed in either of two ways: by partitioning or by replication.

With a partitioned database, a certain item of information is stored at only one location in a distributed system. Distributed systems designed for such applications as sales order processing, automated shipping, inventory control, and computerized reservation booking often partition their databases geographically. Geographic partitioning is well suited to the horizontal distribution structure described above, but it is only practical where access to specific information is geographically determined. This is rarely the case with bibliographic data. A method that is perhaps more appropriate for library applications involves hierarchical partitioning, in which unique local databases are maintained by satellite processors. The totality of local databases forms the system's master database. As an example, the online catalogs of individual libraries in a cooperative network might be maintained as local databases controlled by satellite processors. A host computer could then handle requests from one satellite processor to access information maintained by others.

In the replicated approach to database distribution, copies of all or parts of a database are stored in two or more locations. As with partitioning, databases can be replicated horizontally or, more commonly, hierarchically, with one or more satellite processors maintaining copies of those partitions of a master database that are most relevant for local operations. As an example, a master union catalog might be stored on a host computer located at a library system's headquarters, while satellite processors in the system's individual libraries maintain those subsets of a master catalog that correspond to their own holdings.

Regardless of their structures or database usage patterns, distributed systems offer potentially significant performance advantages when compared to conventional centralized or decentralized data processing configurations. By placing computer hardware and databases closer to their users, problems and costs associated with long-distance telecommunication facilities can often be minimized or eliminated. Problems of contention and delay are generally reduced in a distributed computing configuration. In addition, distributed satellite processors can eliminate the degraded response times that may occur under peak loads when many online terminals are directly connected to a single, centralized computer.

Compared to decentralized data processing configurations, distributed systems offer improved coordination of computing resources. While users are often able to exploit their computing capabilities more directly and effectively than in centralized systems, distributed systems remain amenable to centralized enforcement of standard operating procedures. Furthermore, distributed systems offer somewhat greater resistance to hardware or software failure, since the malfunctioning of any one component will only affect a subset of total system operations. Additional protection against the adverse effects of system failure is provided by redundancies in hardware and stored data.

As a cautionary note, distributed systems require careful planning and coordination at multiple sites. They can be more expensive to install and operate than centralized data processing facilities. From a technical standpoint, the design and successful implementation of distributed systems require an understanding of principles of data communications and fundamentals of computer networks.

Computer Networks

Broadly defined, a telecommunication network is a combination of equipment, transmission facilities, and, in some cases, software that supports the communication of information-bearing signals from one location to another. The most familiar telecommunication network, the public telephone network, was originally designed for transmission of voice messages, although it is now also used to transmit computer-processable information. Other telecommunication networks have been developed to transmit messages between telex terminals and facsimile machines. A computer network is a specialized form of telecommunication network. It consists of various combinations of computers, terminals, and related equipment connected by data communication facilities. Computer networks are often categorized by their geographic spans: A wide area network (WAN) links geographically distant computers and related equipment, while a local area network (LAN) links computers and other devices that are located in close proximity to each other. In either case, the complex technical characteristics of computer networks are principally of interest to communications engineers and others responsible for actual network design and implementation. The following discussion is limited to terminology, concepts, and other facets of network design and function that are important for librarians.

In computer network terminology, computers and other hardware components are called "nodes" and communication facilities are called "links." The specific types and combinations of nodes encountered in a computer network will vary with the network's topology or structure. The simplest networks, common in time-shared mainframe and minicomputer configurations, feature a starlike topology in which terminals and other data communication devices are directly connected to a centralized host processor. In contrast, a more complex treelike network topology is better suited to the hierarchical structure characteristic of the distributed computer systems described above. With a treelike topology, terminals and related data communication devices are connected to intermediate nodes, which are, in turn, connected to a host processor or, in some cases, to other intermediate nodes. In most hierarchical distributed systems, the intermediate nodes are minicomputers that function as satellite processors. In some cases, however, the intermediate nodes may be special-purpose minicomputers or microcomputers functioning as communication controllers. To maximize the utilization of communication facilities and thereby reduce communication costs, several terminals may be connected to a single communication line, called a "multidrop" or "multipoint" line. In such equipment configurations, a minicomputer or microcomputer functions as an intermediate controller to resolve contention when two or more terminals want to communicate simultaneously.

Horizontal distributed systems, in which multiple computers function as peers, may be better served by a meshed network topology that provides direct connections between nodes. In a fully connected meshed network, each computer can communicate with every other computer. In a partially connected implementation, one node may serve as an intermediary between two other nodes. Compared to starlike and treelike topologies, the meshed network structure offers the advantage of alternative communication routes, so that a circuit failure in one part of the network will not invariably isolate a given node.

In a fourth network alternative, described as a ring topology, nodes are connected in a circular fashion. Each node is linked to two others, and the last node is connected to the first. Information transmitted by a given node is passed around the ring until it reaches a designated recipient node. The ring topology is commonly associated with local area networks. In a variation employed by the IBM Token Ring Network, nodes are connected to hubs in starlike fashion, and the hubs are linked in a ring.

The linear bus, in which nodes are connected to a trunk cable, is another topology employed in local area networks. It is relatively easy to implement, uses less cable than some other topologies, and is readily expandable within limits imposed by the specific local area network in use. In a treelike variant of the linear bus topology, several nodes may be grouped for connection to the trunk cable. The daisy chain, a simpler variation suitable for small local area networks, connects individual nodes directly to one another. As in ring networks, information must be relayed from one node to another until it reaches its destination.

Two or more topologies may be combined in a network installation. For example, a time-shared mainframe or minicomputer that serves as the host processor in a starlike network may also be a node in a meshed network. Similarly, a local area network that uses a ring or linear bus topology to link microcomputers may provide a node for a minicomputer- or mainframe-based library automation system that supports online catalog access.

Communication links vary with network topologies and geographic spans. Wide area networks have historically relied on analog telephone lines in switched or dedicated varieties. With conventional dial-up analog telephone lines, properly described as "switched lines," a communication circuit is established between two nodes for the duration of a given transmission. The connection is terminated when transmission is completed. Subsequent transmissions between the same nodes require reconnection, which may employ different circuits of possibly varying quality. Reflecting their original purpose, conventional switched telephone lines are customarily described as voice-grade rather than data-grade. Recognizing the potential for interference, which can impede reliable transmission and reception, communication over switched telephone lines has traditionally occurred at relatively low speeds. Switched analog telephone lines are typically categorized as "narrowband" communication links because they respond to the bandwidth, or range of frequencies, that are characteristic of the human voice. In data communication, transmission speed is limited by available bandwidth; the narrower the bandwidth, the lower the speed. While newer smart modems support high bit rates over conventional switched telephone lines, they do not permit fast transmission in every circumstance. As previously noted, such modems will reduce transmission speeds when interference is encountered.

Narrowband communication links are appropriate for much terminal-to-computer interaction, where a user's typing rate and reaction time are often limiting factors. "Wideband" communication facilities, which support consis-

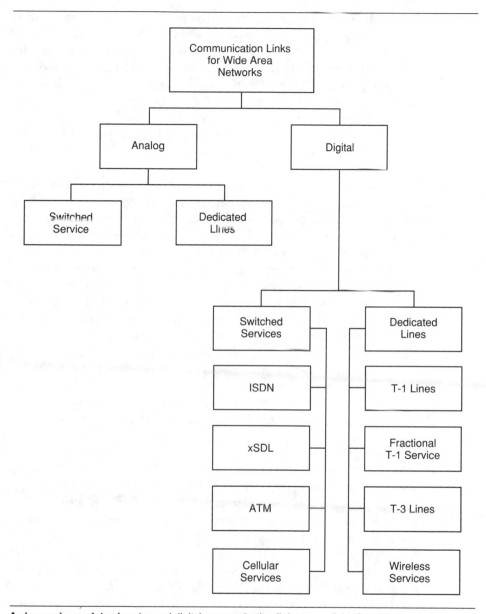

An increasing variety of analog and digital communication links are available for wide area networks.

tently fast bit rates, are normally required for file exchanges or other bulk transmission of large quantities of information between computers, as is the case in the distributed system implementations described above. Computer networks that support distributed systems typically employ dedicated telephone lines as communication links. Such lines are often described as leased lines because the customer pays a flat monthly fee for their unlimited use, as opposed to switched, dial-up lines for which monthly charges vary with the frequency, duration, and distance of specific calls.

As their name suggests, dedicated lines provide a permanent connection between two nodes in a computer network, thereby eliminating the quality variations associated with switched telephone lines. Dedicated analog telephone lines have been used for data communication for several decades. While such lines are normally considered voice-grade, their reliability can be improved through a technique called "conditioning," which minimizes interference and enhances the ability to transmit computer-processable information accurately at high speed. When conditioned for data transmission, a single analog dedicated line can support communication speeds up to 19,200 bits per second, while multiple conditioned analog lines can be combined to create wideband communication links capable of transmission rates in excess of 50,000 bits per second. In many computer networks, special purpose computer-based devices called "multiplexers" and "concentrators" route traffic from low-speed to high-speed lines, thus permitting such relatively expensive facilities to be used in the most cost-effective manner.

Whether switched or dedicated, analog telephone lines require modems to convert the digital signals generated by computers, terminals, and related communication devices to analog form prior to transmission. As an alternative, computer networks increasingly rely on communication facilities that are specifically intended for transmission of digital signals. As its principal advantage, digital transmission is much less susceptible to interference and distortion than its analog counterpart. It is consequently better suited to reliable communication at high signaling rates.

Telephone companies and other telecommunication providers offer a growing variety of switched and dedicated digital communication services. The switched services are the digital counterparts of conventional telephone lines. Integrated Services Digital Network (ISDN), the oldest and best known example, is a switched service for digital transmission of computer data, images, and voice at speeds up to 128 kilobits (12,800 characters) per second. ISDN technology can support a variety of telecommunication services, including enhanced telephony, high-speed data and message transmission, home telemetry, and videoconferencing. ISDN services and products have been available for over a decade, but their acceptance by corporations, government agencies, and other organizations has been slower than anticipated. An advanced version, called Broadband-ISDN (B-ISDN), supports data rates up to 1.5 megabits (150,000 characters) per second over fiber-optic cables, thin strands of glass that carry digital-coded information as pulses of light. Fiber-optic cables are also used by other telecommunication technologies. Compared to copper wires and other metal cables, their advantages include compact size, limited signal loss over long distances, durability under adverse environmental conditions, and immunity to electromagnetic and radio frequency interference.

Among other switched services for digital data communication, Asymmetric Digital Subscriber Line (ADSL) technology supports transmission (uploading) of information at speeds up to 640 kilobits (64,000 characters) per second and reception (downloading) at speeds exceeding 1.5 megabits (150,000 characters) per second. Symmetric Digital Subscriber Line, a related service, supports data rates up to 3 megabits (300,000 characters) per second for both transmission and reception. These services are collectively described as xDSL, a designation that includes High-data-rate Digital Subscriber Line (HDSL), Single-line Digital Subscriber Line (SDSL), and other variants. Cable modem service uses cable television wiring, discussed in chapter 4, for data communications at rates of 768 kilobits (76,800 characters) per second for transmission and up to 10 megabits (1 million characters) per second for reception. Availability is obviously limited to geographic locations served by cable television operators. Asynchronous Transfer Mode (ATM), which supports data rates from 25 to more than 600 megabits (2.5 to 60 million characters) per second, is intended for wide or local area networks. Gigabit-level ATM transmission has been demonstrated. Suitable for a variety of information management applications, ATM technology can carry video and voice signals as well as computer-processible information.

As alternatives to the dedicated analog connections described above, digital leased lines have been available for more than a decade. Early examples, which remain in use, operated at speeds up to 56 kilobits (5,600 characters) per second. T-1 lines, the most widely publicized dedicated digital communication service, support data rates of 1.54 megabits (154,000 characters) per second. A T-1 line actually consists of 24 channels, each supporting a data rate of 64 kilobits (6,400 characters) per second. Many telephone companies and other data communication service providers offer fractional T-1 lines in increments of 56 kilobits per second. A fractional T-1 line corresponds to a 64-kilobit-per-second T-1 channel, with 8 kilobits per second being used for data management. Some data communication service providers offer double T-1 lines with twice the bandwidth of a single line. Intended for very high volume computer networks, T-3 lines support data rates of 43 megabits (430,000 characters) per second. A T-3 line, also known as a DS3 line, consists of 672 channels, each of which operates at 64 kilobits per second. Where less capacity is required, some data communication providers offer partial T-3 service.

Several wireless communication technologies offer data communication alternatives for wide area networks where wire-based links are unavailable or impractical. Terrestrial microwave technology, one of the oldest forms of wireless communication, can transmit information at speeds of 56 kilobits per second or greater, which is comparable to data rates supported by dedicated telephone lines. As the name suggests, terrestrial microwave signals carry information directly between two points on the earth's surface. Terrestrial microwave transmission facilities are not, however, as geographically wide-ranging or as versatile as telephone lines. There must be a clear line of sight between the transmission and reception points. This requirement limits the utility of terrestrial microwaves for long-distance communication. To prevent deflection by temporary or permanent obstacles in the communication path, microwave signals are usually transmitted by highly directional antennas spaced at maximum distances of twenty to thirty miles. As a further complication, there is considerable congestion of currently allocated microwave frequencies in major metropolitan areas.

These problems can be minimized or overcome if microwave signals are first transmitted to satellites for amplification and retransmitted to earth stations located at or near the intended reception point. Satellites suitable for data communication are positioned in the so-called geosynchronous or geostationary orbit, which is located perpendicular to the equator approximately 22,300 miles above the earth's surface. In that orbit, the satellites revolve around the earth at the same speed at which the earth revolves around its own axis. They consequently occupy a constant position relative to earthbound antennas and serve as stationary relay devices in the sky.

Satellites have been used for military applications, international video broadcasting, and telephony since the 1960s. While newly industrialized nations, which lack a wire-based communications infrastructure, have long recognized their potential for domestic voice and data transmission, U.S. interest in satellites for those applications dates from the early 1980s. Since that time, several companies have introduced satellite communication services designed specifically for the transmission of business data at speeds ranging from several hundred thousand to several million bits per second. While they never experienced the spectacular growth that some industry analysts and entrepreneurs originally anticipated, these satellite communication services offer effective, high-speed transmission capabilities suitable for wide area networks with high-volume transmission requirements. As a recent development, companies that offer digital television transmission via satellite, as described in chapter 4, have added data communication capabilities. Such services are the wireless counterparts of the cable modem technology described above.

Among other wireless transmission options, cellular telephone service providers offer data as well as voice communication capabilities. Cellular data communication is particularly attractive for portable computing devices. A special cellular modem is required. Cellular data communication gives business travelers convenient access to databases, electronic mail, and other computer resources. Transmission quality is affected by several factors, including the user's proximity to cellular radio antennas. In some cases, cellular signals may not be able to reach all locations within large buildings.

Wide area data communication networks may be publicly accessible or intended for the private use of one or more corporations, government agencies, or other organizations. In the former category, a group of companies, collectively called "value-added carriers," have created international data communication networks that link computers, terminals, and other data communication devices. Wide area networks developed by such companies are termed "value-added networks." Examples include Tymnet and Sprintnet. Unlike the conventional telephone network, which uses a single communication circuit to establish a transmission link between two points, value-added networks employ packet-switching technology. Information is divided into segments called packets, each of which may be transmitted to its intended destination by a different network route. At the destination point, the packets are assembled in the proper sequence under computer control. Packet-switching technology is covered by the ANSI X.25 networking protocol, published by the American National Standards Institute. Packet-switching networks are consequently described as X.25 networks. As its principal advantage, packet-switching technology promotes the efficient use of telephone lines and other communication facilities with a resulting reduction in communication costs, especially in applications that require long-distance data transmission.

Historically, libraries have used value-added networks to access the online information services and bibliographic utilities described in later chapters. For some library applications, however, the value-added networks have been supplanted by the Internet, the best known example of a publicly accessible wide area computer network. The Internet is an outgrowth of ARPANet, a computer network developed for the Advanced Research Projects Agency of the U.S. Department of Defense. As part of the ARPANet initiative, a special packet-switching methodology, the Transmission Control Protocol/Internet Protocol (TCP/IP) was developed to support data transmission between computer sites. Originally designed to link government agencies, universities, scientific laboratories, and other research institutions, the Internet has expanded rapidly and dramatically into a multipurpose global information network that connects millions of computers and more than 100 million users. (The Internet's original purpose has been revived in Internet2, a collaborative university-based effort, and the Next Generation Internet initiative, a multiagency government research initiative to develop advanced networking technologies.) Libraries associated with universities, government agencies, and corporations typically access the Internet through nodes operated by their parent institutions. Other types of libraries contract with Internet Service Providers (ISPs) or commercial online services that provide Internet access in addition to other information resources.

The Internet is, in effect, a loose confederation of computer networks located throughout the world. Network policies and procedures are defined by several organizations, including the Internet Society, Internet Engineering Steering Group, Internet Engineering Task Force, Internet Architecture Board, Internet Research Task Force, and Internet Assigned Numbers Authority. Internet computers, called hosts, are connected to the network's main lines, which are known as the Internet backbone. It consists principally of the T-3 lines described above.

The Internet provides access to many library catalogs, as well as a variety of reference and research databases. Examples are discussed in later chapters. The telnet program, which is supported by Internet Service Providers, can be used to connect to specific Internet hosts, which are identified by alphabetic or numeric addresses. Typically, a VT100-compatible computer terminal, as described above, is required. The file transfer protocol (FTP) supports uploading and downloading of files from specified Internet hosts. Menu-oriented tools, called gophers, and various searchable indexes help users locate pertinent Internet hosts. Increasingly, however, these Internet resources have been supplanted by the World Wide Web (WWW), a subset of the Internet that provides online access to collections of interlinked documents called Web pages. The World Wide Web is a client/server system that embodies the distributing processing concepts defined above. Web clients are usually microcomputers equipped with special software called Web browsers. The computers that store Web pages are called Web servers. Each Web server is identified by a unique address called a Universal Resource Locator (URL).

The World Wide Web employs the hypertext transfer protocol (HTTP), a set of rules for exchanging information. The hypertext markup language (HTML) is used to encode and format Web pages maintained at a given site. Various software tools support the design and implementation of Web pages containing combinations of text and graphics, including images and, in some cases, video and audio clips. Web pages are designed for display by Web browsers, which may be preloaded on new microcomputers or obtained from Internet Service Providers. The majority of Web pages are designed for compatibility with the two most widely installed Web browsers, Netscape Navigator and Microsoft Internet Explorer. Information in a given Web page may be linked to related information contained in other pages at the same site or at different sites. Such links, termed hyperlinks, are often highlighted within Web pages. Web policies and procedures are defined by the World Wide Web Consortium (W3C).

As defined above, the Internet is a publicly accessible wide area network. Some corporations, government agencies, and other organizations have established private wide area networks based on Internet and World Wide Web technologies. Intended for closed user groups, such private Internets are called intranets. They utilize TCP/IP to transmit information between linked computer sites and HTML to create Web pages for display by browser programs. Compared to conventional wide area networks, intranets can prove less expensive to implement and easier to use. Strictly defined, intranet access is limited to an organization's own employees. If an intranet is connected to the Internet—in order to let employees search the World Wide Web, for example—public access to private information is typically restricted by a set of security measures called a firewall, which isolates the intranet's computers. In some implementations, intranet access is extended to contractors, suppliers, or other organizations with which the intranet operator has a business relationship. In such cases, the intranet is described as an extranet.

Local Area Networks

Since the late 1970s, local area network concepts and technologies have played an increasingly prominent role in the planning, implementation, and operation of computer networks in general and microcomputer networks in particular. As previously defined, a local area network connects computers and related devices that are located within a narrowly circumscribed geographic area, such as a college campus, an industrial park, a school, an office building, a military base, a warehouse, a factory, or a library. The geographic span of a local area network— defined as the maximum distance between the farthest nodes—may be several miles, but most installations involve a much smaller area. Another essential attribute of local area networks is full intercommunication capabilities, meaning that every network node must be able to communicate with every other network node. A local area network is a computer network for independent devices that are capable of autonomous operation. LAN nodes may be computers or autonomous noncomputer devices such as scanners, printers, or facsimile machines that are intended for direct LAN connections. Non-autonomous peripheral devices are not themselves considered nodes, although they may operate as LAN devices attached to nodes.

The autonomous node and intercommunication requirements distinguish local area networks from conventional time-shared systems that support online terminals linked to a host computer. While such time-shared systems may operate within a limited geographic area, they do not share the characteristics of local area networks described in this section. Although time-shared mainframe and minicomputer installations increasingly include autonomous microcomputers operating as intelligent terminals, dumb and smart terminals are usually supported as well. Because dumb and smart terminals, as previously defined, require connection to a host computer in order to function, they do not qualify as autonomous nodes. The time-shared mainframe or minicomputer to which such terminals are attached may itself function as a local area network node, however. As a further limitation, conventional time-sharing systems do not support communication between terminals without host computer intervention.

A number of libraries have installed local area networks. Others have access to LANs implemented by universities, corporations, school systems, municipalities, or other organizations with which they are affiliated. Among their advantages for libraries, local area networks permit sharing of printers, disk drives, and other peripheral devices. Peripherals attached to one LAN node can often be accessed by other nodes, thereby promoting fuller utilization of available equipment and minimizing the total number of peripherals required at a given site. Such peripheral sharing is particularly effective where network participants have an occasional, rather than continuous, need for a relatively expensive output, storage, or communication device. In many local area network installations, designated nodes function as servers that provide particular resources to other network nodes. A print server, for example, provides shared access to printers, plotters, and other output peripherals attached to it. It receives requests for hard copy output from other network nodes and directs them to the appropriate devices, queuing print jobs as necessary. Similarly, file servers provide shared access to high-capacity magnetic disk drives, optical disk autochangers, or other peripherals, permitting centralized storage and control of information. Communication servers provide shared access to modems. While modems are relatively inexpensive, a modem pool minimizes telephone line requirements, with their associated high installation costs and monthly charges. Depending on the installation, a LAN server may be a microcomputer, minicomputer, or mainframe. LAN nodes that receive services are variously called workstations or clients, although the latter term—as defined above—does apply exclusively to local area networks. In some local area networks, specific computers function only as servers. Such LANs are described as dedicated server networks. In other cases, network nodes can function as both workstations and servers. Such LANs are termed peer-to-peer networks.

Local area networks also permit information sharing among nodes. Assuming proper authorization, databases stored by a file server can be accessed by other LAN nodes. In an administrative application, for example, databases of accounting, purchasing, payroll, or personnel information may be referenced, updated, or otherwise processed by LAN participants. Such capabilities are critical for downsizing initiatives in which LAN-based microcomputers support complex applications that were previously implemented on mainframes or minicomputers. Client/server concepts, as described above, play an important role in such downsizing initiatives.

As a potentially attractive form of resource sharing, local area networks can provide multiuser access to prewritten application software stored on hard drives or other peripherals attached to designated file servers. Many software publishers offer LAN licenses that permit simultaneous use by a specified number of computers operating in a local area network. While they are more costly than single-user licenses, LAN licenses usually prove less expensive than the cost of purchasing an equivalent number of copies of a given program for individual microcomputers. Further, software upgrades are much easier to implement if LAN users share a single copy.

As described in later chapters, many library automation programs and CD-ROM information products are available in local area network versions. In LAN implementations, microcomputers can perform different tasks, thereby giving a library considerable flexibility in configuring an automated system. In a six-node microcomputer network that supports circulation control and public catalog access, for example, one microcomputer might function as a database server, two microcomputers might be used as circulation workstations, and the remaining three might serve as public access catalog terminals. In academic, school, government, and corporate installations, a local area network can make a library's computer-based information resources conveniently accessible to faculty, students, researchers, managers, and others working in offices, laboratories, classrooms, dormitories, or other locations within the library's parent organization, thereby improving communication with users and extending the reach of library services beyond the physical confines of the library itself.

Most newer local area networks utilize telephone wires, sometimes described as "twisted-pair wiring," to interconnect nodes. Some long-established local area networks employ coaxial cable, but that medium is more expensive and difficult to install than twisted-pair wiring. Fiber-optic links can support very high data rates, but they are very expensive. Consequently, they are used sparingly. As an alternative to conventional cabling, some local area networks use microwave, infrared, or spread-spectrum radio technology to transmit signals between nodes over the air. As a group, such "wireless" communication links are more easily installed than wire-based LANs, but they are much more expensive and can prove vulnerable to interference. They are typically reserved for special situations, such as a temporary LAN that must be installed quickly to support a short-term project or workgroup.

In local area networks, multiple nodes share the communication link, whether it is twisted-pair wiring or some other medium. As noted above, LAN nodes are autonomous; there is no central processor to mediate among contending users, as is the case in time-shared systems. Instead, media access protocols determine how and when a given device can transmit information over a certain network. Several LAN protocols have been developed for that purpose. In the most widely implemented approach, called Carrier Sense Multiple Access with

Collision Detection (CSMA/CD), LAN nodes desiring to transmit information monitor the network to determine whether it is in use by another node. If the network is idle, a node may transmit immediately. If two or more nodes sense a clear channel and attempt to transmit simultaneously, a "collision" occurs as their signals interfere with one another. Transmission is immediately terminated, and all devices pause for a randomly determined amount of time before retransmitting. If another collision occurs, the procedure is repeated.

The CSMA/CD protocol is used by local area networks that conform to the IEEE 802.3 standard defined by the Institute of Electrical and Electronics Engineers. Such networks are often described as Ethernet LANs. The programs that implement the CSMA/CD protocol reside in read-only memory on special LAN adapters, which must be installed in each node on an Ethernet network. Some microcomputers are factory-equipped with Ethernet adapters; alternatively, adapters can be purchased separately for installation in a computer's expansion slots. Most Ethernet networks employ twisted-pair wiring with a star topology in which LAN nodes are connected to specially designed hubs. Such implementations, which are described as 10-BASE-T networks, support data rates of 10 megabits (1 million characters) per second. Where a higher data rate is required, so-called Fast Ethernet implementations, also known as 100-BASE-T networks, operate at 100 megabits (10 million characters) per second over twisted-pair wiring or fiber-optic links. A Gigabit Ethernet standard, which supports data rates of 1,000 megabits (100 million characters) per second, was approved in 1998 by the Institute of Electrical and Electronics Engineers. Note that these data rates are much higher than those for the wide-area network links described above.

Another popular media access protocol, called token ring, is intended for local area networks with ring topologies. A special signal called a token circulates around the network when all nodes are idle. A node wishing to transmit information to another node must obtain a free token as it passes. When transmission is completed, the token is released for other uses. The token ring protocol is used by local area networks that conform to the IEEE 802.5 standard. The IBM Token Ring LAN is an example of such a network. It supports data rates of 4 megabits (400,000 characters) or 16 megabits (1.6 million characters) per second. The Fiber Distributed Data Interface (FDDI) is a local area network protocol that supports data rates of 100 megabits (10 million characters) per second. Fiber-optic media are preferred for reliability in FDDI networks, but twisted-pair wiring is also permissible. FDDI networks employ token-passing protocols, typically with nodes connected in a ring topology. In businesses and government agencies, FDDI is sometimes used for backbone networks that interconnect several departmental LANs, as described below. Various nonstandard media access protocols have been utilized by other local area networks.

Media access protocols aside, a given local area network can be connected to other local area networks or to wide area communication facilities. In many organizations, multiple small LANs, installed at the departmental or workgroup level, are preferred to a single enterprise-wide LAN. All local area networks place limits on the number of nodes they can support and on the distances between the farthest nodes. Small LANs can be implemented and expanded more easily than complex networks. As an additional advantage, they avoid performance degradations by minimizing the number of users per segment, thus reducing congestion and contention for network access. Where enterprise-wide information exchange is required, bridges and routers are microprocessor-controlled devices that interconnect two or more local area networks within an organization. The two devices differ in their operating methods, but they achieve the same result: full intercommunication between nodes on different LANs, in effect creating one logical network from multiple physical implementations. A device called a "gateway" provides a connection between a local area network and a wide area network for purposes of communicating with external computers, typically on a time-sharing basis. A reference librarian working at a LAN node in an academic or public library, for example, may want to search an online catalog operated by a neighboring library or obtain access to an online information service, a bibliographic utility, or the Internet. Similarly, a corporate or government librarian in a field office location may need to access a proprietary database of research information maintained by a mainframe computer installed in a distant headquarters facility.

SUMMARY

The terms batch and real time denote modes of information processing. In a batch processing system, there is a gap in time between the occurrence of a transaction or other event and the computer's processing of information about that event. Batch processing systems are typically characterized by the offline collection of information for bulk input at prescheduled intervals, the straightforward processing of information recorded on magnetic tape, and the production of printed or microform reports. These reports reflect the condition of a particular application as of the last scheduled processing interval. They cannot reflect transactions or other events occurring after that time. In real-time systems, information about transactions or other events is entered and processed at the time the events occur. As an advantage over batch processing, the information maintained by real-time systems is always up to date. It is typically stored on hard drives or other direct-access devices for reference by online terminals.

Whether information is processed in the batch or real-time mode, computer applications rely on interactive software that prompts and guides users in the performance of various tasks. Well-designed interactive programs are simple to use, forgive user errors, and allow the user to control the pace of interaction. While interactive programs provide an intellectual interface between the computer and the user, online terminals serve as the required physical interface. An online terminal is a device that allows users to transmit data to, and receive data from, a time-shared computer system. Terminals designed for interactive applications can be categorized by their innate information processing capabilities, by their output methods, by the nature of their components, or by their communication characteristics. Dumb terminals derive all of their information processing capabilities from the computer with which they are communicating.

Smart terminals are essentially dumb terminals with more features. Intelligent terminals are actually programmable microcomputers that can also function as terminals. Communication software is required for that purpose. With reference to their output capabilities, terminals can be categorized as video displays or teleprinters. In terms of its components, a terminal can be configured with a keyboard for interactive communication, without a keyboard for receive-only operation, or with a recording device for uploading and downloading information. Most interactive terminals support ASCII asynchronous communication capabilities, which are compatible with a wide variety of computer systems. Some applications may require a specific model of ASCII terminal, such as a VT100. Bisynchronous, 3270-type terminals are principally intended for communication with mainframe computers.

Regardless of the mode in which it is processed or the type of terminal used to access it, information stored on disks or tapes must be organized in a structured format. In terms of physical location, information is recorded on a given device, such as a disk drive or tape unit, in a physical container called a "volume," which is, in the case of disks, divided into cylinders or tracks. The unit of information that can be read or recorded in a single operation is called a "physical record." In terms of logical structure, information is typically organized into files, which may contain data, text, images, or sound. Data files usually consist of one or more logical records that are subdivided into fields. The loading of this logical structure onto physical storage devices and media is accomplished by the computer's operating system or other system software in a manner that is largely transparent to the user. Various methods can be used to arrange stored records. In a sequentially organized file, for example, logical records are ordered by a designated key field. Where multiple retrieval parameters are involved, various indexing techniques may be employed.

In many data processing applications, individual files are specifically designed to meet the requirements of a particular application program—an approach that results in redundant information, wasted storage space, high storage costs, and other problems. As an alternative, the database approach replaces separate files with an integrated accumulation of computer-processible information organized in a manner that can address a variety of application requirements. Among its advantages, the integration of separate files eliminates redundancy, reduces storage costs, and improves the accuracy and integrity of information. Implementation of an integrated database is accomplished through a set of programs called a database management system (DBMS). Such programs are available for computers of all types and sizes. Among their most important features, database management systems feature nonprocedural query languages that simplify application development and permit information retrieval without formal programming. In some organizations, information required for decision making is extracted from databases to create centralized data warehouses. Smaller versions, called data marts, may be implemented at the departmental level.

Centralized computing facilities have often been criticized for failing to respond to the information processing requirements of remote users. Since the mid-1970s, many organizations have adopted distributed data processing systems that are designed to place computing power and information resources closer to the end user. A distributed system is an integrated configuration of computers that performs the work of a given application or group of applications. Distributed systems may be organized along horizontal or hierarchical lines. The former includes client/server implementations, which are an important component of downsizing initiatives that replace older mainframe and minicomputer applications. In some distributed computer systems, databases are distributed as well. In the partitioned approach to database distribution, selected information is stored at specific sites in a distributed system. In the replicated approach, all information is stored at all sites.

The interconnected computers, communication facilities, and related devices in a distributed information processing system constitute a computer network. Computer networks vary in their topologies, geographic spans, and communications facilities. Wide area networks (WANs), which have no geographic restrictions, may utilize combinations of switched analog or digital telephone lines, dedicated (leased) analog or digital telephone lines, or wireless communication technologies such as terrestrial microwave, or cellular data transmission. Wide area networks may be publicly accessible or implemented by a corporation, government agency, or other organization for its own use. The Internet is the most important example of a publicly accessible wide area network. It is actually a loose confederation of independent computer networks that are operated by a variety of organizations. The World Wide Web, a subset of the Internet based on client/server technology, contains specially formatted "pages" of information that are designed for display by browser software. Intranets and extranets are private computer networks that employ Internet technologies.

Local area networks (LANs) are distinguished by their narrowly circumscribed geographic spans, among other characteristics. They typically employ twisted-pair wiring as communications media, but coaxial cable, fiber optics, and wireless links are also possible. Local area networks have proven especially popular in microcomputer installations. Among their advantages, local area networks permit sharing of hardware resources, software, and information. Many library automation systems and related information products are available in LAN versions. Ethernet networks, which are available in several versions, are the most widely implemented local area networks.

4

Automated Office Systems and Related Technologies

While data processing in general—and library automation in particular—are dominated by the computer and data communication concepts and technologies described in preceding chapters, a broader view of automated information processing includes document preparation and reproduction technologies, video-based information systems, and such electronic message transmission systems as facsimile, voice mail, and telex. These technologies and the products that embody them are often collectively characterized as automated office systems because they are widely applied to the creation, storage, retrieval, reproduction, and dissemination of information in an office environment. Although several of the technologies discussed in this chapter have been commercially available for over half a century, their popularity and applications have increased dramatically since the 1980s, when widely acknowledged concerns about the productivity of the rapidly growing office workforce brought them to prominence.

From the mid-1970s through the early 1980s, the developed nations of North America and Western Europe experienced both a marked decline in historical patterns of productivity improvement and a significant shift in workforce composition. Some economists and other observers saw a causal relationship between the two trends. They attributed declining productivity to the increasing migration of workers from highly automated, relatively productive manufacturing jobs to managerial and clerical white-collar positions in offices, where much work was being performed manually or with rather primitive mechanical devices such as typewriters.

Viewing this situation with alarm, many information specialists contended that a more pervasive application of technology would significantly increase the productivity of the rapidly growing white-collar workforce, just as intensified automation had previously improved the productivity of factory and farm workers. Admittedly, computers had been used to automate office operations since the 1960s, but data processing applications through the late 1970s were largely limited to such routine transaction-oriented tasks as payroll processing, accounts payable, and accounts receivable. Seeking greater productivity, many government agencies, corporations, and other organizations significantly expanded their automation initiatives during the early to mid-1980s, broadening the range of their computer operations and applying other technologies to information processing tasks that computers could not successfully address. By the late 1980s, many office activities had been successfully automated. Today, the role of technology as an indispensable workplace component is widely recognized, and most of the devices described in this chapter are routinely encountered in a variety of work environments, including libraries.

With a high percentage of professional and clerical employees, library work environments are overwhelmingly white-collar in composition and include a significant office component. At a time when rising operating costs coincide with significant budgetary retrenchment, productivity improvements are essential to the continued delivery of library services. With proper planning, the technologies described in this chapter can prove useful in a broad range of library operations.

DOCUMENT PREPARATION

Word processing, discussed briefly in chapter 2 and more fully below, is the foundation for automated document preparation in offices and libraries. Since its introduction in the mid-1970s, the phrase "word processing" has intentionally conveyed the impression that conventional data processing, the historically dominant manifestation of business computing, emphasizes numbers to the exclusion of textual information. In the broadest sense, word processing encompasses a group of technologies, concepts, and methods that facilitate the preparation and production of textual documents ranging from ordinary business correspondence and reports to published books and articles. In keeping with this broad definition, a fully and ideally configured word processing system would include equipment for the creation, storage, retrieval, reproduction, and dissemination of textual information. Typically, however, the phrase is used in a much narrower sense to denote the application of technology to the preparation, editing, and printing of typewritten documents. This narrower definition reflects word processing's origins in the German term *textverarbeitung*—literally, the making of text.

As originally conceived, word processing technology was embodied in two different types of products: dictation systems and text-editing systems. The latter product group, described later in this chapter, has attracted so much attention that word processing is usually equated with text editing, to the extent that the latter phrase is now rarely encountered. While dictation systems have long been utilized in a wide range of general business applications, libraries have been slow to incorporate them into their established work patterns, and there is virtually no recent literature on their selection and use in library applications. With some justification, information specialists often view dictation systems as old-fashioned precomputer products. Ultimately, their viability is threatened by the computer skills of professional workers, who increasingly type their own documents, and by newer technologies, such as the voice recognition software discussed in chapter 1. Dictation systems remain useful, however, in a variety of situations, and new products are effectively integrated with computer technologies. The following discussion surveys the advantages of machine dictation and describes typical equipment configurations, features, and functions.

Dictation Systems

In a fully configured word processing installation, document preparation begins with the conversion of the thoughts of a person called a "word originator" to a form suitable for transcription by a typist. In library applications, the word originator may be an administrator composing correspondence, a cataloger creating bibliographic descriptions, an archivist inventorying newly accessioned records, a bibliographic instruction librarian preparing teaching materials, or an information specialist preparing a citation list or literature review. Assuming that the word originator lacks typing skills, the required conversion of thoughts to recorded words can be accomplished in three ways: by writing them in longhand, by dictating them to a stenographer, or by dictating them to a voice recording machine. While all methods have their advantages, they differ significantly in the type and amount of labor involved.

With longhand writing, special equipment, training, and working conditions are unnecessary. Longhand writing can be performed almost anywhere—in an office, at home, while traveling. Secretarial assistance is not required. The longhand method is especially well suited to such library tasks as the drafting of literature reviews that contain esoteric terminology or bibliographies that include foreign language citations. Assuming legible handwriting, the transcribing typist should experience little difficulty with unusual spelling or punctuation. Longhand writing is likewise appropriate for the composition of multipage management reports, policy statements, standard operating procedures, and other long documents where reference to previously written passages is essential. As an obvious disadvantage, longhand writing is a slow process that can consume much of the word originator's workday.

Because the salaries of librarians/word originators are higher than those of clerical support personnel, dictation to a stenographer can reduce the cost of documents. When the word originator is properly prepared and the stenographer appropriately skilled, shorthand dictation can prove several times faster than longhand writing. While this approach requires the labor of two workers, the resulting savings in the word originator's time can offset the added cost of clerical involvement. In addition, immediate interaction between the word originator and stenographer can clarify ambiguous terminology, spelling, or punctuation, thus simplifying eventual transcription by a typist. Usually, typing must be performed by the stenographer to whom the document was dictated, since most stenographers have difficulty deciphering shorthand written by others. Some flexibility in the assignment of work to clerical personnel must consequently be relinquished. As a further limitation, many libraries are unable to hire stenographers and, when available, they are usually paid more than ordinary secretaries.

The speed advantages of voice dictation can be retained, however, by using recording equipment. Often, document preparation costs can be reduced as well. The business case for machine dictation was convincingly articulated decades ago. Because dictation to a machine can occur at a faster rate than dictation to a stenographer, the word originator's involvement in document creation is minimized. A stenographer's presence is not required—an important consideration for libraries with a low ratio of clerical to professional employees and in applications such as cataloging, where many word originators may be involved and the typical unit of work (a bibliographic description) is relatively short. Given the availability of portable voice recorders, dictation technology can be used effectively by traveling library administrators, by literature searchers extracting citations from printed indexes and abstracting journals, and by archivists and manuscript librarians who must inventory records in crowded storage areas. The absence of stenographic involvement in dictation results in a significant reduction in the clerical costs associated with document creation. As an additional advantage that simplifies the hiring of clerical personnel, training in shorthand is not required. Clerical productivity is likewise improved because typing or other work need not be interrupted to take dictation.

Turning from advantages to equipment configurations, a dictation system consists of two basic components: a recorder and a transcriber. The most commonly encountered recorders are desktop devices that capture spoken words on magnetic tape cassettes. Older models, which are widely installed and continue to be manufactured, use analog recording technology. Newer devices, as described below, employ digital recording technology and media. All available recorders provide some playback capabilities to allow the word originator to review previously recorded material. When dictation is completed, the recording medium is physically removed from the recorder and taken to a typist who inserts it into a transcriber, a device that plays the recorded signals through a speaker or earphones. While dual-purpose devices suitable for both recording and transcription are available, the typical transcriber is a less expensive, single-purpose unit designed to play back previously recorded media.

In addition to the basic operations familiar to users of mass-market cassette recorders, most dictation equipment incorporates features that facilitate the work of both word originators and typists. As an example, well-designed desktop recorders feature ergonomically designed microphones that filter out background sounds, thus permitting dictation in busy offices and other noisy work environments. Foot-pedal controls permit hands-free dictation and transcription. Some recorders employ voice-operated relay technology in which the recording mechanism is activated only when the word originator is actually speaking, thus eliminating tape-wasting gaps during periods of thought or other pauses. Word originators can employ electronic coding or other techniques to mark the locations of special instructions or priority documents within cassettes. Some transcribers are equipped with variable speed controls that allow the typist to adjust the playback rate to match typing speed without excessive voice distortions. Following pauses for typing, most transcribers can be set to repeat previously played words before playing new material. Some vendors offer multifunctional "voice processing" products that combine dictation and telephone equipment in a single unit. In addition to recording, such devices can store telephone numbers, perform automatic dialing, send prerecorded messages, and function as telephone answering machines.

Although a desktop recorder with a separate transcriber is the most widely encountered dictation system configuration, certain library applications may be better served by other types of recording and transcribing equipment. Portable cassette recorders, for example, are handheld devices that extend the utility of dictation systems to work environments where desktop units are impractical. Such devices typically record communications on magnetic tape cassette for replay on a compatible transcriber. Portable recorders often serve as auxiliary recording units in desktop recorder/transcriber configurations. So-called micro-cassettes permit compact recorder designs, although some portable units will accept the familiar standard-size cassette used in consumer audio products.

As noted above, the newest dictation systems employ digital recording techniques. Since the mid-1990s, several companies have introduced dictation software that operates on Windows based microcomputers equipped with microphones for recording and earphones for transcription. Voice dictation is digitized for recording on the microcomputer's hard drive. It can later be transferred to a digital audiotape (DAT) cassette or other medium and taken to a typist for transcription on another microcomputer. The transcribing computer is typically equipped with earphones and foot-pedal controls for convenient playback. Some portable digital recorders capture voice dictation on a PCMCIA card that can be loaded into a microcomputer for transcription. While they are more expensive than analog devices, digital recorders are more versatile. They permit lengthy insertion in previously dictated documents, use special codes to identify instructions pertaining to particular communications, and allow operators to easily transcribe communications out of their recorded sequence, thereby accommodating priority jobs.

Centralized dictation systems offer highly functional alternatives to portable and desktop units with the self-contained recording capabilities. Analog systems, which date from the 1960s, are accessed by desktop microphones or ordinary telephones that are wired to a centrally located recorder/transcriber to which one or more typists are connected by earphones. As new communications are dictated, previously recorded material is being transcribed. Depending on the equipment configuration, centralized analog systems can accommodate dozens to hundreds of hours of voice recording using automatic cassette changers.

Centralized digital systems, the most sophisticated dictation configurations, employ computer networking technology to connect word originators and typists. Documents dictated at desktop or portable computers are transferred over local or wide area networks to servers, where they await transcription by word processing operators. The transcriptionists, as described above, work at Windows-based microcomputers equipped with earphones and foot-pedal controls. For efficient storage and transmission, the digitized speech files are typically stored in a compressed format. Increasingly, developers of digital dictation systems are integrating their products with voice recognition software that converts dictated documents to character-coded form suitable for editing by a word processing program. While voice recognition technology, as previously noted, may ultimately supplant conventional dictation systems, available products do not offer sufficient reliability for direct voice-to-printer operation without operator intervention. The text usually contains some incorrect words, omissions, and other mistakes. With digital dictation systems, word processing operators can proofread the recognized text while listening to the dictated version, making any required corrections.

Whether they employ digital or analog recording techniques, newer centralized dictation systems are computer-controlled. Using a video display terminal, a supervisor can determine the status and estimated completion time of particular jobs, expedite the typing of priority material, equitably allocate workload, monitor the productivity of individual typists, review transcribed documents, and archive or delete voice recordings following transcription. Software can generate a variety of management reports, productivity statistics, and other documents. Such computer-controlled dictation systems are installed in large government agencies, corporations, law firms, and health care organizations, among other work environments. Special system configurations have been developed for transcription of medical records, public safety applications, testimony management, and call center monitoring. Libraries affiliated with businesses, government agencies, and other organizations may be able to use centralized dictation systems for their own document preparation applications.

WORD PROCESSING

Dictation systems facilitate the conversion of a word originator's thoughts to a spoken form suitable for transcription. Until voice recognition technology is perfected, the transcription process will continue to require keystroking. The typewriter was one of the first business machines to be used for library work, and typewritten documents remain important communication media in library administration, technical services, and information services. As with dictation systems, the business case for word processing as a document preparation technology is well developed and widely acknowledged. While word processing systems have virtually replaced typewriters in most offices, the technology was originally intended for preparation of documents with specific characteristics.

Library systems analysts, like their counterparts in corporations and government agencies, have long recognized that diminished productivity and consequently increased costs are the inevitable result of some obvious shortcomings inherent in conventional typing. As an often-cited example, repetitive text—such as the information contained in an acknowledgment letter sent to job applicants—must be manually retyped to produce additional typewritten originals, with the possibility of errors occurring in each retyping. Whether multiple originals are involved or not, typing is an error-prone activity and mistakes are inevitable. When they occur, the usual methods of correction—erasure, overlay with opaque material, or starting over—interrupt keystroking, take considerable time, and sometimes deface documents. As perhaps the most significant shortcoming of conventional typing, entire documents must be retyped to accommodate even minor content revisions and format changes. Bibliographies, for example, must be completely retyped to insert a single additional entry in alphabetical sequence. Similarly, cataloging records must be retyped to produce accession lists.

As work methods analysts point out, a clerical employee who ostensibly types sixty words per minute may actually produce finished work at less than

25 percent of that rate when all retyping and error correction routines are considered. Word processing technology improves typing productivity by recording keystrokes in machine-readable form on magnetic media before producing human-readable paper documents. Once recorded in this manner, text segments can be edited (altered, moved, deleted, or otherwise manipulated) without extensive retyping. Mistakes are easily corrected by overtyping. Global change capabilities can correct all occurrences of a given typing error with a single action. Line lengths are automatically adjusted to accommodate margin changes. To enhance the appearance of printed output, an operator can justify or otherwise control the contour of a page's right margin. Once the machine-readable version of a document has been corrected or revised to the operator's satisfaction, it is sent to a printer, which produces a presumably perfect paper copy. The machine readable version, typically recorded on a hard drive or other media, can be retained for later editing or other uses.

Certain word processing capabilities are particularly useful for commonly encountered library tasks. An academic librarian responsible for assembling and updating a collection of college catalogs may prepare periodic mass mailing to be sent to registrars or other information officers. The text of each mailed request will usually vary only slightly, if it all, from the text of all others. The inside address and salutation will be different, and selected sentences in the body of the letter may request information about specific academic programs, but the majority of the letters' contents will be identical. Such document production tasks are increasingly common as public and other libraries extend their activities to include job information centers, community referral programs, and similar services that require written information requests. Conventional document creation methodologies may approach such applications through a combination of photocopying and original typing. In addition to requiring considerable handling, the resulting letter will have an impersonal, unimpressive appearance that may fail to gain the attention of the intended recipient. Consequently, additional labor will be required for follow-up mailings.

Word processing offers document assembly capabilities that greatly simplify the creation of such nearly identical typewritten communications. While the specific approach varies from system to system, prerecorded text—such as the body of a letter to be used in a mass mailing—is automatically merged at printing time with prerecorded variable information, such as the names and addresses of recipients. As an attractive feature, some word processing systems combine document assembly with a sort/select capability that automatically selects specified names or other text from a prestored list for merging with the body of a letter or other document. If desired, the list can be sorted into a specified sequence—by zip code, for example—prior to printing. From the standpoint of clerical productivity in library applications, document assembly addresses one of the most severe limitations of conventional typewriting: the inability to use previously typed text to create multiple output products.

Originally, word processing capabilities were implemented by specially designed, computer-like devices that performed text-editing exclusively and could not be programmed for other purposes. Marketed by dozens of companies, such dedicated word processors dominated office automation from the late 1960s through the early 1980s. Much more expensive than typewriters, they were typically reserved for applications with repetitive typing, extensive editing, or document assembly requirements. Dedicated word processors were eventually replaced by less expensive microcomputers equipped with word processing software. Introduced in the early 1980s, the earliest microcomputer-based word processing programs gave little indication of their future potential as typewriter replacements. They were difficult to use and lacked essential text-editing capabilities, but successive refinements eventually yielded excellent products that can address a broad range of document preparation requirements. Improvements in computer hardware have similarly enhanced the effectiveness of microcomputer-based word processing. Ink jet and laser printers can produce high-quality documents with varied typographic characteristics. High-capacity hard drives simplify text storage. Local area networks, as described in chapter 3, permit shared access to word processing software, documents, and peripheral devices.

The best word processing programs are suitable for complex corporate, government, and institutional applications that require a broad range of editing and formatting capabilities. Such programs can produce attractively formatted documents in multiple type fonts, styles, and sizes. Diacritics, mathematical symbols, and other special characters can be inserted into documents. Information can be printed in multiple columns with borders, dividing lines, shading, or other ornamentation. Text can be combined with digitized illustrations, photographs, or other graphics generated by document scanners or transferred from other programs. Some word processing programs even incorporate drawing tools and chart production capabilities. In addition to elaborate editing and formatting capabilities, word processing programs typically support spelling verification, an electronic thesaurus, mailing list management, grammar checking, document outlining, and other special features. To simplify the preparation of scholarly documents, word processing programs can automatically number footnotes and print them at the bottoms of appropriate pages or as endnotes. Some word processing programs can automatically generate indexes and tables of contents from marked text segments or typed phrases. For compatibility with Internet and intranet implementations, word processing programs can create Web pages in addition to printed documents.

Electronic Typewriters

As described above, word processing technology was originally intended for complex document production requirements, but microcomputer-based word processing systems have become the preferred devices for most typing tasks. Typewriters, however, remain useful for certain purposes, such as the preparation of envelopes or multipart business forms. With word processing programs, considerable trial and error may be required to print information in the correct position within a form. As additional constraints, some computer printers cannot conveniently accommodate envelopes, and nonimpact devices, such as ink jet and laser printers, cannot produce carbon copies.

In such situations, electronic typewriters are a useful adjunct to word processing systems. They offer the familiarity and relative simplicity of typewriting, while supporting error correction, repetitive typing, and other capabilities that expedite straightforward typing tasks. Electronic typewriters are microprocessor-controlled devices. Their enhanced typing capabilities are derived from programs that are stored in read-only memories. Random-access memory circuits provide storage for a small amount of typed information.

Electronic typewriters represent a significant improvement in functionality and convenience when compared to conventional typewriters, but they cannot approach the text-editing and document formatting capabilities of even the simplest computer-based word processing programs. Most models feature a single-line liquid crystal display that simplifies the detection and correction of typing errors before they are recorded on paper. Most electronic typewriters can perform automatic centering of text and margin alignment. A given model may support a variety of horizontal character spacing, and store frequently used phrases in random-access memory for rapid recall. Some models include spelling verification programs that use an internally stored dictionary to check individual words as they are typed. An alarm sounds when a possible misspelling is detected. Some electronic typewriters can be equipped with a floppy disk drive for exchange of information with microcomputer-based word processing programs.

DOCUMENT IMAGING TECHNOLOGIES

A document imaging system is an integrated configuration of hardware and/or software components that produces pictorial copies (images) of book pages, journal articles, technical reports, office records, and other documents for storage, retrieval, dissemination, or other purposes. This broad definition encompasses technologies and devices with widely varying characteristics and capabilities. Familiar examples of document imaging products include photocopiers, which make full-size or near-size reproductions of documents, and micrographic systems, which record source documents as miniaturized images on microfilm, microfiche, or other microforms. Such widely encountered imaging devices typically employ photographic technologies for document recording. Electronic document imaging systems, by contrast, use scanners to create computer-processible images for storage on magnetic or optical media.

Electronic Document Imaging

Electronic document imaging systems provide a completely computerized approach to document storage and retrieval. Broadly defined, an electronic document imaging system is a combination of hardware and software that converts documents to digitized images for computer storage and retrieval. The systems described in this section are specifically designed for document retrieval and dissemination, usually as high-performance alternatives to paper filing methodologies or microfilm technology. From the hardware standpoint, a basic electronic document imaging configuration includes a computer, one or more scanning stations for conversion of paper documents to digitized images, one or more input stations for image inspection and entry of index data, one or more retrieval stations for display of index data and document images, one or more laser printers for hard copy output, an appropriate group of computer storage peripherals, and cabling or a computer network to interconnect the various system components.

The characteristics of document scanners (document digitizers) as image-oriented input devices were described in chapter 1. Depending on the volume of documents to be stored and the required retrieval speed, the digitized document images generated by such scanners may be recorded on magnetic disks, optical disks, or magnetic tapes. In many implementations, optical disks provide the most favorable combination of high storage capacity and direct-access capabilities for rapid retrieval. As previously described, write-once and rewritable optical disks are removable storage media; autochangers can provide unattended, near line access within several seconds to very large quantities of information. Hard drives offer superior retrieval performance, but they may lack sufficient storage capacity for very high-volume imaging applications. Certain magnetic tape formats offer high capacities, but their retrieval performance is limited by the serial access characteristics described in chapter 1.

Regardless of the medium employed, a computer-maintained database serves as an index to recorded images. The database is typically stored on a hard drive. It contains one record for each indexable document stored by the system. An indexable document consists of one or more pages, each recorded as an electronic image. Database records contain fields that correspond to index categories specified by an information systems analyst or other application designer. Index data entry, file maintenance, and retrieval operations are supported by database management software. Retrieval operations begin with a database search to determine the existence and media addresses of electronic document images that satisfy specified retrieval parameters. Potentially relevant index records associated with a particular document image are displayed on a video monitor for operator perusal. A field in each index record identifies the particular medium on which the associated image is recorded. If a desired imaging is stored on an online medium, such as a hard drive, it can be retrieved and displayed on operator command. Removable media, such as optical disk cartridges or magnetic tapes, must be obtained from their storage locations and mounted in an appropriate peripheral device for online access. Autochangers, as previously noted, can eliminate manual media handling. Once a given medium is mounted, the database management program locates the desired image and displays it for operator examination. Printed copies can be produced for reference purposes.

Electronic document imaging implementations can yield significant benefits. Improved retrieval capability when compared to paper-based document management methodologies is perhaps the most frequently cited motive. While specific retrieval characteristics and capabilities depend on the software employed by a given system, database searches and their associated image retrieval operations will usually prove more convenient and much faster than browsing through paper filing cabinets or library shelves. Most electronic document imaging systems can also perform complex searches involving a combination of fields and truncated search terms. Such searches may be difficult or impossible to perform in conventional paper-based filing or classification systems. Electronic document imaging systems can further improve retrieval by delivering needed documents quickly and conveniently to requesters. In conventional library or filing room installations, physical proximity to documents is a precondition for access and use. Electronic document imaging systems, by contrast, permit online access to index records and document images by remote users through local or wide area computer networks. Depending on the hardware and software configuration, retrieved document images can be routed through an electronic messaging system or faxed to designated locations.

Shelving or filing newly received books, reports, or other documents; removing them when requested for reference purposes; and reshelving or refiling them following retrieval activity are essential but time-consuming operations in libraries, offices, and other paper-based document repositories. They are also error-prone activities; misfiling is a common reason for loss of valuable documents, and considerable time and effort may be wasted in searches for misfiled or incorrectly shelved materials. Additional complications are posed by documents that have been removed from library shelves or files for reference or other purposes. Such documents must be tracked to determine their locations in the event that they are needed for reference purposes and to ensure that they are returned to the library in a timely manner following use. Even when extensive precautions are taken, documents removed from a library may be misplaced, stolen, or damaged by accident or through malicious intent. Frequently referenced documents are also subject to cumulative wear and tear, which may impair their utility.

Electronic document imaging systems can simplify file maintenance by eliminating filing, refiling, and the potential for misfiling. Scanning and indexing replace shelving and filing for newly received items. In many implementations, documents are converted to electronic images in the order of their arrival at a scanning station. Time-consuming sorting procedures are eliminated. The media locations of specific document images are system assigned; as previously noted, access is obtained through database records, which serve as an index to stored images. File integrity is likewise enhanced. Once documents are recorded as digitized images on magnetic or optical media, their sequence is fixed. Removal or misfiling of individual pages is impossible. Because electronic images are not removed from storage media for reference purposes, circulation control and other document tracking requirements are eliminated. Instead, copies of images are transferred electronically to retrieval stations over computer networks. The document images themselves are unaffected by reference activity. Unlike paper records, they cannot be damaged by use, stolen, or misplaced.

Automated workflow capabilities are among the most widely publicized and dramatically effective characteristics of electronic document imaging systems. In acquisitions and other transaction-oriented library applications, documents may be routed among designated employees in a formally defined sequence in order to obtain approvals, perform designated operations, or otherwise complete specific tasks. Each employee adds information to or extracts information from a given document, and passes it along to the next person in the predefined routing path. Depending on employee proximity and the urgency with which particular operations must be completed, documents may be hand-carried from person to person; alternatively, interdepartmental mail or other physical delivery methodologies may be employed. Both approaches are time-consuming and subject to delays. Unless routing procedures are closely monitored, documents may be misplaced or allowed to languish in the in-baskets of recipients. Operations that must await the arrival of documents cannot proceed.

Automated workflow can address these problems. Under program control, electronic images of essential documents can be routed from one workstation to another over a local area network or other data communication facility. The workflow program defines the routing procedure and monitors each document's progress. Such automated workflow implementations can ensure that documents will be processed into correct sequence. They also increase the likelihood that specific operations will be performed in a timely, accurate manner.

As a further advantage, electronic document image systems can significantly reduce storage space requirements for a given quantity of books, journals, reports, or other documents, thereby freeing floor space for other purposes. While space savings are rarely the sole justification for an electronic document imaging implementation, they can be an important secondary motive. Depending on media size, recording density, and other system characteristics, an optical disk can store tens of thousands of document images. Optical disk autochangers can provide unattended, near line access to millions of pages. In this respect, electronic document imaging systems compare favorably with micrographics technology; some optical disks, for example, can store the equivalent of dozens of rolls of microfilm or hundreds of microfiche.

Electronic document imaging systems can be custom-designed for particular applications, purchased as preconfigured combinations of hardware and software, or implemented as prewritten software packages on a library's own computer equipment. Customized electronic document imaging implementations are tailored to particular applications by contractors called "systems integrators." They are often based on specifications, requirement statements, and expectations delineated in requests for proposals (RFPs) or similar procurement documents. Alternatively, the systems integrator may consult with the customer to analyze application characteristics and determine required document imaging capabilities; analysis of requirements and preparation of systems specifications are among the services offered by most systems integrators. Whether specifications are developed independently or with a systems integrator's assistance, the integrator obtains or develops hardware and software components appropriate to the specifications. The first electronic document imaging system in the United States was implemented in the mid-1980s by a systems integrator for the Library of Congress. Since that time, customized imaging systems have been installed in diverse information management environments, including banks, pharmaceutical companies, government agencies, military bases, engineering organizations, and nuclear power plants.

As their most obvious disadvantage, customized electronic document imaging systems can be time-consuming and expensive to develop and implement. As a faster, less expensive (but not necessarily inexpensive) alternative, numerous vendors offer preselected hardware and prewritten software components that are offered for sale as a bundled package designed for straightforward implementation and operation by nontechnical personnel. Ideally, the customer can install the system and begin scanning documents with a minimum of software modifications and setup routines. Often, however, some customized programming or other vendor intervention is required to accommodate special application requirements. An interesting and rapidly growing group of electronic document imaging systems is purchased as prewritten software packages for use with specific hardware components, which the customer must furnish. Such packages are available for various types of computers, including Windows-based microcomputers in stand-alone and networked configurations. They support document scanning, database creation, document retrieval, image display, and other operations. As with all purchased software, the customer's computer configuration must meet minimum requirements. The software developer provides a list of compatible peripherals and other hardware components, which customers are free to purchase at the best available price from any source they choose.

In an alternative approach to software-based implementations, electronic document imaging capabilities can be added to existing database management systems, electronic mail systems, workgroup programs, and other software products. When such programs are augmented by the incorporation of document images, they are said to be "image-enabled." In a library's acquisition department, for example, a database of order records may provide online access to most of the information needed to respond to inquiries about deliveries and payments, but some inquiries may require examination of purchase orders, invoices, or other source documents. In such cases, the required documents must be obtained from office files or other storage locations—a procedure that can prove time-consuming and labor-intensive. To facilitate responses to inquiries, images of the source documents can be added to the database. Typically, the images are stored in separate files that are linked to database records by customized programming. When database records are retrieved, operators have the option of viewing any associated document images.

Micrographics

Micrographics is a specialized field of information processing that is concerned with the making and use of microforms—photographic information carriers that contain images, properly called "microimages," that are greatly reduced in size. The reduction is so extreme that microimages require magnification for legibility. Among specific types of microforms, 35 mm microfilm is usually wound on plastic reels in lengths of 100 feet or less. It is widely encountered in library applications that involve newspapers, historical manuscripts, and other research materials. Sixteen-millimeter microfilm, which may be wound onto reels or loaded into the self-threading cartridges, is routinely used to record office documents as well as some research materials, particularly in corporate and government libraries.

Microfiche are rectangular pieces of film on which document images are recorded in a grid pattern of rows and columns. The most common size of microfiche measures 105 mm wide by 148 mm high. With capacities ranging from 60 to more than 400 images, microfiche are used for technical reports, computer printouts, serial publications, and various other documents. Microfilm jackets are transparent acetate or polyester carriers that feature sleeves or channels for the insertion of strips of 16 mm or 35 mm microfilm cut from rolls. Microfilm jackets have been used by libraries to store vertical file materials and other collections that require periodic addition of new documents. Aperture cards are tabulating-size cards that feature a hole or aperture designed to contain one frame of 35 mm microfilm. They are the microforms of choice for engineering drawings, maps, architectural renderings, and other large documents, copies of which are sometimes encountered in technical libraries.

Regardless of type, microforms can be created in either of two ways: (1) Source document microfilming uses specially designed cameras equipped with reducing lenses to record paper documents as miniaturized images. (2) As discussed in chapter 1, computer-output microfilm (COM) technology permits the direct recording of computer-processable, machine-readable information on microfilm or microfiche without first creating paper documents. In either case, a microfilm camera or a COM recorder produces latent (potentially visible) images that must be developed to become usable. The required development is performed by a separate machine called a "microfilm processor." Most source document cameras employ silver gelatin microfilm, which requires development by liquid chemicals. Some COM recorders use a thermally processed microfilm, which is conveniently developed by heat without chemicals. Processed microforms are usually reproduced by a duplicator to create one or more working copies. Following duplication, camera-original microforms are usually placed in a secure, environmentally controlled storage location; when properly processed and stored, silver gelatin microfilm will remain stable for hundreds of years. Working copies, intended for reference or research, can be displayed by magnifying devices called "microform readers." When hard copies are required, reader/printers can produce paper enlargements of displayed images. If high-volume printing activity is required, enlarger/printers can make high-speed paper prints of all or specified microimages from a roll of microfilm, sheet of microfiche, or stack of aperture cards.

Source document microfilming, the focus of this discussion, is a well-established technology that has been routinely and successfully utilized in business applications since the 1920s. Library applications date from the same period, when several American research libraries began using microfilm cameras to reproduce scholarly materials contained in European libraries and archives. Since that time, microforms have been used by libraries of all types and sizes for collection development, to preserve the content of newspapers and other ephemeral materials, as an alternative to binding for serial backfiles, and to reduce storage space requirements for library materials.

Although some larger libraries have established microfilming facilities for in-house recording of source documents, most library microform collections contain materials purchased from third parties called "micropublishers."

Broadly defined, micropublishing is the publication of information in multiple microform copies for sale or distribution. The term encompasses original micropublications, which contain information published for the first time in any form, and retrospective micropublications, which contain material previously published in paper form. The earliest micropublishers, active from 1930 to about 1960, followed the lead of library-administered microfilming projects in emphasizing research materials from foreign repositories as well as doctoral dissertations and similar specialized documents of narrow subject interest. Their projects involved original micropublishing of archives and manuscripts, as well as retrospective micropublishing of rare books. With the rapid expansion of higher education during the 1960s, a number of micropublishers began offering selected library core collections consisting of microform versions of important out-of-print monographs essential for students' term papers and recommended readings. At about the same time, micropublished versions of annual volumes of newspapers and serials became widely available.

Micropublications play such an important role in library installations that library administrators and collection development specialists have emphasized them to the virtual exclusion of other aspects of micrographics. While many libraries own microform readers and reader/printers, budgetary constraints and a lack of technical expertise have limited the implementation of in-house microform production facilities. Compared to their business counterparts, fewer libraries own microfilm cameras, even though such devices can prove useful for filming technical reports and laboratory notebooks in industrial libraries, preserving local newspapers in public libraries, and storing manuscripts and vertical file materials in historical societies and special collections. Although some microfilm cameras and related production equipment are expensive to purchase and complex to operate, the micrographics industry does offer simpler, less costly products that are designed for operation by clerical personnel with a modest amount of training in an office rather than a laboratory environment.

Widespread business interest in so-called paperless information systems has led to important developments in micrographics technology that are potentially significant for library applications. Through the mid-1970s, micrographics equipment relied heavily on mechanical components. Since that time, however, manufacturers have emphasized "intelligent" micrographics products that incorporate microprocessors, read-only memories, and other electronic components to enhance versatility and reliability. Microprocessor-controlled retrieval units, for example, can be programmed to automatically display or print specified sequences of frames within a given microform. Similarly, microprocessor-controlled microfilm cameras can record documents in a variety of formats and reductions.

Information specialists who advocate micrographics as a document storage alternative emphasize the so-called computer/micrographics interface—a phrase that denotes the combined use of computer and micrographics technologies to satisfy information processing requirements that cannot be as effectively accommodated by either technology alone. Computer-output microfilm (COM) is the most common manifestation of the computer/micrographics interface. As described in chapter 1, a COM recorder is essentially a computer printer that offers a compact alternative to paper output for reports and other

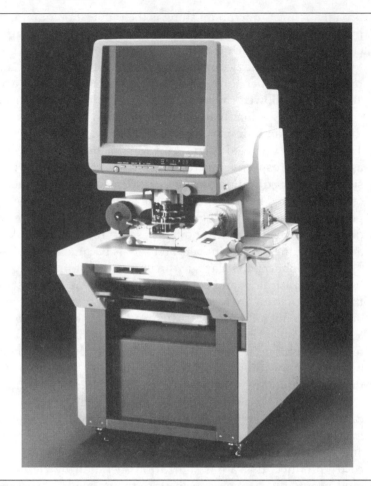

Reader/printers, a popular type of micrographics equipment in library installations, can display enlarged microimages and print paper copies on demand. (Courtesy of Minolta Corporation; used by permission)

computer-generated documents. Computer-assisted retrieval (CAR), another example of the computer/micrographics interface, makes straightforward use of the unique advantages of computer and micrographics technologies. CAR systems use computers to create, maintain, and search an online index to document images that are recorded on microfilm. In a typical retrieval operation, the index is searched to determine the existence and microform locations of document images that satisfy specified retrieval parameters. In a library application involving technical reports, for example, the index may be searched by combinations of author, subject, or other categories of information. In this respect, the CAR concept resembles the database management systems discussed in chapter 3, the critical difference being that retrieved index information directs the operator to specific frames in a separate file of microforms. When a designated microform is obtained from that file, it is loaded into a special retrieval unit that locates and displays desired frames. Paper enlargement can be printed for reference purposes.

CAR systems combine space savings, media stability, and other advantages of microform with the ability of computers to rapidly manipulate index information. Although CAR technology is widely promoted in government and business installations, it has its roots in library applications. The idea of automated microform retrieval for research documents was first discussed in the 1940s. Basic concepts were developed during the 1950s and 1960s, when a number of experimental microfilm-based systems were implemented for the storage and retrieval of scientific and technical documentation. The most famous of these experiments, implemented as part of Project Intrex at the Massachusetts Institute of Technology, was designed to provide scientists with rapid, automated retrieval of technical publications stored on microfiche. Commercially available CAR systems were introduced in the early 1970s. They consisted of integrated configurations of micrographic equipment, computer hardware, and prewritten database management software. Today, CAR implementations are often based on conventional database management programs that are adapted for document indexing and microform retrieval. Microcomputer software packages have proven particularly effective in extending the range and affordability of CAR technology.

As their name implies, microform scanners convert microimages to digitized form for computer storage, retrieval, and dissemination. Designed to integrate micrographics with electronic document imaging systems, they are the microform counterparts of the document scanners described in chapter 1. Production-level models can digitize large quantities of microimages at relatively high speed with little or no operator intervention. They are used for microform backfile conversions, which are often one-time occurrences. Service bureaus consequently constitute the primary market for such devices. A reader/scanner combines the capabilities of a microform reader and an image digitizer. It creates electronic versions of magnified images that are displayed on a microform reader. The images must be individually located and positioned prior to scanning. Reader/scanners can also be equipped with fax modems to transmit digitized microimages to fax machines. Alternatively, a reader/scanner can be combined with a laser printer to create a digital reader/printer.

Copiers and Duplicators

The term reprographics denotes the field of information processing that is concerned with equipment and technologies for document reproduction. Given this broad definition, the micrographics and electronic document imaging systems described above can be considered specialized facets of reprographics, but the term is usually applied more narrowly to photocopying and duplicating equipment that makes paper copies of paper documents. The difference between a copier and a duplicator is difficult to delineate precisely. Traditionally, a copier has been defined as a machine that is designed to make one or several copies of a given document, while a duplicator offers faster multicopy speeds and is better suited to applications requiring ten or more copies of a given document. For high-volume applications, some duplicators can produce several copies per second. The traditional distinction between copiers and duplicators may not be observed in product specifications, however, and it is often ignored in practice; many libraries use copiers for duplicating and duplicators for copying.

While most of the attention given to library automation is properly focused on computers as the most powerful, versatile, and complex of available information processing machines, a strong case can be made for copiers and duplicators as historically the most important category of automated equipment in library applications. Every year, libraries make millions of copies to meet administrative needs and to provide users with convenient access to journal articles, reports, portions of books, and other materials. Copiers have revolutionized research. Interlibrary loan of journal articles and other materials would be unthinkable without them. Conventional and coin-operated copiers are ubiquitous and indispensable devices in libraries of all types and sizes, and the extent and potential impact of library copying activity have been major factors in revisions of copyright legislation.

Despite their obvious and continuing importance, copiers and duplicators are sometimes cited as "mature" products that are unlikely to experience significant future growth or change. The xerographic (plain-paper) variant of the electrostatic process, the dominant photocopying technology, has completely supplanted coated-paper processes in office installations and offers a viable alternative to offset duplication in certain high-volume printing applications. No competing reprographic technologies are on the horizon. Apart from improvements in the performance of specific machines, it is difficult to envision how the currently high level of xerographic copy quality can be significantly improved; in some cases, copies are of higher quality than the original documents from which they were made.

Although photocopying technology has not changed radically since the invention of xerography and its subsequent refinement during the 1960s and 1970s, copying and duplicating machines continue to acquire new operating capabilities and convenient features. Operating under the control of integral microprocessors and programs stored in read-only memories, copiers and duplicators use flat-panel video displays to prompt operators and provide diagnostic information. Shortened paper paths and increased use of electronic components have significantly improved reliability and reduced equipment size. Many models support such special features as job interruption and recovery, two-sided copying, variable reduction and enlargement, automatic erasure of dark borders, margin shifting, and multiple paper trays with automatic selection of the correct copy size. Standard or optional attachments permit automatic feeding of documents, automatic sorting of multiple copies of multipage documents, and automatic stapling or binding of copy sets. Digital copiers and duplicators permit image editing and other manipulations; where documents contain proprietary or confidential information, for example, such machines can suppress the reproduction of specific portions of a page. Color copiers, the subject of several innovative product developments since the late 1980s, can prove useful in various library applications.

From the standpoint of computer systems, the most important development in photocopying technology has been the introduction of multifunctional xerographic devices that can operate as copiers, scanners, fax machines, and computer printers. Such devices are sometimes described as "intelligent" copiers.

ELECTRONIC MAIL AND MESSAGING SYSTEMS

The phrase "electronic mail and messaging systems" (EMMS) encompasses a group of technologies that permit the electronic transmission of messages between compatible devices. As its name suggests, electronic mail provides a high-speed alternative to the physical delivery of messages by conventional mail service or private courier. In the broadest sense, voice communications by telephone can be considered a form of electronic mail and message system, but the scope of this group of automated office products is usually limited to systems that transmit written messages generated by handwriting, typewriters, word processing programs, or any of the several special terminals described later in this section. As a notable exception, voice mail systems support non-interactive spoken communications.

Facsimile

Systems designed for the electronic transmission of written messages can be divided into two groups: those that transmit images of message-bearing documents and those that transmit the content of messages as a sequence of encoded characters. Facsimile, also known as telefacsimile or simply fax, is the oldest of the image-oriented message transmission technologies. In a facsimile system, an encoded image of a document is transmitted electronically from one location to another. At the reception point, the document image is usually printed to create a paper copy or facsimile, hence the name. As described below, certain computer-based facsimile products capture document images in machine-readable form at the reception point. The captured images may then be displayed on a video monitor rather than printed.

Facsimile's potential for library applications is obvious. It can be used to transmit library documents ranging from purchase orders and claiming notices for missing issues of periodicals to copies of journal articles, technical reports, and even entire books. From the mid-1960s to the early 1970s, a number of academic and public libraries experimented with facsimile transmission, primarily as a high-speed document delivery alternative for interlibrary loan applications. Those experiments were not successful; participating libraries reported significant problems with output quality, transmission time, equipment reliability, and compatibility. Since the 1980s, however, facsimile technology has changed dramatically. Output quality is now acceptable for many library documents. As discussed below, transmission speed and reliability have improved, and compatibility problems have been resolved. In addition, drastic reductions in equipment costs, combined with the availability of facsimile components for computer installations, have made the technology affordable and ubiquitous.

As with other electronic mail and message technologies, a facsimile system is an integrated configuration of equipment and communication facilities designed for the transmission of information-bearing signals between two points. In most cases, the transmission medium is an ordinary, voice-grade telephone line to which a facsimile machine is connected by means of a modem, although facsimile signals can also be transmitted by terrestrial microwave carriers, satellites, coaxial cable, or other communication facilities. The signal itself originates at a source terminal called a "facsimile transmitter," which combines the attributes of a document scanner and a communication device. The document being scanned, which is called the "subject copy," may contain textual or graphic information. Although facsimile transmitters for bound volumes have been demonstrated, most commercially available devices feature a pass-through document feeder that can only accept individual sheets of paper. Some models can accept computer-printout-size (11-by-14-inch) or ledger-size (11-by-17-inch) pages, although documents larger than letter-size may be automatically reduced prior to transmission.

Like the document scanners described in chapter 1, a facsimile transmitter divides a subject copy into a grid of picture elements, or pixels, each of which is analyzed for its light-reflectance characteristics. Information about the tonal values of successfully encountered pixels is transmitted, in encoded form, over telephone lines or other communication links to a receiving device, which produces a printed facsimile of the subject copy. In effect, the fax receiver draws the incoming image by making a dark mark on a page wherever a dark pixel appears in the subject copy. A facsimile implementation can thus be viewed as a kind of remote copying system in which the copier's platen is located at one end of a telephone line and the out-tray is located at the other. Depending on the receiver's characteristics, the facsimile copy may be printed on plain or coated paper.

The earliest fax machines used analog coding techniques and required as long as six minutes to transmit a letter-size page. During the 1960s, when long-distance telephone rates were much higher than they are today, analog fax machines proved inconvenient and costly to operate. Digital facsimile systems, introduced in the early 1970s, revolutionized the technology by employing image compression techniques to achieve sub-minute transmission speeds, but the earliest models were very expensive and incompatible with their analog counterparts. As a further complication, the analog and digital machines of different manufacturers were often incompatible with one another. Through the 1970s, such incompatibilities impeded the acceptance and implementation of facsimile systems, despite general acknowledgment that the technology satisfied a widely encountered need for rapid delivery of time-sensitive documents.

Beginning in the late 1970s, the Consultative Committee on International Telephony and Telegraphy (CCITT), now known as the International Telecommunications Union (ITU), addressed this problem by issuing standards for four groups of facsimile devices. The Group 1 (G.1) and Group 2 (G.2) standards applied to analog facsimile equipment, which is now obsolete. Group 3 (G.3) facsimile devices, which employ digital coding techniques, have dominated fax technology since the 1980s. Digital fax machines encode pixels as 1 or 0 bit, depending on their relative lightness or darkness. As noted above, digital fax machines utilize image compression to achieve sub-minute transmission speeds over ordinary switched telephone lines. In some circumstances, a letter-size page can be transmitted in less than fifteen seconds, but actual speeds may vary considerably. The least expensive Group 3 facsimile machines are equipped with step-down modems that operate at a maximum rate of 9,600 bits per second. The actual rate attained in specific situations depends on telephone line conditions. Step-down modems, as their name indicates, automatically decrease the transmission rate to 7,200, 4,800, or 2,400 bits per second when interference or other telecommunication problems are detected. Faster fax machines can operate at 14,400 or 33,600 bits per second when communicating with like devices, again assuming that telephone line conditions support those high rates. In most cases, 28,800 bits per second is the maximum attainable rate. Facsimile transmission speed is also affected by the characteristics of subject copies. The highest degree of image compression and fastest transmission rate are obtained with documents that have wide margins and open spacing between lines. Densely printed pages, which are not as readily compressed, require longer to transmit.

Group 3 fax machines employ digital coding of document images, as described above, but the encoded information must be converted to analog form for transmission over ordinary switched telephone lines. Where faster transmission is required, Group 4 (G.4) fax machines can operate at 64,000 bits per second over ISDN lines. Because ISDN lines carry digital rather than analog signals, the transmission rate will not vary. A few Group 3 fax machines can also operate in the Group 1 and Group 2 modes for communication with older analog devices. Librarians should be aware, however, that Group 1 and Group 2 products have not been manufactured for many years, and their installed base has dwindled to the point where communication with them is rarely, if ever, required.

Typically, a facsimile transmitter and receiver are configured together as a dual-purpose device that is properly described as a "facsimile transceiver." New models make extensive use of microprocessors and other electronic circuitry to simplify work steps and improve reliability. For improved management and control of electronic message traffic, many models can produce activity logs that list all transmissions and receptions, including such information as starting time, elapsed transmission time, and a remote terminal identifier for each transaction. Unattended reception is a standard feature with all available fax machines. To eliminate confusion associated with documents received at night or during other periods of unattended operation, some machines stamp copies with the date and time of reception. Some models feature an automatic dialer for speed dialing for the day and unattended transmission during evening or nighttime hours, when long-distance telephone rates are lower.

Since the early 1990s, considerable attention has been given to the integration of computer and facsimile technologies. Some Group 3 facsimile transceivers are equipped with an industry standard serial interface that permits attachment to an external computer system, allowing a fax machine to operate as an input peripheral for document digitization. As described above, certain multifunctional computer peripherals combine facsimile technology with photocopying, document scanning, and printing capabilities. As an alternative to a single-purpose facsimile transceiver, a document scanner can be linked to a computer equipped with a fax modem and software. The scanner generates digitized document images, which are converted by the fax modem and software for transmission over telephone lines to Group 3 fax machines or to other computers equipped with Group 3–compatible fax modems.

Fax modems and software are widely available for many types of computers. Most microcomputer modems routinely combine data and fax transmission capabilities. In some local area networks, fax modems and software are implemented on a network node, which functions as a fax server for multiple workstations with occasional document transmission requirements. As an attractive feature, fax software typically supports store-and-forward operations, in which digitized images are scheduled for transmission at a designated future time. As perhaps their most convenient capability, fax modems can convert word processing files, spreadsheet files, and other computer-processible information to a form suitable for facsimile transmission, thereby eliminating the need to print such files as paper documents for scanning.

Character-Oriented Message Systems

Facsimile signals, as described above, encode the light-reflectance characteristics of successively encountered pixels within a subject copy. Character-oriented message systems, in contrast, transmit information as a sequence of individually encoded characters, in the manner of the computer terminals described in chapter 3. Most character-oriented message systems employ keyboard send-receive (KSR) terminals or microcomputers for message preparation. This is the case, for example, with telex—a long-established, character-oriented message transmission technology that has been utilized by libraries for more than a quarter of a century. As originally conceived, the telex communication network supported message transmission between specially designed terminals. The original telex terminal was an electromechanical teletypewriter with limited typographic characteristics, an unusual three-row keyboard, and minimal message transmission capabilities. Some devices were equipped with a paper tape punch for offline preparation of messages prior to transmission. As a more convenient alternative, software packages now permit preparation of telex messages by microcomputers. Typically, microcomputer-originated messages are sent to an intermediary carrier, which routes them to a designated telex address.

While other, newer technologies offer faster and more varied message transmission capabilities, the telex network provides exceptional geographic coverage, particularly where international message transmission is required. Even in countries with primitive telecommunications infrastructures, libraries, businesses, and other organizations can usually be reached by telex. In the simplest telex configuration, a message, such as an interlibrary loan request, is key-entered from any terminal for transmission to a designated compatible receiver, where it is printed on paper. The message reception does not require an operator in attendance. Like other character-oriented transmission devices, the originating telex terminal converts an operator's keystrokes into a coded sequence .

of bits that represent the individual characters in a message. Often criticized as an old-fashioned, telegraph-derivative technology, telex transmits messages at 50 bps (66 words) using International Telegraph Code No. 2, which is also known as the Baudot code. The Teletypewriter Exchange (TWX), a similar telegraph-derivative service that supported terminal-to-terminal message transmission within North America, was discontinued in 1991. Through the mid-1980s, TWX was utilized for transmission of interlibrary loan requests. It has been supplanted by more convenient messaging and interlibrary loan systems described in later chapters. Except for its continued utility in international communications, telex would have shared TWX's fate.

Like facsimile machines, telex technology is designed to deliver messages to designated terminals. As such, it is well suited to time-sensitive communications that would lose their value if subjected to the delays and uncertainties inherent in conventional mail delivery. Such time-sensitive messages must often be conveyed in written form, making the use of voice communication inappropriate. They do not require interaction or intermediate recipient response, apart from a simple acknowledgment of successful transmission. Interlibrary loan requests are an obvious category of messages having such characteristics. They must be transmitted to lending institutions quickly; their contents must be conveyed in writing to avoid confusion; and, assuming a clear request, immediate interaction between borrower and lender is not required. While computers may be used in such message transmission applications, their role is largely limited to routing messages between terminals.

In another approach to character-oriented message transmission, computers play a more significant role as intermediaries that accept messages, notify recipients, and store messages for varying periods of time as directed by the sender or recipient. Variously called computer-based message systems, electronic mail systems, or simply "e-mail" systems, such character-based message transmission capabilities are provided by computer software packages. Unlike the telex service discussed above, computer based message systems transmit messages to specified persons rather than to designated terminals. Recipients can receive messages at any compatible terminal, regardless of location. Also in contrast to telex service, computer-based message systems are used less for transmission of time-sensitive messages than as alternatives to interdepartmental memoranda, telephone conversations, and other traditional modes of communication when interaction or an immediate response is not required or necessarily desired. In businesses and government agencies, they have proven particularly popular as a means of facilitating communication among members of project teams, committees, task forces, or other groups involved in cooperative work activities.

Software packages for electronic mail are available for computers of all types and sizes. As an alternative to in-house implementation, computer-based messaging services are offered by service bureaus, online information services, telecommunications companies, and other providers. The Internet, as discussed in chapter 3, links computer-based messaging capabilities implemented on many computers, allowing librarians to conveniently communicate with researchers and colleagues throughout the world.

In the typical e-mail implementation, a user working at an online terminal directs a computer's operating system to make a message preparation program available. The program prompts the user for the addressee's name or identification number, the subject of the message, and the text itself. Most computer-based message systems provide a simple but effective text-editing subsystem for typing, error correction, and revisions. Alternatively, the text of a message may be prepared by a word processing program and imported by the message input program. In either case, the computer passively accepts the text without regard to its content or format and stores the message on a hard drive or other direct-access medium in a location that can be viewed as the recipient's "electronic mailbox." When the designated recipient signs onto the computer, he or she is notified of the existence of new messages. With most systems, the recipient can peruse a list of dates, senders, and subjects for newly received messages. Alternatively, the entire text of any or all messages can be printed or displayed. Most systems likewise offer a range of message disposition options. Messages can, for example, be deleted once read, stored for later reexamination, filed under designated subject headings, or forwarded to other parties for further action.

In a variant form of computer-based message systems called "computer conferencing," three or more persons can communicate with one another. In the simplest computer conferencing configurations, one participant sends a message to multiple recipients for comments. Individual responses are appended to the original message and can be reviewed by other participants. These in turn may provoke responses that are themselves made available for review and comment. The result is a computer-stored dialog that can be reviewed in whole or in part by all authorized persons. Internet discussion groups are the most widely encountered examples of such computer conferencing.

As is true of conventional computer-based message systems, computer conferencing removes barriers of time and geography, allowing individuals to participate at their own pace without the interruptions and contention that often characterize conventional meetings and conference telephone calls. As a further advantage, a transcript of the interaction is automatically created and can be stored for later retrieval and reference. As discussed in this context, computer conferencing is one of several attempts to use technology to improve communication among participants in group endeavors. Improved communication among workgroups is likewise a goal of the videoconferencing systems described in a later chapter.

Voice Mail

Introduced in the early 1980s, voice mail systems support the transmission of spoken messages between designated recipients. The messages, spoken into a telephone, are transmitted to recipients indirectly by a central computer that stores them on magnetic disks or other direct-access media as digitized audio signals. At a later time, the designated recipient uses a Touch-Tone telephone to enter command codes to recall and play back the stored messages.

Voice mail systems differ from conventional answering machines in several important respects. A voice mail system connects all participants to a computer system on which voice mail software resides. An answering machine, in contrast, is connected to a single telephone. Voice mail messages are encoded digitally for computer storage rather than in the analog form employed by most answering machines. Voice mail messages are stored on disks rather than the tape cassettes used in answering machines; disk storage, as previously noted, permits rapid access to messages for convenient playback. As a further distinction, voice mail is designated for a specific recipient; it is not accessible to others without authorization. A single answering machine may receive messages for several persons. Finally, voice mail systems are much more versatile than answering machines. Depending on the particular system employed and nature of the message, a spoken response may be made by the recipient, the message may be saved for further reference, or the original message may be forwarded with comments or instructions to a third party.

Voice mail systems are widely implemented on computers operated by corporations, government agencies, and other organizations on in-house computer systems. Alternatively, telephone companies offer voice mail services. The latest technology emphasizes the integration of voice mail with other types of electronic messaging, particularly character-based e-mail systems. Integrated messaging software, which is offered by a growing number of vendors, uses speech synthesis to convert character-based messages to spoken form, allowing users to receive e-mail from Touch-Tone telephones. Similarly, speech recognition technology is used to convert voice mail to character-coded form for retrieval and display by computers. With integrated messaging systems, recipients can respond to messages in voice- or character-based formats. Computer files can be appended to voice mail messages, and voice and character-coded messages can be appended to one another. Internet links permit the transmission of voice mail messages to other organizations, in the manner of character-based e-mail. Alternatively, a converted voice mail message can be faxed to a designated location.

VIDEO-BASED INFORMATION SYSTEMS

Many libraries use video technology to record and display visual information. Video cameras and videocassette recorders are commonplace devices in libraries of all types and sizes. In communities with cable television, some libraries have established video studio facilities that produce programs for broadcast over public access channels. On a less ambitious scale, many public libraries submit information about their hours, services, or special events for display on the "electronic bulletin boards" operated by some cable television franchises. In addition, libraries of all types maintain collections of prerecorded video material ranging from industrial training courses to commercial motion pictures. Since the mid-1980s, a number of public and academic libraries have circulated prerecorded videocassettes and videodiscs.

But while these library activities emphasize the relationship between video technology and television systems, the scope of video technology encompasses a wide range of products and services, some of which are potentially significant for library information processing. In particular, increasingly close links are being established between video technology and computers. The earliest microcomputers utilized television receivers as display devices. Electronics companies offer microcomputer adapter boards that permit the display of full-motion television images, in a separate window, on a computer monitor. Alternatively, several manufacturers have developed dual-purpose computer/television units. Many cable television services feature one or more "cable text" channels that continuously display news headlines, weather forecasts, sports results, and other computer-generated textual information. In some areas, the coaxial cables that deliver television signals to homes are also used by businesses for high-speed data transmission between computer installations. Cable modems, which provide high-speed access to the Internet, were described in chapter 3.

As a related development, the design of video equipment is increasingly influenced by computer technology. Television receivers, for example, routinely incorporate microprocessors and other electronic circuitry. Component television systems resemble computers in their emphasis on a central tuner/controller that can support a video monitor, audio speakers, a videocassette recorder, a video disk player, and other peripherals. So-called digital televisions and videocassette recorders, described below, use internal computers to refine and enhance received signals prior to display, simultaneously display multiple images, and support a variety of other special effects and features. Increasingly, the convergence of television and computer technologies relies on so-called set-top boxes, addressable electronic devices that transmit, receive, and decode data and video programming, thereby augmenting the capabilities of television receivers. The simplest set-top boxes support reception of video and audio signals generated by cable or satellite television services. More complex devices, such as the set-top boxes employed by the WebTV system, support Internet access, electronic mail, and other computer services. Among its most interesting features, WebTV provides online access to local television broadcast schedules and permits the simultaneous display of television programs and related Web pages. A printer can be attached for hard-copy output.

Digital Television and HDTV

Since the inception of the television industry, video signals have been encoded and broadcast in analog form. Television peripherals, such as videocassette recorders and videodisc players, likewise employ analog coding techniques. As part of the emerging integration of computers and television, however, the video industry is rapidly moving toward digital technology. Direct broadcast satellite services, which compete with conventional cable television systems in consumer markets, have utilized digital coding and transmission since the early 1990s. The eventual replacement of analog technology in other video products and services is expected.

The transition to digital video technology is closely associated with the widely publicized development of high-definition television (HDTV). The definition, or amount of detail visible in a video image, is determined by the number of scan lines that form the image. Prevailing broadcast standards specify video images that consist of 525 or 625 scan lines. The 525-line standard, developed by the National Television Systems Committee (NTSC), is utilized in North America, Japan, the Caribbean, much of Latin America, Saudi Arabia, and a few other parts of the world. The 625-line Phase Alternation Line (PAL) standard is used in the United Kingdom, West Germany, some other Western European countries, and parts of South America, Asia, and Africa. The Sequential Couleur a Memoire (SECAM) standard, which likewise specifies 625 lines per video image, is employed in France, Russia, other former Soviet republics, and parts of the Middle East.

As technology analysts, video engineers, and other critics frequently point out, the NTSC, PAL, and SECAM standards were developed over half a century ago when television was just emerging. They advocate the implementation of new television formats that will take advantage of the significant technological advances that have occurred since that time. Such formats are collectively described as high-definition television. Employing 800 to 1,200 scan lines, they provide noticeably sharper images than those offered by existing television systems. High-definition images approach motion picture quality in their presentation of detail. As a further advantage with broad information processing implications, a video format that offers high-definition images transcends television programming in its potential applications. It is suitable for sophisticated computer graphics and for the display of textual information, including images of typewritten or printed documents.

High-definition television is not a new concept. Research activity dates from the 1950s, and prototype HDTV systems and components were demonstrated in the 1970s. An operational HDTV system with 1,125 scan lines was introduced in the 1980s by NHK, the Japanese Broadcasting Company, although the technology has never enjoyed wide acceptance. Most HDTV receivers are installed in Japanese department stores and other public locations rather than in individual homes and offices. As its principal shortcoming, the Japanese HDTV system employs analog rather than digital coding and transmission of video signals. In the United States, the Federal Communications Commission (FCC) has approved a digital HDTV format with 1,080 scan lines. Similar digital HDTV initiatives are under way in other parts of the world. Because high-definition television signals contain more information than their conventional counterparts, they require a greater allocation of bandwidth within the television broadcast spectrum. A single HDTV channel can require the transmission bandwidth of five NTSC channels. As their principal advantage, digital HDTV systems permit image compression for more efficient utilization of available broadcasting facilities.

The FCC has mandated that HDTV broadcasting be available in the thirty largest U.S. television markets, which account for more than half of all U.S. households, by the fall of 1999. HDTV receivers, marketed as digital televisions, entered the U.S. market in mid-1998. Compared to conventional televisions, they feature wider screens that approximate the width-to-height ratio of motion picture screens. HDTV videocassette recorders and other video peripheral devices have also been developed.

According to the FCC plan, HDTV will eventually replace conventional NTSC television broadcasting, which is scheduled to terminate by 2006 in the United States. Some television station operators and industry analysts, however, have advocated a standard-resolution digital television system that will retain 525 lines per image but use video compression to expand the channel capacities of existing bandwidth allocations. If implemented, that plan will employ digital technology to provide more television programming rather than higher-definition images, although such standard-resolution television systems will offer some quality improvements through enhancement of digitally coded images. They will also take advantage of the special capabilities of digital video peripherals, such as the DVD systems described below, and digital videocassette recorders. The latter devices, which were introduced in the late 1990s, offer significantly improved image quality when compared to analog videocassette technology. They also support a variety of visual effects, program indexing capabilities, and CD-quality audio recording.

Analog Optical Videodiscs and DVD

The analog optical videodisc is a platter-shaped medium designed to store conventional television images and accompanying stereo audio signals. Also known as "laser discs," "laser video discs," "Laservision discs," or simply "LV discs," they were introduced in 1978 as the first commercially available optical storage media. While videodisc systems that permit direct recording of television images have been developed, most analog optical videodiscs are read-only media that contain prerecorded information. They are produced by mastering and replication techniques in special production facilities where program material is transferred from videotapes, motion picture film, or other media to a photosensitive master disk. The master is used to create one or more intermediates from which individual plastic copies are produced. Compact discs, as discussed elsewhere in this book, are manufactured in a similar manner, but analog optical videodiscs should not be confused with CD-ROMs or with the read/write optical disks described in chapter 1. While such media employ optical storage technologies, the information they contain is encoded in digital rather than analog form. The analog optical videodiscs must be further distinguished from such non-optical videodiscs as the RCA Capacitance Electronic Disk (CED), which was discontinued in the 1980s, and the Video High Density (VDH) videodisc system, which was never marketed in the United States.

An analog optical videodisc features a platter-shaped plastic substrate with a reflective metal layer and protective coating. Within the reflective layer, recorded information is represented by microscopic pits of varying sizes and spacing. (With digital optical disks, by contrast, information is represented by the presence or absence of microscopic pits of uniform size.) A 12-inch analog optical videodisc, the original and most popular size, can store 54,000 still images or 60 minutes of continuous, full-motion video accompanied by stereo audio signals on each of two sides. Videodiscs are also available in an eight-inch size that can store 44,000 still images or 13.5 minutes of continuous full-motion video plus stereo audio per side. Both sizes of videodiscs are read by specially designed players that display recorded images on a television receiver or video monitor. The most versatile models can retrieve and display specified video frames in a matter of seconds. Designed to operate under computer control, they support still-frame displays with sound, variable playback speeds, and seamless branching between images. Integral character generators can overlay video signals with one or more lines of text in various fonts, sizes, and colors.

Analog optical videodiscs were initially developed and promoted as high-performance alternatives to videotape for feature films and other entertainment programming. Compared to videotape, videodisc recordings are much sharper and feature truer colors. While widely admired by video enthusiasts seeking high-quality components for home theater installations, analog optical videodiscs could not compete with videocassette recorders in the broad consumer market for which they were originally intended. They are, however, important information storage media for interactive training, computer-assisted instruction (CAI), and other applications involving full-motion video images. Analog optical videodiscs are well suited to nonlinear applications in which the user controls the sequence in which specific information will be displayed. Operating under computer control, interactive videodisc implementations utilize branching techniques to display appropriate program segments in response to commands or data entered at a keyboard or other input device. In a self-paced instruction application, for example, specific video segments may be repeated if an operator's responses to computer-displayed questions do not indicate mastery of particular topics. Alternatively, correct answers may initiate the display of video segments dealing with more detailed and difficult material. Such nonlinear programming relies heavily on freeze-frame, slow motion, random frame access, and other visual effects and search capabilities supported by videodisc players.

U.S. government agencies, particularly the military, have utilized videodiscs as interactive alternatives to conventional motion picture films and printed materials in a variety of training and recruitment applications. Some corporations have likewise employed them for product-specific training. The substantial advantages of self-paced learning with minimal supervision make the analog optical videodisc a popular medium for interactive continuing education programs intended for physicians, nurses, and other health care professionals. Recognizing the potential of medical markets, several organizations have produced analog optical videodiscs for patient education. Among other popular interactive applications, analog optical videodiscs have been successfully employed in point-of-purchase customer information systems and tourist orientation systems. Implemented as kiosk-type workstations, such systems have been widely installed in retail outlets, convention centers, hotels, and other public places.

With its high storage capacity and excellent image retrieval capabilities, the analog optical videodisc has also been used to publish visual databases, an application that is of considerable interest for librarians, archivists, museum curators, and others responsible for large collections of photographs or other pictorial documents. Well-publicized early examples of such applications included the videodisc catalog produced by the National Gallery of Art and the videodisc edition of photograph collections from the National Air and Space Museum. Because they store video images that conform to prevailing broadcast television standards, analog optical videodiscs do not provide sufficient resolution for the consistently legible reproduction of textual information contained in most typewritten or printed documents. Several companies have developed videodisc formats that combine analog-coded video images with digitally coded, computer-processable information, but such hybrid formats have not been widely adopted.

In recent years, designers of multimedia information systems have preferred CD-ROM to analog optical videodiscs, but CD-ROM cannot match the quality or recording capacity of analog optical videodiscs in applications involving full-motion video images. The continued viability of analog optical videodiscs in such situations is threatened, however, by the increasing availability of digital television technologies. As discussed elsewhere in this chapter, digital coding systems offer quality and capacity advantages over their analog counterparts. DVD, originally known as the Digital Video Disk, competes directly with analog optical videodisc technology in consumer, educational, and business applications involving full-motion video images. The high-capacity successor to the compact disc, DVD uses digital coding and image compression to store a feature-length movie with accompanying stereo audio on a 4.75-inch disk. That format is called DVD-Video to distinguish it from the DVD-ROM and DVD-RAM data recording formats discussed in chapter 1.

Like analog optical videodiscs, DVD-Video disks are read-only media created by a mastering and replication process. DVD disks themselves closely resemble compact discs, but they can store more information. Compared to compact discs, DVD media feature smaller pits and more closely spaced tracks. In their initial configurations DVD-Video disks store up to 4.7 gigabytes on single-layer, single-sided media. An industry-defined migration path calls for a doubling of capacity to 9.4 gigabytes on dual-layer, single-sided media, followed by a fourfold improvement in storage capacity to 17 gigabytes on dual-layer, double-sided media. The first DVD-Video titles were introduced in 1997, and many new movies are issued simultaneously on videocassettes and DVD. Some DVD-Video disks contain a movie in wide-screen and television aspect ratios. They may also contain subtitles and/or soundtrack dubbing in multiple languages. DVD-Video media are encrypted to prevent unauthorized duplication of their contents. DVD-Video players, which are smaller and more widely available than their analog optical videodisc counterparts, support a variety of special features and can read compact discs.

Videoconferencing

Broadly defined, videoconferencing systems utilize video and audio technology to conduct interactive meetings between geographically separated persons or groups. As such, videoconferencing is a form of teleconferencing. The latter is a generic term that denotes the combined use of telecommunications and electronic technologies as an alternative to in-person meetings. Other forms of teleconferencing include audio conferencing, which uses the familiar conference telephone call to establish a voice link between three or more people, and computer conferencing, a variant form of electronic message system described earlier in this chapter. As applied to videoconferencing, the term "meeting" encompasses a broad spectrum of activities ranging from small-scale planning sessions involving two or three people to elaborate product introductions, press conferences, and educational presentations with hundreds of participants. Regardless of a meeting's size and scope, an emphasis on interactive communication among participants distinguishes videoconferencing from the mere televising or video recording of such presentations.

First implemented in video telephone products, full-motion, two-way videoconferencing is the most interesting, sophisticated, and fully interactive form of videoconferencing. In its most elaborate configurations, full-motion, two-way videoconferencing requires special studio facilities equipped with voice-activated cameras, multiple video monitors, microphones, and related equipment. It provides both video and audio coverage of all participants and offers the most realistic approximation of in-person meetings. Full-motion, two-way videoconferencing is best suited to planning sessions, project review meetings, or other small conferences that involve two geographically distant groups, each consisting of perhaps five to ten people. In a typical videoconferencing facility, participants sit on one side of a specially designed conference table, facing a group of video monitors that display participants at a remote site. Wall-mounted video cameras transmit close-up and overview images of conference participants. Additional cameras may be dedicated to the display of chalkboards, flip charts, projected visuals, and similar graphic materials. Some videoconferencing studios also provide electronic stylus systems that can transmit information written on a sensitized surface, the most widely publicized example being a touch-sensitive device that resembles a conventional blackboard or whiteboard. Support equipment may include telephone lines for private voice communication, computers for electronic message transmission, videocassette recorders, and fax machines for document transmission and reception. In most cases, satellite communication facilities link the two videoconferencing sites.

One-way, full-motion videoconferencing with two-way audio capabilities provides a simpler and less expensive alternative to two-way systems. The technology is well suited to large group meetings that involve a televised presentation by a single speaker or a panel of participants, followed by questions from an audience located at one or more geographically distant sites. Particularly useful for educational sessions, stockholder meetings, product introductions, and other special events, one-way videoconferences must be carefully planned and formally produced. The specially equipped meeting rooms used for two-way videoconferencing are replaced by a conventional television studio that is connected to one or more audience sites by satellite communication facilities. The audience sites are sometimes described as "downlinks." Audiences may be seated in small rooms or large auditoriums; many hotels offer downlink capabilities. Projection television systems may be used for large-screen display, and microphones are provided for audience questions and comments, which are transmitted to the main site by telephone lines. The audience sites are not televised; participants at the main site can hear questions from audience members, but they cannot see the audience.

The full-motion, one-way and two-way videoconferencing systems described above are expensive and complicated to implement. They require special video production facilities, satellite communication links, and elaborate planning. Microcomputer-based videoconferencing, also known as desktop videoconferencing (DTVC), offers a simpler, less costly alternative that is effective for many applications. As its name suggests, desktop videoconferencing relies on specially configured personal computers that are equipped with circuit boards for transmission and reception of video signals with accompanying audio. The video signals may be generated by handheld or tripod-mounted cameras that photograph videoconferencing participants at one or more sites. That approach is well suited to small group meetings or a panel of presenters. Microphones capture the participants' voices, while loudspeakers attached to a personal computer's audio board reproduce the spoken words. For person-to-person communication in the manner of video telephones, various vendors offer small, inexpensive video cameras that are designed for installation on the top of a computer monitor. Desktop videoconferencing software supports the transfer of key-entered notes or computer files between sites. Drawing tools may also be included.

The full-motion videoconferencing systems described above support broadcast-quality television signals that require a transmission rate of 90 million bits per second, hence the use of satellite communication to link participating sites. With broadcast-quality television, thirty video images (frames) are transmitted per second. Desktop videoconferencing, by contrast, lowers the frame change rate to ten to twenty frames per second, thereby reducing bandwidth requirements by minimizing the amount of information that must be transmitted. Desktop videoconferencing systems may also reduce the video resolution. In some cases, quality suffers; the resulting images may appear blurry or choppy, particularly where there is a lot of movement from frame to frame. Further, desktop videoconferencing systems compress video and audio signals for efficient transmission over switched analog telephone lines or the digital ISDN lines described in chapter 3. Alternatively, video and audio signals may be carried by an organization's local area network or transmitted over the public Internet or private intranets and extranets. Transmission delays and quality problems can arise, however, when videoconferencing information is interleaved with other network traffic.

Because video and audio signals are compressed, they must be decompressed for display at the reception point. Compression and decompression are performed by CODEC components that are installed in personal computers. Some desktop videoconferencing systems employ proprietary compression and transmission protocols. In the late 1990s, the International Telecommunications Union (ITU) introduced standards for compression, transmission, and other attributes of video and audio signals in desktop videoconferencing installations. These standards facilitate interoperability of videoconferencing systems and components of different manufacturers.

Videotext Services

The term videotext has been defined in several potentially confusing ways. It sometimes denotes a computer-based information service that is intended principally for consumer markets. According to that definition, which was utilized in the United States during the 1980s, the computer-based information services offered by such companies as America Online and Delphi are considered videotext services. In library literature and other publications, descriptions of such services often employed the variant spelling "videotex." That usage is seldom encountered now. In the United States, the Internet—particularly the World Wide Web—has largely supplanted the types of information resources offered by videotext services, although some online information services continue to offer proprietary content.

Today, videotext is essentially a European technology, and this discussion will adopt a definition that relates videotext to its European origins. In Europe, videotext services combine video and database technologies to distribute combinations of computer-generated textual and graphic information to modified television receivers or other relatively inexpensive terminals. Unlike ordinary television systems, the textual content of videotext information is of primary significance, and visual materials play a complementary or, in some cases, decorative role. Although animation is possible, videotext information typically consists of preformatted still frames that deal with specific topics. While some business-oriented systems have been implemented, most videotext systems offer consumer or personal services information of general interest and utility. Web pages, a competing technology, are more elaborately formatted and provide a much greater volume and diversity of information, but videotext systems predate the World Wide Web and reach the many European homes that are not connected to the Internet.

Typical videotext databases emphasize news stories, weather forecasts, traffic reports, and sports results; financial information, including business news, stock market reports, and commodity prices; and such household information as grocery prices, recipes, postal rates, theater schedules, real estate listings, airline and train schedules, gardening tips, horoscopes, and descriptions of cultural events and local tourist attractions. Videotext information providers include government agencies, nonprofit organizations, and businesses. In some cases, entire frames are devoted to product advertisements. Alternatively, a brief advertiser's logo or message may appear in the top or bottom margin of a frame that contains news or other information. Thus, in the manner of commercial television, a brewery may sponsor frames that contain sports reports, or a pharmaceutical company may sponsor frames that provide health news. The World Wide Web has made these advertising practices commonplace for computer users.

Since their introduction in the early 1970s, videotext systems have been divided into two varieties—teletext and viewdata—which are differentiated by their information dissemination methodologies. Teletext systems, sometimes called "broadcast videotext," utilize an otherwise unused portion of conventional television signals to transmit digitally coded information over the air or through cable services. Closed captioning of television programs, which displays subtitles in a superimposed window, was the original application for teletext technology. Teletext systems, however, utilize the entire screen for information display, suppressing the television picture and accompanying audio.

Drawing on terminology from the publishing industry, teletext information is usually formatted as a "magazine" composed of a predetermined number of pages or television frames that are continuously broadcast on a recirculating basis. Teletext subscribers are equipped with specially modified television receivers. After consulting a table-of-contents frame, the subscriber selects a desired information frame and enters its number into a keypad that operates with a television receiver equipped with a teletext decoder, which may be built into the receiver or implemented as a set-top box. The decoder captures the indicated frame when it is rebroadcast. The frame is stored in the decoder's memory, from which it is displayed on the television screen. To achieve a reasonable retrieval time, most teletext magazines contain about 100 information frames. Thus, the entire collection of frames is rebroadcast every two seconds.

Viewdata systems, like their teletext counterparts, present information that is formatted into frames, but the frames are maintained as a computerized database on hard drives or other direct access storage devices, where they await retrieval commands issued by user terminals that are connected to the database by telephone lines. The simplest terminal is a television receiver equipped with a viewdata decoder, typewriter-like keyboard, and modem. The decoder is typically a set-top box, although some viewdata implementations employ specially designed terminals or microcomputers equipped with viewdata software. Viewdata systems resemble conventional time-sharing computer services, although the information they offer is a distinctively packaged combination of text and graphics. The size of a viewdata database is limited only by the amount of available online storage, and systems that offer several hundred thousand frames have been implemented. Compared to viewdata technology, teletext systems are simpler, both conceptually and technically. They require no special telecommunications or computer facilities, but their interactive capabilities are limited to the selection of desired pages from a recirculating collection of frames. With viewdata systems, the use of a telephone line permits interactive communication.

Given their computer-like attributes, viewdata systems can address a broader range of information requirements than their teletext counterparts. For example, they can be expanded to offer conventional computing services, electronic message transmission, home banking, and home shopping, although they must compete with the Internet in those applications. While teletext systems do not permit such expanded services, the two technologies can coexist, teletext being used for news headlines or other rapidly changing information, while viewdata serves users with more varied and detailed retrieval requirements.

The existing body of knowledge and assumptions about videotext is principally based on experience in European countries, especially the United Kingdom, where videotext experiments date from the 1970s. British teletext systems have been implemented as a logical extension of other broadcasting activities. Conceptualized as a kind of "printed radio," they provide alternative treatment of topics that are covered by conventional broadcasting services. Compared to radio and television, teletext can immediately report news stories, weather forecasts, sports results, and similar developments that other broadcasting methodologies must usually delay until regularly scheduled intervals. As a further advantage over conventional broadcasting techniques, teletext viewers can select pages of interest and examine them at their leisure in any sequence. In this respect, teletext differs from the cabletext services mentioned above; such services display information frames in a predefined sequence. While most, if not all, of the information provided by teletext services is accessible through the World Wide Web, teletext has much simpler equipment requirements—an appropriately configured television set versus the computer, software, and data communication components needed for Internet access. Viewdata systems, however, are more directly threatened with replacement by the Internet.

In France, videotext service was introduced in the 1970s as part of a government-sponsored plan to expand the country's computer and telecommunications industries, with the specific intention of developing technology for export. The German Bildschirmtext viewdata system was developed by the national postal and telecommunications agency. Other videotext services have been implemented, on an experimental or operational basis, in other European countries, including the Netherlands, Denmark, Sweden, Norway, and Austria. Non-European examples include the Character and Pattern Telephone Access Information Network (CAPTAIN), a Japanese videotext service developed by Nippon Telegraph and Telephone, and various videotext experiments undertaken by the Canadian Broadcasting Corporation. There was considerable U.S. interest in videotext technology during the 1980s, when a number of experimental systems were implemented by broadcasting and communication companies. One of these experiments, jointly sponsored by the Online Computer Library Center (OCLC) and Bank One, provided reference and educational information, including an online encyclopedia and the catalog of the Public Library of Columbus and Franklin County, to selected customers in Columbus, Ohio. The development of operational U.S. videotext systems was ultimately impeded, however, by uncertainties about their commercial viability. In Europe, where telecommunication and broadcasting services are largely nationalized, videotext research and implementations have been subsidized by national governments. Profitability is not an issue.

While videotext was originally conceived as a consumer-oriented technology for publicly available information services, some of the most interesting and successful implementations have involved small user groups. Such systems are used by corporations, government agencies, universities, hotels, convention centers, banks, and other organizations to display news bulletins, daily activity listings, schedules of community events, telephone directories, mass transit schedules, and other information. With their menu-oriented retrieval approach, such videotext systems are easy to use, although organizations increasingly prefer intranet technology for computer-literate users.

SUMMARY

As a group, the automated office systems and other products described in this chapter are designed to improve the productivity of white-collar workers by automating, and presumably facilitating, a variety of information processing tasks. Since the library workforce is overwhelmingly white-collar in character and includes a significant office component, such systems are potentially of great importance.

Word processing denotes a group of concepts, technologies, and techniques that are designed to simplify the production of typewritten and other textual documents. In the broadest sense, it encompasses the dictation systems and automated text-editing systems. As an alternative to longhand drafting or the use of a stenographer, dictation equipment can facilitate the conversion of thoughts to a form suitable for transcription by a typist. Available equipment configurations range from inexpensive desktop units to complex centralized systems that feature digitized voice recordings and operate under computer control. The most sophisticated dictation systems incorporate voice recognition capabilities for direct conversion of spoken words to text. Portable recorders are available for use outside conventional office settings.

Automated text-editing systems are often called "word processors." They are designed to simplify typing by creating a machine-readable version of a textual document from which a printed copy can be produced. The machine-readable version, which is usually recorded on magnetic media, can be modified or otherwise processed to create successive drafts or multiple copies of typewritten documents. Since the mid-1980s, microcomputer software packages of increasing power and complexity have dominated word processing implementations. They have virtually replaced the special-purpose word processors that dominated office installations in the 1970s and early 1980s.

As an alternative to paper and machine-readable storage, micrographics technology offers compact storage, simplified handling, and other advantages. While libraries have used microforms since the 1920s, they have tended to purchase them from micropublishers rather than create them in-house. Although relatively few libraries have established microform production facilities, a variety of source document cameras are available for operation by non-technical personnel. Much recent attention has been given to the interrelationships of computer and micrographics technologies. Computer-output microfilm (COM), discussed in chapter 1, uses microforms as alternatives to paper for the production and distribution of computer-generated reports. Computer-assisted retrieval (CAR) systems combine the space-saving advantages of microforms for document storage with the ability of computers to rapidly manipulate index data.

Electronic document imaging systems offer a completely computerized approach to document storage and retrieval. Designed as an alternative to paper filing systems and micrographics technology, they utilize scanners to convert documents to digitized images suitable for computer storage, retrieval, and distribution. In most cases, the images are recorded on high-capacity optical disks. Index information is stored on hard drives, in the manner of CAR systems.

Retrieved images can be displayed on video monitors or printed on paper. Some electronic document imaging systems incorporate optical disk autochangers that provide convenient, unattended access to large document collections.

Copiers and duplicators, long commonplace and important in library applications, are increasingly incorporating features and accessories that enhance flexibility and improve operator productivity. Examples include color reproduction capabilities, two-sided copying, image reduction and enlargement, automatic page sorting, automatic document feeding, and automatic stapling and binding. Some companies offer multifunctional devices that can operate as copiers, computer printers, document scanners, and fax machines.

Electronic mail and message systems offer a high-speed alternative to conventional mail service or other physical message-delivery methodologies. Facsimile technology, one of the oldest forms of electronic mail, uses telephone lines or other communication facilities to transmit an image of a document to a remote location where it is reconstructed as a paper copy. In recent years, facsimile has improved steadily and significantly in reliability, output quality, speed of transmission, and compatibility. Most facsimile devices conform to Group 3 standards, which permit interoperability of different brands and models. Depending on document characteristics and other factors, Group 3 fax machines can transmit a letter-size page over ordinary telephone lines in as little as fifteen seconds. Faster Group 4 devices are available for transmission over digital telephone lines.

While fax machines transmit images of documents, the telex network transmits typed messages composed of encoded characters. In libraries, telex terminals have been used for the transmission of interlibrary loan requests. Increasingly, however, they have been replaced by computer-based message systems, in which a computer serves as an intermediary for the temporary storage of messages transmitted between individuals or organizations. In most medium-size and larger organizations, this form of electronic mail is as commonplace as telephony. Using the Internet, computer-originated messages can be transmitted to recipients located anywhere in the world. A variant form of computer-based message system, called "computer teleconferencing," allows users to send messages to multiple recipients for comment, with each recipient having access to all responses. Voice mail systems store spoken messages in digitized form. The newest products incorporate speech synthesis and speech recognition components for integration with conventional computer-based messaging.

A group of automated office products employs video technology alone or in combination with computers. High-definition television (HDTV) provides video images that are significantly sharper and more detailed than those supported by conventional television technology. Relying on digital coding and transmission technology, it also offers potential for computer graphic applications and electronic image storage. Analog optical videodiscs are an important storage medium in interactive training applications that involve full-motion video information. Although their limited resolution capabilities cannot support consistently legible reproduction of textual documents, analog optical videodiscs can store photographs, illustrations, and other visual materials encountered in library picture collections. As an alternative to videodiscs, DVD technology employs digital coding and compression techniques to store full-motion images and other information on a 4.75-inch optical disk.

Videoconferencing combines voice and image transmission to permit communication between two or more groups of people in geographically scattered locations. Desktop videoconferencing relies on computers equipped with video cameras and other components. Older videoconferencing configurations, which require special studio facilities and elaborate production techniques, remain available but are expensive. Videotext systems deliver information to specially modified television receivers. They have been implemented in European countries and other locations where they are often funded by government subsidies. In the United States, videotext systems have been implemented on an experimental basis, but their commercial viability has never been demonstrated. For computer users, videotext technology must compete with the World Wide Web, which provides the same type of information in a more attractive format.

Library Automation, Systems, and Services

5

Computers and Descriptive Cataloging

The purpose of descriptive cataloging is to produce informative bibliographic and physical descriptions of library materials in sufficient detail to permit the conclusive identification of a given item and to differentiate it from other, possibly similar items. In most academic and larger public libraries, where the library catalog is considered a bibliographic tool as well as a finding aid, descriptive cataloging is performed according to the detailed set of instructions embodied in the Anglo-American Cataloguing Rules, the latest in a 125-year series of efforts to standardize cataloging practices in American libraries. Smaller public libraries, school libraries, and many corporate libraries may follow locally developed cataloging practices that are presumably better suited to their collections and clienteles, although such local practices can complicate the implementation of computer-based cataloging systems.

Regardless of their source, rules for descriptive cataloging specify the choice and form of the names or other terms under which a given item will be entered in a library catalog or other bibliographic product. They further specify the words or phrases to be used in describing an item and the order in which descriptive elements are to be recorded. In most libraries, the description of an item also includes subject headings and a classification number. The end product of descriptive cataloging is a series of entries for inclusion in a library's catalog, which may be in a card, book, or online format.

Apart from any particular physical representation of catalogs, librarians have long recognized the problems associated with manual approaches to descriptive cataloging. As an intellectual activity requiring considerable decision making, descriptive cataloging is time-consuming. Many libraries consequently experience significant cataloging backlogs that impede the flow of materials into circulating and reference collections, thereby preventing library catalogs from representing those collections fully and accurately. In some research libraries, for example, materials of presumably limited interest may be placed in offsite storage facilities with only an abbreviated catalog record being created.

In most libraries, conventional descriptive cataloging is not even considered for individual titles in large microform sets, even though such titles often significantly augment a library's resources in particular subject areas and the failure to catalog them may impair their usefulness. Analytic cataloging, involving the making of additional catalog entries for individual contributions within anthologized works or to individual chapters of monographs, is rarely done. As a labor-intensive activity requiring special training and sometimes considerable experience, descriptive cataloging can prove expensive, so much so that the cost of cataloging a given item may approach or even exceed the value of the item itself. Consequently, many libraries do not catalog paperback books, low-cost government publications, or other relatively inexpensive items. Similarly, the cost of cataloging can make a library reluctant to accept gifts and bequests.

In an attempt to simplify decision making, save time, and reduce the costs associated with descriptive cataloging, libraries have historically relied on a practice called "cataloging with copy," in which published library catalogs and bibliographies are searched for descriptive cataloging information prepared by other libraries. For older publications, the various printed catalogs of the Library of Congress are among the most widely consulted sources of such cataloging copy. The purchase of printed card sets from book jobbers or other sources is a variant form of cataloging with copy. Through the late 1990s, when the service was discontinued, the Library of Congress was the leading supplier of such printed catalog cards. While cataloging with copy is generally faster and less costly than original cataloging, the time-consuming and labor-intensive work steps characteristic of manual cataloging systems are not entirely eliminated. Many libraries, for example, modify cataloging copy to conform to local practices regarding the choice and form of main and added entries. Unless printed cards are ordered, a library must type or otherwise prepare entries for inclusion in its catalog. Even when printed cards are used, some combination of typing and copying is usually required to prepare complete card sets.

In the early 1960s, librarians became increasingly aware that descriptive cataloging might be simplified if cataloging copy could be obtained in machine-readable, computer-processable form. The Library of Congress, as the nation's primary source of cataloging copy, commissioned several studies of the potential and problems inherent in the development of such an alternative bibliographic product. Those studies, which indicated the feasibility and potential advantages of recording LC cataloging data in machine-readable form, were discussed at a series of conferences in 1965 and 1966. The outcome of those conferences was the MARC (Machine Readable Cataloging) Pilot Project.

THE MARC PROGRAM

Funded by the Council on Library Resources, the MARC Pilot Project established a format now known as the MARC I format for recording bibliographic data in machine-readable form. From November 1966 through June 1968, the MARC Pilot Project distributed some 50,000 machine-readable cataloging records in that format to sixteen participating libraries. The records were distributed weekly on magnetic tapes that came to be known as MARC tapes. They contained descriptive cataloging data that also appeared in human-readable form in LC printed catalogs and cards. Participating libraries used MARC tapes, together with their institutional computers and locally developed software, to produce catalog cards, book catalogs, and specialized bibliographic lists.

While the MARC Pilot Project allowed participating libraries to experiment with the manipulation of machine-readable cataloging records, the MARC I format required revision before the Library of Congress and other libraries could develop extensive programs based on the interchange of bibliographic data in machine-readable form. Those revisions are embodied in the MARC II communications format. Introduced in 1967, the MARC II format is designed to facilitate the exchange of bibliographic data about all types of materials by a wide range of libraries using varied computer equipment and software. The MARC II format—now termed the USMARC or LC MARC format to distinguish it from MARC formats developed in other countries—is described in detail in various publications of the Library of Congress, on which the following summary is based.

The USMARC Format

The USMARC format specifies a basic structure for machine-readable bibliographic records that consists of three components:

1. A leader, composed of fixed length fields, provides information about the length, type, and bibliographic level of the ensuing record. Record types are designated by codes that identify the cataloged work as a printed book, manuscript, microform, map, music, or other entity. Codes for bibliographic level indicate whether the work is a self-contained monograph, a part of a series, a serial publication, an analytic component within a larger bibliographic work, or a collection of manuscripts, pamphlets, or other items cataloged as a single unit.

2. A record directory indicates the locations of specific variable fields within each record. It is analogous to the table of contents of a book. Each record directory entry includes a content designator, or tag, that identifies the variable fields within the record; an indication of the length of the variable fields; and the position of the first character within the record. The record directory facilitates the retrieval of selected fields from within a MARC record.

3. The variable fields within each MARC record contain bibliographic data accompanied by numeric tags that reflect the content of the fields and any subfields into which they may have been divided.

Logically related groups of MARC tags are assigned to specific types of bibliographic data. The "100" tag, for example, denotes a personal name as main entry; the "110" tag is used for a corporate name as main entry; while the "111" tag denotes a conference or meeting name as main entry. Similarly, the "400" tag denotes a series statement that consists of a personal name; the "410" tag is used for a series statement that consists of a corporate name; while the "411" tag identifies a series statement that consists of a conference or meeting name. The "600" tag identifies a personal name as a subject added entry; the "610" tag denotes a corporate name as a subject added entry; while the "611" tag is used for a conference or meeting name as a subject added entry. The "650" tag identifies one of the most common data elements, a topical heading as a subject added entry, while the "651" tag is used for a geographic name as a subject added entry. Some fields associated with specific tags are identified by letter designations. For the "245" tag, for example, subfield code "a" identifies a short title or title proper, while subfield code "b" identifies the remainder of the title.

The USMARC record structure is an implementation of standards for information interchange that have been adopted by the American National Standards Institute (ANSI) and the International Standardization Organization (ISO). Those organizations have not, however, standardized the content designators and subfield codes that identify the elements within records or the rules for creation of the data content of the records themselves. Bibliographic record formats developed by other organizations are based on the USMARC record structure, although they may differ in the content of their variable fields and the specific MARC tags used as content designators. This is the case, for example, with MARC records created by such organizations as the Institution of Electrical Engineers, the European Association of Scientific Information Dissemination Centers (EUSIDIC), and the Educational Research Information Center (ERIC).

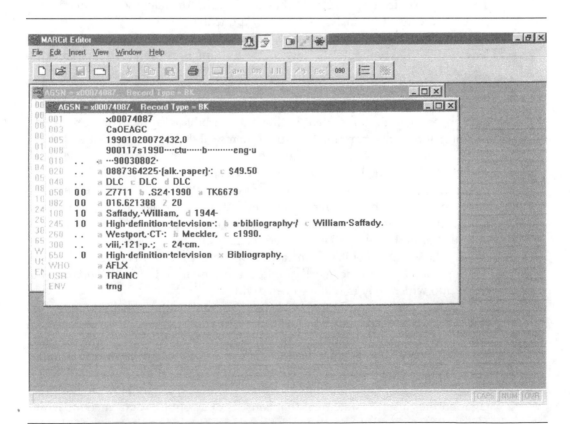

A MARC record displayed with tags.

Considerable variation in content designators is also characteristic of MARC formats developed by national libraries in Canada, Great Britain, France, Germany, Italy, Australia, Denmark, Sweden, Norway, Japan, and other countries. The Canadian MARC (CANMARC) format, for example, uses more content designators than are permitted by the Library of Congress. The United Kingdom UKMARC and French INTERMARC formats permit a wider range of content designators than the Canadian format does. The International Federation of Library Associations and Institutions (IFLA) has endorsed a UNIMARC format that facilitates the international exchange of bibliographic data in machine-readable form.

In the United States, the Library of Congress has developed MARC formats for various types of library materials, including books, serials, maps, visual materials, archives and manuscripts, musical scores, and computer files. USMARC formats have also been developed for authorities, including names, subjects, series titles, and uniform titles; for holdings information about serial and non serial items; for classification information, including the Library of Congress classification system, Dewey Decimal System, and other classification schemes; and for community information, including records for organizations, services, and events. These USMARC formats are maintained and revised, as necessary, by the Library of Congress in consultation with various interested parties, including the MARC Advisory Committee and the Machine Readable Bibliographic Information (MARBI) committee of the American Library Association.

The Library of Congress has distributed magnetic tapes containing MARC records on a subscription basis since 1969. The scope of the MARC program, which was initially limited to English-language monographs, has broadened to include all monographs written in languages that use roman scripts as well as certain non-roman languages and various non-monographic materials regardless of language. Cataloging-in-Publication (CIP) data were added to the MARC program in 1971.

The LC MARC Database

The LC MARC database is the name given to the accumulation of machine-readable cataloging records produced and distributed by the Library of Congress. While its scope and content have changed over the years, the database is usually subdivided by the types of materials being cataloged. At the time of this writing, the LC Cataloging Distribution Service offered MARC records on an annual subscription basis for the following categories and subcategories of bibliographic materials:

1. As noted above, the distribution of machine-readable cataloging records for English-language books dates from the inception of the MARC program in 1968. Cataloging records for books written in French, German, Spanish, Portuguese, Italian, Dutch, and other languages employing the roman alphabet were added to the LC MARC database in stages between 1973 and 1977. Romanized records for books written in eastern Slavic, Greek, Arabic, Hebrew, Yiddish, Persian, Chinese, Japanese, Korean, and Southeast Asian languages were added between 1979 and 1985. Since 1987, the Library of Congress has distributed Chinese, Japanese, and Korean cataloging records in vernacular as well as romanized form. As discussed elsewhere in this chapter, such records are created on the RLIN system. Hebrew cataloging records have been distributed in vernacular form since 1989. Distribution of vernacular cataloging records for books published in Arabic and Persian began in 1991. At the time of this writing, the Books All segment of the LC MARC database contained over 4.5 million bibliographic records for monographs cataloged by the Library of Congress, including Cataloging-in-Publication (CIP), minimal level cataloging (MLC), and preliminary level records. Records for monographs published in non-roman alphabets are in romanized form. Vernacular cataloging records must be purchased separately. Over half a million records are added to the Books All segment of the LC MARC database annually. Of these, about 40 percent are new records. The remainder update CIP or other incomplete records. A Books English subset of the Books All segment of the LC MARC database is limited to bibliographic records for English-language monographs published in the United States and elsewhere. At the time of this writing, it contained over 2.5 million cataloging records. Approximately 330,000 records are added to the Books English subset annually. One-third of them are new records. A Book U.S. subset of the Books All segment is limited to bibliographic records for books published in the United States, regardless of language. At the time of this writing, it contained approximately 1.8 million cataloging records. Approximately 250,000 cataloging records are added to the Books U.S. subset annually, of which about 80,000 are new records.

   2. As an alternative to the widely criticized practice of romanization, the Library of Congress offers vernacular cataloging records in machine-readable form for books published in certain languages. The Books CJK segment of the LC MARC database contains both vernacular and romanized cataloging records for monographs published in the Chinese, Japanese, and Korean languages. At the time of this writing, it contained approximately 300,000 bibliographic records. About 38,000 records, 45 percent of them new, are added to the Books CJK segment annually. The Books Arabic segment of the LC MARC database contains vernacular and romanized cataloging records for monographs published in the Arabic and Persian languages. At the time of this writing, it contained approximately 12,000 bibliographic records. About 5,000 records are added to the Books Arabic segment annually. About 60 percent are new records. The Hebrew segment of the LC MARC database contains both vernacular and romanized cataloging records for monographs published in Hebrew and Yiddish. At the time of this writing, it contained over 30,000 bibliographic records. Approximately 7,000 records, 45 percent of them new, are added to the Hebrew segment annually.

   3. LC MARC cataloging records for cartographic materials cover single- and multisheet maps, globes, map sets, and maps treated as serials. This segment of the LC MARC database dates from 1973. At the time of this writing, it contained approximately 175,000 records. Approximately 15,000 records are added to the Maps segment annually. Of these, approximately 50 percent are new records.

   4. Cataloging records for serial publications in languages that utilize roman alphabets, as well as romanized versions of serial publications in other languages, were added to the LC MARC database in 1973. Cataloging records for newspapers were added to the database in 1975. The Library of Congress also distributes serials cataloging records authenticated by the Cooperative On-line Serials (CONSER) program. CONSER reviews records for accuracy, appropriateness of headings, completeness of descriptive elements, and conformity to specified cataloging practices. At the time of this writing, the Serials segment of the LC MARC database contained over 900,000 bibliographic records. About 120,000 records are added to the Serials segment annually. Approximately 45 percent are new records. Available separately, the Serials CJK segment of the LC MARC database includes vernacular and romanized cataloging records for serials published in the Chinese, Japanese, and Korean languages. At the time of this writing, it contained approximately 6,000 bibliographic records dating from 1991. Approximately 1,600 cataloging records are added to the Serials CJK segment annually. About 60 percent are new records.

5. The Library of Congress has distributed cataloging records for music— including printed and manuscript musical scores, as well as musical and non-musical sound recordings—since 1984. Materials in non-roman languages are cataloged in romanized form. At the time of this writing, the Music segment of the LC MARC database contained approximately 210,000 bibliographic records. About 23,000 records are added annually. Approximately 45 percent are new records.

6. The Visual Materials segment of the LC MARC database includes bibliographic records for films, film strips, video recordings, transparencies, media kits, and other graphic materials cataloged by the Library of Congress since 1972. Prior to 1992, this database segment included some records that were cataloged by other libraries. At the time of this writing, the Visual Materials segment of the LC MARC database contained approximately 140,000 bibliographic records. About 3,400 records are added annually. Approximately 60 percent are new records. The LC Cataloging Distribution Service also offers a nitrate film file, which contains MARC-format records for nitrate-based motion pictures held by the Library of Congress and for nitrate safety transfer copies created since the early 1980s.

7. The Computer Files segment of the LC MARC database contains bibliographic records for machine-readable data files and computer software cataloged by the Library of Congress since 1990. At the time of this writing, the Computer Files segment contained approximately 3,500 records. About 650 records are added annually. Approximately two-thirds are new records.

LC cataloging records for books are distributed weekly on magnetic tape or daily through electronic transfer using the Internet's file transfer protocol (FTP). Cataloging records for serials, maps, music, visual materials, CJK books, and CJK serials are distributed monthly on magnetic tape. Cataloging records for computer files, Arabic books, and Hebrew books are distributed quarterly on magnetic tape.

In addition to the LC MARC database, the LC Cataloging Distribution Service distributes cataloging records produced by organizations other than the Library of Congress. The GPO cataloging file, for example, contains bibliographic records that are produced by the U.S. Government Printing Office and published in the *Monthly Catalog of U.S. Government Publications* and its several supplements. Covering monographs, serials, maps, and visual materials, GPO cataloging records have been distributed in the MARC format since 1976. Since 1991, the Government Printing Office has used the OCLC system, described below, for its original cataloging. At the time of this writing, the GPO cataloging file contained approximately 475,000 bibliographic records. About 19,000 records are added to the file annually. About 70 percent are new records.

The LC Cataloging Distribution Service also offers cataloging records produced by several national libraries. The Books Canada file, for example, contains cataloging records produced by the National Library of Canada for monographs pertaining to Canada or bearing Canadian imprints. The records, which date from 1975, are received by the Library of Congress in the CAN-MARC format. They are converted to the USMARC format prior to distribution. At the time of this writing, the Books Canada file contained approximately 630,000 bibliographic records. Approximately 40,000 records are added annually. The file is updated weekly. The British National Bibliography (BNB) file contains cataloging records produced by the British Library for books and first issues of serials published in the United Kingdom. The records are chiefly for English-language imprints. At the time of this writing, the BNB file contained over 750,000 records dating from 1984. Approximately 60,000 records are added annually. The BNB file is produced by the British Library in the UKMARC format. It is converted to the USMARC format by the Library of Congress prior to distribution. The file is updated weekly.

The Australia/New Zealand file contains cataloging records produced by the national libraries of those countries. Records from each library are distributed in separate segments. The National Library of Australia segment contains bibliographic records for books and serials. The National Library of New Zealand segment contains bibliographic records for books, maps, music, and serials. At the time of this writing, the file contained approximately 400,000 records dating from 1972 for Australia and from 1982 for New Zealand. Approximately 40,000 records are added annually. The file is updated monthly. The Library of Congress also distributes cataloging records produced by Die Deutsche Bibliothek for German-language monographs and selected non-monographic materials published in Germany, Austria, and Switzerland. The file, which is updated monthly, contained approximately 900,000 records at the time of this writing. About 150,000 records are added annually. Cataloging records produced by the National Diet Library of Japan are distributed by the Library of Congress on a monthly basis. The records contain both romanized and vernacular entries. About 75,000 records are shipped annually.

Like most machine-readable databases, MARC tapes are prospective in that they emphasize items cataloged by the Library of Congress since the inception of the MARC program. Several projects have, however, extended the scope of the LC MARC database retrospectively. The RECON Pilot Project, funded by the Council on Library Resources in 1969, provided an initial exploration of the feasibility of retrospective conversion. The project converted some 58,000 titles identified by a study of the most frequently ordered printed catalog cards. Its most important technical achievement, however, was refinement of automatic format recognition (AFR) techniques for the simplified creation of MARC records. When conventional conversion techniques are used, content designators are manually assigned to each variable field by catalogers for technical assistance before input. With automatic format recognition, however, computer programs recognize the variable fields in a given MARC record and assign appropriate content designators to them. While the potential for error still necessitates proofreading by human editors, some keystroking labor is saved by the elimination of content designators from the input data. The International Standard Bibliographic Description (ISBD), which uses specified combinations of punctuation symbols to separate the various elements in a cataloging record, was developed in part to facilitate the use of automatic format recognition techniques, especially where foreign language records are involved.

To avoid possible confusion, it is important to distinguish automatic format recognition from optical character recognition (OCR). As defined in chapter 1, OCR is a method of converting human-readable information to the machine-readable form required for computer processing. Automatic format recognition is a computer processing technique that requires the prior conversion of bibliographic data to machine-readable form. Such conversion may be accomplished by means of OCR, but, for reasons discussed in chapter 1, key-entry methodologies are more often used. Ideally, retrospective conversion of cataloging records to the MARC format might be accomplished by using an OCR reader to input data from existing catalog cards to an automatic format recognition program. Such capabilities are not, however, within the current state-of-the-art data entry technology.

Following the RECON Pilot Project, which ended in 1971, a number of libraries participated in a conference to explore the interchange of machine-readable bibliographic data at which the possibility of sharing locally converted MARC records was discussed. The Cooperative MARC (COMARC) Project was the outcome of the discussion. Funded by the Council on Library Resources in 1974, it represented a further attempt to extend the LC MARC database retrospectively. As participating libraries converted cataloging records from the National Union Catalog, LC printed cards, or other LC cataloging copy to machine-readable form, they transmitted them in the USMARC format to the Library of Congress, where they were reprocessed as required and made available to subscribers through the Cataloging Distribution Service, just as non-LC cataloging appears in the *National Union Catalog*. COMARC Project participants included the Washington State Library, University of Chicago, Northwestern University, Cornell University, Yale University, University of Illinois, University of Tennessee, University of Wisconsin, Boston Theological Institute, and 3M Company. The project ended in 1978.

While the RECON and COMARC projects resulted in the addition of some older cataloging records to the LC MARC database, the most ambitious MARC retrospective conversion project was undertaken by a private firm, the Carrollton Press. Begun in 1980, the REMARC (Retrospective MARC) project converted over 4.5 million records cataloged by the Library of Congress from 1897 through the inception of the MARC program. (English-language works are included through 1968; works in other languages are included at the time they entered the MARC program.) All REMARC records observe the USMARC format, with non-roman scripts being transliterated.

MARC-DERIVATIVE CATALOGING PRODUCTS

At the inception of the MARC program it was felt that, in the manner of the *National Union Catalog* and LC printed cards, libraries would acquire MARC tapes for use in locally developed cataloging systems implemented on their own computing equipment. It was further assumed that libraries would develop, purchase, or otherwise obtain software to print catalog cards or book catalogs, perform bibliographic searching, or perform other operations involving MARC records. The Library of Congress itself has offered no software for the processing of MARC data beyond the programs distributed to participants in the original MARC Pilot Project. As a result, the earliest applications of MARC tapes were primarily developed by a relatively small number of research libraries and public library systems with access to the computer hardware, programming resources, and funds required for systems analysis and software development.

From 1969 to the mid-1970s, library databases derived from MARC tapes, supplemented by the local input of additional cataloging records, were used to print catalog cards, book catalogs, and other bibliographic products at such institutions as the New York Public Library, Stanford University, Rice University, University of California, California State Library, Orange County Public Library, Hennepin County Public Library, Trinity University in San Antonio, and the University of Guelph in Ontario. The Library of Congress itself makes extensive use of MARC records for various purposes, including production of book catalogs and catalog cards. As an alternative to acquiring and processing MARC tapes, however, libraries of all types and sizes can obtain access to MARC records through products and services developed by publishers, computer system developers, time-sharing services, and other intermediaries. Computer-output microfilm (COM) publications were among the earliest examples of such MARC-derivative products. Many libraries used them during the 1970s. While they remain available, microfiche publications are no longer the preferred sources for cataloging with copy, although they can prove useful for bibliographic verification in acquisitions, interlibrary loan, and related operations. For most libraries, MARC-derivative CD-ROM products or bibliographic utilities provide more effective cataloging support.

Microfiche Cataloging Tools

Prior to the implementation of the MARC program, many libraries relied on the printed catalogs of the Library of Congress, particularly the *National Union Catalog,* as authoritative sources of cataloging copy. Librarians often complained, however, that delays associated with the publication and distribution of LC printed catalogs seriously impaired their utility for cataloging and other purposes. When mailed at lower postage rates, conventionally printed issues of the NUC typically arrived several weeks after their cover dates. Limited access points for identification of pertinent cataloging copy also posed problems. Because bibliographic records in the printed NUC were arranged in main entry sequence, considerable familiarity with LC cataloging practices was required to locate desired information. These problems were addressed by microfiche cataloging tools. With their compact size and low weight, they can be mailed economically at first-class postage rates. Further, they provide excellent indexing to simplify identification of LC cataloging records for specific works.

The Library of Congress replaced the conventionally printed NUC with a COM-generated microfiche version, produced from the LC MARC database, in 1983. Issued monthly, *National Union Catalog: Books* has supplanted its hard-copy predecessor as well as *LC Books: Subjects*. It contains cataloging records for books, pamphlets, manuscripts, map atlases, microform masters, and monographic government publications. Three related COM-generated publications, the *National Union Catalog: Audiovisual Materials,* the *National Union Catalog: Cartographic Materials,* and the *Music Catalog on Microfiche* are issued quarterly. All of these publications present complete cataloging records in the traditional main entry format. Individual entries are arranged by an LC-assigned registry number. The user consults name, title, series, and subject indexes to determine the registry numbers associated with works to be cataloged. Index entries contain brief data—including publisher, date, and LC card number—that may satisfy some information requirements and eliminate the two-step retrieval procedure. The indexes, which are arranged alphabetically, cumulate continuously.

While it provides more varied access to bibliographic information than its conventional printed predecessor, the COM-generated version of the *National Union Catalog* retains the printed edition's monthly publication frequency. Where more frequent access to cataloging information is required, MARC-FICHE is distributed weekly by The Library Corporation, a company that is best known for CD-ROM and online cataloging products and services described below. The weekly subscription gives libraries access to Library of Congress cataloging records within a few days of the distribution of MARC tapes. MARCFICHE includes LC MARC cataloging records since 1967, COMARC-contributed cataloging, cataloging records for Canadiana produced by the National Library of Canada, and cataloging records for 90,000 additional twentieth-century imprints that are not included in the LC MARC database. As with the COM-generated NUC, individual entries conform to the traditional main entry format and are recorded in control number sequence on microfiche. Access to desired cataloging records is obtained by consulting indexes to main entry/title, LC Card Number, LC class number, and International Standard Book Number. The indexes themselves are on COM-generated microfiche and cumulate quarterly. Index updates cumulate weekly between quarters. Other index cumulations and publication frequencies are optionally available.

Books in English (BIE) is a COM-generated cataloging and bibliographic reference tool produced by the British Library from a combination of the British National Bibliography (UKMARC) and LC MARC databases. BIE is a bi-monthly alphabetical author/title listing of English-language books cataloged by the British Library or the Library of Congress. It thus approximates the scope of H. W. Wilson's *Cumulative Book Index* but, like the *National Union Catalog*, its entries contain full cataloging data. Originally published ultrafiche for maximum compactness, BIE is now issued on conventional COM-generated fiche. Information is current through the month preceding publication. Each entry includes LC and Dewey class numbers, LC Card Numbers, added entries, and subject headings. Successive issues cumulate continuously and contain all cataloging records published since the beginning of the current year. Various cumulations are available for earlier years.

CD-ROM Cataloging Systems

As their principal shortcoming, microfiche cataloging tools make no provision for preparation of catalog entries or for convenient transfer of bibliographic records into a library's online catalog. Once located on microfiche, individual catalog entries must be key-entered into a library's database or typed onto cards. In either case, considerable labor is required. CD-ROM cataloging support products address these limitations. They combine computer-based information retrieval capabilities with word processing functionality for rapid identification, modification, and output of cataloging records.

As described in chapter 1, CD-ROM is a read-only optical disk format for computer-processible information. It is particularly useful for database publishing and distribution. CD-ROM cataloging products, as their name indicates, provide databases of bibliographic records on compact discs. The CD-ROMs are distributed to customer sites for local processing by cataloging support software that operates on microcomputer-based workstations. While specific hardware requirements vary from product to product, the microcomputer configuration must include a hard drive and one or more CD-ROM drives. A printer is required for card or label production.

The earliest CD-ROM cataloging product, BiblioFile, was introduced in the mid-1980s by The Library Corporation. Besides The Library Corporation, other vendors include Brodart Automation, Follett Software, Gaylord Information Systems, General Research Corporation, and Online Computer Library Center (OCLC). Three of these vendors—Brodart Automation, OCLC, and The Library Corporation—also operate bibliographic utilities that are described later in this chapter. In the early 1990s, the Library of Congress introduced its own CD-ROM implementation of the LC MARC database, but that product has been discontinued.

While they differ in detail, available CD-ROM cataloging products feature similar capabilities and operating procedures. Designed to support both current cataloging operations and retrospective conversion projects, they typically include all or part of the LC MARC database on one or more compact discs. In some cases, LC cataloging data is supplemented by bibliographic records obtained from other sources such as the National Library of Medicine, the National Library of Canada, the British Library, or the National Information Center for Educational Media (NICEM). Some CD-ROM products also include original cataloging records prepared by academic, public, or school libraries. Regardless of source, the records are stored on CD-ROM in the USMARC formats associated with specific types of library materials. With some products, the cataloging database is subdivided into English- and foreign-language components, which are recorded on separate compact discs. With others, cataloging records are grouped on compact discs by date, by type of library material, by topical themes, or by cataloging source. Some CD-ROM cataloging systems include authority records—typically, the LC Name Authority File (NAF) and LC Subject Authority File (SAF)—in addition to bibliographic records.

To support cataloging operations, CD-ROM cataloging products provide prewritten software that permits the retrieval of bibliographic records by various parameters, modification of cataloging copy for conformity with local practices, retention of the modified records in machine-readable form, and printing of catalog card sets and labels. As with the microfiche cataloging tools described above, indexes are searched to identify bibliographic records for particular works. While specific retrieval capabilities vary from product to product, typical indexing parameters include the Library of Congress Card Number (LCCN), International Standard Book Number (ISBN), International Standard Serial Number (ISSN), music publisher's number, author, title, series title, publication date, and media type. Other possibilities include a European access number, government publication number, report number, CODEN, LC or Dewey class number, or language of publication. Searches by conclusive identifiers, such as the LCCN or ISBN, are preferred because they usually retrieve a single cataloging record. If cataloging records are recorded on multiple compact discs and the microcomputer configuration includes a single CD-ROM drive, media handling may be required to mount the proper compact disc for record retrieval. Multiple CD-ROM drives can minimize or eliminate such media handling.

Retrieved cataloging records are displayed in the MARC format with tags, content indicators, and subfield information. They can be modified to meet local requirements and to add a location indicator, call number, control number, or other holdings information. Word processing-like functionality is provided for that purpose. CD-ROM cataloging software also supports the creation of original cataloging records using displayed workforms for simplified data entry. Predefined workforms are typically provided for the types of library materials for which USMARC formats have been developed: books, serials, visual materials, music, computer files, maps, and archives and manuscripts. Customized workforms can be created for other materials or special applications.

When completed, cataloging records are stored in a work file on the microcomputer's hard drive, from which they can be copied onto diskettes or magnetic tapes for transfer into a library's online catalog. CD-ROM cataloging products are utilized by many smaller libraries that operate microcomputer-based integrated systems of the type described in chapter 6. Such systems typically accept cataloging records on diskettes in the MicroLIF or USMARC MicroLIF Protocol formats.

For some libraries, CD-ROM cataloging systems offer a potentially cost-effective alternative to the bibliographic utilities described in the next section. Certain bibliographic utilities charge libraries for specific cataloging transactions as they are performed. Charges are incurred, for example, each time a cataloging record is retrieved or whenever output products are ordered. By contrast, libraries that utilize CD-ROM cataloging systems pay a fixed annual subscription fee of several hundred to a thousand dollars or more, depending on the product and the subscription option selected. The annual subscription fee provides unlimited database access without additional transaction charges. Thus, CD-ROM cataloging products are particularly attractive for high-volume current cataloging operations or retrospective conversion projects, where a low unit cost per cataloging transaction can be achieved.

Comparisons between CD-ROM cataloging systems and bibliographic utilities assume, of course, that CD-ROM databases are appropriate for the items being cataloged by a given library. As a potentially significant limitation, CD-ROM products may provide fewer cataloging records than the bibliographic utilities. Some CD-ROM products rely principally or exclusively on the LC MARC database, which may be segmented or offered as a series of separately priced subsets. Because most CD-ROM databases are updated at monthly or quarterly intervals, they may not contain full cataloging records for a library's most recently acquired items. By contrast, the databases maintained by bibliographic utilities are updated at regular, frequent intervals through subscriptions to resource files. The LC Cataloging Distribution Service issues MARC tapes on a weekly or monthly basis for most library materials, and some bibliographic utilities receive daily updates of LC MARC cataloging records through electronic transfers. In addition, as discussed below, databases maintained by the bibliographic utilities are updated continuously by participants' original cataloging activities. Further, the bibliographic utilities offer capabilities appropriate to resource sharing, acquisitions, and other library operations that are not addressed by CD-ROM cataloging products. Because the cataloging records maintained by most bibliographic utilities include library holdings symbols as well as bibliographic data, they can support interlibrary loan activities. Cost considerations aside, such capabilities may give bibliographic utilities a functional advantage over CD-ROM systems in certain library situations.

BIBLIOGRAPHIC UTILITIES

"Bibliographic utilities" is the collective name for a group of computer service organizations that maintain large databases of cataloging records and offer various cataloging support services and related products to libraries and other customers who access those records on an online, time-sharing basis using microcomputers or other specified terminals. The databases maintained by most bibliographic utilities are essentially online union catalogs. As discussed below, all bibliographic utilities acquire cataloging records in machine-readable form from the Library of Congress and other subscription sources. In most cases, their databases also include cataloging records contributed by participating libraries. Regardless of source, databases maintained by bibliographic utilities contain two kinds of information: (1) descriptive cataloging and classification data in the MARC format appropriate to the items being cataloged and (2) holdings information for libraries that have added specific items to their collections.

While their size and content varies in a manner discussed below, the databases maintained by bibliographic utilities are designed to automate cataloging with copy, among other library operations. As time-sharing computer services, all bibliographic utilities support the interactive retrieval of cataloging records using online workstations. While specific retrieval capabilities vary from utility to utility, their general search procedures will prove familiar to librarians accustomed to other online information services. In brief, the workstation operator enters a retrieval specification in a prescribed format. The system consults one or more indexes and responds with information that satisfies the retrieval specification. All bibliographic utilities can retrieve cataloging records by system-assigned control numbers, Library of Congress Card Numbers, International Standard Book Numbers, and International Standard Serial Numbers. Other numeric retrieval parameters—such as government publication numbers, music publishers' numbers, and CODEN identifiers for serials—are selectively supported for specific types of bibliographic records. Author, title, subject, and keyword retrieval capabilities may be supported as well.

Where multiple cataloging records satisfy a retrieval specification, they are initially displayed in an abbreviated format for operator perusal and selection of records for more detailed display. The order in which records are displayed is variously determined by a utility's default operating parameters, by a profile established at the time a library becomes a utility participant, or by operator preferences. To support cataloging and other technical services operations, all bibliographic utilities can display records in the full MARC format, with content indicators and subfield codes. For reference applications, certain bibliographic utilities will replace MARC tags with field labels.

A workstation operator can add, move, change, delete, or otherwise edit individual field values to meet local cataloging requirements. At a minimum, the operator must enter local holdings information. When modifications are completed, output products, such as machine-readable records on magnetic tape or catalog card sets, can be ordered. The magnetic tapes, often described as "archival tapes," permit the transfer of cataloging records to a library's online catalog or other local automation system. Alternatively, cataloging records can be downloaded for transfer to a local system. Assuming an appropriate workstation configuration, all bibliographic utilities support local printing of book pocket and spine labels. Other output products are selectively available. Examples include CD-ROM catalogs, computer-output microfilm (COM) catalogs, and printed bibliographies.

Bibliographic utilities principally compete with the CD-ROM cataloging systems described above. Because they are larger and updated more frequently than their CD-ROM counterparts, the databases maintained by bibliographic utilities will presumably satisfy a greater percentage of a given library's copy cataloging requirements, thereby minimizing original cataloging. If a database search fails to identify an appropriate cataloging record, however, the workstation operator can place the system in the original cataloging mode. Typically, bibliographic data is key-entered into a workform appropriate to the type of item being cataloged. In most cases, the entered cataloging record becomes available to other utility participants. The completeness and quality of original cataloging records contributed by utility participants has been a topic of discussion and concern since the early 1970s. Ideally, contributed records will conform to the Anglo-American Cataloguing Rules, the Standard Bibliographic Description, Library of Congress name and subject authorities, and the full MARC data-entry format, but most utilities permit the creation of briefer records under certain circumstances.

Recognizing the close relationship between acquisitions and cataloging in the technical services workstream, several bibliographic utilities offer online acquisition subsystems that support a variety of procurement situations. These acquisitions subsystems facilitate order preparation by transferring bibliographic information from cataloging records to order workforms. They provide online directories for procurement source selection and can transmit orders electronically to certain publishers, book jobbers, and other vendors. Where cataloging records are combined with local holdings information, the databases maintained by bibliographic utilities promote resource sharing among participants. Most bibliographic utilities provide an interlibrary loan component to facilitate such resource sharing. Specific operational differences aside, those components permit the identification of prospective lenders and the preparation of interlibrary loan requests. To expedite interlibrary loan transactions, requests are electronically routed to designated libraries, which may accept, decline, or refer them to other institutions.

While bibliographic utilities offer capabilities appropriate to a broad range of library operations, their continued emphasis on cooperative cataloging clearly distinguishes them from other online information services that provide time-shared access to similar bibliographic records. The LC MARC database of cataloging records produced by the Library of Congress, for example, has long been available online through the DIALOG information service, which is discussed in chapter 7; but that implementation is intended for reference and research applications rather than for technical processing. It is a good source for bibliographic verification, but DIALOG does not support online entry of original cataloging data, record editing, card production, or other services that specifically support cataloging operations.

The following sections describe six North American organizations that operate bibliographic utilities: the Online Computer Library Center (OCLC); the Research Libraries Group (RLG), which operates the Research Libraries Information Network (RLIN); Auto-Graphics, Incorporated, which operates the Impact/ONLINE CAT service; A-G Canada, a subsidiary of Auto-Graphics that operates Impact/MARCit, a bibliographic utility originally developed by Utlas; Brodart Automation, which operates the Interactive Access System (IAS); and The Library Corporation, a well-known supplier of CD-ROM cataloging systems that also offers the ITS.MARC online cataloging service. Other bibliographic utilities operate in Europe, the Pacific Rim, and elsewhere. They maintain similar databases of cataloging records, but are generally unavailable to North American libraries. Examples include the British Library's BLAISE-LINE service, The Dutch Project for Integrated Catalogue Automation (PICA), SIBIL France, the Australian Bibliographic Network (ABN), and SABINET, a South African bibliographic utility.

OCLC

The Online Computer Library Center (OCLC) is the world's largest, best-known, and most widely analyzed supplier of computer-based cataloging services. It was incorporated in 1967 as the Ohio College Library Center, a not-for-profit organization intended to function as a computerized regional processing center for academic libraries in Ohio. OCLC implemented an offline catalog card production system in 1970, using a database of LC MARC records. An online system for shared cataloging became operational in 1971 and was employed by 54 academic libraries by the end of that year. In 1972, OCLC participation was extended to non-academic libraries in Ohio. Interstate operations were initiated with the installation of several terminals in Pennsylvania libraries in late 1972. In 1973, OCLC abandoned its regional orientation, offering membership to libraries outside Ohio and setting the stage for a rapid expansion of its customer base. By the end of the decade, OCLC had library customers in all 50 states. The organization's national—and, since the late 1980s, increasingly international—orientation has been reflected in two name changes: to OCLC, Incorporated, in 1977 and to the Online Computer Library Center, Incorporated, in 1981.

OCLC participation is open to libraries of all types and sizes, regardless of geographic location. At the time of this writing, OCLC provided approximately 26,000 libraries with computerized cataloging, reference, and other services; of these, over 7,000 rely on OCLC for online cataloging support. OCLC's cataloging customers can be divided into two broad groups: (1) online cataloging members who agree to use the OCLC online system for all of their current cataloging activity and to contribute original cataloging records and holdings information to the OCLC database; (2) tapeloading members who do a portion of their current cataloging online and contribute the remainder of their current cataloging on magnetic tape for inclusion in the OCLC database. Tapeloading membership is designed for libraries that utilize a different bibliographic utility, a CD-ROM product, or another methodology for part of their current cataloging activities. OCLC online and tapeloading members are eligible to participate in the organization's governance.

Other libraries may utilize OCLC for specific, limited services. As an example, group access capability (GAC) permits local and regional use of the OCLC online system by non-member libraries that are part of consortia or other preformed groups. Each group must include at least one OCLC member. Non-member libraries, termed "selective users," can access brief bibliographic records and holdings information for libraries within a consortium. Because selective users do not contribute bibliographic or location information to the online database, they cannot access records contributed by libraries outside their group. OCLC also provides a serials union list capability that can be utilized by members and non-members, but only members have online access to serials listings. Non-members may receive copies of union lists on paper, microfiche, or magnetic tapes. OCLC grants special or partial user status to national libraries, library schools, and certain other organizations.

While independent participation is possible, OCLC encourages U.S. libraries to become members through regional networks that operate as its authorized agents. Such regional networks and their service areas include the AMIGOS Bibliographic Council (Arizona, Arkansas, Oklahoma, New Mexico, and Texas, with additional members in Kansas, Louisiana, and Nevada); BCR, the Bibliographic Center for Research (Colorado, Idaho, Iowa, Kansas, Montana, Nevada, Utah, and Wyoming); CAPCON Library Network (the District of Columbia, Maryland, and Virginia); Federal Library and Information Center Committee, FEDLINK (U.S. government libraries); ILLINET (Illinois); the Indiana Cooperative Library Services Authority, INCOLSA (Indiana); the Michigan Library Consortium (Michigan); MINITEX Information Network (Minnesota, North Dakota, and South Dakota); Missouri Library Network Corporation (Missouri); NEBASE (Nebraska); NELINET (Connecticut, Massachusetts, Maine, New Hampshire, Rhode Island, and Vermont); OHIONET (Ohio); PALINET (Delaware, the District of Columbia, Maryland, and eastern Pennsylvania); PRLC (western Pennsylvania and West Virginia); the Southeastern Library Network, SOLINET (Alabama, Florida, Georgia, Kentucky, Louisiana, Mississippi, North Carolina, Puerto Rico, South Carolina, Tennessee, Virginia, and Virgin Islands); SUNY/OCLC (New York); WILS (Wisconsin); and OCLC Pacific (California, Alaska, Washington, Oregon, Idaho, Montana, and Hawaii).

As a group, the regional networks help member libraries install OCLC equipment and implement OCLC operations. They provide system documentation in the form of operators' manuals, equipment selection aids, newsletters, and other written communications; conduct training courses; collect fees for OCLC usage; and generally serve as liaison agencies between OCLC and member libraries. Most regional networks operate as not-for-profit corporations or as subsidiaries or ancillary activities associated with not-for-profit institutions. In recent years, some regional networks have expanded their activities, offering CD-ROM information products, group discounts on online searching, Internet access, professional education, and other products and services to attract libraries that do not use OCLC for cataloging.

While OCLC continues to gain customers among U.S. libraries, international markets offer the most significant opportunities for future expansion. As described below, the OCLC database is international in scope. It contains bibliographic records in more than 300 languages and includes numerous Canadian, European, Asian, and Latin American imprints. Because libraries outside the United States purchase many U.S. publications, the OCLC database offers them a comprehensive and convenient source of cataloging copy for those materials. International participation in OCLC benefits the utility's U.S. customers by increasing the availability of cataloging records for foreign imprints and providing greater opportunities for resource sharing.

OCLC has library customers in over 60 countries. Their participation ranges from full cataloging membership to applications that involve a single OCLC service, such as retrospective conversion or resource sharing. The OCLC Europe office, located in Birmingham, England, was established in 1981. It serves libraries in the United Kingdom, continental Europe, the Middle East, and Africa. The OCLC Asia-Pacific Services Office, located at OCLC headquarters in Ohio, was established in 1986. It serves libraries in Asia and the Pacific Rim. National libraries in Australia, New Zealand, Singapore, and Taiwan provide online access to OCLC in their countries. The OCLC Latin American and Caribbean Office was established in 1995. Located at OCLC headquarters, it serves Mexico, the Caribbean, Central America, and South America. OCLC serves Canadian libraries from an office in Quebec.

Like other bibliographic utilities, OCLC provides online access to a large database of cataloging records that supports descriptive cataloging, subject cataloging, classification, preorder bibliographic verification, interlibrary loan, and other library operations. The OCLC database, formerly known as the Online Union Catalog, is now called WorldCat. At the time of this writing, it contained approximately 40 million cataloging records, making it the world's largest collection of cataloging information measured by the number of bibliographic records for unique editions. As discussed below, cataloging databases offered by certain other bibliographic utilities are larger, but they contain multiple records for individual editions. Approximately 2 million cataloging records are added to the WorldCat database each year.

The WorldCat database contains information from two sources: (1) resource files of cataloging records from subscription services and (2) cataloging records contributed by participating libraries. Providing a solid foundation for participants' current cataloging activities, various machine-readable resource files are loaded into the WorldCat database at regular intervals. Like other bibliographic utilities, OCLC obtains Library of Congress cataloging records on magnetic tape or through electronic file transfer. The LC MARC database is the largest source component of WorldCat. Among other resource files, OCLC acquires the CATLINE and AV-LINE databases, which contain bibliographic records for books and audiovisual materials cataloged by the National Library of Medicine. The WorldCat database also contains CANMARC records, produced by the National Library of Canada for Canadian publications and books about Canada, and UKMARC records, produced by the British Library for works about or published in the United Kingdom. OCLC obtains the CANMARC and UKMARC data files from the Library of Congress, which also supplies Australian and New Zealand MARC records.

In addition to the WorldCat database, online cataloging users can access a collection of bibliographic records for rare books created jointly by OCLC and Harvard University, as well the EUR-OP database of bibliographic records for documents published by the Office of Official Publications for European Communities. OCLC also loads cataloging records obtained from certain book vendors, such as Casalini Libri and Puvill Libros. These vendor records are stored in WorldCat, where they constitute a database within a database.

During OCLC's first several years of operation, LC MARC records constituted the major portion of the WorldCat database. By 1973, however, contributed cataloging represented almost half of the online records. Its relative percentage has increased steadily and significantly since that time, as participating libraries have contributed cataloging records for older imprints and other items not included on LC MARC tapes. Since the mid-1990s, contributed cataloging and bibliographic records acquired from non-LC sources have accounted for about 85 percent of the records in the WorldCat database. The phenomenal growth of the contributed cataloging portion of WorldCat is in large part attributable to the previously discussed broadening of OCLC's customer base since the 1970s, as well as to retrospective conversion projects undertaken by OCLC participants to support the implementation of local library automation systems. As their principal contribution to WorldCat, such retrospective conversion projects have added cataloging records for older imprints that predate the LC MARC program and the inception of OCLC's online cataloging system.

To catalog an item, an OCLC member first searches the WorldCat database for appropriate cataloging copy. Since its inception, OCLC's online cataloging system has supported the retrieval of bibliographic records by numeric identifiers and derived search keys. The former permit searches by Library of Congress Card Number (LCCN), International Standard Book Number (ISBN), International Standard Serial Number (ISSN), CODEN, government document number, music publisher's number, and OCLC control number. Where numeric identifiers are involved, search procedures are straightforward. To retrieve a record by Library of Congress Card Number, for example, an OCLC workstation operator simply enters the number. Because the numeric identifiers listed above are usually unique to specific bibliographic records, they will yield the fastest retrieval results and are consequently preferred where appropriate.

Derived search keys permit retrieval of bibliographic records by personal or corporate author (whether in main or added entries), title, or a combination of author and title. Derived search keys are based on specified combinations of characters from individual words in a desired name or title. An author search key, for example, is composed of the first four or fewer characters of the author's surname; the first three or fewer characters of the author's first name; and, where applicable, the author's middle initial. Thus, the derived author search key for George V. Higgins would be "higg,geo,v"—the individual segments being entered in lowercase characters, separated by commas. Search keys for corporate authors are constructed in much the same way, although the OCLC search system includes a stop list of commonly encountered words in corporate authors' names. Such words can be omitted when deriving the search key, thereby limiting the retrieval of irrelevant records.

Similar rules apply to the formulation of title and combined author/title search keys. The search key for a given title consists of the first three or fewer characters of the first word in the title; the first two or fewer characters in each of the next two words; and, where applicable, the first character of the fourth word. Initial articles are ignored. Thus, the key for a title search for James M. Cain's *The Postman Always Rings Twice* would be "pos,al,ri,t." The derived key for a combined author/title search consists of the first four or fewer characters of the author's surname and the first four or fewer characters of the first non-article word in the title. Thus, the author/title search key for the above example would be "cain,post."

While such parameters as the LCCN and ISBN are unique and usually retrieve just one record, the derived keys for author, title, and combined author/title searches are not necessarily unique. They often retrieve multiple, irrelevant records along with the desired items. Considerable numbers of records may be retrieved, for example, in author/title searches where truncation results in search keys of a common form, such as "john,hist."

Other bibliographic utilities permit the direct entry of authors' names and titles, singly or in combination. They also support a broader range of retrieval parameters, as well as search statements with multiple retrieval parameters linked by Boolean operators. Since the early 1990s, OCLC has expanded its retrieval capabilities to permit combined key searches, title browsing, title phrase searches, keyword searches of designated fields, and limited Boolean operations. While these features facilitate the identification of bibliographic records for technical processing, they cannot satisfy the diverse retrieval requirements of reference and research applications. Because OCLC's keyword searching feature does not permit subject retrieval, libraries requiring greater retrieval functionality involving the WorldCat database must use OCLC's FirstSearch service, which is designed specifically for reference and research applications. That service is described in chapter 7.

When one bibliographic record is retrieved by a given search, it is displayed in the full MARC format with labeled fields. Multiple records are initially displayed in an abbreviated format for operator inspection and selection of those for which a full MARC display is desired. OCLC's cataloging software simplifies editing of database records to meet local requirements. Any OCLC member can modify database records to conform to local cataloging requirements or add holdings information. Such modifications are reflected in magnetic tapes, catalog cards, and other output products that the library may order, but the database records themselves are never changed. Theoretically then, the WorldCat database contains just one cataloging record for each edition obtained from source files or contributed by participants. Although OCLC cautions participating libraries against creating duplicate records, some duplication inevitably results from mechanical problems such as typographical errors during data entry and from intellectual factors such as variations in descriptive cataloging practices and difficulties in distinguishing among different printings and editions of a given title.

As previously noted, OCLC members agree to use the utility for all cataloging operations. If the WorldCat database does not contain bibliographic records for items to be cataloged, OCLC members must promptly perform original cataloging and contribute the records to the database. Original cataloging records are input in the MARC format, using displayed workforms that consist of labeled fields with adjacent blank spaces for data entry. Member-contributed cataloging creates database records that will be used by other OCLC participants. Contributed records remain in the WorldCat database until they are superseded by Library of Congress cataloging. OCLC has established bibliographic standards, based on MARC formats and Library of Congress practice, for member-contributed cataloging records. Full-level cataloging, previously known as level I cataloging, corresponds closely to the second level of description in the Anglo-American Cataloguing Rules (AACR). It is the most complete and consequently preferred cataloging level. Core level cataloging meets the requirements of first-level description and some of the requirements of second-level description as specified in AACR. Minimal-level cataloging, previously known as K-level cataloging, corresponds closely to first-level description in AACR. It is used for library materials that otherwise might not be cataloged.

Examples include dissertations, pamphlets, exhibition catalogs, audiovisual materials, and locally produced publications of limited interest outside their issuing organizations.

OCLC's cataloging software performs certain data validation routines to prevent the entry of inappropriate data elements in specific fields. OCLC's automated authority control software corrects and modernizes headings for personal names, corporate names, series titles, and subjects. It also identifies and corrects certain form errors, coding errors, and typographical errors in headings. OCLC's staff does not review contributed cataloging records for correctness prior to their inclusion in the WorldCat database. Such reviews are instead left to the contributing libraries. Because the quality of cataloging copy decisively influences the effectiveness of a shared cataloging system in which only one version of a record is available online, OCLC participants have been much concerned about the quality of member-contributed cataloging practices. OCLC encourages members to report errors or omissions in bibliographic records. The Enhance program, which was established by OCLC in 1983, authorizes certain libraries to correct and replace records contributed by other OCLC participants. Enhance libraries are selected for inclusion in the program on the basis of their high-quality cataloging. Participants receive training in OCLC enhancement policies and procedures.

To improve cataloging quality through convenient selection of standardized headings, OCLC offers online access to the OCLC authority file, Library of Congress Name Authority File, and Library of Congress Subject Authority File. These files are implemented as search-only information resources for authorized headings and cross-references. The OCLC authority file contains headings and cross-references for personal names, corporate names, conference names, genre names, geographic names, uniform titles, and subject headings. The Library of Congress Name Authority File contains headings for personal, corporate, conference, and geographic names, plus some headings for uniform titles and series. The records are created by the Library of Congress and by participants in the National Coordinated Cataloging Operations (NACO) program. They are added to the OCLC system daily by electronic transfer. LC subject authority records are added weekly. OCLC also offers an authority control service that automatically corrects and modernizes headings in a library's bibliographic records.

Once an original cataloging record is entered, or modifications to an existing database record are completed, an OCLC workstation operator can order printed card sets, which will be produced offline according to the specifications or profile prepared when the ordering library became an OCLC participant. Printed cards and other output products reflect modifications that a library makes to specific cataloging records. Online database records, as previously noted, are unaffected by such changes.

As libraries convert from card to online catalogs, the number of cards printed by OCLC has declined. Libraries with local automation systems can order machine-readable copies of their cataloging records on magnetic tapes. Produced at weekly, biweekly, monthly, quarterly, or semiannual intervals, such tapes contain bibliographic records that reflect the ordering library's cataloging transactions, including original cataloging as well as modified or unmodified versions of existing database records. To support the initial implementation of local automation systems, OCLC can provide magnetic tapes that contain part or all of the cataloging records produced by a particular library since the inception of its OCLC activity or for another specified time period. Tapes containing cataloging records of multiple libraries are available, provided that appropriate permission is obtained. As an alternative to archival tapes, the OCLC system can electronically transfer cataloging and authority records in the MARC format to a local library automation system. As its principal advantage, this electronic transfer capability permits immediate updating of local databases, eliminating the delays inherent in ordering, receipt, and loading of cataloging records on magnetic tape.

RLIN

The Research Libraries Information Network (RLIN) is a bibliographic utility and online information retrieval system that is owned and operated by the Research Libraries Group (RLG). Designed to support cataloging and other library operations, RLIN was established in 1978 as an outgrowth of BALLOTS, a library automation program developed by Stanford University. BALLOTS—an acronym for Bibliographic Automation of Large Library Operations using a Timesharing System—was ambitiously conceived as an integrated information processing system in which shared bibliographic and other data files would support both technical processing operations and information retrieval activities. The latter component of the BALLOTS program was an outgrowth of the Stanford Physics Information Retrieval System (SPIRES), an interactive online retrieval system developed in 1967. A prototype BALLOTS implementation, introduced in 1969, was followed by a production system for the Stanford University libraries in 1972. In 1976, BALLOTS became available to other California libraries as a shared cataloging service. At that time, it was widely regarded as a potential alternative to OCLC for West Coast libraries.

BALLOTS' destiny was significantly altered in 1978, however, when it was selected by the Research Libraries Group as the system with the greatest potential for meeting its requirements for automated bibliographic control. RLG was founded in 1974 by Harvard University, Columbia University, Yale University, and the New York Public Library as a resource-sharing consortium. One of the group's original goals was the establishment of a computer-based bibliographic processing system. It initially experimented with an online link to the Library of Congress but ultimately adopted BALLOTS as its bibliographic utility. When that decision was made, Harvard withdrew from RLG. It was replaced by Stanford, which became the utility's host institution. BALLOTS provided the technical base for the RLIN system.

Although they are specifically intended for large or specialized research libraries, RLIN's cataloging services are similar to those offered by other bibliographic utilities. Available to libraries of all types and sizes, RLIN has two broad categories of participants: RLG members and others. RLG membership is open to research libraries, archives, museums, historical agencies, scholarly societies, and other not-for-profit institutions with educational, cultural, or scientific missions. Two categories of RLG membership are available: (1) general members serve a clientele of more than 5,000 faculty, researchers, students, professionals, or others; (2) special members are institutions that serve 5,000 or fewer users. At the time of this writing, RLG had more than 155 members. For the most part, the general members are large university and national libraries, while the special members have highly focused educational missions or strong research collections in particular subject areas. Libraries outside North America are a growing component of RLG's membership.

Participation in RLIN is not required of RLG members in either category, although most members use RLIN to support some activities. Libraries other than RLG members can become RLIN participants by submitting an order form and executing the required service agreement, both of which can be obtained from RLG. RLIN distinguishes technical processing customers, who have full access to the system's cataloging support and related capabilities, from search service users, who are limited to retrieval of database records for reference purposes. RLIN also permits search-only access by individuals rather than institutions, as well as instructional access by graduate-level library education programs. RLIN users who are not members of RLG do not participate in the organization's governance.

The principal components of the RLIN database, the so-called central bibliographic files, form an online union catalog of library materials held by the utility's participants. Like their counterparts in other bibliographic utilities, RLIN's central bibliographic files contain records from two broad sources: subscription files and cataloging contributed by participating libraries. RLIN obtains cataloging records for books, serials, maps, music, visual materials, and computer files from the Library of Congress. It also loads cataloging records produced by the U.S. Government Printing Office; CANMARC records produced by the National Library of Canada for Canadian imprints and books about Canada; and UKMARC records produced by the British Library for books about the United Kingdom or bearing United Kingdom imprints. In addition, RLIN subscribes to the CATLINE database, which contains cataloging records produced by the National Library of Medicine.

Through the RLG European Library Data Initiative, RLIN will significantly increase its supply of cataloging records for Western European imprints and provide shared access to the holdings of major European libraries, some of which are RLG members. Initial participants in the project are the national libraries of France, Spain, and Switzerland. In 1997, RLIN began loading current cataloging records from the Biblioteca Nacional de España (BNE). In early 1998, RLIN began adding current cataloging records for monographs from the Bibliotheque Nationale de France (BNF). RLG claims that 85 percent of the BNE records and 90 percent of the BNF records are unique to the RLIN database. To further enhance its international coverage, RLIN has loaded cataloging records from the European Register of Microform Masters (EROMM), to which thirty European libraries contribute.

RLIN also obtains bibliographic records from book vendors such as Blackwell North America and Iberbook International. Blackwell's Enhanced Library of Congress Cataloging in Publication records change CIP information that differs from the published work. Blackwell's Table of Contents records contain transcribed tables of contents, detailed summaries, or both, for collected works, anthologies, conference proceedings, festschrifts, monographs, and works of fiction. Iberbook International provides cataloging records for new Spanish books, sound recordings, and video recordings. Other book vendors that contribute in-process cataloging records to the RLIN database include Puvill Libros, for Spanish and South American imprints, Casalini Libri for Italian publications, and the National Yiddish Book Center for current and older Yiddish-language publications.

Records from subscription sources are added to the central bibliographic file shortly after their receipt by RLIN through electronic file transfer or on magnetic tape. The Library of Congress itself uses the RLIN system for online entry of MARC cataloging records in Chinese, Japanese, Korean, Hebrew, and Arabic scripts.

Unlike the OCLC WorldCat database, which maintains all bibliographic records in a single repository, RLIN's central bibliographic files are divided into separate segments that correspond to the eight types of library materials recognized by USMARC formats. The RLIN books file accounts for about 90 percent of the cataloging records in the central bibliographic files. Other files contain cataloging records for serials, musical scores, sound recordings, visual materials, maps, machine-readable data, and archives and manuscripts. The last of these, known as the AMC file, contains records for complete archival collections, parts of collections, and single items held by university libraries and public libraries, government archives, historical societies, museums, and other research institutions. The file incorporates the complete records of the National Union Catalog Manuscript Collections (NUCMC) since 1987.

At the time of this writing, RLIN's central bibliographic files contained over 85 million cataloging records. Measured by total database size, RLIN is the largest bibliographic utility, but the storage of duplicate and variant records for the same editions cataloged by different libraries complicates comparisons of databases offered by the various bibliographic utilities. As discussed elsewhere in this chapter, the OCLC database maintains—at least ideally—a single bibliographic record for each edition of a given work. As a result, this database contains fewer cataloging records than its RLIN counterpart.

Among its advantages, the storage of duplicate and variant records gives RLIN participants a broader range of choices for cataloging copy. It also simplifies interlibrary loan transactions by providing online access to exact cataloging and holdings information contributed by RLIN participants. While comparisons are rarely published, the OCLC online union catalog is larger than the RLIN database when measured by the number of cataloging records that it contains for unique editions. At the time of this writing, RLIN's central bibliographic files contained cataloging records for approximately 30 million unique editions as compared with approximately 40 million unique editions in the OCLC Online Union Catalog.

Most RLIN participants use online data entry to contribute bibliographic records that reflect their current cataloging activities. Cataloging records produced by retrospective conversion projects or transferred from other systems, such as OCLC, are typically loaded into RLIN via magnetic tapes. Given RLIN's role as a bibliographic utility for research libraries, it is not surprising that the central bibliographic files contain contributed catalog records that reflect the highly specialized, often distinctive materials held by RLIN participants. Such materials include publications in over 365 languages. While works written in English account for over half of the titles in the RLIN database, fifteen other languages are represented by at least 100,000 titles each. RLIN has a well-deserved reputation for innovations that facilitate cataloging in nonroman scripts. The RLIN system supports input and retrieval of bibliographic records in the so-called JACKPHY languages (Japanese, Arabic, Chinese, Korean, Persian, Hebrew, and Yiddish) plus Cyrillic. The RLIN database contains more than 1.5 million CJK cataloging records contributed by RLIN participants and the Library of Congress, which uses the RLIN system for that purpose. The RLIN database also contains the largest collection of bibliographic records in Middle Eastern languages.

Since the early 1980s, RLG has devoted considerable attention to the bibliographic control of library materials in specific subject areas, such as East Asian studies and art and architecture. Among the bibliographic utilities, RLIN has most actively encouraged the entry of information about archival and management collections. Its involvement with such materials dates from 1983, when RLG established an archives and manuscripts task force to promote the development of a national database of primary source materials. To accommodate the requirements of archives and manuscript repositories, the RLIN system permits the repeated modification of a bibliographic record as an individual collection progresses through various stages of processing. It should be noted, however, that the databases maintained by other bibliographic utilities also contain cataloging records for distinctive and important research materials. The OCLC WorldCat database, in particular, includes many cataloging records contributed by special collections departments in participating libraries.

The RLIN system's sophisticated information retrieval component supports bibliographic verification, copy cataloging, literature searches, interlibrary loan, and other library operations. As described above, the RLIN database is divided into files that correspond to the various types of library materials covered by MARC formats. To retrieve bibliographic records, an RLIN user must specify the data file to be searched. Indexes support the retrieval of cataloging records by various numeric and textual parameters. As a group, numeric parameters permit faster, more efficient searches than their textual counterparts and are consequently preferred where appropriate. Numeric search parameters include the Library of Congress Card Number (LCCN), International Standard Book Number (ISBN), International Standard Serial Number (ISSN), RLIN control number, U.S. government document number, GPO monthly catalog number, music publisher's number, report number, or a Dewey, LC, or other classification number.

RLIN's textual search parameters can retrieve cataloging records by personal, corporate, and conference names; titles; and subjects. Name indexing covers main and added entries, including authors, editors, illustrators, and compilers. Personal names can be entered in normal or inverted order. The searcher can specify an exact or partial form of a personal name to be matched. Corporate and conference names, titles, and subject headings can be searched for words or phrases. Regardless of the particular search parameters employed, RLIN's retrieval procedures are straightforward and should be easily mastered by librarians familiar with other online information services. The RLIN workstation operator simply enters a retrieval command accompanied by a field name and search term. Unlike OCLC, with its derived retrieval keys, RLIN users enter search terms directly. Search terms can be truncated to compensate for uncertain spelling or to retrieve all field values with a common root. To further enhance retrieval flexibility, the Boolean AND, OR, and NOT operators can be used to combine multiple search specifications.

Like other bibliographic utilities, RLIN supports both original cataloging and cataloging with copy. Cataloging operations typically begin with a search of RLIN's central bibliographic files. If an appropriate bibliographic record is identified, it must be used. Retrieved records can be modified by adding, moving, or deleting information to meet local cataloging requirements. When modifications are completed, the system assigns a unique control number, adds a copy of the record—incorporating all modifications plus an identifier for the contributing library—to the central bibliographic files, and updates the appropriate indexes. The cataloging record on which the modified record was based is unaffected by any changes made by RLIN customers. Once entered in the central bibliographic files, a contributed cataloging record is available to other RLIN participants. A record will remain in the central bibliographic files until it is deleted by the library that contributed it.

If a database search fails to identify an appropriate cataloging record, the RLIN operator can place the system in the original cataloging mode. The operator indicates the desired MARC input format, and the system responds by displaying an appropriate workform. RLG standards for original cataloging are based on the Anglo-American Cataloguing Rules, as interpreted by the Library of Congress; LC practice for names and subject headings; and the USMARC formats for specific library materials. RLIN recognizes three levels of detail for original cataloging. Full-level original cataloging conforms to RLG standards and is based on National Level Bibliographic Record standards. Full-level cataloging consists of complete MARC records with authority control for name and subject headings. Core or base-level original cataloging employs the MARC format and RLG cataloging standards but omits some fields associated with full-level records. Briefer cataloging records do not conform to RLIN cataloging standards. Each record in the central bibliographic files contains a field that identifies its cataloging standard. RLIN participants are encouraged to upgrade brief cataloging records to full level.

Original cataloging is not reviewed by RLIN staff prior to inclusion in an appropriate bibliographic file. Participants may correct cataloging errors detected in their own records, but they are not permitted to correct errors in records contributed by others. Because the RLIN database makes all modified versions of cataloging records available to all participants, formal error detection procedures are less important than they are in the OCLC system, which maintains just one copy of each cataloging record.

To facilitate cataloging decisions, RLIN provides online search-only access to Library of Congress authority files. Authority records can be retrieved by a variety of parameters, including personal names, subject words, and subdivisions, as well as words or phrases in corporate names, conference names, and titles. The LC Name Authority File is updated daily through electronic file transfers. Participants in the National Coordinated Cataloging Operations project can use the RLIN system to contribute records to the LC Name Authority File. The LC Subject Authority File is updated weekly.

RLIN participants can have their cataloging records converted to MARC-format magnetic tapes suitable for input to a local library automation system or other uses. RLIN tapes contain a library's newly added or updated cataloging records for a specified time period. Tape content can be limited to cataloging records from a particular bibliographic file, such as the books file. Custom tapes can be created by searching the RLIN database for cataloging records that satisfy specific search parameters. Alternatively, RLIN records can be transferred electronically to a library's online catalog or other local database. RLIN can also print catalog cards in a wide range of formats.

In addition to its central bibliographic files, RLIN provides online access to various subject-oriented databases that support reference and research activities, as opposed to cataloging and other technical services operations. Access to such databases is provided in the search-only mode. In this respect, RLIN combines the attributes of a bibliographic utility with those of an online search service. While RLIN's reference and research databases lack the breadth and depth of subject coverage offered by the largest online services discussed in chapter 7, they are potentially useful information resources for RLIN participants and increasingly important components of the RLIN service.

RLIN's subject-oriented databases in the humanities provide noteworthy coverage of disciplines that are too often neglected by commercial online information services. The Avery On-Line Index, for example, contains bibliographic citations from hundreds of architecture periodicals. The Art and Architecture Thesaurus is an online authority file produced by the Art History Information Program of the J. Paul Getty Trust. The SCIPIO (Sales Catalog Index Project Input Online) database contains bibliographic records for art auction catalogs held by art libraries and museums. SCIPIO headings are contained in a special authority file. The English Short Title Catalog (ESTC) database contains bibliographic records for books, broadsides, and other works published in Great Britain and its colonies, as well as for items printed in English anywhere in the world between 1400 and 1800. RLIN's CitaDel service, which was introduced in 1992, provides online access to approximately one dozen bibliographic databases produced by a variety of organizations. Initially, CitaDel offered a number of popular databases that were widely available from other online services. At the time of this writing, however, the CitaDel service emphasized specialized information sources. Examples include the BIBLIOGRAPHY OF THE HISTORY OF ART, the Chicano Database, the Index to Foreign Legal Periodicals, the Hispanic American Periodicals Index, Russian Academy of Sciences Bibliographies, and the World Law Index, which covers Hispanic legislation.

Impact/ONLINE CAT

Impact/ONLINE is the broad designation for a group of interrelated information services offered by Auto-Graphics, Incorporated, a well-known supplier of library automation systems and services. The Impact/ONLINE CAT system, which provides online cataloging capabilities, is an outgrowth of the Auto-Graphics Interactive Library Exchange (AGILE), a bibliographic utility introduced in the early 1980s and significantly augmented in subsequent years. Like its predecessor, Impact/ONLINE CAT is a general-purpose bibliographic utility for libraries of all types and sizes, regardless of geographic location. It is particularly well suited to multibranch library systems, consortia, and other cooperative arrangements at the local, regional, or state level. Other Impact/ONLINE services support inter-library loan, union catalog implementations, and reference databases.

Like other bibliographic utilities, the Impact/ONLINE CAT system provides online, time-shared access to a large database that contains cataloging records from two broad sources: (1) resource files obtained on a subscription basis and (2) cataloging records contributed by participants. As its largest and most important subscription resource file, the Impact/ONLINE CAT system provides online access to LC MARC cataloging records. Its coverage includes English-language monographs cataloged by the Library of Congress since 1968, which corresponds to the Books English subset of the LC MARC database. As explained above, cataloging records for books published in other languages were phased into the LC MARC database during the 1970s. The Impact/ONLINE database does not include CANMARC or CJK cataloging records for books. The database does contain LC MARC cataloging records for serials, maps, visual materials, musical scores, and sound recordings. At the time of this writing, the total database size exceeded 12 million unique bibliographic records.

As a supplementary bibliographic resource, the Impact/ONLINE CAT system provides online access to a file of cataloging records prepared by Auto-Graphics for pre-1968 imprints not included in the LC MARC database. The Auto-Graphics resource file contains over half a million cataloging records for books published in various languages, plus additional records for serials, musical scores, sound recordings, visual materials, and maps. The LC MARC and Auto-Graphics resource files are available to all Impact/ONLINE CAT customers. Through the optional Impact/ACCESS GDCS component, Impact/ONLINE CAT customers can access Auto-Graphics' Government Document Cataloging Service, an enhanced and corrected implementation of the *Monthly Catalog of U.S. Government Publications.* As another option, Impact/ONLINE CAT participants can access the Impact/MARCit database, which is operated by A-G Canada. That database, which contains over 50 million cataloging records and a broad range of resource files, is described below. Impact/ONLINE CAT users can also access the RLIN database for cataloging records that are not available in either Impact/ONLINE CAT or Impact/MARCit.

Like RLIN, the Impact/ONLINE CAT system stores individual participants' cataloging records—including original cataloging as well as modified versions of cataloging records created by the Library of Congress or other participants—

in separate, individually identifiable and searchable segments of the database. By providing online access to cataloging records and individual libraries' holdings information, the system is an effective vehicle for resource sharing, but participation in that aspect of system operation is voluntary. Impact/ONLINE CAT users have the option of storing their cataloging records in shared or private files. If the shared file option is selected, a library's cataloging records are available on a reciprocal basis to other Impact/ONLINE CAT participants. Cataloging records stored in private files are not accessible to other participants. Libraries that select the private file option cannot access other participants' files.

As one of its most attractive features, the Impact/ONLINE CAT system supports a flexible and convenient group of online retrieval capabilities that are well suited to cataloging support and resource-sharing applications. An Impact/ONLINE CAT user begins a retrieval operation by specifying a search path to be employed. Created by one of the system's administrative functions, search paths specify the segments of the database to be searched for cataloging records and the sequence in which searches will be performed. As an example, a user may specify that a library's own cataloging file will be searched first, followed by the LC MARC file, followed by other libraries' files—assuming, as discussed above, that they are shared files. Participants can specify different search paths to meet different requirements and select among them at the time a retrieval operation is performed.

Once a database segment is selected, the Impact/ONLINE CAT system supports a variety of search parameters, including author, title, subject headings, internal accession number, Library of Congress Card Number (LCCN), International Standard Book Number (ISBN), International Standard Serial Number (ISSN), GPO Monthly Catalog number, and Superintendent of Documents (SuDocs) number, among others. Search procedures are straightforward. The operator specifies the field to be searched and a search term. Searches based on author, title, subject headings, or numeric parameters can be limited by publication date, record type, or language. Keyword qualifiers can be applied to author, title, or subject searches.

The Impact/ONLINE CAT system is accessed through the Internet. The required cataloging workstation is a Windows-based microcomputer equipped with a Web browser. Auto-Graphics supplies software that interacts with the Web browser to support original and copy cataloging in any of the eight MARC formats. The software can also be purchased separately as a general-purpose cataloging tool for use with MARC records from other sources. To catalog books, serial publications, or other items, an Impact/ONLINE CAT operator searches the database. If an appropriate record is available, it is copied into a working file. During this transfer procedure, Impact/ONLINE CAT eliminates data elements, such as local call numbers, that are specific to the source from which the record was derived. The working file copy is then displayed for editing by moving, changing, deleting, or otherwise modifying individual field values to satisfy local cataloging requirements.

When all modifications to a given record are completed, the system assigns a unique accession number. Batch processing routines will later add the new record to the library's segments of the Impact/ONLINE CAT database. The cataloging record on which the edited record was based is unaffected by any changes made to it. Once entered into a shared file, the modified cataloging record is available to other Impact/ONLINE CAT participants. Newly entered records are indexed prior to inclusion in the database and are immediately searchable. A record will remain in a library's segment of the database until it is deleted by the library that entered it.

If a database search fails to identify an appropriate cataloging record, the Impact/ONLINE CAT operator places the system in the original cataloging mode and contributes a new record to the database. If the contributing library is a shared file participant, the new record will be accessible to other Impact/ONLINE CAT customers. In the original cataloging mode, an operator specifies a format (book, serial, map, etc.) for the item to be cataloged, and Impact/ONLINE CAT displays a data entry workform appropriate to that format. If desired, cataloging workforms can be customized by a system administrator. Unlike OCLC, Auto-Graphics does not require that participants use the Impact/ONLINE CAT system for all of their cataloging activities, although it is presumably advantageous for them to do so.

For both original and copy cataloging, Impact/ONLINE CAT automatically validates MARC tags, indicators, and subfield codes for each field in which data are entered or modified. The validation process compares tags, indicators, and codes to those listed in a tag table to ensure correct entry. It also confirms that required fields are present and that fields are not improperly repeated. The program displays a warning message if errors are detected, and it will not store the incorrect record unless the user specifically overrides the validation. The Impact/ONLINE system does not impose minimum cataloging standards, nor does it provide formal mechanisms for reporting, detecting, and correcting cataloging errors. Original cataloging is not reviewed by Auto-Graphics staff prior to inclusion in the database, and no libraries are authorized to correct errors detected in contributed cataloging records. Because the Impact/ONLINE database makes all modified versions of cataloging records available to all participants, formal error detection procedures are less important than they are for bibliographic utilities that maintain just one copy of a cataloging record.

In addition to maintaining cataloging records, the Impact/ONLINE CAT system can store a library's name authority records and subject authority records in the MARC format for online access. As an unusual feature of particular interest to public libraries, Impact/ONLINE CAT customers can create information and referral (I&R) records to describe government agencies, professional associations, and other organizations that provide community services of interest to a given library's clientele.

The Impact/ONLINE CAT system supports local printing of catalog cards, as well as pocket and spine labels. Libraries can also download cataloging records or order copies in the MARC format on magnetic tape. Auto-Graphics can produce CD-ROM catalogs, COM catalogs, and printed bibliographies to customer specifications.

Impact/MARCit

Impact/MARCit is an online cataloging service operated by A-G Canada, a wholly owned subsidiary of Auto-Graphics, Incorporated. A-G Canada was formed in June 1997 when Auto-Graphics purchased bibliographic utility services and related software previously marketed by ISM Library Information Services. ISM itself had purchased its bibliographic utility, known as the Cataloging Support System (CATSS), from Utlas International Canada, one of the most important organizations in the history of library automation.

CATSS was an outgrowth of library automation activities at the University of Toronto. In the late 1960s, the University of Toronto Library established a systems department and began to convert its bibliographic records to machine-readable form. From its inception, the systems department was charged with responsibility for developing automated systems and services for the library community in general. In 1971, the department was reorganized as a separate administrative entity and renamed the University of Toronto Library Automation System. The new unit was popularly identified by the uppercase, acronymic designation UTLAS. It introduced an online cataloging support system in 1973, initially to serve public and academic libraries in Ontario and Quebec. In the mid-1970s, UTLAS broadened its focus to include other Canadian libraries. In 1980, the Rochester Institute of Technology became the first UTLAS participant in the United States.

In 1977, UTLAS was removed from the library and made an ancillary enterprise of the University of Toronto. In 1983, UTLAS was incorporated as an Ontario company wholly owned by the University of Toronto. In early 1985, it was acquired by the International Thomson Organization, a Canadian-based multinational company with broad interests in publishing and information services. UTLAS was renamed Utlas International Canada; the uppercase form of the name, retained for a time in some product literature, was eventually dropped. In late 1992, Utlas International Canada was acquired by ISM Information Systems Management Corporation, Canada's largest computer service bureau and outsourcing contractor. As noted above, ISM sold its Library Information Services Division to Auto-Graphics, Incorporated in mid-1997. The acquisition included CATSS, the Utlas bibliographic utility, and related software products, including interlibrary loan components. A-G Canada redesigned the CATSS system and renamed it Impact/MARCit. Although Canadian libraries dominate its customer list, the system operates on computers located at Auto-Graphics' corporate headquarters in California. It is accessed through the Internet. Customers must have a Windows-based microcomputer equipped with a Web browser and special cataloging support software that is available from A-G Canada.

Impact/MARCit provides online access to a very large database of cataloging records that are obtained from subscription sources and contributed by participating libraries. The Impact/MARCit database incorporates an extensive and varied group of resource files. Like other bibliographic utilities, A-G Canada obtains MARC records for books, serials, maps, music, visual materials, and computer files from the LC Cataloging Distribution Service. Coverage for those records dates from the time they were included in the LC MARC database. The Impact/MARCit database also includes LC Cataloging-in-Publication (CIP) records; LC cataloging records for Chinese, Japanese, Korean, and Hebrew books; LC minimal-level cataloging records from 1983 to 1988; and U.S. Government Printing Office cataloging records.

In addition, the Impact/MARCit database includes the CATLINE file of cataloging records for books and serials produced by the National Library of Medicine; the CANMARC file of cataloging records for books, serials, and music produced by the National Library of Canada; the UKMARC file of cataloging records produced by the British Library; the AUSMARC file of cataloging records created by the National Library of Australia; and the New Zealand MARC file of cataloging records created by the National Library of New Zealand. Alone among the bibliographic utilities, Impact/MARCit provides online access to the REMARC database, which contains cataloging records for English-language works published prior to the inception of the MARC program and for various non–English-language works published prior to the inclusion of those languages in the LC MARC database. The Impact/MARCit database also contains cataloging records for monographs and serials published by Statistics Canada; the CISTI resource file of cataloging records produced by the Canadian Institute for Scientific and Technical Information (CISTI), Canada's national science library; the CIHM file of MARC records issued by the Canadian Institute for Historical Microreproductions; and cataloging records produced by the Bibliotheque Nationale du Québec.

The distinctive characteristics of the contributed cataloging segment of a given bibliographic utility's database are determined by the number and nature of its customers. Given its history and largely Canadian customer base, Impact/MARCit is the best online resource for cataloging records pertaining to Canadian imprints, works about Canada, and specialized materials held by Canadian government, corporate, technical, and academic libraries. Since most of the books purchased and cataloged by Canadian libraries are imported from foreign publishers, however, the Impact/MARCit database is necessarily international in scope. The Impact/MARCit database contains cataloging records for works published in almost 400 languages, many of which utilize non-roman scripts. Unlike OCLC and RLIN, A-G Canada does not support vernacular cataloging. Instead, cataloging records for works written in Russian, Chinese, Japanese, Korean, and other languages that employ non-roman scripts are romanized for entry into the Impact/MARCit database.

At the time of this writing, the Impact/MARCit database contained over 50 million bibliographic records, including both resource files and contributed cataloging. Measured by the number of records available online, Impact/MARCit is second only to RLIN among the bibliographic utilities discussed in this chapter, but the size of the Impact/MARCit database is increased by storage of duplicate and variant cataloging records produced by participating libraries. The Impact/MARCit database contains approximately 20 million unique cataloging records, which is about half as many as the OCLC WorldCat database. The Impact/MARCit resource files account for approximately one-half of the database's unique bibliographic records. About 60 percent of newly created records are contributed by participating libraries.

Impact/MARCit offers powerful and flexible retrieval capabilities that are equally well suited to cataloging and reference operations. English- and French-language interfaces are operator-selectable. The Impact/MARCit database can be searched by various numeric and textual parameters, including a system-defined record sequence number, OCLC control number for records that originated in the WorldCat database, Library of Congress Card Number (LCCN), International Standard Book Number (ISBN), International Standard Serial Number (ISSN), government documents control number, National Library of Canada (NLC) control number, music publisher's number, government document classification number, author, title, series title, and subject headings. Searches based on numeric identifiers are limited to exact matches. For author, title, series, and subject searches, an operator can select an exact match of a specified search term, a match that contains the search term in addition to other words, or a match based on right-truncation of the search term. Searches can also be limited to a particular owning library, by the media type, by a publication date or range of dates, and by language. The Boolean AND operator is supported on a limited basis.

Impact/MARCit responds to search operations with a brief list of bibliographic records that satisfy the retrieval specification. Brief listings are hyperlinked to full bibliographic records. Any record in the brief list can be selected for a full MARC display, including tags and content designators, for cataloging or other purposes. If no matching records are found, the system displays a browsable, alphabetical list of headings that most closely match the search term. Any heading can be selected for a more detailed display. For general bibliographic searching, interlibrary loan, and other public service applications, Impact/MARCit provides a reference-oriented retrieval component that utilizes the same search procedures as the cataloging component but displays bibliographic records with labeled fields rather than MARC content designators. Displayed information includes the author, title, publisher, subject headings, language, call number, and Library of Congress Card Number. Retrieved records not owned by the library can be hyperlinked to an interlibrary loan workform that prompts the requester for additional information. The completed request can then be transmitted electronically to a lending source through A-G Canada's interlibrary loan component.

Like other bibliographic utilities, Impact/MARCit supports both original cataloging and cataloging with copy obtained from resource files or contributed by other Impact/MARCit participants. All cataloging records in the database are available to all participants. To catalog an item, an operator searches the Impact/MARCit database for a desired bibliographic record. As previously noted, Impact/MARCit stores multiple cataloging records for items held by more than one library. The records may differ only slightly from one another if they differ at all. When multiple cataloging records are retrieved, they are sorted in a manner specified in the library's profile, with records from the library's preferred cataloging source at the top of the list. When an appropriate record is selected, it is transfered to the Impact/MARCit editing program for modification or augmentation.

When a database search fails to identify an appropriate bibliographic record, the Impact/MARCit editing program supports original cataloging through displayed workforms that correspond to the types of library materials for which MARC formats have been developed. The workforms include MARC content designators. Libraries can modify workforms to address special cata-

loging requirements. Unlike OCLC, A-G Canada does not require its participants to use the Impact/MARCit system for all of their cataloging activity, although it is presumably convenient and advantageous for them to do so. A-G
Canada does not impose minimum cataloging standards, nor does it provide
formal mechanisms for reporting, detecting, and correcting cataloging errors.
Original cataloging is not reviewed by A-G Canada staff prior to inclusion in
the Impact/MARCit database, and no libraries are authorized to correct errors
detected in contributed cataloging records. Since the Impact/MARCit database
stores modified versions of cataloging records and makes the various versions
available to all participants, formal error-correction procedures are less important than they are for bibliographic utilities, like OCLC, that maintain just one
copy of a cataloging record.

Impact/MARCit supports flexible, interactive authority control capabilities
that link bibliographic records to headings in specified authority files. The link-
ages ensure that the most current forms of headings are contained in bibliographic records, regardless of when the records were created. The Impact/
MARCit system supports several authority control files, including the Library
of Congress Name Authority File (NAF), the Library of Congress Subject Authority File (SAF), the CANMARC Name Authority File, the Medical Subject
Headings (MeSH) file prepared by the National Library of Medicine, the Repertoire de Vedettes Matiere (RVM) File of French-language subject headings issued by Laval University, a file of children's subject headings, files of cross-
references for obsolete and variant headings in LC authority files, and a file of
pseudonymous headings. Impact/MARCit participants can also create their
own authority records to reflect local cataloging practices.

Impact/MARCit participants can transfer cataloging records electronically
into local library automation systems. Alternatively, A-G Canada can provide
cataloging records in the MARC format on magnetic tapes. Catalog cards, microfiche catalogs, and CD-ROM catalogs are also available.

Interactive Access System

The Interactive Access System (IAS) is a bibliographic utility introduced in 1982
by Brodart Automation. It is used for online cataloging by a number of public
libraries, school library systems, and academic libraries. The IAS database contains more than fourteen million cataloging records derived from resource files
and contributed by participants. As its largest and most important resource file,
the IAS database includes the books, serials, maps, music, sound recordings,
and visual materials segments of the LC MARC database. The Interactive Access System also provides online access to GPO cataloging records produced by
the U.S. Government Printing Office and to CANMARC cataloging records
produced by the National Library of Canada for Canadian imprints and books
about Canada. The IAS database does not include CJK cataloging records from
the LC MARC database. LC MARC cataloging records account for about one-
quarter of the IAS database. To simplify searching, they are divided into two
files: MARC Current, which contains cataloging records for the current year,
and MARC Retro, which contains cataloging records for previous years.

As a supplementary cataloging resource, the Brodart MARC database contains approximately three million bibliographic records created by Brodart's Books Division and by retrospective conversion projects undertaken by Brodart Automation for specific customers. Such records are stored in several data files, which are subdivided by date and media type. New records are added to the Brodart resource file daily. Brodart's Books Division uses the Interactive Access System to upgrade Cataloging-in-Publication records received from the Library of Congress. That upgrade service is available to IAS customers.

The Interactive Access System also provides online access to sizable files of cataloging records created by various Brodart customers. Like RLIN and Impact/ONLINE CAT, the Interactive Access System stores individual participants' cataloging records in separate, individually identifiable and searchable segments of the IAS database. IAS participants have access to cataloging records created by other participants, unless a given library specifically prohibits access to its data file. When libraries become IAS participants, they obtain access to the LC MARC and Brodart MARC data files, plus their choice of data files created by other IAS participants. The Interactive Access System stores all cataloging records in the MARC format.

The IAS database can be searched by various numeric and textual parameters, including a system-assigned control number, Library of Congress Card Number (LCCN), International Standard Book Number (ISBN), International Standard Serial Number (ISSN), author, title, and subject headings. As a potentially useful feature that is supported by some online public access catalog programs, the Interactive Access System supports "anyword" searches across all indexed fields. Boolean operations are supported. Searches can be limited by publication date or type of material. Any retrieved record can be selected for a full MARC display.

To catalog an item, an IAS participant searches the database for an appropriate bibliographic record. The Interactive Access System stores records contributed by individual libraries in separate data files. The system searches a library's own data file first to confirm that the library has not already cataloged the item in question. Failing to locate an appropriate record, the system will then search other files in a sequence specified by a profile created when a library becomes an IAS participant.

A retrieved bibliographic record is copied into the user's working file and displayed with MARC tags for review and editing to meet local requirements. The original cataloging record is unaffected by such changes. While any field within a bibliographic record can be modified, the Interactive Access System can restrict the editing capabilities of specific users to designated fields. In a multibranch or consortium installation, where cataloging is performed by a central staff, for example, individual libraries' modifications might be limited to holdings fields within database records. Specific editing privileges are determined by passwords. When all modifications are completed, the Interactive Access System adds the record to the library's data file.

If an appropriate bibliographic record cannot be located in IAS resource files, the workstation operator activates the original cataloging mode. The system displays a formatted screen that includes commonly used MARC tags.

Other tags can be added as needed. Brodart does not require IAS participants to contribute original cataloging records, but most libraries will find the system simpler and easier to use than conventional cataloging methodologies. IAS participants can delete records from their data files at any time. Brodart does not impose minimum cataloging standards on IAS participants, nor does it provide formal mechanisms for reporting, detecting, and correcting cataloging errors in database records. Original cataloging is not reviewed by Brodart's staff prior to inclusion in the database, and no libraries are authorized to correct errors detected in cataloging records contributed by other participants. In addition to cataloging records, the Interactive Access System supports online retrieval of LC name and subject authority records.

The Interactive Access System supports online printing of catalog cards, pocket labels, and spine labels by locally installed printers. Cataloging records can be downloaded to a microcomputer workstation for transfer to a local library automation system or for other purposes. IAS participants also can obtain machine-readable cataloging records in the USMARC or OCLC MARC format on magnetic tape. Brodart Automation can produce printed book catalogs, subject bibliographies, microfiche catalogs, CD-ROM catalogs, and other output products to address specific customer requirements.

ITS.MARC

ITS.MARC is a Web-based online cataloging service operated by The Library Corporation, a company that is best known for its CD-ROM cataloging products. Introduced in 1997, ITS.MARC is the first bibliographic utility developed specifically and exclusively for the World Wide Web. Customers require a Windows-based microcomputer, a Web browser, and special cataloging support software supplied by The Library Corporation.

Like other bibliographic utilities, ITS.MARC provides online access to a variety of cataloging resource files that are obtained on a subscription basis from national libraries and other producers. The LC MARC English Language data file contains cataloging records produced by the Library of Congress for works published in English. For online access, this data file is divided into current and backfile segments. The LC MARC Current segment contains records for English-language works cataloged by the Library of Congress from 1990 to the present. A selectable portion of the LC MARC Current segment contains cataloging records produced by the Library of Congress within the past five days. The LC MARC Current segment is updated daily. The LC MARC Foreign Language data file contains cataloging records produced by the Library of Congress for works published in languages other than English. This file is updated monthly.

The A/V Access data file contains MARC-format records for popular audio and visual items cataloged by the Library of Congress and by Professional Media Service Corporation, while the NICEM A-V MARC data file contains records for audiovisual materials cataloged by the National Information Center for Educational Media. The Canadian MARC data file contains CANMARC records produced by the National Library of Canada, supplemented by cataloging from the Library of Congress, for works published in Canada or about Canada. The British MARC data file contains UKMARC cataloging records produced by the British Library for works published in or about the United Kingdom. The MedMARC data file contains bibliographic records from the National Library of Medicine's CATLINE database, supplemented by cataloging records produced by the Library of Congress and the National Library of Canada. The Docufile contains cataloging records for publications by the U.S. government, state governments, foreign countries, and the United Nations. This file is updated monthly.

Among the unusual bibliographic resources offered by ITS.MARC, the Sears Cataloging data file contains MARC-format cataloging records with Sears subject headings and Dewey classification numbers. The MARC en Español data file contains records for Spanish-language works cataloged by the Library of Congress, the National Library of Canada, the U.S. Government Printing Office, and the National Library of Medicine. The MARC en Français contains records for French-language works cataloged by the Library of Congress, the National Library of Canada, and Services Documentaire Multimedia Incorporated. ITS.MARC provides online access to an Authorities database that contains the Library of Congress Name Authority File (NAF), the Library of Congress Subject Authority File (SAF), Sears subject headings, and Medical Subject Headings (MeSH) produced by the National Library of Medicine.

Unlike most other bibliographic utilities, ITS.MARC does not store cataloging records created by participating libraries. It provides two files of cataloging records produced by preselected libraries. The Contributed Research and Academic data file contains MARC-format records for works cataloged by The Library Corporation's customers in academic and research libraries. Approximately 60 percent of these records pertain to pre-1968 imprints that are not included in the LC MARC data file. The Contributed School and Public data file contains MARC-format records for works cataloged by The Library Corporation's customers in school and public libraries. The contributed cataloging files are available exclusively from The Library Corporation. All data files are available to ITS.MARC subscribers. Catalogers have the option of searching a specific data file or all data files. In the latter case, the LC MARC Current file is searched first.

ITS.MARC subscribers can retrieve cataloging records by various textual and numeric parameters, including author, title, subject headings, Library of Congress Card Number (LCCN), International Standard Book Number (ISBN), International Standard Serial Number (ISSN), U.S. Government Printing Office (GPO) monthly catalog number, Superintendent of Documents (SuDocs) number, music publisher's number, report number, National Library of Canada (NLC) control number; and classification number. Subscribers can also retrieve cataloging records by combinations of author and title, author and subject heading, and title and subject heading. Other permissible retrieval operations include an alphabetical search for field values that begin with a specified character string, a keyword search for field values that contain a specified character string, and a phrase search, which implies adjacency of multiple search terms. Searches can also be limited by year of publication, a range of publication dates, format (books, serials, films, etc.), or language (English, French, Spanish, German, or Italian).

At the operator's option, search results can be displayed with labeled field values or in the MARC format. The display format can be changed during a cataloging session. When cataloging records are retrieved, authors, titles, subject headings, and other indexed field values appear as hyperlinks. When a hyperlink is selected, ITS.MARC will retrieve other cataloging records that contain the indicated value. Failing to find a cataloging record in one of the ITS.MARC databases, subscribers can access the RLIN database at no additional charge. As a unique feature among the bibliographic utilities discussed in this chapter, an ITS.MARC subscription includes CD-ROM updates of the LC MARC English Language database for fast access to the most frequently retrieved cataloging records.

ITS.MARC cataloging software provides word-processing like capabilities to facilitate editing of bibliographic records. It also supports original cataloging based on workforms (templates) that correspond to the type of material being cataloged. Workforms can be customized to meet special requirements. Cataloging records retrieved can be transferred to a library's local automation system. Catalog card sets and labels can be printed locally.

SUMMARY

Computerization of descriptive cataloging depends on the availability of appropriate bibliographic information (cataloging copy) in machine-readable form. In the late 1960s, the Library of Congress developed the MARC format now known as the USMARC format for the communication of bibliographic information in machine-readable form. The Library of Congress, the nation's principal supplier of cataloging data, has distributed bibliographic records on magnetic tape since that time. The accumulation of such records is known as the LC MARC database. The scope of the MARC program, which was initially limited to English-language monographs, has broadened to include all monographs written in languages that use roman scripts as well as certain non–roman alphabet and ideographic languages and various non-monographic materials regardless of language. Other national libraries and library organizations have established similar MARC formats and distribution programs for machine-readable cataloging records.

MARC formats have been developed for books, serials, and various non-book materials. While MARC tapes that contain machine-readable cataloging records can be purchased from the Library of Congress, most libraries obtain access to MARC data through products and services offered by publishers and other information providers. Computer-generated micropublications, such as MARCFICHE and Books in English, were among the earliest examples of MARC-derivative products. The Library of Congress itself has discontinued the printed *National Union Catalog* in favor of a microfiche version produced from the LC MARC database. Since the mid-1980s, various companies have offered CD-ROM cataloging systems that contain bibliographic data on compact discs, accompanied by software for record retrieval and production of printed card sets and labels. CD-ROM cataloging systems typically include all or part of the LC MARC database, possibly supplemented by additional bibliographic records obtained from other sources, such as the National Library of Medicine, the National Library of Canada, or the British Library. Compared to other cataloging methodologies, CD-ROM systems can prove particularly cost-effective for high-volume retrospective conversion projects. Their suitability for current cataloging depends on their update frequency. CD-ROM databases that are updated monthly or quarterly may not contain full cataloging records for a library's most recently acquired items.

Bibliographic utilities are organizations that maintain large databases of cataloging records that libraries can access on a time-sharing basis. Examples of North American bibliographic utilities include OCLC, RLIN, Impact/ ONLINE CAT, Impact/MARCit, the Interactive Access System, and ITS.MARC. The databases maintained by most bibliographic utilities are essentially online union catalogs that combine descriptive cataloging records with holdings information. All bibliographic utilities acquire cataloging records in machine-readable form from the Library of Congress and other subscription sources. In most cases, their databases also include cataloging records contributed by participating libraries. Using microcomputer workstations, participating libraries can retrieve cataloging copy, modify it to meet local requirements, and order machine-readable bibliographic records or printed card sets. Failing to locate appropriate cataloging copy, libraries can perform original cataloging online.

The bibliographic utilities differ in database size and composition, the number and nature of their subscribers, and the specific cataloging and retrieval capabilities they support. Some utilities store one cataloging record for each edition of an item. Others store duplicate and variant records contributed by participants. Several utilities support vernacular cataloging of works published in non-roman scripts. Some bibliographic utilities have online acquisitions and interlibrary loan subsystems.

Bibliographic utilities principally compete with CD-ROM cataloging systems. Because they are larger and updated more frequently than their CD-ROM counterparts, the databases maintained by bibliographic utilities will presumably satisfy a greater percentage of a given library's copy cataloging requirements, thereby minimizing original cataloging.

6

Integrated
Library Systems

Broadly defined, an integrated library system—variously termed an "integrated online library system" (IOLS) or simply an "integrated system"—is a computer-based information system that uses a single bibliographic database and a set of interrelated application programs to automate multiple library applications. That straightforward definition belies the product group's diversity. As described below, integrated library systems are marketed by dozens of vendors. They may operate on mainframes, minicomputers, or microcomputers. They may be implemented by small libraries or large multilibrary consortia. They may be purchased as preconfigured combinations of hardware and software or as prewritten programs for use with separately purchased computing equipment.

The earliest integrated library systems date from the late 1970s. Prior to that time, library automation was dominated by single-purpose computer systems intended for specific applications, particularly circulation control, which was one of the first library operations to be successfully computerized. During the late 1970s and early 1980s, vendors of circulation control systems began offering online public access catalogs (OPACs) as widely publicized enhancements. The resulting products were often described as library management systems to reflect their expanded functionality, although their OPAC implementations were primitive by today's standards and libraries were slow to adopt them. As late as 1985, for example, only about one-third of libraries that utilized CLSI circulation control systems, then the most widely installed products of their type, had implemented that vendor's public access catalog module. Similarly, Data Research Associates implemented its first integrated system at Cleveland Public Library in 1978, but it made only three additional installations in the next five years. Product availability and customer acceptance increased in the mid-1980s, however. By the end of that decade, there was little interest in single-purpose library automation systems.

Most integrated systems are modular in design. Vendors offer suites of interrelated programs that automate specific library operations. Core functionality is provided by certain application modules that are required in all installations; optional modules, which automate specific operations, can usually be added at any time. A minimal, but fully functional, implementation typically incorporates three application modules: cataloging, online catalog access, and circulation control. Of these, the cataloging module—which supports data entry, database management capabilities, and, in some cases, authority control—is required. Online public catalog access is often the principal motive for implementing an integrated system. Consequently, OPAC modules are widely installed. Circulation control, while not essential, may be inextricably integrated with cataloging and online catalog access as a standard product configuration.

Acquisitions and serials management are popular but usually optional additions to a basic system configuration. They may be implemented during the initial installation of an integrated product or added at a later time. Other application modules, which are selectively available and almost invariably optional, include media booking, a community bulletin board, community information and referral, homebound access, reference databases, Internet access, electronic imaging, full-text retrieval, and electronic mail capabilities. Reserve room capability may be implemented as a separate module or incorporated into circulation control. Some vendors also offer a report generator that supplements the integral output capabilities of the various application modules by producing lists, notices, and other printed documents in a variety of customized formats.

The following discussion surveys important capabilities and features associated with specific integrated system components. Integrated library systems are offered by several dozen vendors. Examples include Ameritech Library Services, Best-Seller Incorporated, Brodart Automation, CARL Corporation, CASPR Library Systems, Comstow Information Services, Contec Data Systems, Data Research Associates, Endeavor Information Systems, EOS International, Ex Libris Limited, Extended Library Access Solutions, Follett Software Company, Fretwell-Downing Informatics, Gaylord Information Systems, Geac Computers, Gores Technology Group, Innovative Interfaces, International Library Systems, MAX-CESS Library Systems, Nichols Advanced Technologies, SIRS Incorporated, SIRSI Corporation, The Library Corporation, Winnebago Software Company, and VTLS. Some of these vendors offer multiple product lines.

In library publications, integrated systems are often divided into two broad groups: (1) minicomputer- and mainframe-based products, which are principally installed in medium-size and larger academic and public libraries, and (2) microcomputer-based products, which are intended for smaller public, community college, school, corporate, and government libraries. That distinction, while once meaningful, is increasingly artificial. As technology narrows the performance differences between traditional categories of computing devices, several vendors of minicomputer-based integrated systems have introduced microcomputer implementations with comparable functionality.

While integrated library systems are available for many types of computers, the newest product configurations are intended for Unix, Windows, or Windows NT installations. Mainframe-based integrated systems, which were popular among large libraries in the 1980s, are now out of favor. Throughout the 1990s, older integrated systems that operated on proprietary minicomputers, such as VAX processors from Digital Equipment Corporation, were steadily replaced by Unix-based products, which offer excellent price/performance characteristics and expandability. At the time of this writing, the newest integrated systems were designed for the Windows NT operating system and client/server implementations in which computing tasks are distributed among a shared computer (a server) and microcomputer-based workstations (the clients). Specific computer configurations aside, integrated systems may be sold as prewritten software packages for implementation on library-supplied computers or as turnkey combinations of preselected computer hardware and prewritten software.

ONLINE CATALOGS

All integrated systems support cataloging as a core application module that permits the creation, updating, and management of a library's bibliographic database. Certain cataloging capabilities are so widely implemented that they provide little basis for product differentiation, although system-specific variations can affect the convenience with which particular tasks are performed. All integrated systems, for example, support MARC records for those types of library materials for which USMARC formats have been developed. Some systems also support other national implementations of the MARC format, such as CANMARC, UKMARC, UNIMARC, or AUSMARC. At least one integrated library system supports the COSATI/CENDI format developed by the U.S. Department of Defense for technical reports and similar documentation. Most integrated systems permit partial MARC records that employ the USMARC format with some fields left blank. Some systems also support non-MARC formats with library-defined fields. Typically MARC and non-MARC records can coexist within a library's database.

All integrated library systems permit key-entry of original cataloging data as well as the transfer of cataloging records from machine-readable sources. Original cataloging is typically facilitated by displayed workforms that correspond to USMARC formats for specific types of library materials. Depending on the system or customer preferences, newly entered cataloging records may update a library's database immediately or at scheduled intervals. Most integrated library systems can import machine-readable cataloging records from MARC-format tapes produced by national libraries, bibliographic utilities, retrospective conversion services, book jobbers, or other sources. Vendors typically provide a list of source tapes that have been successfully loaded into their systems. Microcomputer-based products may transfer machine-readable records from diskettes rather than magnetic tapes. Many integrated systems also do electronic transfer of machine-readable cataloging records from bibliographic utilities, CD-ROM information products, or other sources.

Depending on the system, authority control may be incorporated into the cataloging module or offered as a separately purchased component. In either case, authority control establishes and maintains authorized forms and cross-references for designated field values. As bibliographic records are entered, field values subject to authority control are automatically checked against authorized forms, with new or questionable names and headings being flagged for review. System-specific variations determine the fields to which authority control can be applied. Authors' names, uniform titles, series titles, and subject headings are the most commonly controlled fields. Depending on the system, authority records may be key-entered, generated from existing headings in a library's catalog, or imported in machine-readable form from external sources. Global editing capabilities facilitate the modification of headings. Some integrated library systems permit multiple authority files. Some integrated systems support thesaurus-like cross-reference structures that include broader terms, narrower terms, related terms, and scope notes, in addition to the familiar "see" and "see also" entries.

The Problem of Card Catalogs

As discussed above, the introduction of effective online public access catalog (OPAC) modules in the late 1970s and early 1980s signaled the transition from single-purpose circulation control systems to true integrated library systems that support online retrieval of bibliographic records in addition to mere transaction processing. For many libraries, card catalog replacement is the principal motive for implementing an integrated system.

Librarians have long recognized the many problems associated with the production, maintenance, and use of card catalogs. Writing in the 1940s, Fremont Rider pointed out the substantial amounts of space consumed by the card catalogs of research libraries. Since that time, high construction costs and greatly diminished capital funds for new library buildings have made the efficient use of available floor space an important concern for libraries of all sizes and types. Assuming an average of 20 square feet per card catalog cabinet and its required adjacent aisle and work space, the card catalog for a collection of 100,000 titles will occupy approximately 280 square feet of contiguous floor space, a portion of which might be put to other uses were the catalog converted to a more compact format. At a rate of 10,000 new titles per year, an additional 30 square feet will be required to accommodate annual catalog growth. If the collection is not weeded, the size of the catalog will double in ten years.

In addition to occupying valuable floor space, card catalog cabinets are expensive. A frequently cited 1969 study by R&D Consultants found that a typical sixty-drawer cabinet contained about 43,000 catalog cards when filled to 60 percent of capacity. At the time of this writing, such a cabinet cost several thousand dollars. Assuming an average of six cards per title, the catalog of a library with a monograph collection of 100,000 titles would occupy more than $30,000 worth of cabinets. Assuming a new acquisition rate of 10,000 titles per year, over $6,000 would have to be spent every two years for new cabinets. Additional expenditures and floor space will be required for tables or other furnishings that are customarily provided in the card catalog area.

For most libraries, the labor required to create and maintain card catalogs will prove more costly than the floor space and cabinets that such catalogs occupy. Catalog cards must be printed internally or purchased in preprinted sets.

New cards must be sorted and interfiled, while existing cards must be removed, modified, and refiled to reflect changes in the library's collection. Additional labor is required to create and maintain guide cards, cross-reference cards, and authority files. Of these tasks, only the production of catalog card sets has been directly affected by the automated systems and services described in chapter 5. Computer-produced cards can be ordered from bibliographic utilities, printed locally by CD-ROM cataloging systems, or purchased from book jobbers or other suppliers. These automated systems and services do nothing, however, for other aspects of catalog maintenance. While cards may be printed automatically, they must still be filed manually, a potentially time-consuming task. At six cards per set, for example, the annual acquisition of 10,000 new titles will generate 60,000 catalog cards. At a sustained filing rate of one card per minute, 1,000 hours of labor, or one-half of a person-year, will be required. In many libraries, this expenditure is increased by the additional labor required to check newly filed cards for correct placement before adding them to the catalog. In some cases, the lack of sufficient labor for catalog maintenance results in considerable delays in filing of newly produced bibliographic records. Consequently, some cards never enter the catalog. As an example, libraries that acquire micropublished collections consisting of multiple titles are often unable to allocate the labor required to file the printed catalog cards that may accompany such collections.

Similar substantial costs are incurred to remove previously filed cards as collections are weeded, location information is added to or deleted from union catalogs, or existing file headings are modified to conform to revised cataloging practices. The cost of such heading modifications gained considerable prominence when the Anglo-American Cataloguing Rules were revised. A study by the Library of Congress indicated that full implementation of the provisions of AACR2 would require changes in at least 37 percent of the form of headings then in use by LC, and changes would require modification of at least 49 percent of LC catalog cards. High as they are, such percentages do not reflect the impact of revised rules for corporate authorship that necessitate additional card modifications to reflect changes in the choice of headings. Presumably, comparable modifications are required by other libraries, each modification involving the removal and refiling of the affected cards. As a further source of potential expenditures to those libraries desiring to make their cataloging practices conform to those of the Library of Congress, LC closed its card catalog in favor of a computer-based system in 1981. As several librarians have pointed out, the Library of Congress was previously constrained in changing headings by the inconvenience inherent in having to manually modify its own card catalog. Such constraints no longer apply.

The cost of file maintenance aside, card catalogs offer only limited performance and convenience, both for library users and for libraries themselves. Except where telephone inquiries are accepted, a user must visit a library to consult its card catalog, even though time might potentially be saved if users could determine in advance whether a given item is in the library's holdings. Ideally, an academic library's catalog should be readily accessible to faculty members in individual departments; a technical library's catalog should be available in user work areas; and a public library's catalog might be consulted in schools, stores, and even homes. Unfortunately, the cost of card production, floor space, cabinets, and file maintenance discussed above prevent the replication of all or portions of conventional card catalogs. In multibranch libraries and library systems, the necessity of maintaining a union catalog in a system headquarters or other centralized location is especially constrained. In such cases, library users are denied convenient access to information about system-wide holdings. In addition, the time and cost of resource sharing transactions may be significantly increased by the need to route all interlibrary loan requests to the central union catalog where library locations can alone be determined. If the union catalog were conveniently accessible to individual libraries, the holding libraries for desired items could be determined and contacted directly by the borrowing institutions.

Additional limitations make card catalogs inconvenient for library users. As an example, individual cards cannot be removed from the catalog for photo-copying. Instead, the user must take notes, usually while standing at a table. Although many libraries consider the card catalog an important local biblio-graphic resource rather than a mere location device, they rarely provide a com-fortable work setting for its prolonged use. Critics of card catalogs further point out the limited number of access points they provide; they note, for example, that users cannot retrieve books by title keywords or conveniently perform searches that involve multiple headings. While there is no intellectual impedi-ment to the production of additional catalog cards for title keywords or other retrieval parameters, such a practice would significantly increase the cost of card production and file maintenance. It would also increase the size of the cat-alog, compounding the space consumption problems and cabinet costs noted above. Expense aside, the logical coordination of multiple headings cannot be conveniently implemented with card-form catalogs.

Among their other problems, card catalogs are vulnerable to intentional or inadvertent damage or destruction. Individual cards are subject to wear and tear in daily use, and the entire card catalog or substantial portions of it can be destroyed by fire or vandalism. Because the card catalog is a unique and vital operating record, which if damaged or destroyed would seriously impair a li-brary's ability to function, a protective microfilming program is typically advis-able to create a backup copy for offsite storage. In addition, older catalog cards that are in poor condition must be periodically replaced, thus further increasing maintenance costs.

Retrospective Conversion

Presumably, some or all of the problems discussed in the preceding section can be minimized or eliminated by replacing card catalogs with online catalogs. The implementation of such catalogs requires, however, the conversion of a li-brary's cataloging records to machine-readable, computer-processible form. Such conversion can be accomplished relatively easily for cataloging records pertaining to a library's recent or ongoing acquisitions. As discussed in chapter 5, libraries that obtained cataloging services from bibliographic utilities can order archival magnetic tapes that contain machine-readable records for the items they have cataloged since becoming utility customers. Depending on the particular bibliographic utility and library requirements, such archival tapes may be available on a monthly, weekly, or more frequent basis. Alternatively, some bibliographic utilities support electronic transfer (downloading) of cataloging records, either individually or in batches, into a library's local automation system. Libraries that utilize CD-ROM cataloging products also create machine-readable versions of cataloging records. As another source of machine-readable cataloging data, libraries that purchase books and other materials from jobbers or other suppliers can often obtain magnetic tapes containing computer-processible cataloging records that reflect their acquisitions for specified time periods. Some book jobbers maintain machine-readable databases of LC MARC records supplemented by local cataloging that can be used for this purpose.

Thus, many libraries can readily obtain machine-readable versions of records acquired and cataloged since the late 1960s, when the MARC program began. Retrospective conversion of a library's catalog—that is, the conversion of older catalog records to machine-readable form—is a more complicated undertaking, however. Such records can, of course, be converted by direct data entry—that is, by typing them at a computer terminal or other input devices in the manner discussed in chapter 1—but that is a conversion technique of last resort. The preferred retrospective conversion method involves the use of abbreviated keystroking to search for and obtain machine-readable copies of cataloging records from existing resource databases. While a few libraries have purchased or otherwise acquired the machine-readable catalogs of comparable libraries against which their own holdings can be matched, the databases offered by bibliographic utilities and CD-ROM cataloging systems are the most important and widely used sources of cataloging copy for retrospective conversion. Although the LC MARC resource records maintained by all bibliographic utilities and CD-ROM cataloging products primarily pertain to post-1968 imprints, the LC MARC database does include cataloging records for some earlier titles. As previously discussed, MARC-format records for selected pre-1968 imprints were created by the RECON project and COMARC program. In addition, occasional pre-1968 imprints have been acquired and cataloged by the Library of Congress since the inception of the MARC program. More importantly, cataloging contributed by subscribers of bibliographic utilities includes many records for older imprints entered by libraries that either have recently acquired and cataloged those items or had previously contributed them as part of their own retrospective conversion projects. Certain CD-ROM cataloging systems also contain cataloging records for older imprints, but they cannot match the huge resource databases offered by the largest bibliographic utilities. For retrospective conversion, as with current cataloging, a large resource database increases the likelihood of retrieving suitable cataloging copy for a given item.

The use of bibliographic utilities and CD-ROM cataloging systems for retrospective conversion involves straightforward work steps. A bibliographic database is searched to obtain cataloging copy for each record in a library's shelflist or card catalog. To simplify input and speed response, the resource database is typically searched by Library of Congress Card Number (LCCN) or another unique identifier. Many library shelflists contain LC printed cards that include the LCCN. If an appropriate bibliographic record is retrieved, it can be edited to conform to local cataloging practice, as reflected in the shelflist card. In the case of certain bibliographic utilities, the library's holding symbol is added to the cataloging record. Records processed in this manner can be ordered from a bibliographic utility in machine-readable form on magnetic tape or transferred electronically into a library's local automation system. With CD-ROM cataloging support products, the records are transferred from the CD-ROM database to a hard disk, from which they may later be copied onto tapes or diskettes.

The retrieval and modification of existing resource records, while still time-consuming and labor-intensive for large retrospective conversion projects, will prove faster and less expensive than full keystroking of the information content of a library's shelflist. Use of a resource database to retrieve cataloging copy produces a MARC-format record with the least effort. Full keystroking of original cataloging records remains necessary, however, for items that are not found in databases provided by bibliographic utilities or CD-ROM cataloging systems. In such cases, a library uses cataloging copy from its shelflist or card catalog as the basis for input. Original cataloging records can be entered directly into an integrated library system's database, using the cataloging module described above. Alternatively, a bibliographic utility or CD-ROM cataloging system can be used for original cataloging and the resulting records transferred to the library's local system through electronic transfer, magnetic tape, or diskettes.

Several bibliographic utilities offer products that simplify retrospective conversion through offline preparation of information about the records to be converted. The prepared information is then processed against the utility's database in the batch mode. With OCLC's Cataloging Micro Enhancer program, for example, a library prepares diskettes that contain search keys for cataloging records to be retrieved from the WorldCat database. The diskettes also include call numbers, holdings information, and other local cataloging information from the library's shelflist. The diskettes are shipped to OCLC, which retrieves the indicated MARC-format cataloging records from WorldCat, enters the library-supplied local information, and transfers the results to magnetic tapes or diskettes for delivery to the library. RLIN's Marcadia service offers similar capabilities. A library creates brief search records that contain minimal bibliographic information plus call numbers and other holdings data for the titles to be converted. The search records are submitted to the Marcadia service on computer media or via the Internet for matching against the RLIN database. Search records that match entries in the RLIN database generate new cataloging records based on the information provided.

As an alternative to in-house conversion projects, several bibliographic utilities and other companies offer fee-based retrospective conversion services that draw on their own resource databases and cataloging expertise. As an example, OCLC RETROCON is a customized conversion service in which OCLC staff members, working under the supervision of experienced catalogers, convert a library's shelflist to full MARC records by editing existing records retrieved from the WorldCat database and performing original cataloging, as required, to library specifications. OCLC staff members also enter the library's holding symbol for converted items. Similarly, the OCLC provides additional database preparation and authority control capabilities for retrospective conversion and other applications. In addition to converting a library's shelflist to machine-readable form, OCLC will compare, validate, and update authority headings in bibliographic records by matching them against specified authority files. It will upgrade unauthorized headings to authorized forms, expand abbreviations, and correct obsolete subdivisions. Other capabilities include preparation of smart barcodes for circulation control, manual review of bibliographic records, and enrichment of cataloging records with table of contents information. As described above, libraries typically supply lists of LC Card Numbers or other identifiers for the records to be converted. Alternatively, a library may send its entire shelflist, or a copy thereof, to the retrospective conversion service. In either case, the conversion company typically furnishes MARC-format cataloging records on magnetic tape for input to mainframe or minicomputer-based integrated systems or on diskettes for input to microcomputer-based systems. In the latter case, the cataloging records are typically provided in the MicroLIF format, which is accepted by most microcomputer-based integrated library systems.

While bibliographic utilities, CD-ROM cataloging systems, or other sources of machine-readable data can facilitate retrospective conversion, a conversion project may prove too expensive or time-consuming for a given library. Consequently, some libraries that have implemented online catalogs have decided to "close" or "freeze" their card catalogs rather than convert existing records to machine-readable form. In this context, closing means that no additional records will be entered into the card catalog after some predetermined date. In effect, a static, retrospective card catalog will coexist with a growing online catalog. As time passes, the online catalog will represent an increasingly large percentage of the library's collection. Further, it will contain cataloging records for newly acquired titles, which are presumably of great interest to library users. In some cases, closing the card catalog is a temporary expedient that permits the implementation of an online catalog within an available budget. The library may intend to convert all or part of the closed catalog at some future time when funding is available.

In actual practice, the complexity of library activities and bibliographic records rarely permits the complete closing of a card catalog. The most common closing strategies rely on cataloging date or imprint date. Each approach is limited in several important respects. In the former instance, all records for items cataloged after a predetermined date are entered into a library's online catalog, regardless of the imprint date of the item. While this is probably the simplest closing strategy from the cataloging department's standpoint, open entries for serials, series, and multivolume sets must be removed and converted before the card catalog can be closed. As a source of potential confusion, users seeking older imprints must consult both the retrospective and current catalogs, as must the library staff when using the catalog for bibliographic verification and reference.

A closing strategy based on an item's imprint date may be more convenient for the library user, but it does not permit a complete closing of the card catalog, since older imprints may be acquired and cataloged in the future. Records for such items must be added to the card catalog. If different practices for choice and form of headings are applied to the old and new catalogs, catalogers must be trained in both sets of rules. A closing strategy based on imprint date does, however, permit continued maintenance of open entries in the card catalog. As an additional problem for research libraries and some special collections, neither of these closing strategies addresses the problem of cataloging records in non-roman languages. While some integrated library systems can accommodate vernacular records in Cyrillic, Hebrew, Arabic, and other non-roman alphabets, most cannot. Unless transliteration is acceptable, the card catalog must remain open for such records, as well as for those containing the ideographic symbols used in the Chinese, Japanese, and Korean languages.

Even when a card catalog is completely closed, a library must continue to maintain it. Cards will remain subject to wear and tear, which necessitates some replacement activity. Similarly, some heading changes will be required to maintain compatibility with a library's online catalog. If different rules for the choice and form of headings apply to each catalog, some cross-references will be required.

OPAC Characteristics

Broadly defined, an online public access catalog is an organized, machine-readable collection of bibliographic records that represents a library's holdings. The records are stored on hard drives or other direct-access computer storage media for convenient retrieval by library users working at interactive terminals or appropriately configured microcomputers. As its name suggests, an OPAC has characteristics and capabilities that are designed for library users as opposed to library staff members, although librarians will use it as well. When compared to card catalogs, online catalogs offer a number of advantages. Software permitting, online catalogs permit information retrieval operations that are not possible with card catalogs; as previously discussed, practical considerations prevent the expansion of a card catalog's access points to include such additional parameters as keywords in titles, series, or subject headings. Online catalogs can retrieve records that contain specified combinations of retrieval parameters. Assuming appropriate communication arrangements, an OPAC can be accessed from any location by authorized persons equipped with compatible terminals. Thus, a scientist or engineer working in a field office can consult the catalog of a technical library implemented at a headquarters location. Similarly, faculty members can access the online catalog of an academic library to determine the availability of needed research materials. High school students working on term papers can use home computers to search public library catalogs to identify relevant books. Further, the labor-intensive file maintenance routines associated with card catalogs are eliminated. If desired, online catalogs can be updated in real time, with records being added or removed as items are cataloged or weeded. Typically, however, changes to the catalog are made in the batch mode on a daily or other periodic basis. Because catalog records are stored on hard drives, they can be conveniently backed up on magnetic tape, which can be stored offsite for vital records protection.

Online catalogs can be implemented in several ways. Libraries that subscribe to certain bibliographic utilities, for example, already have a portion of their catalog records accessible online. As discussed in chapter 5, several bibliographic utilities store duplicate and variant cataloging records contributed by participants. Such records accurately represent a given library's holdings, including local call numbers. Increasingly, bibliographic utilities offer powerful information retrieval capabilities that support keyword searching and logical coordination of search parameters, as well as conventional author, title, and subject searches. It is consequently conceivable that a given library could use a bibliographic utility's database as its online catalog. Similarly, some online information services discussed in chapter 7 offer "private file" capabilities that allow customers to establish their own bibliographic or other data files for access through the same retrieval software that is used to access publicly available data files. Such private files can contain a library's online catalog.

While interesting, these implementation options are limited in several important respects. An online catalog maintained by a bibliographic utility would be limited to those records that a given library had cataloged with the utility. Unless a retrospective conversion project is undertaken, a card catalog must still be maintained for older records not in machine-readable form. The wide-area networking arrangements required to connect a library's OPAC terminals to a remote bibliographic utility or online information service can prove costly to implement, and a library must pay online charges or other fees to search its own catalog. Library users must be trained in the search procedures employed by the bibliographic utility or online information service. While some utilities and online services feature graphical user interfaces, others employ conventional retrieval procedures that require memorization of commands. Finally, libraries that rely on bibliographic utilities or online information services for OPAC implementations will relinquish direct control over system priorities and the management of downtime and response time.

For most libraries, an online catalog implemented on a local computer is a more practical approach. During the 1970s and 1980s, some libraries implemented online catalogs based on custom-developed software. Examples include the Library Computer System (LCS) at Ohio State University, the MELVYL system at the University of California, the LIAS system at Pennsylvania State University, the Catalog Access System at Mankato State University, the LSCAN system at the Dallas Public Library, the SULIRS system at Syracuse University, the Phoenix system at the University of New Brunswick, and the Dartmouth Online Catalog at Dartmouth College. While some of these systems remain in use, customized software development requires a substantial investment of resources. As discussed in chapter 2, it is rarely the preferred approach to computer implementations. It is possible to use a prewritten database management program to implement an online catalog or other bibliographic database—and several programs, such as INMAGIC from Inmagic Incorporated and the STAR product line from Cuadra Associates, have been developed for that purpose—but most libraries will be better served by an integrated system that includes an OPAC module among its functional components. The OPAC modules of integrated library systems have improved steadily and significantly over the past decade. The best integrated systems support a versatile and flexible repertoire of catalog access capabilities that can address users' information retrieval requirements in many types of libraries.

The sizable body of library literature dealing with online public access catalogs differentiates command-driven from menu-oriented systems. In command-driven implementations, a user enters a search string that specifies the field to be searched followed by a specific value to be matched in that field. Often, mnemonic abbreviations—such as "A=," "T=," and "S="—are used for author, title, and subject fields. While some command-driven systems provide excellent instruction screens with concise directions that enable new users to begin searching quickly, others require formal initial training for effective utilization. Menu-driven systems are consequently preferred for inexperienced or occasional users.

Most OPAC modules are menu-driven, although a command-driven mode may also be provided for experienced users or library staff members. Menu-driven interfaces are essential for institutions such as public libraries that serve diverse clienteles and have limited opportunities to train their user populations. Command-mode searching will appeal most strongly to academic or special libraries, where faculty members, graduate students, scientists, or other frequent users with complex retrieval requirements can be trained in advanced search techniques. Command-mode searching is also potentially useful for reference librarians, enabling them to initiate retrieval operations that are cumbersome or impossible to perform with menu-based searching.

Designed for novice users, menu-driven OPAC modules are characteristically straightforward in concept and operation. Search options, identified by abbreviations or numbers, are typically listed in introductory screens for operator selection. Brief instructions explain search procedures and indicate the proper syntax for search statements. More detailed information is presented in help screens that may be invoked by function keys. While vendors supply the initial text of help screens, libraries can often edit their contents to incorporate local information.

Most minicomputer- and mainframe-based integrated systems support conventional character-based video terminals as OPAC workstations. In microcomputer systems and client/server implementations, however, OPAC workstations are Windows-based microcomputers or, less commonly, Macintosh microcomputers. Such systems rely on pulldown menus, dialog boxes, mouse operations, and other graphical user interface components to simplify the entry of search commands and formatting of retrieved information. Several vendors have implemented special OPAC interfaces for children. One popular example, the Kid's Catalog, was developed by CARL Corporation in collaboration with the Denver Public Library. Icons that represent broad topical areas, subject headings, or names of popular authors simplify searches for children with limited typing skills. It also compensates for failed searches due to typing errors, misspellings, inaccurate punctuation, or improper syntax.

As a recent development stimulated by the Internet's immense popularity, some integrated library systems support OPAC searches by microcomputers equipped with popular Web browsers, such as Netscape Navigator or Microsoft Internet Explorer. Some vendors also provide Web server components that make a library's catalog accessible to remote users through the World Wide

Web. Since the mid-1990s, hundreds of library catalogs have been publicly available, either through the World Wide Web or by using the Internet's telnet capability. Alternatively, the Web access capability might be used to provide access to a library catalog in a corporate or government intranet installation.

Interface characteristics aside, online public access catalogs employ indexes to retrieve bibliographic records. With all integrated systems, the OPAC modules permit searches by author, title, and subject, thereby replicating the traditional retrieval functionality of card catalogs. Typically, a user specifies a field to be searched and a name, subject heading, or other value to be matched. Other retrieval capabilities vary from system to system. Classification number indexes are essential if libraries are to replace their shelflists with computerized records. Many systems support retrieval by one or more unique record identifiers, such as a system control number, Library of Congress Card Number (LCCN), or International Standard Book Number (ISBN), but such capabilities are more appropriate for library staff members than for library users. Other possible search parameters include publisher, publication date, country of publication, language of publication, and media type. With some integrated systems, a previously entered search statement can be qualified by these parameters.

For maximum flexibility, some integrated systems allow any library-designated field within bibliographic records to be indexed for retrieval purposes. In other cases, indexed fields are predetermined by the system's vendor, but the list is often sufficiently broad to satisfy diverse library requirements. Root-word searching, relational expressions in search statements, and Boolean operations for logical coordination of multiple search terms are commonplace. Some integrated systems permit keyword searching of designated fields, particularly corporate and conference names, titles, series, and subject headings. An "anyword" capability will search all indexed fields for a specified value. Several integrated library systems support proximity commands, wildcard characters, and other capabilities commonly associated with full-text retrieval systems. Such capabilities are most relevant for bibliographic records that contain abstracts or other long text segments. They are difficult for uninstructed searchers to use effectively. In consortia or other multilibrary installations, OPAC searches can often be limited to the collection of a specific library, usually the one in which the searcher is located. Some integrated systems allow a library to define a portion of its holdings, such as a special collections catalog, that can be searched separately.

If only one bibliographic record satisfies a retrieval specification, it is usually displayed immediately and completely. Where other search results are obtained, responses vary. If multiple records are retrieved by a given search, most OPAC modules provide a count of the number of retrieved items, followed by a scrollable display of brief bibliographic records that include some combination of author, title, publication date, and call number. The searcher can then request a more detailed display for all or selected items.

Full bibliographic records are usually displayed with field labels that clearly identify specific data elements. With some integrated systems, display formats are predetermined for specific types of library materials; in other cases, a library can specify the fields to be included in brief and full record displays. The inclusion of holdings information, such as the locations of copies and their circulation status, in retrieved records is an essential attribute of integrated library systems. Such information is often contained in continuation screens that can be displayed at the searcher's option. Some integrated library systems can display full MARC records with tags and subfield codes, but that format is more appropriate for technical processing operations than for public catalog access.

When no bibliographic records are retrieved by a given search, most OPAC modules display a scrollable, alphabetized list of field values that most closely match the search term. If authority control is implemented, cross-references are displayed for invalid or related headings. In some cases, the referenced heading is automatically substituted for an invalid term. In the absence of a cross-reference, some systems will automatically substitute the closest matching name or word for a search term that fails to retrieve bibliographic records, the assumption being that a typographical error or misspelling led to the retrieval failure.

To expand their functionality, integrated library systems increasingly incorporate external information resources into OPAC searches. Reference databases, obtained on magnetic tapes from information publishers, can be locally mounted and listed as OPAC menu items for operator selection. Such databases will be discussed in chapter 7. Some vendors of integrated library systems also provide interfaces to CD-ROM information products, online information services, and Internet sites. Some integrated systems also support local mounting of library-produced databases. As noted above, an information and referral module is offered as an optional application component by some integrated system vendors. It gives OPAC users access to information about community groups and local events. Depending on the system, community information can be retrieved by the name of the sponsoring organization, the title or date of the event, and keywords.

Since the mid-1980s, integrated systems have provided access to the catalogs of other libraries. The NISO Z39.50 standard is widely supported for that purpose. It defines an interface that permits communication between the compliant computer systems of different vendors. It allows an OPAC terminal of one integrated system to search an external computer system using the retrieval commands and operating procedures associated with the terminal's host system. The Z39.50 standard is based on client/server technology. The integrated system to be searched must be equipped with Z39.50 server software, while the integrated system at which searching originates must be equipped with Z39.50 client software. Z39.50-compatibility is not limited to integrated library systems. It has also been implemented by online information services, CD-ROM information products, and Internet sites.

CIRCULATION CONTROL

With the exception of archives, manuscript libraries, rare book collections, and other special repositories, the circulation of books and other materials is an important part of a library's mission. People who visit a public, academic, school, corporate, or government library expect to be able to borrow materials for predetermined periods of time for use in their homes or offices—assuming, of course, that they qualify as authorized borrowers. The principal purpose of circulation control is to maintain records about the withdrawal of specific books or other library materials. Circulation records protect a library's investment in its collections by fixing the responsibility and date for the return of borrowed items. In addition, circulation records contain information about the use of library materials, which, when extracted and properly analyzed, constitutes a valuable aid to collection development, resource allocation, and decision making.

In manual implementations, a library's master circulation file usually consists of paper cards or slips, each of which contains information about a particular circulation transaction. The specific information content of these records may include a brief description of the item (author, title, and call number, for example), its due date, and the borrower's identification number, name, and perhaps address. This master file reflects the library materials in circulation at any given moment. It is typically arranged in a manner that enables a library to obtain information about the status of a given item. In many public libraries, for example, circulation cards are filed by due date for simplified identification and reprocessing of overdue items. In academic and special libraries, where it is often necessary to recall a given circulating item before the expiration of its loan period, the card file may be arranged by call number or author/title. In such situations, it can be difficult to identify overdue items.

In addition to a master circulation file, most libraries also maintain records about authorized borrowers. Such records, which may be maintained on cards or sheet-form rosters, usually include some combination of the following information for each borrower: an identification number, name, address, telephone number, registration and card expiration dates, privilege category (such as adult or juvenile in a public library, faculty or student in an academic library), and the name of the issuing branch or library (in multibranch or multilibrary systems). Additional files may be created to address the special circulation requirements. Some libraries, for example, maintain lists of delinquent borrowers or of circulating items to be held for specified borrowers on their return. Likewise, libraries may maintain circulation cards for returned items in a historical transaction file that is used for statistical analysis. Many scientific, technical, and business libraries maintain profiles of borrowers' interests that can be matched against newly acquired items. This approach to library service, sometimes described as the selective dissemination of information (SDI), is often considered a facet of reference service, but it can also be viewed as a form of anticipatory circulation.

Since the 1930s, libraries have sought, and more or less successfully applied, automated alternatives to the manual circulation control methodologies described above. The following discussion examines the transaction processing and recordkeeping problems inherent in circulation control and surveys the characteristics and capabilities of circulation control modules included with integrated library systems.

Problems of Circulation Control

Library interest in computerized circulation is, in large part, based on a long-standing recognition of certain problems inherent in manual circulation systems. Specifically, the recordkeeping operations associated with manual circulation control procedures are characteristically labor-intensive. They involve such time-consuming work routines as filing single- or multicopy book cards, checking card files to determine the circulation status of specific items, identifying overdue items with the subsequent preparation of borrower notices, and calculating fines and other charges for overdue or lost materials. Assuming, for example, an average of just one minute of work time associated with filing, removal, and other handling of each card in a master circulation file, a library with an annual circulation of 200,000 items must spend about 3,500 hours on file maintenance each year. At a labor rate of just $8 per hour, the annual cost of file maintenance will approach $28,000. In many public and academic libraries, this required labor commitment is increased by a high volume of circulation activity, long hours of service, and, in the case of multibranch library systems, multiple service points.

As a further complication, most circulation control operations are clerical rather than professional in nature. Their routine character contributes to errors in filing and related recordkeeping tasks, as well as to low employee motivation and high staff turnover, with its associated retraining costs. Academic libraries, for example, often employ students as part-time circulation clerks, paying them lower hourly wages than would be required for full-time clerical personnel. Such students rarely find the job sufficiently challenging to maintain their interest. As a consequence, they may make errors or require considerable supervision, which, in turn, increases total system costs.

Errors and staff turnover aside, the scope of manual circulation systems is necessarily limited to activities directly related to the charging and discharging of library materials. In most cases, accurate circulation statistics—which are essential to the informed management of collection development activities and appropriate expenditure of limited acquisitions budgets—are very difficult or impossible to derive. Properly prepared and presented, circulation statistics can assist bibliographers and other librarians in determining when additional copies of a given item are required and in identifying portions of a library's collection that are infrequently utilized and may consequently warrant a reevaluation of prevailing selection policies. Given the high prices libraries must pay for books and other materials, the ability to avoid inappropriate purchases is of obvious importance.

As a further constraint, there is typically little or no relationship between a manual circulation system's card or paper files and a library's catalog or other records that contain much of the same bibliographic information. Thus, a user who consults a library's catalog for the call number of a specified book cannot immediately determine the item's circulation status. Finally, from the service standpoint, manual circulation systems place much of the workload on the borrower, who must fill out charge slips or cards for each item to be circulated. This inconvenience, combined with long waiting times attributable to the slowness of manual check-out procedures, can lead to user dissatisfaction. These problems are not unique to library circulation control. They are characteristic of many business applications that involve the maintenance and control of large document files. Such applications are widely encountered in insurance companies, hospitals and medical clinics, personnel departments within corporations and government agencies, registrars' offices in colleges and universities, law offices, police departments, and other paper-intensive work environments. Record tracking systems developed for business applications are often based on library circulation control models.

Although computerized circulation systems are the subject of this discussion, there are other alternatives to manual circulation control. Through the mid-1970s, for example, some small and medium-size public libraries utilized photographic charging systems in which a book identification card, borrower identification card, and date information pertaining to successive circulation transactions were recorded on microfilm using a specially designed camera. While such precomputer approaches to circulation control remain in use in a few libraries, they are outdated in concept and offer limited functionality. More radical alternatives to manual circulation control have been suggested but, for the most part, dismissed. Few library administrators would, for example, abandon circulation control in favor of an honor system in which borrowers assume personal responsibility for returning books after a specified period of time. Even if most borrowed materials were returned on time or eventually, such a circulation method leaves a library with little or no information about the status and use of its collection at any point in time. Still, the idea of abolishing circulation control cannot be dismissed completely. Some libraries apply it selectively to library materials, such as paperback fiction titles, that are not permanent collection resources or that cost more to circulate than to replace.

A somewhat less radical, but still striking, departure from conventional circulation control concepts involves the substitution of duplication for circulation. In a paper delivered at the 1962 convention of the National Microfilm Association, Laurence Heilprin first outlined the concept of a duplicating library in which an inviolate collection of books and other materials, in full-size or microform, would be copied on demand and distributed to library users as an alternative to circulation. Recipients could keep the copies or dispose of them. The cost of duplication would presumably be defrayed by the elimination of circulation-related expenses associated with recordkeeping, the recall of overdue materials, and the replacement of nonreturned items. In addition, since they are not removed from the library, materials are continuously available and multiple-copy purchases can consequently be minimized.

Unfortunately, the relative economics of a wholesale conversion from circulation to duplication have never been fully explored. In addition, copyright restrictions may prevent copying of certain materials or significantly increase the cost and complexity of duplication. Although it is probably not a viable alternative for all library applications, the duplicating concept has been selectively adopted for certain types of library materials. It is, for example, the prevailing method of providing journal articles through interlibrary loan. Similarly, some libraries employ duplication as an alternative to the circulation of microfiche. Rather than circulating the library's master fiche, the requester is given a copy for personal use and disposition. Desktop microfiche duplicators are available for this purpose. In the case of microfiche report collections produced by the Educational Research Information Center (ERIC), National Technical Information Service (NTIS), and other government agencies, there is no copyright impediment to such duplication. Copyright restrictions may apply, however, to the duplication of microforms purchased from commercial micropublishers.

In the broadest sense, the widespread availability of coin-operated copiers in libraries probably constitutes the most common and effective implementation of duplication as an alternative to circulation. A would-be borrower who is not interested in an entire book or serial publication can copy relevant sections. The user, of course, pays for the copies made, but in many libraries the total cost of copier operation is not recovered through such charges. Presumably, those libraries that subsidize coin-vend or other copying operations are doing so to encourage their use and to achieve a corresponding reduction in circulation-related costs.

Evolution of Computerized Circulation Systems

Although the concepts and methods described above have been successfully applied in certain library situations, only computerized systems offer broadly applicable solutions to the problems of manual circulation control. Perhaps more than any other library activity, the historical development of automated circulation control has reflected changes in the state of the art in data processing technology. As early as the 1930s and extending into the 1960s, a number of libraries used punched cards in combination with sorters, collators, and other unit record equipment as an alternative to manual recordkeeping. Tabulating cards punched with information about books, borrowers, and due dates could be sorted, for example, to select overdue items or to identify all books on loan to a given person.

Such precomputer data processing systems were typically based on inventory control models used in business. With the introduction of computers for business applications in the mid-1960s, a number of libraries developed computerized circulation control systems based on batch processing techniques. Typically, such systems were implemented on a computer located in a data processing center operated by a university, municipality, or corporation with which the library was affiliated. Information about circulation transactions was recorded on punched cards or magnetic tape for processing against a master circulation file at predetermined intervals. Following processing, a list of circulating items arranged by call number or title, with due dates, was printed for reference purposes. Periodically, the master circulation file and borrower information files were further processed to identify overdue items, produce recall notices, derive circulation statistics, or print special lists. While they eliminated the maintenance of paper files and the time-consuming preparation of overdue and recall notices, such batch processing systems were limited in several important respects. They could not provide accurate information about items in circulation at a given moment; some information in printed lists was necessarily invalidated by circulation transactions occurring between processing intervals. Batch processing systems could not effectively identify items to be held for specific library users when returned from circulation, and they provided no method of blocking circulation transactions for delinquent borrowers or under other exceptional conditions.

By the mid-1970s, computer manufacturers and information specialists had begun to concentrate on the development of online, real-time systems. Following their lead, several libraries implemented real-time circulation control systems that processed check-out and check-in transactions as they occurred. Widely publicized examples included the Library Computer System (LCS), which was developed at Ohio State University and subsequently replicated at the University of Illinois and State University of New York at Albany; the Bell Laboratories Library Real-Time Loan (BELLREL) system; and a self-service charge-out system developed by Northwestern University. Addressing the limitations of their batch processing predecessors, these real-time systems established the pattern for all subsequent developments in computerized circulation control. Because master circulation files are updated immediately rather than at predetermined intervals, real-time systems accurately reflect the current status of a library's circulating collection. Computer-processible files of items on hold and delinquent borrowers can be automatically checked as items are charged out or returned. Online terminals are used to inquire about the circulation status of given items. Most printed listings are consequently eliminated, although overdue notices, recall notices, and other documents must still be produced in the batch mode.

Through the mid-1970s, computerized circulation control systems, whether operating in the batch or real-time mode, were developed and implemented on a customized basis for a particular library. Following a detailed systems analysis, equipment was selected and programs written to meet the specific needs of a given application. As might be expected, the most interesting and innovative systems were developed by large academic, public, and corporate libraries that had access to institutional computing resources and technical expertise. For the typical medium- to large-size library, however, the computing facilities required to develop a customized circulation control system were too often unavailable. In most organizations, access to computing resources is allocated according to preestablished priorities, and the library's requirements are sometimes given inadequate consideration.

Even when a library is able to obtain appropriate computer hardware, problems of software development can prove significant. In computer applications generally, it is the absence of suitable software that constitutes the most formidable obstacle to automation. Comparatively few libraries have resident systems analysts or programmers. Institutional computing centers allocate software support personnel in much the same manner as hardware resources. In many cases, there is a long waiting list to consult a systems analyst or programmer/analyst, and, once begun, customized software development is a slow, labor-intensive, and error-prone activity.

Prewritten circulation control software addresses this problem. It recognizes that certain aspects of circulation control are performed in more or less the same way, regardless of their specific library setting. As its principal advantages, prewritten circulation control programs can be implemented far more quickly and at lower cost than customized installations. While custom-developed software is funded by a single library, the development cost of prewritten programs is shared by multiple customers. Speed of implementation is especially important in applications where automation of the circulation activity will yield a cost reduction or improved service when compared to the manual system it is designed to replace. Prewritten circulation control software minimizes or eliminates requirements for local computer expertise. Libraries acquiring such products do not need to hire programming staff or take programming courses. In fact, customer programming is usually prohibited by most vendors. Because the system design is predetermined, user training is limited to operational considerations.

The earliest examples of prewritten circulation control programs, introduced in the 1970s, were single-purpose products designed specifically and exclusively for circulation control. Initially, they were marketed as turnkey systems—that is, preconfigured combinations of computer hardware and prewritten programs sold as a package. In most cases, such turnkey circulation control systems included minicomputers that were installed in and operated by the library itself; in the 1970s, mainframe computers were far too expensive for most libraries, and useful microcomputers did not become available until the early 1980s. As an alternative to turnkey configurations, some vendors offered prewritten circulation control software for implementation on separately purchased minicomputers, including equipment already owned by a library or its parent institution.

During the 1980s, as previously noted, single-purpose circulation control programs were supplanted by integrated library systems, in which circulation control is one component or application module. Along with cataloging and online public catalog access, it is typically a core module rather than an optional component. The circulation modules of integrated library systems effectively automate a variety of tasks, including check-out, check-in, and renewal of library materials; placement of holds; fines calculation, collection, and record-keeping; creation, maintenance, and retrieval of borrower records; and printing of reports and notices. These capabilities are described in the following section.

Circulation Control Capabilities

All computerized circulation control systems maintain machine-readable information pertaining to a library's circulating collection and its borrowers. With integrated systems, holdings information about individual copies of specific titles is linked to bibliographic records in a library's catalog. Such holdings information is essential to the circulation activity, since a library circulates copies rather than bibliographic entities. Subject to product- and application-specific variations, typical holdings information includes some combination of a barcode number or other item identifier, a copy number, a loan period category, a local call number, the item's normal location or branch, a temporary location or branch, the media type, the original price, the replacement cost, the item's circulation status (on shelf, checked out, or other), the borrower's identifier and due date for items in circulation, and the date of last circulation activity.

A borrower file contains one machine-readable record for each registered library user. In public libraries that serve medium-size and larger cities, this file may contain 100,000 or more records. Academic, school, and special libraries, by contrast, usually have smaller clienteles. File size aside, common data fields include the borrower's name, address, and telephone number; the date registered, expiration date, and date of last circulation activity; the borrower's privilege category (such as faculty member, graduate student, or undergraduate student in an academic library, adult or juvenile in a public library); the borrower's card number, social security number, or other identifier; the name of the issuing library or branch in a multilibrary system; an indication of delinquency status with a reason for delinquency; a count of the number of items in circulation; and a message field for several lines of text. Several circulation control modules maintain a count of the number of lost books, claimed returns, and similar problems associated with individual borrowers. Some programs also provide optional data fields for personal and demographic information—such as age group, occupation, and primary language—that supports statistical analysis of circulation activity for particular types of library users. Additional data fields may be provided for special situations. Academic libraries, for example, typically include students' campus and home addresses in borrower records. Similarly, corporate and government libraries may record both office and home addresses and telephone numbers. School libraries may require data fields for a student's homeroom and parent's name.

Regardless of content, the creation of borrower files is a potentially time-consuming and costly activity. Key-entry of borrower information, a method of last resort, is often necessary. As an alternative, some integrated systems can import machine-readable borrower records from a previously implemented circulation control system, registrars' files, personnel databases, or other sources. Although special programs must be written to convert the transferred records to a format required by the circulation control module, the cost of required programming usually compares favorably with the cost of key-entry labor. In most cases, vendors of integrated library systems will develop such conversion programs for a negotiated fee. Rather than loading borrower records from external sources, some public libraries reregister all their borrowers at the time an integrated system is installed, upgraded, or replaced, thereby purging their files of obsolete records.

All integrated systems support three broad types of circulation control operations: charging and discharging of library materials, online file inquiries, and offline printing of reports and notices. With the earliest circulation control programs, libraries were forced to accept predetermined loan periods, borrower categories, and other operating conditions. Newer products, however, are much more flexible. Drawing on three decades of library experience with computer-based circulation management, the circulation control modules supported by integrated systems are very well developed and highly parameterized—that is, they allow libraries to specify the conditions under which items will be circulated, file inquiries made, and printed output generated. Rather than being written into programs, particular operating parameters are selected by libraries from a range of possibilities.

With some integrated systems, vendor representatives establish circulation control parameters during a preinstallation "profiling" session. Alternatively, the system may include a programmable module that allows libraries to define or change their own operating parameters. In either case, a library can define the period of time—in days, weeks, or other measures—that specific types of items will be loaned to, and renewed for, specific types of borrowers. Some systems permit renewal periods that differ from the original loan period. Addressing a commonly encountered academic library requirement, most circulation control modules can charge out items until the end of a semester or another fixed date. If desired, this option can be limited to specific borrower categories—faculty members and graduate students, for example—or to particular types of library materials. Addressing the common practice among corporate and government libraries of maintaining selected items in the work areas where they are most frequently utilized, some circulation control modules permit permanent loans to desk or laboratory locations rather than individuals. For chargeback purposes, some integrated systems can link the use of specific items to individual departments or cost centers within a corporation or government agency.

A library can differentiate fine rates by item or borrower type, specify fine immunity for particular types of borrowers, grant a specified number of grace days before fines are incurred, and specify the number of overdue notices that different types of borrowers will receive. Libraries can also impose limits on the amount of fines that specific types of borrowers can incur before circulation privileges are revoked. To ensure that holidays are not used in fine calculation and that due dates do not fall on holidays, most circulation control modules maintain a calendar of dates that the library is closed. For maximum flexibility, circulation parameters can be defined separately for individual participants in consortia or other multilibrary arrangements. If desired, borrower privileges can be limited to specific branches or libraries within a multilibrary system.

All circulation control modules perform check-out, check-in, and renewal operations in real time—that is, all item and borrower records are immediately updated when library materials are charged out or checked in and the circulation status of specific copies is immediately reflected in OPAC displays. With most integrated systems, circulation control is accorded the highest priority for execution, so that circulation transactions are performed before catalog searches or other operations.

Check-out procedures are straightforward. Working at a designated terminal, a circulation clerk enters book and borrower identifiers. Applying predetermined circulation rules, the system retrieves the appropriate records, calculates the due date, and updates holdings information for the circulating item. All circulation control modules support barcode recognition to simplify the entry of item and borrower identifiers. As discussed in chapter 1, barcodes use predetermined patterns of alternating vertical lines and spaces to encode numeric identifiers. In library applications, barcodes are typically printed on adhesive labels that are affixed to circulating materials and borrower identification cards. Barcode labels may be ordered preprinted or produced by the library itself.

In either case, specific numbered labels must be associated with the particular items to which they are attached. This can be done in several ways. In one method, a barcode label is attached to a book or other item, the database record for the item is retrieved by title or some other parameter, the barcode is scanned, and its number is entered in the barcode field within the record. The database record is then saved and the item is shelved. Alternatively, duplicate labels can be affixed to library materials and shelflist cards. When the shelflist is converted, the barcode label for each title is scanned into the database record. This method is particularly useful where a bibliographic utility or other company will perform retrospective conversion from a library's shelflist. Another popular method involves "smart" barcodes that include preprinted call numbers, titles, or other human-readable identifiers for library materials. Smart barcodes are produced from a library's database and must be attached to the materials for which they are intended. Smart barcodes are typically printed in shelflist sequence to simplify the labeling of items.

Regardless of the method employed, barcoding a library's collection is a time-consuming procedure that can take weeks or months to complete. Various types of barcodes are available. Most formats encode fourteen to sixteen digits. Often, the first digit is used to distinguish item and borrower barcodes. The next several digits identify the library in a multilibrary installation, and the remainder identify the item or the borrower. A check digit, used for error detection, is often appended. Circulation control programs are designed to read barcode labels in one or more formats, and different formats cannot be intermixed within a given library collection. Incompatibility of barcodes can pose problems and necessitate relabeling of items and borrower cards in libraries that change circulation control systems.

Though not as common as barcodes, some circulation control modules can read OCR labels. As discussed in chapter 1, optical character recognition uses reflected light to determine the character content of input documents. OCR labels are usually printed in a specially designed type font, such as OCR-A or OCR-B, that is optimized for machine recognition. If barcodes or OCR labels are absent or damaged, item and borrower identifiers can be key-entered. Key-entry is also used for telephone renewals. As an increasingly popular capability, some integrated library systems support self-service circulation terminals.

All circulation control modules block check-out transactions when borrower delinquencies or other exceptional conditions are encountered. Examples include borrowers with overdue items or outstanding fines, borrowers who have exceeded the library's predefined charge-out limit, borrowers who are using an identification card reported lost or stolen, items that are being held for another library user, items that are already checked out to another borrower, or items that are not part of a library's circulating collection. Some integrated systems will automatically block circulation transactions if a borrower's circulation privileges will expire before an item's due date. Most systems distinguish between "soft" blocks, which can be overridden by a circulation clerk or other authorized person, and "hard" blocks, which require correction of the exceptional condition before the circulation transaction can be completed.

With most circulation control modules, check-in of library materials is a repeating transaction that is initiated by a command, followed by scanning of barcodes for the returned items. The check-in command is entered once for multiple items. During check-in, most integrated systems will automatically detect such exceptional conditions as items that are on hold for other borrowers, items that were never properly charged out, and items returned to the wrong location. To reflect the in-house use of library materials in statistical reports, some circulation control modules permit the discharging of items removed from shelves but never checked out. Fines can be calculated for immediate collection when overdue items are checked in. If overdue items are dropped in book bins, or the borrowers are otherwise unavailable or unable to pay the fines, the amounts are typically added to their records. In most cases, a library can specify the amount of fines that borrowers can owe before circulation privileges are revoked. Some systems support amnesty days, when all fines for overdue items are forgiven.

To facilitate the completion of specific circulation transactions, item records can be retrieved by barcode numbers or by any of the search parameters supported by the integrated system's online public access catalog. Once a desired bibliographic record is retrieved, its associated item records can be displayed. Borrower records are usually retrievable by card number or other numeric identifiers or the borrower's name. The content of displayed records varies from system to system. Typical data elements include the borrower's name, address, telephone number, home library (in a multilibrary installation), the date borrowing privileges were granted, and the date of last circulation activity. An operator can usually request additional information, such as a list of the specific items charged out to the borrower, any items the borrower has requested, a list of the borrower's overdue items, and the borrower's delinquency status. Library permitting, some integrated systems give registered borrowers online access to their records, thereby reducing staff time spent on borrower inquiries. Borrowers can review items they have in circulation, items they have on hold, fines owing, and any blocks on their records.

Effective management of holds and recalls is one of the features that clearly distinguish real-time circulation control systems from their batch-oriented predecessors. As used in this context, a hold causes an item in circulation to be trapped on its return and held for a borrower who previously requested it. A hold is a passive request. The borrower waits for the desired item to be returned, although he or she must usually specify a cancellation date after which the item will no longer be required. A recall, in contrast, is an active request that changes the due date for a circulating item in order to obtain its immediate return.

Most circulation control modules support the placement of holds at the bibliographic level—that is, on all copies of a specified title—or on a specific copy only. Bibliographic-level requests will trap the first available copy of a specified title involved in any circulation transaction. In multibranch or consortium installations, copy-level requests are usually made by borrowers who do not want to travel to another location to obtain an item. Recalls are usually placed at the copy level and backed up with holds at the title level. When multiple requests are received for a given item, a hold queue is established. In most cases, the request date determines a borrower's position in the queue, although authorized library staff members can prioritize requests. Some circulation control modules will generate a purchase alert when the hold queue for a given title exceeds a specified number of names. Library permitting, borrowers can use OPAC terminals to place holds on circulating items retrieved through catalog searches. Depending on the system, holds may also be placed on items that are on order or awaiting cataloging.

To conserve computer resources and preserve response time for online operations, integrated library systems typically print circulation reports and notices at night or during other off-peak hours. Most circulation control modules provide a selection of preconfigured operational and statistical reports that address a broad range of library requirements. Some integrated systems also support a general-purpose report-writing program that the library can utilize to generate additional or customized circulation reports. Examples of preconfigured circulation reports include borrower rosters with identification numbers, addresses, phone numbers, and similar information; lists of borrower records added or changed since a specified date; lists of borrowers with excessive overdue items, fines, or other delinquencies; lists of borrowers with more than a specified number of items in circulation; lists of items being held for specific borrowers, lists of items on hold in call number or title sequence; lists of exceptional items on hold, including lost, missing, or long overdue items; lists of items with hold queues longer than a specified number of names; lists of requesters, with phone numbers, for items on hold; lists of fine receipts by workstation location; and lists of overdue items for shelf searching prior to printing borrower notices. Examples of circulation reports that support inventory control activities include lists of lost or missing items arranged by call number, material type, or other parameters; lists of items withdrawn from the library's collection since a specified date; lists of delinquent items claimed to be returned; and lists of unsatisfied holds since a specified date.

Statistical reports provide useful information for collection development as well as for management of the circulation activity itself. Perhaps the most important example provides circulation totals for specified call number groups. It may be produced monthly, quarterly, or at other specified intervals. For comparison purposes, such reports often provide statistics for the same period during the preceding year. Other useful statistical reports summarize circulation activity by borrower category or the type of library material; charge-out, check-in, and hold activity for specified time periods; and workstation activity by day, week, month, or other time periods.

All circulation control modules can generate overdue notices, recall notices, fine notices, hold availability notices, and similar borrower notices, as well as bills for lost items. Libraries can specify the content of borrower notices. They are usually printed on letter-size paper with the borrower's address formatted for compatibility with window envelopes. Some systems can also print notices on postcards. Notices may be sorted by zip code prior to printing. As an alternative to printed notices, some integrated systems support an automatic telephone dialing and voice notification capability for holds and overdue items. Such capabilities, which utilize voice synthesis technology, can store multiple message scripts.

Designed specifically for academic and school libraries, reserve room capabilities maintain circulation records that are linked to courses and instructors. With some integrated library systems, reserve room capabilities are incorporated into the circulation control module; in other cases, a separate reserve room module is available as an optional component. Implementation pattern aside, reserve room materials are identified in the online public access catalog as subject to special, usually short, loan periods. Records for items on reserve can be retrieved through OPAC searches or by course number or instructor. In addition to managing items from a library's own holdings, most reserve room modules can create brief catalog records for photocopies and instructors' personal copies. Circulation periods for reserve materials are customarily measured in hours or even minutes, although most systems will permit overnight circulation if the allowable charge-out period extends beyond the library's closing time. Most integrated systems will print lists of items on reserve for particular courses, reports of charge-out activity arranged by course number and item, lists of reserve items that are overdue, and lists of items to be withdrawn from reserve.

As another optional system component, some integrated library systems support a media booking module that provides circulation control for videotapes, films, and other audiovisual media, as well as equipment and facilities, that are subject to advance reservations. An online calendar is consulted to determine availability and reserve items for specific dates. Holiday and weekend reservations can be prohibited. Check-out and check-in functions are similar to those for circulation control. Reservation records may be accessed by borrower name, item identifier, or other parameters. Typical management reports and notices include media catalogs, pick lists, packing slips, mailing lists and labels, reservation work slips and schedules, media activity reports, overdue notices, and usage summaries. The media booking module is typically integrated with other system components. With some integrated systems, OPAC users can make reservations for media or items.

ACQUISITIONS AND SERIALS MANAGEMENT

As previously discussed, most integrated library systems support acquisitions and serials management modules as optional application components. While acquisitions and serials management are often relegated to separate departments within a given library, they share an important function: the procurement of library materials. This discussion will follow common library practice in using the term "acquisitions" to collectively denote those tasks that support the procurement of library materials that are published on a nonrecurring basis, including books, technical reports, government publications, musical scores, sound recordings, and visual materials. The acquisition of journals, magazines, and other periodical publications is considered a facet of serials management, the scope of which extends to such activities as cataloging and binding of serial publications. The distinction between acquisitions and serials management is rarely unequivocal, however, since annuals or irregularly published materials may be treated as monographs in one library and as serials in another.

Since acquisitions and serials management initiate the procurement of library materials that will eventually be cataloged and circulated, they would seem to be more appropriately discussed at the beginning rather than at the end of this chapter. They are treated here, however, because an understanding of automated acquisitions and serials management requires some familiarity with the application components described above.

Acquisitions

As with automated circulation control and computerized catalog production, libraries have had decades of experience with automated acquisitions. Precomputer book ordering systems—using keypunch equipment, card sorters, and tabulating machines—were developed in the late 1950s by public and academic libraries. The first computer-based acquisitions systems, implemented by a number of academic libraries in the early to mid-1960s, employed batch processing technology to automate procurement and recordkeeping tasks. During the late 1960s and early 1970s, several academic libraries developed online acquisitions systems. Widely publicized examples included the Book Order and Selection System (BOSS) at the University of Massachusetts, the Library On-Line Information and Text Access (LOLITA) system at Oregon State University, and the acquisitions component of the previously discussed BALLOTS system at Stanford University. The first minicomputer-based turnkey acquisitions system was installed by CLSI at the Cleveland Public Library in 1972. Other vendors subsequently introduced similar special-purpose products; the most popular example, the INNOVACQ system from Innovative Interfaces, automated both acquisitions and serials management.

Integrated library systems began incorporating acquisitions modules as optional application components in the 1980s. The earliest examples were noticeably weaker than their OPAC and circulation control counterparts, but they have improved steadily and significantly in recent years. As described below, the latest versions offer excellent functionality for ordering, fund accounting, and recordkeeping. For many libraries, particularly those that operate an integrated system for online catalog access and circulation control, the addition of an acquisitions module is the simplest, least expensive way to automate that activity.

Library motives for computerizing acquisitions operations are well established. Acquisitions funds represent a large and important component of the typical library budget, and library administration is accountable for their responsible expenditure. As with circulation control, manual acquisitions and fund accounting systems cannot readily generate the financial and statistical information essential to scientific planning and management. In libraries where book budgets are allocated annually, for example, certain acquisitions funds may remain characteristically underspent over a period of many months, necessitating intensified expenditures at the year's end, a situation that is not conducive to carefully considered selection practices. Similarly, certain funds may be expended too quickly, leaving little reserve for important materials published later in the year.

In either case, periodic reports of fund status can alert subject bibliographers and library administrators to exceptional situations that require attention and possible corrective action. While such reports can be produced manually, the available labor in most manual acquisitions systems is fully occupied with paperwork processing, accounting, and related work routines pertaining to book orders. Among other advantages, computer-based acquisitions can reduce clerical labor requirements and costs, thereby making more money available for collection development and professional services. Cost reduction aside, many librarians perceive an added value in the potentially faster paperwork processing and more timely receipt of materials permitted by computerized acquisitions capability. Further, automation of acquisitions promotes the integration of library operations. Bibliographic information, captured in machine-readable form at the time an item is ordered, can later be enhanced or modified to support information retrieval, circulation control, or other library operations. In integrated system implementations, a library's online public access catalog can contain information about materials that are on order or awaiting cataloging.

While differences in purchasing practices and procurement regulations may lead to local variations, most library acquisitions departments share certain basic characteristics and work steps. Depending on the type of library involved, a request to purchase a specific item may be transmitted to the acquisitions department by subject bibliographers, other library staff members, library users, or other persons or groups. Typically, the library's own acquisitions files and catalog are first consulted to determine whether the item is on order or already in its collection. Assuming that the item is not already owned or that an additional copy will be purchased, the bibliographic information in the request must be verified, the item's availability and price determined, and a vendor selected. A purchase order is then prepared in multiple copies, several of which are filed by the acquisitions department. When an item is received, the corresponding documents are removed from files and updated as required to reflect the full or partial receipt of an order. Payment is then authorized and a payment voucher or check is issued.

Automated acquisitions systems retain these basic characteristics but replace typing, filing, and related manual work steps with data entry and computer processing. Automated acquisitions control typically employs a combination of three data files: (1) an order file, sometimes called an in-process file, contains one record for each item purchased; (2) a vendor file contains one record for each publisher, book jobber, or other procurement source; and (3) a fund file contains one record for each account that supports the purchase of library materials. While specific details will necessarily vary from one installation to another, most order files contain a combination of bibliographic and order-specific data, including author, title, and imprint information; an edition statement; an International Standard Book Number (ISBN) or other unique numeric identifier; an order number; the order date; a fund account number; a vendor number, code, or similar identifier; the type of procurement (conventional order, standing order, prepayment, approval item, etc.); the number of copies ordered; the price, plus discounts and service charges; the currency type; the estimated receipt date; the ordering branch, department, or agency; and the name of the requester, bibliographer, or other person who initiated the order. Some systems also include a text field for free-form messages intended for acquisitions clerks, catalogers, or others.

As noted above, vendor files contain one record for each publisher, book jobber, dealer, sales agent, or other procurement source. To accommodate gifts and exchanges, the vendor file may also include donor records. Again subject to variation from installation to installation, commonly encountered data fields include the vendor's name, address, telephone number, fax or telex number, and e-mail address; an assigned numeric or other coded identifier that links specific order records to the vendor file; pertinent contract numbers and dates;

applicable discount schedules; a claim period indicator that specifies the intervals at which notices will be sent for overdue orders; and the total volume of vendor order activity, as an item count or dollar value, for a specified period of time. Some vendor files also incorporate performance statistics, such as the average time each vendor requires to fill an order and the number of claims or cancellations experienced in a specified time period.

Most fund files contain one record for each account or other budgetary unit established by the library for acquisitions purposes. These funds may reflect subdivisions of a library's collections, academic departments within a college or university, branch libraries within a public library system, special accounts established for the purchase of particular types of materials, or gifts from specific individuals or groups. For each fund file record, typical data fields include the account number, a brief account description, the original dollar amount allocated at the beginning of the budgetary cycle, total expenditures since the beginning of the budgetary cycle, encumbrances for items ordered but not yet received, and the current fund balance.

Some automated acquisitions systems also include a requester file, which contains names, addresses, and other pertinent information for persons or organizations, including branch libraries, that may initiate acquisition requests. It may be used to print notification slips when requested material is received by the acquisitions department or as other information about the status of requested items becomes available. In some cases, the requester file and vendor file are merged in a master name and address file, although vendor records may contain more information than requester records. A few automated acquisitions systems maintain invoice files to permit the retrieval of information by invoice number in answer to questions about the payment status or history of particular transactions. Similarly, some systems feature an online desiderata file that contains records for items being considered for purchase. In the case of antiquarian or out-of-print items, lists of desiderata records may be printed for circulation to book dealers.

Vendor, fund, and requester files are typically created in advance of system operation, although new records may be added to them at any time. In most cases, their information content is derived from files of source documents used by the automated system's manual predecessor. Records in the order file are key-entered when items are ordered.

The acquisitions modules supported by integrated library systems can accommodate a broad range of procurement transactions, including new orders, multicopy and multivolume orders, standing orders, subscriptions, blanket orders, approval plans, depository items, rental books, items obtained through memberships, prepaid orders, gifts, and exchanges. Like their circulation control counterparts, acquisitions modules are highly parameterized. Libraries, or individual branches in a library system, can specify file contents and operating conditions. Because acquisitions modules are fully integrated with other system components, records for ordered items are included in a library's bibliographic database, and on-order status is reflected in the online public access catalog. With some integrated systems, as previously noted, library users can place holds on materials that are on order. Further, the integrated system's bibliographic database can be used for preorder searching to identify items that are already on order or owned by the library. While this capability does not eliminate the need for external reference sources for bibliographic verification, it can prove especially useful for minimizing duplicate ordering in multilibrary or multibranch installations where the integrated system maintains a union catalog. In most cases, bibliographic information retrieved from the online catalog can be transferred directly into order records, thereby reducing key-entry requirements.

One of the principal advantages of automated acquisitions is the substitution of computer-based file maintenance for the labor-intensive sorting, filing, and other paper-handling procedures associated with manual acquisitions systems. When an order record is entered, the acquisitions module automatically encumbers the estimated purchase price in the indicated fund account. As items are received, order records are searched and their status updated to reflect full or partial shipments. When an order is closed, the corresponding records can be automatically purged from the order file to a historical file. Acquisitions modules can produce claiming and cancellation notices, thereby eliminating a time-consuming work step encountered in manual systems.

Superior file inquiry and order tracking capabilities further distinguish automated acquisitions systems from their manual counterparts. Acquisitions modules permit the online retrieval of order records by bibliographic and acquisitions-specific parameters, including an order control number, purchase order number, order date, vendor identifier, requester identifier, or fund number. Retrieved records typically include brief bibliographic data, accompanied by a summary of the order's essential characteristics and status, including vendor and fund information. Operators can usually request more detailed displays, which may include the number of copies ordered, the price, the payment type, the currency type, the vendor's discount, and the specified cancellation date. Vendor files are typically searchable by vendor name or code. Fund records can be retrieved by account number, account name, or, occasionally, account balance.

More than any other library activity, the acquisitions activity relies on printed output for many operations. The acquisitions modules supported by integrated library systems can produce procurement documents, notices, and reports in a variety of formats. The most important examples of procurement documents are purchase orders and payment documents, including checks and vouchers. As an alternative or complement to printed output, acquisitions modules increasingly support the electronic transmission of order information to publishers, book jobbers, or other vendors. Claiming of overdue orders has a direct counterpart in the circulation activity. Automated acquisitions systems will print claiming and cancellation notices to vendors at predetermined intervals and arrival notices to requesters when items are received. In some cases, librarians must specify an anticipated arrival date for ordered items; in other cases, the acquisitions module uses performance statistics stored in vendor records to calculate an anticipated arrival date. Most systems can generate lists of overdue orders for operator examination prior to printing claiming notices.

While online file inquiry can be used to quickly determine the status of a given order or fund balance, most acquisitions modules rely on printed reports to provide aggregate financial, statistical, or other information on a regularly

National Library of Medicine: Internet Grateful Med Search Screen

| | Perform Search | M Find MeSH/ Meta Terms | Other Databases | Analyze Search | Specify Journals | Clear Search |

Log off IGM

Internet Grateful Med is currently set to search file MEDLINE

Tip: bookmark the IGM front screen, not this page. Here's why.

Enter Query Terms:

Search for

⦿ [   ] as Subject [   ]   [Add OR]

AND search for

○ [   ] as Subject [   ]   [Add OR]

AND search for

○ [   ] as Subject [   ]   [Add OR]

Apply Limits:

Languages:	All		Publ Types:	All
Study Groups:	All		Gender:	All
Age Groups:	All		Journals:	All
Year range:	Begin year 1966	through	End year	1998

Internet Grateful Med is currently set to search file MEDLINE

| | Perform Search | M Find MeSH/ Meta Terms | Other Databases | Analyze Search | Specify Journals | Clear Search |

Log off IGM

Web-based search services make effective use of dialog boxes to simplify the entry of retrieval parameters.

---

scheduled or demand basis. Examples of such reports include fund status summaries, arranged by account number; fund history reports that list closed orders by title within each account; lists of daily accounting transactions; charts of accounts; purchase order lists arranged by title, vendor, fund, workstation, or other parameters; claimed item lists; lists of canceled orders; lists of open orders; lists of orders outstanding longer than a specified period of time; lists of orders received but not invoiced after a specified number of days; vendor rosters, including discounts and performance statistics; lists of newly acquired items arranged by author, title, call number, or other parameters; and lists of ordered items on hold for requesters.

Unlike online catalog access and circulation control, where integrated systems have supplanted other automation options, libraries have several alternatives to the acquisitions modules offered by integrated system vendors. Customized software development is, of course, an alternative in every computer application. As noted above, a number of libraries developed customized acquisitions systems during the 1960s and 1970s, and some of those systems remain in operation. For the most part, they are implemented on mainframes or minicomputers operated by a university, municipality, corporation, government agency, or other organization with which a library is affiliated. Since the 1980s, some small to medium-size libraries have utilized microcomputers and database management software to develop acquisitions systems.

As its principal disadvantage, customized software development can be time-consuming and expensive. Libraries developing customized acquisitions systems run the risk of significant delays in implementation and substantial, often unanticipated costs. Postimplementation costs will likewise be incurred for software modification and other maintenance to address changing application requirements. Consequently, customized development is often viewed as an implementation alternative of last resort, to be considered only in those situations where other approaches to automated acquisitions are clearly unacceptable.

Among the bibliographic utilities, RLIN offers an acquisitions subsystem that libraries can access on a time-sharing basis. The RLIN acquisition system is integrated with bibliographic records and supports a variety of program activities and situations, including selection decisions, single item procurement, direct extensions, and standing orders. Acquisitions records can be created by adding in-process information to the RLIN database. RLIN's central bibliographic files can be used for preorder verification and derivation of bibliographic data for a given title. Order numbers, prices, supplier identifiers, claiming intervals, shipping instructions, fund numbers, encumbrances, and other acquisitions-related information are entered in fields provided for that purpose. To simplify input procedures, codes can be defined for suppliers' names and addresses, selector and requester names, shipping and billing locations, fund codes, and other frequently repeated data values. Default data values can also be specified. The RLIN acquisitions module will track the status of orders through receipt and cataloging. Claims can be generated automatically or on demand. Printed output includes purchase orders, claims, cancellation notices, transaction logs, and fiscal reports.

Among its advantages, the RLIN acquisitions subsystem can draw on a large cataloging database for bibliographic verification. The ability to transfer bibliographic data from cataloging records to order records can facilitate order preparation, while the online availability of holdings information for other libraries is useful in cooperative collection development. The use of a single system for acquisitions and cataloging also simplifies staff training requirements and promotes the integration of technical services operations. As disadvantages, the RLIN acquisitions subsystem may not meet local accounting or auditing requirements. Compared to acquisitions modules supported by integrated library systems, it provides less flexibility for production of information or statistical reports, although certain types of financial reports, such as fund activity and history reports, are offered. Finally, the RLIN acquisitions subsystem does not offer check-writing capabilities.

As an alternative, various booksellers offer software and time-sharing services for online ordering of library materials. Such systems not only automate the creation and maintenance of acquisitions records but also transmit orders to the bookseller electronically. Because their developers are in the business of selling books and other library materials, their online ordering systems are designed to expedite delivery to customers, although they may also help libraries manage their acquisitions operations by maintaining records and preparing purchase orders for materials to be acquired from other vendors.

Online ordering systems provide time-shared access to booksellers' computer systems. In the manner of the bibliographic utilities, formatted screens simplify order entry. File maintenance and fund accounting are performed automatically, and online inquiries about the status of a given order are supported. Libraries receive periodic reports that reflect their acquisitions and fund accounting activities. Because the booksellers' databases contain inventory information, the availability of a given item can be immediately determined.

Serials Management Modules

As previously defined, the term serials denotes publications that are issued in successive parts on a recurring basis, usually, but not necessarily, at regularly scheduled intervals. In additional to scholarly journals, popular magazines, and other periodical publications, the term encompasses newspapers, proceedings and transactions of professional societies, newsletters, and numbered monographic series. Unlike multivolume books, which may likewise be issued in successive parts, serials are characteristically open-ended. The publication of successive issues is expected to continue indefinitely, although external circumstances may force the eventual suspension of a given serial.

Since the 1960s, library interest in automated serials processing systems has been motivated by the same factors that have encouraged the development of automated approaches to acquisitions, circulation control, and cataloging—the desire for improved operating efficiencies and cost reduction. The cost of acquiring and maintaining serial publications represents a significant percentage of many libraries' budgets. In technical, medical, and business libraries, for example, serials typically constitute the major collection component, and ordering, claiming, binding, and related paperwork processing tasks can require many hours of labor. Even in academic and public libraries, where the ratio of serial to monographic publications is usually lower, serials departments may have large staffs. At a time of simultaneously rising subscription prices and reduced library budgets, operational economies are essential if a library's serials collection is to be maintained at its present level, let alone increased.

Although library interest is high and cost-reduction potential considerable, the widespread development and implementation of effective computer-based serials processing systems are complicated by certain peculiarities of serial publications. Circulation control, cataloging, and, to a lesser extent, acquisitions are characterized by well-defined, predictable work steps that are performed in a predetermined sequence on a regular basis. Serials processing tasks, on the other hand, are distinguished by a variety of exceptional circumstances that must be anticipated in the design of any automated system. While bibliographic information pertaining to monographs remains relatively stable once entered into a library catalog or other computer database, it is a rare serials record that will not eventually require some change in title, publisher, issuing agent, frequency of publication, numbering sequence, or other attributes. Such changes can render a computer-generated union list obsolete, complicate the development of an automated claims processing system, or alter previously established binding practices for a given serial. While changes and exceptional conditions can be handled by computer programs, they increase the complexity of automated serials implementations.

Over the past two decades, a number of libraries and vendors have developed systems that automate one or more aspects of serials processing, including the production of serials holdings lists for single or multiple libraries and ordering, check-in claiming, and routing of received issues to designated persons. As with monographic acquisitions, various academic, public, and special libraries developed customized serials control systems during the 1960s and 1970s. Examples include the University of California at San Diego, where an automated serials check-in system was implemented as early as 1961; the Washington University School of Medicine, which introduced its much-publicized PHILSOM serials management system in 1962; the UCLA Biomedical Library; the San Francisco Public Library; the University of Massachusetts; the University of Arizona; the University of Washington; Brigham Young University; and the Université Laval in Quebec, one of the first libraries to implement an online serials control system.

During the 1970s and 1980s, several vendors introduced special-purpose serials control systems and prewritten software. One of the most widely installed examples, the INNOVACQ system from Innovative Interfaces, was mentioned in the preceding discussion of automated acquisitions. Since the 1980s, most integrated system vendors have offered serials control modules as optional application components. As with their acquisitions counterparts, some early versions were not as well developed as other system components, but serials control modules have improved steadily and significantly in recent years. For libraries that operate an integrated system for cataloging and circulation control, they usually offer the simplest, least expensive method of automating serials management.

The serials control modules supported by integrated systems are designed to manage magazines, journals, newspapers, monographic series, and other materials that libraries receive on a continuing basis, whether at regular intervals or as irregular supplements or special publications. With some integrated library systems, ordering and cancellation of serial subscriptions, as well as claims for missing or damaged issues, are handled by the acquisitions module, while the serials control module supports check-in, routing, and binding of received issues. Alternatively, a serials control module may handle all aspects of serials management, including procurement and claiming. That approach does not require implementation of the acquisitions module as a precondition for serials control. With a few integrated systems, acquisitions and serials management are combined in a single module.

In any case, order and renewal of serial subscriptions are typically performed online, although purchase orders and renewal orders may be printed in batches. Received issues are checked in at computer workstations by retrieving the appropriate serials record and modifying designated holdings fields. The most flexible systems simplify data entry by displaying information about an expected issue, including the volume and issue number, cover date, and number of copies anticipated. The workstation operator simply modifies those data elements requiring correction. When all modifications are completed, the new record enters the serials data file. If serial publications circulate, item records can be created for individual issues.

Serials management modules keep track of publication patterns and will predict the receipt of specific issues. The library specifies the periodicity for successive issues and the number of days after the anticipated receipt when claiming notices are to be sent. The most flexible predictive algorithms can accommodate a variety of publication patterns. When overdue issues are to be claimed, the system searches the serials data file for issues that have not arrived according to their previously defined frequencies. Claiming notices for missing issues may be produced manually or automatically. Query notices, rather than claims, can be generated for irregular publications. Based on information stored in serials holdings records, most serials control systems will also prepare bindery orders, print instruction slips, check in items on their return from binding, and print claiming notices for items that have not been returned on schedule.

Some integrated systems support electronic transmission of subscription orders and claims for missing issues. Serials holdings information is included in the library's online catalog, which is updated automatically when new issues are received. Typical management and statistical reports include serials catalogs and union lists, on-order lists, lists of issues received, lists of issues past due, lists of claiming notices sent, and vendor performance reports. Some integrated systems will also print routing slips for received issues and pull-slips for items to be sent to the bindery.

As an alternative to the serials management modules supported by integrated library systems, several serials subscription services offer computerized serials management capabilities on a time-sharing basis. Such services provide online access to large databases of bibliographic records for serials titles and monographic serials, including the serials segment of the LC MARC database. Records can be retrieved by various parameters, including International Standard Serial Number (ISSN), title, and publisher. Serials management capabilities include online ordering, subscription renewal, and claiming of missing issues; confirmation of transactions via electronic mail; online access to account balances, payment histories, and other financial information; and electronic transfer of serials records to a library's local automation system.

SUMMARY

An integrated library system is a computer-based information system that uses a single bibliographic database and a set of interrelated application programs to automate multiple library operations. Since the mid-1980s, integrated library systems have steadily supplanted custom-developed software and single-purpose library automation products that were designed for specific applications, such as circulation control or acquisitions. Integrated systems are offered by several dozen vendors for various types of computers. Products are available for libraries of all types and sizes.

Most integrated library systems are modular in design. Vendors offer suites of interrelated programs that automate specific library operations. Core functionality is provided by certain application modules that are required in all installations, while optional modules, which automate specific operations, can usually be added at any time. In most cases, the standard system modules support cataloging, an online public access catalog (OPAC), and circulation control. Acquisitions and serials management are popular but usually optional additions to a basic system configuration. Other optional application modules, not necessarily offered by all vendors, include media booking, a community bulletin board, community information and referral, homebound access, reference databases, reserve room capability, a report generator, Internet access, electronic imaging, full-text retrieval, and electronic mail capabilities.

All integrated systems support cataloging as a core application module that permits the creation, updating, and management of a library's bibliographic database. All integrated systems support MARC records for those types of library materials for which USMARC formats have been developed. Most integrated systems permit partial MARC records that employ the USMARC format with some fields left blank. Some systems also support non-MARC formats with library-defined fields. Typically MARC and non-MARC records can coexist within a library's database. Cataloging records can be key-entered or transferred from machine-readable sources, either electronically or on magnetic tapes or diskettes. Depending on the system, authority control may be incorporated into the cataloging module or offered as a separately purchased component.

The replacement of a card catalog by an online public access catalog is often the principal motive for implementing an integrated library system. Suitable for novice users who receive little or no training in information retrieval, most OPAC modules are menu-driven, although a command-driven mode may be provided for experienced users or library staff members. Some systems provide graphical user interfaces with pulldown menus, dialog boxes, mouse operations, and other features that simplify the entry of search commands and formatting of retrieved information. Several vendors have implemented special OPAC interfaces for children. As a recent development that is likely to be widely adopted, some integrated library systems support OPAC searches by microcomputers equipped with popular Web browsers such as Netscape Navigator or Microsoft Internet Explorer.

All OPAC modules permit searches by author, title, and subject, thereby replicating the traditional retrieval functionality of card catalogs. Typically, a user specifies a field to be searched and a name, subject heading, or other value to be matched. Other search parameters, selectively supported, include a classification number, Library of Congress Card Number, International Standard Book Number, publisher, publication date, country of publication, language of publication, and media type. For maximum flexibility, some integrated systems allow any library-designated field within bibliographic records to be indexed for retrieval purposes. Special retrieval capabilities include keyword searching, root-word searching, and Boolean operations.

To expand their functionality, integrated library systems increasingly incorporate external information resources, such as locally mounted reference databases and CD-ROM information products, into OPAC searches. Some systems also provide Internet access from OPAC terminals. If an integrated system supports the NISO Z39.50 standard, OPAC users can search the compliant computer systems of other vendors. With some systems an optional information and referral module gives OPAC users access to information about community groups and local events.

Drawing on three decades of library experience with computer-based circulation management, the circulation control modules supported by integrated systems are very well developed and highly parameterized—that is, they allow libraries to specify the conditions under which items will be circulated, file inquiries made, and printed output generated. All circulation control modules perform check-out, check-in, and renewal operations in real time. Circulation procedures are straightforward. Barcodes are typically used to simplify the entry of item and borrower identifiers. Circulation transactions are blocked when borrower delinquencies or other exceptional conditions are encountered. Holds can be placed at the title or copy level. Most circulation control modules provide a selection of preconfigured operational and statistical reports that address a broad range of library requirements.

Designed specifically for academic and school libraries, reserve room capabilities maintain circulation records that are linked to courses and instructors. Records for items on reserve can be retrieved through OPAC searches or by course number or instructor. In addition to managing items from a library's own holdings, most reserve room modules can create brief catalog records for photocopies and instructors' personal copies. Some integrated library systems support a media booking module that provides circulation control for videotapes, films, and other audiovisual media, as well as equipment and facilities, that are subject to advance reservations.

The acquisitions modules supported by integrated library systems can accommodate a broad range of procurement transactions, including new orders, multicopy and multivolume orders, standing orders, subscriptions, blanket orders, approval plans, depository items, rental books, items obtained through memberships, prepaid orders, gifts, and exchanges. Because acquisitions modules are fully integrated with other system components, records for ordered items are included in a library's bibliographic database, and on-order status is reflected in the online public access catalog.

The serials control modules supported by integrated systems are designed to manage magazines, journals, newspapers, monographic series, and other materials that libraries receive on a continuing basis, whether at regular intervals or as irregular supplements or special publications. Capabilities include online ordering and renewal of subscriptions, check-in of received issues, claiming of missing or damaged issues, and control of bindery orders. Some integrated systems support electronic transmission of subscription orders and claims. Serials holdings information is included in the library's online catalog, which is updated automatically when new issues are received.

7

Automated Reference Service

Broadly defined, the function of reference service is to help library users obtain access to required information. While such activities as circulation control and cataloging reflect the custodial and bibliographic aspects of librarianship, reference is a public service activity in which librarians function as professionally trained information specialists. Reference service is usually provided in response to questions or problems posed by library users. Such questions range from simple inquiries about the physical locations of particular library facilities and resources to complex research requests requiring retrieval and analysis of information in specialized subject disciplines. Much of the reference work for which librarians are specially trained involves two types of transactions: (1) so-called ready reference questions that require straightforward factual responses—for example, the population of a specified city, the quantity of a given product manufactured in a particular location during a specified time period, or the reported earnings of a particular corporation; and (2) literature searching—the preparation of the bibliographies on specified topics.

Similar reference methodologies are employed in both types of transactions. A reference librarian first interviews the requester to clarify information requirements and determine the desired outcome. A reference strategy is then formulated, and appropriate books or other sources likely to contain the required information are identified. In some cases, the requester is merely directed to those sources and perhaps provided with instruction in their use. In others, the reference librarian actually performs the search and provides the requester with the needed information in the form of facts or bibliographic citations. Following discussion and evaluation of the initial search results, additional searching, perhaps based on a modified reference strategy, may be undertaken. This process is repeated until satisfactory results are obtained or available information sources are exhausted. This fuller type of reference service is common in technical and business libraries within corporations and government agencies where considerable staff time may be devoted to literature searching and other reference-related activities.

While the reference methodology described above is time-consuming, certain work steps—notably, the reference interview and the evaluation of search results—depend on interaction between persons. Apart from using electronic mail to clarify requirements and exchange opinions, they are not generally amenable to automation. Although some information retrieval systems allow users to type their reference inquiries in conventional paragraph form for automatic analysis by a computer program, such systems have typically been implemented in experimental applications involving relatively small, specialized collections of information sources. Neither their cost-effectiveness nor their viability in a broad range of library applications has been demonstrated. While a few libraries have developed computer-based orientation and bibliographic instruction programs that can assist users in locating specific physical facilities and identify potentially relevant information resources, the most prevalent and effective approaches to the automation of reference service concentrate on the search procedure itself—that is, the consultation of appropriate reference books and other information resources for facts and bibliographic citations.

As in the case of cataloging with copy, the availability of machine-readable reference sources is a precondition for computer-based reference service. The opening section of this chapter cites examples of machine-readable bibliographic and non-bibliographic databases, indicating the specific subject disciplines that they primarily support. Subsequent sections discuss the ways in which libraries currently access and use those databases, as well as some economic and operational implications of automated reference service.

MACHINE-READABLE REFERENCE SOURCES

Performed manually, literature searching—that is, the preparation of bibliographies on specified topics—relies heavily on printed indexing and abstracting journals, bibliographic lists, and other sources that facilitate subject or other access to monographs, periodical literature, technical records, and other published and unpublished materials. These printed bibliographic sources are produced by a variety of organizations, including government agencies, professional associations, and private companies. During the 1960s and early 1970s, many publishers of printed bibliographies and indexes attempted to simplify and reduce their production costs by using computer-based text-editing and phototypesetting technologies. Such publishing methods, which are now commonplace, require the conversion of bibliographic data to machine-readable form before a work is typeset and published. Thus, the earliest machine-readable bibliographic databases were created as by-products of efficiencies in the production of printed reference works.

Bibliographic Databases

The late 1960s and early 1970s were, coincidentally, characterized by emerging interest in the application of computers to information storage and retrieval. Recognizing the value of machine-readable data to organizations interested in automating information-processing systems, publishers of indexing and abstracting journals and bibliographies began selling machine-readable versions of their products in addition to, or in place of, their printed counterparts. Such machine-readable versions were, and still are, offered to prospective purchasers on magnetic tape, together with descriptive information about their format. The LC MARC tapes discussed in chapter 5 were among the earliest examples of such machine-readable bibliographic products.

Today, hundreds of printed indexing and abstracting journals and bibliographies are available in machine-readable versions, and a growing number of bibliographic products have been introduced specifically for use in computer-based information retrieval systems. These machine-readable products are sometimes called "bibliographic databases." Given its prevalence in library literature, that usage will be followed in this chapter. As discussed in chapter 3, however, the term database broadly denotes an integrated accumulation of computer-processible information organized in a manner suited to multiple applications. Following that definition, the bibliographic products discussed here are more accurately considered data files, because they must usually be reorganized to meet specific application requirements. Thus, LC MARC records distributed on magnetic tape by the Library of Congress comprise a data file, while OCLC WorldCat, which incorporates those LC MARC records along with other cataloging information, is a database that supports online searching, shared cataloging, catalog card production, and other applications.

Some machine-readable bibliographic databases are interdisciplinary in character and can consequently be viewed as the computer-processible counterparts of general reference sources. This is the case, for example, with the previously discussed LC MARC, CANMARC, UKMARC, and REMARC databases, which contain cataloging records pertaining to published materials on a wide variety of subjects. Interdisciplinary scope likewise characterizes such news, current affairs, and general interest databases as IAC NATIONAL NEWSPAPER INDEX, IAC NEWSEARCH, and IAC MAGAZINE DATABASE, produced by Information Access Company, the NEWSPAPER ABSTRACTS and PERIODICALS ABSTRACTS databases, produced by UMI; the EBSCO MASTERFILE, produced by EBSCO Publishing; the READERS' GUIDE TO PERIODICAL LITERATURE, READERS' GUIDE ABSTRACTS, and BOOK REVIEW DIGEST databases from H. W. Wilson; the BOOK REVIEW INDEX, produced by Gale Research; BOOKS IN PRINT, produced by R. R. Bowker; and BRITISH BOOKS IN PRINT, produced by J. Whitaker and Sons Limited. Other examples of interdisciplinary bibliographic databases include the COMPREHENSIVE DISSERTATION INDEX, produced by UMI; the CONFERENCE PAPERS INDEX, produced by Cambridge Scientific Abstracts; the GPO MONTHLY CATALOG and GPO PUBLICATIONS REFERENCE FILE, produced by the U.S. Government Printing Office; and the BRITISH OFFICIAL PUBLICATIONS database, produced by Chadwyck-Healey Limited.

Like their printed counterparts, most machine-readable bibliographic databases cover the literature of one or more specialized disciplines within the sciences, social sciences, or humanities. Since corporate and governmental technical libraries were among the earliest implementers of computer-based reference service, it is not surprising that many bibliographic databases address the literature of science and technology. Some of these databases provide coverage of multiple scientific and technical disciplines. This is the case, for example, with SCISEARCH and CURRENT CONTENTS SEARCH, the machine-readable counterparts of the *Science Citation Index* and *Current Contents* publications of the Institute for Scientific Information; the NTIS database, the machine-readable version of *Government Reports Announcements and Index,* published by the National Technical Information Service of the U.S. Department of Commerce; the PASCAL database, the machine-readable counterpart of *Bibliographie Internationale,* produced by the Institut de l'Information Scientifique et Technique of the French National Research Council; GENERAL SCIENCE ABSTRACTS and APPLIED SCIENCE AND TECHNOLOGY ABSTRACTS, produced by H. W. Wilson; and the various patent databases produced by such organizations as Derwent Publications, the European Patent Office, IFI/Plenum Data Corporation, the International Patent Documentation Center, and Pergamon International.

Databases dedicated to a single scientific or technical discipline are more numerous than general-purpose scientific information resources. Well-known examples include CHEMICAL ABSTRACTS, produced by Chemical Abstracts Service; ANALYTICAL ABSTRACTS and CHEMICAL BUSINESS NEWSBASE, produced by the Royal Society of Chemistry; BIOSIS PREVIEWS, produced by BIOSIS Incorporated as the machine-readable counterpart of *Biological Abstracts and Biological Abstracts/RRM;* Elsevier BIOBASE, an enhanced version of *Current Awareness in Biological Sciences;* the LIFE SCIENCES COLLECTION database, produced by Cambridge Scientific Abstracts; the BIOLOGICAL AND AGRICULTURAL INDEX, produced by H. W. Wilson; the SPIN (Searchable Physics Information Notices) database, produced by the American Institute of Physics; and the MATHSCI database, produced by the American Mathematical Society. Geological and geographic literature is covered by the GEOARCHIVE database, produced by Geosystems; GEOBASE, produced by Elsevier Science; the GEOREF database, produced by the American Geological Society; METEOROLOGICAL AND GEOASTROPHYSICAL ABSTRACTS, produced by the American Meteorological Society; the AESIS database, produced by the Australian Mineral Foundation; and the GEODE database, produced by the French Bureau de Recherches Géologiques et Minières. Databases that cover the literature of aquatic science and oceanography include AQUACULTURE, produced by the National Oceanic and Atmospheric Administration; AQUATIC SCIENCES AND FISHERIES ABSTRACTS, which corresponds to the printed Cambridge Scientific Abstracts publication of the same name; AQUALINE, produced by the Water Research Centre; WATER RESOURCES ABSTRACTS, produced by the U.S. Department of the Interior; WATERNET produced by the American Water Works Association; and AFFE, produced by the Association Française pour l'Étude des Eaux.

The reference requirements of health science libraries are addressed by many bibliographic databases, the most famous being MEDLINE, the machine-readable counterpart of three printed indexes published by the National Library of Medicine: *Index Medicus, Index to Dental Literature,* and *International Nursing Index.* EMBASE, produced by Elsevier Science, is the machine-readable counterpart of the printed *Excerpta Medica.* The IAC HEALTH AND WELL-NESS database, produced by Information Access Company, and MDX HEALTH DIGEST, produced by Medical Data Exchange, provide broad coverage of works on medicine, fitness, and nutrition from a variety of professional and consumer-oriented publications. Specialized aspects of medicine and health care management are covered by various databases, including AIDSLINE, CANCERLIT, and TOXLINE, produced by the National Library of Medicine; HEALTHSTAR, produced jointly by the National Library of Medicine and American Hospital Association; BIOETHICSLINE, produced jointly by the Kennedy Institute of Ethics and National Library of Medicine; Allied and Alternative Medicine, produced by the British Library; EXTRAMED, produced by Informania Limited; MANTIS, produced by Action Potential; and the CUMULATIVE INDEX TO NURSING AND ALLIED HEALTH LITERATURE, produced by CINAHL Information Systems. Pharmaceutical literature is covered by a number of specialized databases, including the DERWENT DRUG FILE, produced by Derwent Information; INTERNATIONAL PHARMACEUTICAL ABSTRACTS, produced by the American Society of Health-System Pharmacists; PHARM-LINE, produced by the Guy's and St. Thomas Hospital Trust in association with the U.K. Drug Information Pharmacists Group; and PHARMACEUTICAL NEWS INDEX, produced by UMI.

The DERWENT VETERINARY DRUG FILE, produced by Derwent Information, and CAB VETERINARY SCIENCES/MEDICINE, produced by CAB International, cover the literature of veterinary medicine. Biotechnology is covered by DERWENT BIOTECHNOLOGY ABSTRACTS; CURRENT BIOTECHNOLOGY ABSTRACTS, produced by the Royal Society of Chemistry; and BIOCOMMERCE ABSTRACTS AND DIRECTORY, produced by BioCommerce Data Limited. Databases that index and abstract the worldwide literature of agriculture, food science, and related subjects play a particularly important role in developing countries, where agricultural librarianship is an important area of professional practice. Well-known information sources include AGRICOLA, produced by the National Library of Agriculture; AGRIS International, produced by the Food and Agriculture Organization of the United Nations; CAB Abstracts, produced by CAB International; FOODLINE, produced by Leatherhead Food Research Association; FOODS ADLIBRA, produced by Foods Adlibra Publications; FOOD SCIENCE AND TECHNOLOGY ABSTRACTS, produced by IFIS Publishing; the DERWENT CROP PROTECTION FILE, produced by Derwent Information; FAIREC, produced by the Institut de Recherches sur les Fruits et Agrumes; and IALINE, produced by the Centre de Documentation des Industries Utilisatrices des Produits Agricoles.

Excellent general coverage of the field of engineering is provided by two well-known databases: EI COMPENDEX, produced by Engineering Information Incorporated as the machine-readable counterpart of the *Engineering Index;* and INSPEC, which corresponds to three printed indexing and abstracting journals published by the Institution of Electrical Engineers: *Physics Abstracts, Electrical and Electronics Abstracts,* and *Computer and Control Abstracts.* Many engineering specialties are further served by one or more databases. The APILIT and APIPAT databases, produced by API EnCompass, cover the literature of petroleum engineering, as does the TULSA database, produced by Petroleum Abstracts. CHEMICAL ENGINEERING AND BIOTECHNOLOGY ABSTRACTS is produced by the Royal Society of Chemistry and DECHEMA, the German Society for Chemical Equipment, Chemical Technology, and Biotechnology. The literature of metallurgical engineering is covered by the METADEX database, ENGINEERED MATERIALS ABSTRACTS, and ALUMINUM INDUSTRY ABSTRACTS, all produced by Cambridge Scientific Abstracts. The ISMEC database, also produced by Cambridge Scientific Abstracts, covers the literature of mechanical engineering. The GLOBAL MOBILITY database, produced by SAE Incorporated, and the VWWW database, produced by Volkswagen AG, deal with published literature on automobiles, ships, and other self-propelled vehicles.

Examples of other databases that support literature searching in specialized engineering disciplines include the AEROSPACE DATABASE, produced by the American Institute of Aeronautics and Astronautics; CERAMICS ABSTRACTS, produced by the American Ceramics Society; FLUIDEX, a fluid engineering database produced by Elsevier Science; ICONDA, an international construction database produced in Germany by the Fraunhofer Information Center for Regional Planning and Building Construction; PAPERCHEM, produced by the Institute of Paper Science and Technology; RAPRA, a database that covers rubber, plastics, and adhesives, produced by Rapra Technology Limited; SAFETY SCIENCE ABSTRACTS, produced by Cambridge Scientific Abstracts; TRIS, produced by the Transportation Research Board; WELDASEARCH, produced by the Welding Institute; MEDITEC, a biomedical engineering database, produced in Germany by FIZ Technik; and WORLD SURFACE COATINGS ABSTRACTS, produced by the Paint Research Association of Great Britain. Databases that cover the literature of environmental engineering and energy management include ENERGY SCIENCE AND TECHNOLOGY and NUCLEAR SCIENCE ABSTRACTS, produced by the U.S. Department of Energy; ENERGYLINE and ENVIROLINE, produced by Congressional Information Service; ENVIRONMENTAL BIBLIOGRAPHY, produced by the Environmental Studies Institute; and POLLUTION ABSTRACTS, produced by Cambridge Scientific Abstracts.

While the earliest bibliographic databases emphasized the sciences and technology, coverage of the social sciences has expanded rapidly since the late 1970s. Combined coverage of the various social science disciplines is provided by the SOCIAL SCISEARCH database, the machine-readable version of the *Social Science Citation Index*, published by the Institute for Scientific Information; APPLIED SOCIAL SCIENCES INDEX AND ABSTRACTS, produced by Bowker-Saur; and SOCIAL SCIENCE ABSTRACTS, produced by H. W. Wilson. ERIC—one of the oldest and most widely available machine-readable bibliographic databases—is the primary information resource in the field of education, broadly interpreted to include such fields as library science. Produced by the Educational Research Information Center of the U.S. Department of Education, the ERIC database is the machine-readable counterpart of two printed publications: the *Current Index to Journals in Education* and *Resources in Education*. Other education databases include AV-ONLINE, a guide to audiovisual materials, produced by Access Innovations; EDUCATION ABSTRACTS, produced by H. W. Wilson; and the BRITISH EDUCATION INDEX, produced by the University of Leeds.

PSYCINFO, produced by the American Psychological Association as the machine-readable counterpart of *Psychological Abstracts,* is the primary bibliographic database in the field of psychology. Other bibliographic databases relevant to psychology include MENTAL HEALTH ABSTRACTS, produced by IFI/Plenum Data Corporation; AGELINE, produced by the American Association of Retired Persons; and LINGUISTICS AND LANGUAGE BEHAVIOR ABSTRACTS, produced by Sociological Abstracts Incorporated, which also produces SOCIOLOGICAL ABSTRACTS, the primary bibliographic database in sociology and related disciplines. Selected facets of sociology, psychology, and related fields are covered by the CRIMINAL JUSTICE PERIODICALS INDEX, produced by UMI, and the NCJRS database, produced by the National Criminal Justice Reference Service. The PAIS INTERNATIONAL database, produced by Public Affairs Information Service, emphasizes public affairs and public policy issues. The ECONOMIC LITERATURE INDEX, produced by the American Economic Association, corresponds to the index sections of the quarterly *Journal of Economic Literature* and the annual *Index to Economic Articles.*

Spurred by increased management awareness of the importance of information for decision making, business-oriented bibliographic databases have grown rapidly in number, scope, and popularity. General business literature is covered by several databases, including ABI/INFORM from UMI; IAC GLOBALBASE, IAC MANAGEMENT CONTENTS, IAC PROMT, and IAC TRADE AND INDUSTRY DATABASE from Information Access Company; BUSINESS & INDUSTRY and BUSINESS & MANAGEMENT PRACTICES, produced by Responsive Database Services; INDUSTRY TRENDS AND ANALYSIS, produced by Decision Resources Incorporated; WILSON BUSINESS ABSTRACTS, produced by H. W. Wilson; MANAGEMENT AND MARKETING ABSTRACTS, produced by Pira International; and CANADIAN BUSINESS AND CURRENT AFFAIRS, produced by MicroMedia Limited. The BUSINESS DATELINE database, produced by UMI, indexes hundreds of North American regional business publications.

Various databases cover publications that deal with specific industries or business activities. Examples include the ACCOUNTING AND TAX DATABASE, BANKING INFORMATION SOURCE, and INSURANCE ABSTRACTS, all produced by UMI; INSURANCE PERIODICALS INDEX, produced by NILS Publishing; INSURANCE INFORMATION ONLINE, produced in Switzerland by Insurance Information Online; CHEMICAL BUSINESS NEWSBASE, produced by the Royal Society of Chemistry; CHEMICAL INDUSTRY NOTES, produced by Chemical Abstracts Service; the BIOBUSINESS database, produced by BIOSIS Incorporated; IAC AEROSPACE/DEFENSE MARKETS AND TECHNOLOGY, IAC COMPUTER DATABASE, and IAC MARKETING AND ADVERTISING REFERENCE SERVICE, produced by Information Access Company; MATERIALS BUSINESS FILE, produced by Cambridge Scientific Abstracts; AUTOMOTIVE INFORMATION AND NEWS, produced by Forecast International; MOTOR INDUSTRY RESEARCH, produced by the Motor Industry Research Association; and PHARMACEUTICAL AND HEALTHCARE IN-DUSTRY NEWS, produced by PJB Publications.

While database coverage of the humanities lags well behind that of the sciences, social sciences, and business, some interesting information resources are available. The ARTS AND HUMANITIES SEARCH database, produced by the Institute for Scientific Information, is the machine-readable counterpart of the *Arts and Humanities Citation Index*. HUMANITIES ABSTRACTS, produced by H. W. Wilson, provides multidisciplinary coverage of the humanities. The FRANCIS database, produced by the Centre de Documentation Sciences Humaines du CNRS, provides extensive coverage of European published literature in the humanities and social sciences. Published historical literature is indexed and abstracted in two databases produced by Clio Press Limited: HISTORICAL ABSTRACTS covers world history from 1450 to the present, excluding publications dealing with the United States and Canada, which are covered in the AMERICA: HISTORY AND LIFE database. Both databases are available in printed versions under the same titles.

Clio Press also produces the ART BIBLIOGRAPHIES MODERN database, which covers monographs, periodicals, exhibition catalogs, and other publications dealing with art and design from 1800 to the present. Art periodicals are also indexed by ART ABSTRACTS, produced by H. W. Wilson, and the BIBLIOGRAPHY OF THE HISTORY OF ART, produced by the J. Paul Getty Trust and the Centre National de la Recherche Scientifique. The ARCHITECTURE DATABASE, produced by the British Architectural Library at the Royal Institute of British Architects, is the machine-readable counterpart of the *Architectural Periodicals Index*. The literature of music is covered by the RILM database, which is produced by Repertoire International de Litterature Musicale. The MLA BIBLIOGRAPHY is the machine-readable version of the well-known printed bibliography produced by the Modern Language Association. The literature of philosophy and related fields, such as religion, is covered by the PHILOSOPHER'S INDEX, produced by the Philosopher's Information Center, and the ATLA RELIGION INDEX, produced by the American Theological Library Association.

Non-bibliographic Databases

The machine-readable databases described in the preceding section contain bibliographic citations and, in some cases, abstracts or the complete texts of cited works. While such databases support computer-based literature searching, they are not directly useful for answering reference questions where the desired response is factual information rather than citations to publications. Such reference applications are addressed by an increasing number of non-bibliographic databases.

As their name suggests, non-bibliographic databases are defined by exclusion. They contain information other than citations to books, journal articles, or other publications. In terms of their utility for library reference service, non-bibliographic databases can be divided into two broad groups: (1) textual databases that contain information equivalent to commonly encountered printed reference sources, such as encyclopedias, directories, and other publications, and (2) numeric databases that contain statistical, financial, or other quantitative information.

Of the two groups, textual databases more closely resemble printed reference sources in concept, are easier to understand, and can be more readily assimilated into the broad spectrum of reference applications. In the 1960s, models of so-called libraries of the future predicted the online availability of computer-stored encyclopedias that could be accessed on demand through terminals. Today, such encyclopedias are widely available through online information services, on the World Wide Web, and as CD-ROM information products. Examples include the *Encyclopaedia Britannica, World Book, Grolier Multimedia Encyclopedia, Compton's Interactive Encyclopedia,* and Microsoft's *Encarta Encyclopedia.* Among specialized encyclopedias available in machine-readable form, the KIRK-OTHMER database corresponds to the *Kirk-Othmer Encyclopedia of Chemical Technology,* published by John Wiley.

Directory-type databases are among the most common non-bibliographic reference sources available in machine-readable form. Gale Research, for example, offers the ENCYCLOPEDIA OF ASSOCIATIONS database, a machine-readable version of its popular printed publication. Machine-readable records for each professional and trade association include such basic descriptive information as address, telephone number, and number of members, together with a summary of the association's scope and purpose. Machine-readable sources of biographical information include the MARQUIS WHO'S WHO database, produced by Reed Reference Electronic Publishing; BOWKER BIOGRAPHICAL DIRECTORY, produced by R. R. Bowker; and STANDARD & POOR'S REGISTER-BIOGRAPHICAL, produced by Standard & Poor's Corporation. The Foundation Center offers machine-readable versions of several of its printed directories. The FOUNDATION DIRECTORY database, for example, provides descriptions of more than 25,000 grant-making foundations, while the FOUNDATION GRANTS INDEX database contains information about grants awarded by American philanthropic foundations. The GRANTS database, produced by Oryx Press, contains information about grant programs that are available through governmental and private sources.

A growing number of databases provide directory-type coverage—including name, address, and similar straightforward descriptive information—for business establishments. As the machine-readable counterpart of a widely utilized business reference resource, the THOMAS REGISTER database, produced by Thomas Publishing Company, contains information about U.S. manufacturers and their products. The AMERICAN BUSINESS DIRECTORY, produced by American Business Information, covers ten million U.S. corporations, partnerships, and other companies. The D&B MILLION DOLLAR DATABASE, produced by Dun & Bradstreet, provides location information, executives' names, and summary characteristics for public and private U.S. companies with annual sales exceeding $1 million. Subsets of that database are offered under various names, including DUN'S ELECTRONIC BUSINESS DIRECTORY and DUN'S MARKET IDENTIFIERS. DUN'S REGIONAL BUSINESS DIRECTORY database provides sales and marketing information about U.S. businesses in selected metropolitan areas. STANDARD & POOR'S REGISTER-CORPORATE, produced by Standard & Poor's, provides directory information for over 50,000 leading public and private corporations.

For libraries in multinational companies, directory databases provide valuable management and financial information about international competitors or prospective business partners. KOMPASS USA, produced by Kompass International Neunschwander, provides directory, ownership, and management information for over 50,000 U.S. businesses. Other Kompass databases provide comparable coverage of businesses in Europe, the Middle East, and elsewhere. The HOPPENSTEDT DIRECTORY OF GERMAN COMPANIES, produced by Hoppenstedt Wirtschaftsdatenbank, provides addresses and general business information for German companies. Similar Hoppenstedt databases are available for Austria and the Benelux countries. The FINEX database, produced by Technimetrics, identifies executives of private companies and government agencies throughout the world. Other machine-readable sources of information about international businesses include D&B PRINCIPAL INTERNATIONAL BUSINESSES, produced by Dun & Bradstreet; the ICC BRITISH COMPANY DIRECTORY, produced by ICC Information Group Limited; ESSOR, a catalog of French companies produced by Union Française des Annuaires Professionnels; and the LATIN AMERICAN COMPANY database, produced by International Company Handbook.

Some business directory databases cover specific industries or activities. Among the many examples that might be cited, the HEALTHCARE ORGANIZATIONS database, produced by Medical Economics Company, provides information about health care group purchasing organizations, health maintenance organizations, and hospital personnel. The ADVERTISER AND AGENCY REDBOOKS databases, produced by National Register Publishing, contain information about advertising agencies and companies that spend more than a specified amount each year to advertise their products. The CORPTECH database, produced by Corporate Technology Information Services, is a directory of U.S. technology companies. The THOMSON/POLK BANKING DATABASE, produced by Thomson Financial Publishing, is a comprehensive directory of banks, credit unions, and other financial institutions. The THOMSON RISK MANAGEMENT DIRECTORY covers banks, brokers, and securities dealers. The DMS CONTRACTORS database, produced by DMS Incorporated, identifies companies involved in international defense and aerospace programs. The growing number of directory-type databases dealing with computer-related topics includes the MICROCOMPUTER SOFTWARE GUIDE, produced by R. R. Bowker, and SOFTBASE, produced by Information Sources Incorporated.

In the field of education, the SCHOOL DIRECTORIES databases, produced by Market Data Retrieval Incorporated, contain information about public and private schools and school districts in the United States. As a source of directory-type information about higher education, PETERSON'S COLLEGE DATABASE is the machine-readable counterpart of *Peterson's Guide to Four-Year Colleges* and *Peterson's Guide to Two-Year Colleges*. The GRADLINE database is equivalent to *Peterson's Annual Survey of Graduate Education*. The RESEARCH CENTERS AND SERVICES DIRECTORY, produced by Gale Research, provides information about university-based and non-profit research organizations worldwide. The

EUROPEAN RESEARCH AND DEVELOPMENT database, produced by Bowker-Saur, covers academic and commercial research activities in a variety of organizations. The EVENTLINE database, produced by Elsevier Science, is a directory of conferences, symposia, conventions, and other events on scientific, medical, technical, and business topics.

An important group of directory-type, non-bibliographic databases contains information about chemical substances. Probably the best known example is the CAS REGISTRY database, produced by Chemical Abstracts Service. It contains CAS registry numbers, molecular formulas, available synonyms, and other information on substances that have been named in documents cited in the CHEMICAL ABSTRACTS database. Other CAS databases include CHEM-CATS, a machine-readable catalog of commercially available chemicals; CAS-REACT, which deals with chemical reactions; and CHEMLIST, which contains information about regulated chemicals. The CHEMSAFE database, produced in Germany by DECHEMA, covers the safety characteristics of flammable substances. The BEILSTEIN database, produced by Chemiedaten und Software GmbH, contains organic chemical structures, numeric property data, and preparation and reaction information. It is the machine-readable counterpart of the *Beilstein Handbook of Organic Chemistry*. The GMELIN database, produced by the Gmelin Institute for Inorganic Chemistry, includes chemical structures, molecular formulas, and numeric data. The CHAPMAN AND HALL CHEMICAL DATABASE contains chemical names, synonyms, chemical and physical properties, hazards, toxicity, and other reference information.

The CHEMTOX database, produced by Research Consultants Incorporated, is a collection of health and safety information for chemical substances. The PESTICIDE FACT FILE, produced by the British Crop Protection Council, provides directory-type information for fungicides, herbicides, insecticides, and other microbial agents and chemicals used in agricultural, veterinary, and other public health applications. The PLASPEC database, produced by IFI/Plenum Data Corporation, contains trade names, chemical descriptions, engineering data, and other information for plastic materials. The MERCK INDEX database, produced by Merck and Company, is the machine-readable version of a widely utilized guide to chemicals, drugs, and biological agents. The DRUG INFORMATION FULLTEXT database, produced by the American Society of Hospital Pharmacists, is the machine-readable counterpart of two printed publications: the *American Hospital Formulary Service* and the *Handbook of Injectable Drugs*. The DRUGS OF THE FUTURE database, produced by Prous Science Publishers, contains information about chemical structures, pharmacokinetics, metabolism, toxicity, and other topics. The USP DICTIONARY, produced by United States Pharmacopeia, is an authoritative listing of drug names. The MARTINDALE PHARMACOPOEIA database, produced by the Royal Pharmaceutical Society of Great Britain, provides information about drugs and medicine, including generic and proprietary names, CAS registry numbers, physical and pharmaceutical properties, dosages, and contraindications.

Numeric databases that contain financial and statistical information have been used for many years by businesses and government agencies to analyze demographic and market trends. Commonly cited and widely available examples include databases produced by the U.S. Bureau of the Census and comparable government agencies in other countries. The DISCLOSURE, DISCLOSURE/SPECTRUM OWNERSHIP, and EDGARPLUS databases, produced by Disclosure Incorporated, contain financial and ownership information pertaining to publicly owned U.S. companies. The SEC ONLINE database, produced by SEC Online Incorporated, contains information filed by public companies with the U.S. Securities and Exchange Commission. The EIU COUNTRY RISKS AND FORECASTS database, produced by the Economist Intelligence Unit, provides information about the creditworthiness and economic outlook for specific countries. The MG FINANCIAL/STOCK STATISTICS database, produced by Media General, and the VALUE LINE database, produced by Value Line Incorporated, contain detailed financial and stock price information for selected public companies. The EXTEL INTERNATIONAL FINANCIAL CARDS database, produced by Extel Financial Limited, provides financial information about large international companies. ICC BRITISH COMPANY FINANCIAL DATASHEETS, produced by ICC Information Group Limited, provides financial information for U.K. companies. The TEIKOKU DATABANK is the largest machine-readable directory of Japanese companies.

Databases that contain historical and predictive economic information are an increasingly common resource in corporate, banking, brokerage, government, and other libraries that support financial planning and econometric analysis. Such databases are produced by various financial analysis and publishing companies, including Citicorp Database Services, DFI/McGraw-Hill, Quest Economics, Responsive Database Services, and the WEFA Group. Examples of machine-readable econometric resources produced by government agencies and non-profit organizations include the CONSUMER PRICE INDEX (CPI) and PRODUCER PRICE INDEX (PPI) databases, produced by the U.S. Bureau of Labor Statistics; the CONFERENCE BOARD DATA BANK, produced by the Conference Board; the CANSIM database, produced by Statistics Canada; the FLOW OF FUNDS and INTERNATIONAL FINANCIAL STATISTICS databases, produced by the International Monetary Fund; the MAIN ECONOMIC INDICATORS database, produced by the OECD; the SPHINX database, produced by the Institut National de la Statistique et des Études Économiques; and the CRONOS-EUROSTAT database, produced by the Statistical Office of the European Communities. In addition to their obvious importance for corporate libraries that support business decision making and for academic libraries that support graduate business curricula and faculty research, such databases will prove attractive to public libraries interested in developing fee-based information services for their local business communities.

ONLINE INFORMATION SERVICES

As previously indicated, libraries can purchase machine-readable bibliographic and non-bibliographic databases on magnetic tape for processing on their own computers using custom-developed information retrieval software. During the late 1960s and early 1970s, a number of such computer-based literature searching systems were implemented to automate the production of comprehensive retrospective bibliographies and current awareness listings. In the typical application, a scientist or other researcher submitted a request for a literature search to a specially trained librarian or information specialist who formulated an appropriate search strategy consisting of a combination of commands and search terms. These search requests were then keypunched and batched for processing against one or more databases at prescheduled intervals, the computer producing lists of citations for each request. Subject to the limitations of offline, non-interactive data processing, these early computer-based systems simplified the performance of certain complex or comprehensive literature searches requiring the logical coordination of multiple search terms.

Custom-developed literature retrieval systems based on the acquisition of bibliographic data in machine-readable form were primarily implemented by large university, corporate, and government libraries, especially those serving researchers in scientific and technical disciplines. As with the acquisition of cataloging information on MARC tapes, most libraries lacked access to the computer resources and programming expertise necessary to take advantage of available machine-readable bibliographic data resources. During the 1960s and early 1970s, the needs of these libraries were addressed by fee-based search services operated by producers of machine-readable databases or by third parties, such as university-based technical information centers. These services, like their in-house counterparts, customarily operated in the offline, batch processing mode.

Taking the MEDLARS search service operated by the National Library of Medicine as an example, librarians in medical schools, hospitals, and other health service facilities first interviewed researchers locally in order to prepare a written statement of their information requirements to be mailed or otherwise transmitted to the National Library of Medicine. There an information specialist analyzed the submitted statement and formulated a search strategy to be executed in a batch with other incoming search requests against the MEDLARS database, the machine readable counterpart of the printed *Index Medicus*. The results, consisting of a printout of retrieved citations, were mailed or otherwise delivered to the originating library for dissemination to the researcher who requested the search. As with in-house literature searching systems, this approach simplified and speeded the completion of lengthy and complex searches that are difficult and time-consuming to perform manually. Without direct interaction between requesters and search specialists, however, such searches lacked precision—that is, some or even many of the retrieved citations proved irrelevant to the researchers' stated or implied information requirements.

Online Search Concepts

As discussed elsewhere in this book, developments in library automation have generally reflected trends in the broad field of data processing. In the early 1970s, the computing industry began to shift its emphasis from offline, batch-oriented data processing to the development of online systems that process requests for information entered at remote terminals in a time-sharing environment. As with offline search systems, a requester's information requirements are delineated and a search strategy, consisting of commands and search terms, is formulated. But rather than being batched for later input, the search strategy is entered at an online terminal, and an immediate indication of the number of presumably relevant citations is obtained. A few citations can then be displayed or printed for immediate examination, and the search strategy modified, if necessary, to improve precision. Once the appropriateness of the search strategy is confirmed, all or selected results can be displayed, downloaded, or printed locally. Alternatively, search results can be printed offline for later distribution to the requester.

A few government and corporate libraries have developed their own online search capabilities, using machine-readable bibliographic databases created locally or purchased from publishers of printed indexing and abstracting services. Most libraries, however, obtain online, time-shared access to bibliographic and non-bibliographic databases through fee-based information services that are variously described as online information services, online search services, or simply online services. As outlined later in this chapter, such services differ in the number and type of databases offered, but they share a common operating methodology: they create, purchase, or otherwise obtain bibliographic and non-bibliographic databases in machine-readable form; convert them to a format required for storage on their own computers; and allow libraries or other subscribers to perform various retrieval operations on the databases using prewritten software. Some services also offer private file capabilities that allow libraries or other customers to establish their own databases for online access. As noted briefly in chapter 6, such private file capabilities can be used for online catalog implementations.

Like the general-purpose database management systems discussed in chapter 3, the bibliographic database management systems implemented and operated by online information services support non-procedural query languages that allow users to initiate literature searches or other retrieval operations by entering a series of commands accompanied by specified retrieval parameters. Although they require study and practice to use effectively, these query languages are easily learned and do not require the memorization of elaborate sets of rules or careful attention to the formulation of algorithms that characterize conventional procedural programming languages.

Taking the query language utilized by the popular Dialog information service as an example, most operations can be performed with a simple set of commands. Following the entry of passwords that identify the terminal user as a valid DIALOG customer, the BEGIN command, followed by the number of a desired database, informs the DIALOG system that the user wants to begin retrieval operations in that database. All DIALOG databases are identified by numbers contained in a master list that is available in printed form or accessible online. Thus, a command of the form

BEGIN 15

will initiate retrieval operations in the ABI/INFORM database, which covers business publications. If desired, several databases can be searched simultaneously, either by entering their identifying numbers or by selecting one of the preformed database groups assembled by DIALOG for subject-oriented information retrieval. The geology subject group, for example, includes GEO-ARCHIVE, GEOREF, GEOBASE, and other databases. Other online services offer similar capabilities, although they may identify databases by names or alphabetic abbreviations rather than numbers.

Once a given database has been selected, DIALOG's EXPAND command, followed by a search term or phrase, enables the searcher to determine whether that term or phrase is listed in the master index for the active database and, if so, how many times it appears in the database's individual records. In effect, the EXPAND command causes the DIALOG system to display that section of the database index where the indicated search term or phrase appears. In many cases, terms or phrases that are alphabetically adjacent to the indicated term may prove relevant to the search. The DIALOG system indexes every significant term that appears in any part of a record. With some databases, the operation of the EXPAND command can be limited to the occurrence of the search term in a specific part of a record, such as the title or assigned subject headings.

The EXPAND command is useful for identifying possible search terms or phrases. Specific retrieval operations are initiated by the SELECT command. When followed by a search term or phrase, the SELECT command instructs the DIALOG system to establish a set of database records indexed with the indicated term or phrase. Thus, the command

SELECT VIDEO

will establish a set of records in which the term video appears. As with the EXPAND command, operation of the SELECT command can be restricted to a specific part of a record. As an interactive search system, DIALOG responds to each SELECT command by assigning a set or statement number to it, indicating the number of index entries for the specified search term or phrase and repeating the command itself for confirmation purposes. Thus, a response of the form

1   408   VIDEO

indicates that the DIALOG system has identified a set of retrieved records that it will hereafter refer to as set number 1, that the set contains 408 records, and that the records contain the search term *video*.

While some literature searches or other information retrieval operations involve a single search term, many are based on combinations of several terms. In the DIALOG system, such retrieval requirements are met by using logical operators to combine the sets created by two or more SELECT commands. As an example, a search for citations on the use of video technology in medicine might be accomplished by the following sequence of search statements:

SELECT VIDEO
1   408   VIDEO
SELECT MEDICINE
2   946   MEDICINE
SELECT S1 AND S2
3   28   S1 AND S2

The last SELECT command instructs the DIALOG system to apply the logical AND operation to citations contained in the sets created by the first two SE-LECT commands. The results constitute a third set that might later be combined with other sets.

Three logical operators are widely encountered in computer-based information retrieval systems: AND, OR, and NOT. These logical operators, which are also supported by some online public access catalog systems, are sometimes called Boolean operators. They are named for George Boole, a nineteenth-century mathematician who pioneered the application of mathematical concepts and algebraic symbols to the field of logic. In the example depicted above, the logical AND operator creates a third set from records that are members of both of two previously established sets—that is, those records that contain the terms *video* and *medicine*. In effect, the AND operation seeks the logical intersection of the two sets. Much of the power of computer-based reference service is derived from the logical AND operator.

The logical OR operator takes two previously established sets and combines them into a third set. It thus establishes the logical union of two sets. In information retrieval applications, it can be used to group synonymous or related terms into a single set for search purposes. Hence, the sequence of search statements:

SELECT VIDEO

1   408   VIDEO

SELECT TELEVISION

2   312   TELEVISION

SELECT S1 OR S2

3   705   S1 OR S2

SELECT MEDICINE

4   946   MEDICINE

SELECT S3 AND S4

5   46   S3 AND S4

combines the sets of records indexed with either the terms *video* or *television* into a third set that is then combined, using the AND operator, with the set of records indexed with the term *medicine*. The result is the retrieval of records indexed with both *video* and *medicine* or with both *television* and *medicine*.

Experienced DIALOG users can perform the same operation with a single command of the form

SELECT (VIDEO OR TELEVISION) AND MEDICINE

In this example, the DIALOG system will perform the parenthesized operation first, responding to the command with a listing of search terms and set numbers.

1   408   VIDEO

2   312   TELEVISION

3   705   VIDEO OR TELEVISION

4   946   MEDICINE

5   46   (VIDEO OR TELEVISION) AND MEDICINE

If desired, the SELECT and EXPAND commands can be combined with a truncation operator to search for terms with common roots. Thus, a command of the form

SELECT VIDEO?

will select records indexed with *videos, videotape, videocassette, videodisc, videotext,* and other singular and plural words that begin with the character string "video." Similarly, the SELECT command can combine with operators that specify the desired proximity of two search terms. Thus, a command of the form

SELECT VIDEO (W) MONITORS

will retrieve records that contain the word "video" immediately followed by the word "monitors." Other DIALOG commands permit the storage of specified command sequences for use in subsequent online sessions.

Records from specified sets can be displayed online, downloaded for local storage and later use, or printed offline in user-specified formats and sequences. Other online information services support similar retrieval capabilities, although the syntax and semantics of particular commands will necessarily vary from one service to another. For inexperienced or untrained users, online services increasingly support menu-driven interfaces. Recently, many services have introduced Internet access via Web browsers that make full use of graphical user interface components. As discussed below, some newer online information services are exclusively available on the World Wide Web, and some industry analysts have questioned the continued viability of conventional online information services with command-mode interfaces, which they criticize as old-fashioned and cumbersome. While menu-driven and Web-based implementations speed learning where searches will be performed by library users, command-mode operation by a trained information specialist may be required for best results, particularly for queries with complex retrieval characteristics.

Interface characteristics aside, an online information service is—as previously defined—a publicly available, fee-based information service that provides online, time-shared access to one or more computer databases. Most online search services operate on mainframe or minicomputer-class hardware that is installed at the search service's headquarters. Customer locations are equipped with compatible terminals and, in some cases, software.

Online information services can be divided into three broad categories, based on their database content and intended audiences:

1. Multidisciplinary online services offer databases on a variety of subjects for a diverse clientele, including scientists, engineers, managers, professional practitioners, and scholars, as well as the general public.

2. News- and business-oriented online services provide multidisciplinary subject coverage but emphasize news and business information of practical significance, as opposed to the scholarly or research-oriented databases offered by most multidisciplinary services.

   3. Specialized search services limit database coverage to particular subject areas, such as science or engineering, or to professional disciplines
   or activities, such as medicine or law.

The following discussion surveys online search services that are suitable for
library reference applications and that count libraries among their most important customers. The survey excludes consumer-oriented online services, such as
America Online, that offer databases in addition to other computer services. It
also excludes certain business-oriented information providers—such as ADP
Network Services, Citicorp Database Services, Desktop Data, DRI/McGraw-Hill,
IBM InfoSage, and WEFA Group—that market online services directly to financial planners, corporate strategists, investment analysts, administrative managers, and business consultants. While such consumer- and business-oriented
services may be used for library reference support, that is not their principal market. Finally, the discussion excludes bibliographic utilities, which provide online
access to large databases that are intended mainly for cataloging support or resource sharing rather than reference service. Products and services offered by
bibliographic utilities are covered in chapter 5.

Multidisciplinary Services

Multidisciplinary online search services, as defined above, provide databases
appropriate to a variety of subject areas and information requirements. While
competitive pricing is an important factor when selecting an online search service for library applications, the availability of relevant databases is the most
critical consideration. While some database producers have exclusive arrangements with a particular online search service, overlapping coverage is increasingly common. Although no online service exactly duplicates the offerings of
any other, certain databases are so widely available that no multidisciplinary
online service can base its competitive position on them. Examples include
ABI/INFORM, BIOSIS PREVIEWS, CHEMICAL ABSTRACTS, EI COMPEN-
DEX, INSPEC, MEDLINE, NTIS, and PSYCINFO. As the following discussion
indicates, individual multidisciplinary services are largely distinguished by the
breadth and depth of their offerings beyond this core group.

   DIALOG, the world's largest multidisciplinary online information service,
is operated by Dialog Corporation, which was formed in 1997 through the
merger of M.A.I.D. plc and Knight-Ridder Information Incorporated. Knight-
Ridder Information had acquired DIALOG in 1988 from the Lockheed Missiles
and Space Company, which introduced the service in 1972. Dialog Corporation
also operates the Data-Star and Profound online services described below.
Among its other library-related operations, Dialog Corporation owns CARL
Corporation, a supplier of integrated library systems, and the UnCover Company, a document delivery service.

   DIALOG's competitive position is firmly established; it is a virtually indispensable information resource for any library with a serious commitment to
computerized reference service. Its offerings have expanded steadily and significantly over the past two decades; excluding practice files and counting split
files as a single database, DIALOG now provides online access to more than 400

databases. While other online services may offer more favorable pricing for certain databases or provide better topical coverage of selected areas, DIALOG is unquestionably the best choice for the broadest possible subject coverage from a single online service. As further competitive advantages, DIALOG offers more databases per subject area than other multidisciplinary services, and many of its offerings are exclusive.

Through the late 1980s, the largest number of DIALOG databases provided bibliographic coverage of scientific and technical subjects. Since that time, however, business interest in online searching has increased dramatically, and DIALOG's business-oriented information resources have expanded accordingly. Now the most numerous subject group, business databases account for about one-third of DIALOG's online offerings, as compared with less than one-fourth for scientific and technical databases. Besides their obvious importance for corporate libraries that retrieve information for business decision making and academic libraries that support graduate business curricula and faculty research, DIALOG's business-oriented databases will prove useful to public libraries that offer fee-based information services to their local business communities.

Although now outnumbered by business information resources, DIALOG's impressive range of scientific and technical databases rivals the offerings of specialized search services described later in this chapter. Chemistry is covered by more than twenty bibliographic and non-bibliographic databases. Bioscientists and medical researchers can draw on over forty databases. Patents are covered by more than a dozen databases. DIALOG offers at least one database for each engineering specialty, including environmental engineering, materials science and metallurgy, geological engineering, textile engineering, fluid engineering, mechanical engineering, polymer science, and packaging technology.

DIALOG's news-oriented coverage includes online access to the complete texts of more than fifty U.S. newspapers published by Knight-Ridder, plus the *New York Times* and selected Canadian and United Kingdom newspapers. Additional news coverage is provided by newswire databases, as well as newspaper indexes that provide conventional bibliographic coverage of news publications. DIALOG's coverage of the social sciences and humanities is comparable in breadth and depth to the offerings of other multidisciplinary search services but much less extensive than its business and scientific offerings. Most major subject disciplines are covered by at least one or two databases. The humanities and social sciences are also covered by certain general reference databases, such as the IAC MAGAZINE DATABASE from Information Access Company, PERIODICALS ABSTRACTS PLUSTEXT from UMI, and such general bibliographic databases as BOOKS IN PRINT, BRITISH BOOKS IN PRINT, LC MARC BOOKS, and REMARC.

In addition to its command-oriented search service described above, DIALOG can be accessed through the World Wide Web. DIALOG Select, a related service, offers a subset of DIALOG databases grouped topically. Suitable for end-user searching, it can be accessed through the World Wide Web or a Windows interface.

The Data-Star online service was established by Radio Suisse in the early 1980s to serve the European market. It subsequently expanded its customer base to other countries, including the United States. As noted above, Data-Star is now owned by Dialog Corporation. Operating on computers located in Berne, Switzerland, it is the largest European online service measured by the number of databases offered. With more than 325 databases available, it is second only to DIALOG among multidisciplinary search services. Data-Star's competitive position is based on its extensive biomedical subject coverage and its distinctive business and news-oriented information resources. In both areas, Data-Star provides certain unique or unusual European databases.

Data-Star's biomedical offerings include widely available databases from the National Library of Medicine and other information providers, as well as health-oriented resources produced in the United Kingdom. Examples include CAB HEALTH, CAB VETERINARY SCIENCES/MEDICINE, DHSS-DATA, DHSS-MEDICAL TOXICOLOGY AND HEALTH, GENERAL PRACTITIONER, and HSELINE. Data-Star's superior pharmaceutical coverage encompasses more than two dozen drug information and regulatory databases from U.S. and European suppliers. Data-Star offers a good selection of chemical databases, but its coverage of other scientific and technical disciplines is unremarkable; engineering and applied science are served by a handful of databases with limited subject specialization. Data-Star provides a few, widely available databases in the social sciences and humanities.

For libraries in multinational companies, Data-Star's superior selection of European business databases provides valuable directory and financial information about international competitors or prospective business partners. Data-Star's European news coverage includes an excellent selection of newswire databases plus online access to the complete texts of selected European newspapers. Many of Data-Star's news and business databases require a reading knowledge of languages other than English. Like DIALOG, Data-Star is available in command-oriented and World Wide Web implementations.

The Questel-Orbit search service was formed in 1994, when Groupe France Telecom, the operator of Questel, acquired Orbit, one of the oldest and most famous online search services. Like DIALOG and Data-Star, the Orbit and Questel services operate on different computers and employ different command-oriented retrieval procedures. Together they offer about 175 databases. While both services provide online access to impressive technical information resources, there is little duplication of database offerings. Questel-Orbit customers receive passwords for both services.

The Orbit search service has changed ownership and market emphasis several times since its inception in 1973. Under its originator, System Development Corporation, Orbit was a general-purpose multidisciplinary search service. Competing directly with DIALOG, it offered databases appropriate to a broad spectrum of research requirements. During the early 1980s, Orbit narrowed its focus considerably. While remaining a nominally multidisciplinary search service, it emphasized exclusive access to important technical and business databases that complemented, rather than competed with, other vendors' offerings. In recent years, however, those databases have become available through competing services. For the most part, Orbit's remaining exclusive databases are useful but lesser known European offerings, such as GEOMECHANICS ABSTRACTS from Elsevier/Geo Abstracts, IMAGING ABSTRACTS from the Royal

Photographic Society, and TROPICAL AGRICULTURE from Koninkijk Instituut voor de Tropen.

Exclusivity aside, Orbit's scientific and technical information resources remain impressive. Strong areas include patent information, chemistry, earth science, engineering, food science, pharmaceuticals, and occupational safety. Orbit's non-technical offerings have fallen off steadily and significantly since the 1980s. Its limited business coverage includes several technical business databases. Orbit no longer offers databases in the social sciences or humanities.

The Questel search service has been available to North American subscribers since 1983, but its merger with Orbit significantly enhanced its visibility among U.S. libraries. Questel's competitive position is based on its European, particularly French, information resources. It will appeal most strongly to research-oriented industrial and technical libraries that require convenient online access to information about international research, business, and news activities. Many of Questel's databases are unique or available only through smaller, less conveniently accessible European search services. While some of Questel's databases are in English, others require a reading knowledge of French, German, or Italian.

Questel's principal topical concentrations are science, technology, and business. Its exclusive scientific and technical offerings emphasize European research publications and activities. An extensive group of patent and trademark databases covers Austria, Belgium, Denmark, France, Germany, Italy, Liechtenstein, Luxembourg, Monaco, the Netherlands, Switzerland, and the United Kingdom. Questel's limited biomedical coverage includes an implementation of the MEDLINE database with French as well as English descriptors. Questel also offers the CHEMICAL ABSTRACTS and PASCAL databases, but other search services, including Orbit, provide broader coverage of science and technology.

Questel's collection of business directory databases will appeal to special libraries in companies with European branch offices, subsidiaries, manufacturing facilities, business partners, or investment interests. Questel's news-oriented databases include the online versions of French newspapers and newsmagazines, as well as newswire databases in French, English, and Spanish. In the social sciences and humanities, Questel's most important offering is the FRANCIS database, produced by the Centre de Documentation Sciences Humaines du CNRS.

Ovid Online, formerly known as BRS Online, offers approximately eighty databases. While multidisciplinary in scope, it is particularly noteworthy for its extensive coverage of biomedical and allied health subjects. In addition to MEDLINE and other familiar information resources, Ovid Online offers several exclusive medical and pharmaceutical databases plus full-text access to selected medical journals. Ovid Online's strong coverage of allied health fields includes databases that deal with nursing, sports medicine, osteopathy, and chiropractic medicine. Technical and business databases are limited to such widely available information resources as ABI/INFORM, EI COMPENDEX, INSPEC, and NTIS. Ovid Online's offerings in the social sciences and humanities are useful but not distinctive. A good selection of general reference databases includes BOOKS IN PRINT, DISSERTATION ABSTRACTS, EXPANDED

ACADEMIC INDEX, NEWSPAPER ABSTRACTS, PERIODICALS ABSTRACTS, and READERS' GUIDE ABSTRACTS.

FirstSearch is a multidisciplinary online search service operated by OCLC. Designed from its inception for end-user searching, it features a menu-driven interface that simplifies retrieval procedures and minimizes training requirements. Alternatively, an implementation developed for the World Wide Web provides attractively formatted displays and graphical user interface components. FirstSearch offers more than seventy databases in a variety of subject areas. Its most important information resource is OCLC WORLDCAT, the world's largest collection of bibliographic records for books and monographs. As discussed in chapter 5, OCLC's bibliographic utility uses the WORLDCAT database for cataloging and resource sharing, but FirstSearch is the only online service that supports subject searching of WORLDCAT. FirstSearch also provides exclusive access to other OCLC-produced databases, including ARTICLEFIRST, which contains citations from the table of contents pages of over 13,000 journals; CONTENTSFIRST, which contains table of contents pages and holdings information; and NETFIRST, which indexes World Wide Web pages, library catalogs, electronic journals, news groups, and other Internet resources. In addition, the PROCEEDINGSFIRST and PAPERFIRST databases provide access to conference papers accessioned by the British Library's Document Supply Centre.

FirstSearch provides good breadth but limited depth of subject coverage. Most disciplines are served by one or two databases. Humanities, social sciences, and general reference offerings compare favorably with other multidisciplinary services, but scientific and business coverage are noticeably weaker. Certain databases, such as BIOSIS PREVIEWS, are offered in abbreviated versions. While some research-oriented databases are provided, FirstSearch is better suited to college, public, and school libraries than to university and technical libraries. Some FirstSearch databases will prove most useful to students writing term papers or to consumers seeking background information about specific topics. Among its noteworthy features, FirstSearch links bibliographic records in certain databases to library holdings symbols.

Addressing the same market as FirstSearch, EBSCOhost is an online information service operated by EBSCO Information Services, a well-known supplier of periodical subscription services, document delivery services, and related information products. EBSCOhost is a Z39.50-compliant system based on client/server technology. It is accessible through direct connection or via the Internet. A World Wide Web implementation is compatible with popular browser programs. Libraries can customize EBSCOhost search screens, control retrieval and display options, and mark titles that are held locally.

EBSCOhost appeals principally to public, academic, and school libraries. Its most important offerings are general- and special-interest databases produced by EBSCO itself. Examples include MASTERFILE FULLTEXT, which indexes 3,000 journals with full text available for about one-third of the titles; PRIMARY SEARCH and MIDDLE SEARCH, which provide full-text access to popular magazines for elementary and middle school students; HEALTH SOURCE and HEALTH SOURCE PLUS, which contain the full text of journals and pamphlets dealing with health and nutrition; BUSINESS SOURCE PLUS and BUSINESS SOURCE ELITE, which cover business periodicals; ACADEMIC SEARCH FULLTEXT and ACADEMIC ABSTRACTS FULLTEXT, which index publications of interest to undergraduate college students; CANADIAN MAS FULLTEXT, which indexes Canadian publications; WORLD MAGAZINE BANK, which is specifically designed for users in the United Kingdom, Australia, and South Africa; and SERIALS DIRECTORY, which contains bibliographic data for 185,000 journals, magazines, and other serial publications. EBSCOhost also offers a small selection of widely available databases from other producers.

ProQuest Direct is a multidisciplinary search service operated by UMI, a leading supplier of databases, documents, micropublications, and related information products. Accessible through the World Wide Web, ProQuest Direct provides online access to databases produced by UMI and other information providers. Examples of UMI databases include ABI/INFORM, ACCOUNTING AND TAX DATABASE, BANKING INFORMATION SOURCE, BUSINESS DATELINE, PERIODICALS ABSTRACTS, the COMPREHENSIVE DISSERTATION INDEX, and PHARMACEUTICAL NEWS INDEX. Most of these databases are offered by other online services. Besides online retrieval of bibliographic citations and abstracts, ProQuest Direct provides full-text access to selected newspapers, journal articles, and other documents from 1991 to the present. ProQuest Direct incorporates the extensive collection of news publications formerly offered by DataTimes, which UMI acquired in 1997. ProQuest Direct also offers online access to digitized page-images for many documents. A unique feature combines full text with images of photos, charts, diagrams, or other graphic components. For documents that are not available online, UMI offers fax or overnight delivery from its huge collection of periodicals, newspapers, and dissertations.

The WilsonWeb search service provides online access to databases produced by H. W. Wilson Company, a well-known publisher of reference tools. As its name suggests, it is accessible through the World Wide Web. Some WilsonWeb databases are computer-searchable versions of printed Wilson indexes, such as the *Readers' Guide to Periodical Literature* and *Business Periodicals Index*, which are widely utilized in public, academic, and school libraries. Other WilsonWeb databases, which contain abstracts and the full text of selected documents, have no printed counterparts. WilsonWeb competes with other multidisciplinary search services, which also offer online access to Wilson-produced databases plus other information resources.

The European Space Agency-Information Retrieval Service (ESA-IRS) has offered online information services since the early 1970s. Operating on computers located in Italy, ESA-IRS has been available to North American libraries since the mid-1980s. While its database catalog is impressive, ESA-IRS lacks the breadth and depth of subject coverage provided by DIALOG and Data-Star. Since its inception, it has emphasized scientific and technical databases, some of which support highly specialized engineering activities. As might be expected, aerospace, including aeronautics and astronomy, is a strong subject area. Distinctive offerings include European technical databases, such as BRIX-

FLAIR, produced by the Building Research Establishment Library, EDF-DOC from Electricité de France, GLASSFILE from Stazione Sperimentale del Vetro, and SHIP ABSTRACTS from the Netherlands Maritime Information Centre.

Measured by the number of databases it offers and the diversity of its topical coverage, QL Systems Limited is the leading online provider of Canadian information. Through the early 1990s, it operated QL QuickSearch, a multidisciplinary search service that provided an excellent selection of Canadian legal, news, and technical information resources. The QL QuickSearch service has been renamed Quicklaw to reflect its legal emphasis. While news and technical databases remain available, legal, legislative, and taxation information dominate Quicklaw offerings, although its subject coverage is sufficiently broad to warrant a multidisciplinary designation.

Some of Quicklaw's legal databases are produced by QL Systems itself. Others are obtained from Canadian government agencies, universities, or legal publishers. Canadian federal and provincial laws and legal decisions are covered in a variety of full-text databases. Quicklaw provides online full-text versions of Canadian law journals, law reviews, legal newspapers, and legal newsletters. Legal index databases such as the INDEX TO CANADIAN LEGAL LITERATURE and CANADIAN LAW SYMPOSIA INDEX provide bibliographic rather than full-text coverage. Quicklaw's news and public affairs databases include several Canadian newswire services and the CANADIAN JOURNALISM DATABASE. Quicklaw's technical offerings include the Certified Products Database, a directory of products that have been tested and certified for sale by the Canadian Standards Association. BOREAL NORTHERN TITLES, ARCTIC SCIENCE AND TECHNOLOGY, SCOTT POLAR RESEARCH INSTITUTE LIBRARY CATALOG, and YUKON BIBLIOGRAPHY contain information about Canada's cold regions. Several Quicklaw databases deal with environmental sciences and metallurgy. Examples include ASBESTOS INFORMATION, produced by the University of Sherbrooke; IEA COAL RESEARCH, produced by the International Energy Agency; and various mining databases produced by Canada Natural Resources.

The OZLINE search service, operated by National Library of Australia, provides online access to approximately forty bibliographic and directory databases that are produced in Australia and deal with Australian topics. Examples include the AUSTRALIAN NATIONAL BIBLIOGRAPHY, which is produced by the National Library of Australia for works published in Australia, about Australia, or by Australians; the RASA database, a register of archival records relating to science in Australia; the AUSTRALIAN EDUCATION INDEX, which covers education at all levels plus library and information science; and the AUSTRALASIAN MEDICAL INDEX, which covers medical publications in Australia and New Zealand. Other OZLINE databases deal with agriculture, engineering, law, criminal justice, and social issues.

Other multidisciplinary search services provide online access to information resources that are not readily available elsewhere. Such services typically offer a small number of databases. SDM, for example, is a French-Canadian search service operated by Services Documentaires Multimedia Incorporated. It provides online access to French-language databases on a variety of subjects.

Most of the databases are produced in Quebec by SDM itself or by provincial government agencies and other organizations. The BLAISE-LINE search service is operated by the National Bibliographic Service unit of the British Library, which produces the majority of BLAISE-LINE's databases. Its online offerings include bibliographic files, which contain cataloging and other information for books and serial publications; British Library catalogs, which cover various departmental collections; and a limited selection of subject databases.

The Belgian Information Dissemination Service (BELINDIS) is operated in Brussels by the Belgian Ministry of Economic Affairs. Its principal offerings are a unique group of legal and public affairs databases produced in and pertaining to the Benelux countries. L'Européenne de Donnes is a French search service that provides online access to databases in five broad subject areas: news and public affairs, law, business and economics, social sciences, and sports. Eurobases, a commercial search service based in Brussels, and ECHO, a non-commercial service operated in Luxembourg by the European Commission Host Organization, provide online access to databases produced by the European Commission. Infoscan, a unit of the Danish Ministry of Research and Technology, operates DIANE Online, a small collection of databases that are accessible free of charge.

A relatively new and rapidly growing group of Web-based multidisciplinary search services provide bibliographic citations and full-text access to selected publications obtained from a variety of sources. As an example, the Electric Library from Infonautics is available in versions for elementary and secondary schools, colleges, public libraries, and consumers. All versions offer online access to dozens of newspapers, newswires, and other news sources; hundreds of popular magazines; and selected reference books, historical works, maps, and photographs. The Electric Library Business Edition, a related service, offers articles from news and business magazines, press releases, television and radio transcripts, company directory and financial information, and market research reports and statistics. The Northern Light search service combines the attributes of an online information service and a Web search engine. In response to retrieval queries, it will deliver information from news, business, popular, and scholarly publications as well as references to pertinent Web sites. Like Infonautics' Electric Library, Northern Light provides full-text access to a well-selected collection of publications on a variety of subjects. Other examples of Web-based multidisciplinary search services include Information Quest and SIRS Researcher. These Web-based services are designed for end-user searching with little or no training, although they do support Boolean operations and other advanced retrieval capabilities for experienced searchers.

News and Business Services

An important category of online search services is multidisciplinary in subject scope but specializes in news information sources, including newspapers, newsmagazines, newsletters, and newswire databases. Given the reference value of news information, the library significance of these search services is obvious. Used alone or in combination with news-oriented databases offered by multidisciplinary services, they combine breadth and depth of subject coverage with rapid, complex information retrieval capabilities that are difficult or impossible to achieve with conventional printed sources. In recent years, most news-oriented services have broadened their coverage to include financial news sources as well as company directories, analytical reports, and other business information. As previously noted, news and business services emphasize practical rather than scholarly information. Full-text and non-bibliographic databases predominate.

NEXIS, the best-known news-oriented search service, was operated by Mead Data Central through 1994, when it was acquired—along with its legal counterpart, LEXIS—by Reed Elsevier, an Anglo-Dutch publishing company. The acquired service operates under the LEXIS-NEXIS name; its news and legal components are separate but related offerings. Just as DIALOG is the model for research-oriented multidisciplinary services, LEXIS-NEXIS sets the standard for online services that provide practical information. The NEXIS database catalog lists several thousand information sources, a much larger number than other online services. Comparisons based on database listings are potentially misleading, however. News-oriented services such as NEXIS do not distinguish between online sources and databases. They typically list each newspaper, magazine, newsletter, or other title as a separate online source, even if they are part of a multititle database, such as the IAC NEWSLETTER DATABASE or BUSINESS DATELINE. In contrast, DIALOG and other multidisciplinary services list such multititle information resources as a single database. Further complicating comparisons, NEXIS information sources are arranged in topical groups called "libraries," which combine selected sources from various databases. Adding to the confusion, some NEXIS databases are components of multiple libraries.

The NEXIS News Library is a voluminous online repository of full-text news information from U.S. and international sources. It contains an impressive selection of U.S. newspapers, including such major national and metropolitan newspapers as the *New York Times* since 1980, *Washington Post* since 1977, *Los Angeles Times* since 1985, *Chicago Tribune* since 1985, *Christian Science Monitor* since 1980, and *USA Today* since 1989. Over the past few years, NEXIS has expanded its full-text coverage of newspapers published in medium-size U.S. cities and state capitals. Hundreds of international newspapers are online as well. Compared to other search services, NEXIS offers a much larger selection of online news magazines. Examples include such general news publications as *Time, Newsweek,* and *U.S. News and World Report;* business newsmagazines like *Business Week, Dun's Review, The Economist, Forbes, Fortune,* and *Industry Week;* general-interest magazines like *People, Life, Money, Sporting News,* and *Sports Illustrated;* and publications that provide news coverage of specific industries or professions, such as *Legal Times, Chemical Week, Electronics, Microwave Systems News, Oil and Gas Journal,* and *Public Relations Journal.* NEXIS also provides a good selection of regional business periodicals.

NEXIS's subject-oriented news collections cover such fields as banking, communications, computers, consumer products, energy, entertainment, the environment, marketing, insurance, and transportation. Among online search services, NEXIS provides the largest, most varied selection of newswire databases. Of particular interest to business and technical libraries, the NEXIS newsletter files emphasize financial and energy-oriented publications. In addition to electronic versions of printed news sources, NEXIS offers online access to transcripts of television and radio programs, including "ABC News," "BBC World Broadcasts," and "MacNeil/Lehrer NewsHour." As a complement to its news-oriented information sources, NEXIS has strengthened its business coverage with an expanded group of bibliographic, directory, and financial databases.

Dow Jones Interactive is the Web-based successor to the Dow Jones News/Retrieval Service, one of the first business search services. It provides online access to various editions of the *Wall Street Journal*, including the Interactive Edition, which is updated continuously and contains material that does not appear in the printed edition. The Dow Jones Publications Library provides online access to the full text of other newspapers, business magazines, and newswires. Like NEXIS, Dow Jones Interactive supplements its news coverage with business-oriented databases that provide company and financial information. Investment-oriented information sources provide information about stocks, bonds, market indexes, options, and exchange rates.

Profound is a news and business information service operated by Dialog Corporation. It features a well-designed user interface, convenient retrieval features, and a useful, effectively organized group of information resources. Profound's databases are topical collections of information assembled from a variety of sources, some of which are offered as separate databases by other online services. This method of database organization, also successfully employed by NEXIS, is well suited to unassisted searching by end-users rather than librarians or other trained intermediaries. Profound users merely select the type of information desired, such as company news, market research reports, financial information, or country background. Familiarity with the scope and content of individual databases is not required. To further simplify searching, Profound's user interface facilitates the entry of retrieval commands, minimizes memorization requirements, and permits cross-database searches. Special retrieval capabilities include automatic searching of synonymous and related terms. Reports, magazine articles, and other documents are displayed in the same format as their printed counterparts, including graphics and color. This capability is particularly useful for market research reports that contain tables or charts. With other online services, such diagrammatic presentations are often omitted from online reports. As an additional feature, Profound users can browse through tables of contents to select sections of documents to be displayed.

Info Globe Online is operated by Globe Information Services, a division of the *Globe and Mail*. Based in Toronto, it combines news-oriented databases with general reference and business information resources. Most of its databases are produced in Canada and emphasize Canadian news and business information. Info Globe's most important database remains its original offering, the GLOBE AND MAIL ONLINE, which contains the full text of Canada's national newspaper since November 1977. The GLOBE AND MAIL ONLINE was the first newspaper database to be available online on the same day the printed edition was published. It was also the first online newspaper database to include every article from each issue of its printed counterpart, although certain items—such as horoscopes, weather reports, and photo captions—are omitted. Info Globe

Online also offers the full text of selected Canadian provincial newspapers, Canadian newswires, and Canadian business databases.

Infomart Online is a Canadian news and business information service operated by Infomart Dialog Limited, a joint venture of Southam Incorporated and Dialog Corporation. It provides online access to more than eighty databases, most of them Canadian in origin and subject focus. Its offerings include an extensive selection of Canadian provincial newspaper, newswires, and special-interest publications in full-text versions. The CANADIAN BUSINESS AND CURRENT AFFAIRS database provides full-text access to articles from Canadian periodicals. Other Infomart databases offer directory and financial information about Canadian businesses.

Since its introduction in the early 1980s, the NewsNet search service has been the leading source for online, full-text access to newsletters and special-interest periodicals, a useful group of publications that are widely encountered in business and technical libraries. The only online service with comparable newsletter coverage is NEXIS, although several multidisciplinary search services offer the IAC NEWSLETTER DATABASE, which contains the full text of many newsletters. NewsNet's subject coverage is multidisciplinary in scope, but most of its information resources are intended for narrowly focused audiences. Its excellent selection of online newsletters and related publications cover recent developments in specific industries or activities, such as aviation and aerospace, banking biotechnology, chemicals, defense, electronics and computers, energy and petroleum engineering, environmental issues, health care, insurance, publishing and broadcasting, and telecommunications. In addition to newsletters, NewsNet provides online access to newswires and selected business databases.

FT Profile, operated in the United Kingdom by Financial Times Electronic Publishing, is a leading European online service for news and business information. It provides online, full-text access to an extensive collection of U.K. newspapers plus selected news publications and newswires from other countries. Business coverage includes directory and financial databases for U.K. and European companies; country intelligence information; full-text versions of market research, economic forecasts, and investment reports; and familiar bibliographic databases produced by Information Access Company, UMI, and others. A limited group of science and technology information resources has a business emphasis. FT Discovery, a related service, is accessible through the World Wide Web. Intended for end-user searching, it offers a subset of the FT Profile databases.

The Nikkei Telecom Japan News and Retrieval service, operated by Nihon Keizai Shimbun Incorporated (Nikkei), is the most comprehensive source for English-language access to Japanese news and business information. Its news-oriented databases provide full-text translations of stories from such Japanese publications as *The Japan Times, Nikkei Weekly, Nikkei Industrial News,* and *Far Eastern Economic Review.* Nikkei Telecom also offers the Knight-Ridder and AFX newswire databases. Additional databases provide directory and financial information for public companies and private businesses in Japan and the Far East, as well as current and historical market quotations and indexes for Japanese stocks and bonds, Japanese and international industrial indicators, macroeconomic statistics, and currency information. In addition to Nikkei Telecom, Nihon Keizai Shimbun produces Nikkei English News (NEN), a newswire service that covers business and financial developments in Japan and the Far East, and the Nikkei Economic Electronic Database Service (NEEDS), which provides comprehensive coverage of Japanese financial markets.

Subject-Oriented Search Services

While several multidisciplinary search services provide in-depth, multidatabase coverage of particular subjects, some online search services are specifically and exclusively designed to support research activities in particular subject areas or professional disciplines such as medicine, science, engineering, and law. The National Library of Medicine (NLM), which formerly operated a fee-based online service called MEDLARS, offers a variety of biomedical databases through its free Web-based search services. The PubMed service provides online access to MEDLINE, the NLM's premier bibliographic database, and PRE-MEDLINE, which contains citations that are in the process of being indexed for inclusion in the MEDLINE database. The Internet Grateful Med service provides online access to other biomedical databases previously offered by the MEDLARS service. For the most part, those databases are produced by the National Library of Medicine. Examples include AIDSLINE, AIDSDRUGS, HEALTHSTAR, HISTLINE, POPLINE, and TOXLINE. The Toxnet on the Web service provides online access to non-bibliographic databases dealing with toxicology and hazardous chemicals.

PaperChase and HealthGate are examples of an emerging group of biomedical information services intended for untrained searchers rather than professional information specialists. Designed for ease of use, their market consists of physicians, nurses, pharmacists, dentists, physical therapists, and other health care providers; medical facility administrators, psychologists, social workers, and other professionals with health care interests; and researchers, graduate students, lawyers, and others who require access to biomedical literature. The PaperChase search service has been operated since the 1980s by Beth Israel Deaconess Medical Center in Boston. It combines the MEDLINE, CANCERLIT, AIDSLINE, and HEALTHSTAR databases into a single information resource for convenient searching. HealthGate, a Web-based service developed and operated by HealthGate Data Corporation, is intended for health care professionals as well as for consumers who require medical information. Its databases—which include MEDLINE, AGELINE, AIDSLINE, CANCERLIT, EMBASE, CINAHL, HEALTHSTAR, and PSYCINFO—are divided into such topical areas as medicine, behavioral health, drug information, patient information, and nursing.

Outside the United States, health scientists and researchers can access MEDLINE and other biomedical databases through the National Library of Medicine's Web-based services or through DIALOG, Data-Star, Ovid Online, and other multidisciplinary search services described above. In Europe and the Pacific Rim, several specialized search services offer unique biomedical information resources. As an example, the MEDIC database, which is available through the Central Medical Library in Helsinki, provides online access to Finnish medical literature, much of which is omitted from international biomedical databases. The MIC information service, operated by the Medicinska Informations Centralen at the Karolinska Institute, offers online access to Swedish databases on alcoholism, occupational medicine, drug reactions, and other biomedical topics.

The most comprehensive non-U.S. source for online access to biomedical information, however, is the DIMDI search service operated by the Deutsches Institut für Medizinische Dokumentation und Information in Köln, Germany. With over 100 databases online, it is one of Europe's largest information services. DIMDI interprets the biosciences broadly to include agriculture, aquatic sciences, food science, gerontology, psychology, and physical fitness. Its health-related subject coverage combines the best elements of other online services, providing a single system to satisfy the database access requirements of scientific researchers and health care practitioners. DIMDI offers MEDLINE and other NLM-produced databases, as well as EMBASE, BIOSIS PREVIEWS, PSYCINFO, SCISEARCH, and other widely available information resources. It also offers a distinctive group of German-language databases that deal with biomedicine and related disciplines. As a convenient feature, DIMDI's "super-bases" are preassembled groups of databases in designated subject areas, including bioethics, biotechnology, drug addiction, nutrition, oncology, social and industrial medicine, sports medicine, toxicology, and veterinary medicine.

Since the inception of online searching, scientific and technical information resources have been important components of the offerings of multidisciplinary search services. In particular, the competitive positions of Orbit, ESA-IRS, and, to a lesser extent, Questel are based on their extensive scientific and technical databases. DIALOG, as previously noted, offers impressive coverage of scientific disciplines and an excellent selection of databases pertaining to engineering specialties. Even multidisciplinary services, such as Data-Star and Ovid Online, that emphasize other subject areas offer certain popular scientific and technical databases, such as EI COMPENDEX and INSPEC.

While multidisciplinary services provide useful support for scientific research and engineering activities, several specialized search services emphasize or concentrate exclusively on scientific and technical databases. Compared to multidisciplinary services, their competitive positions are based on the depth and, in many cases, the exclusivity of their sci-tech offerings. STN International, the largest and best known example of a specialized sci-tech search service, is jointly operated by the American Chemical Society in North America, FIZ Karlsruhe in Europe, and the Japan Information Center for Science and Technology in Japan. STN International's database offerings have expanded steadily and significantly since the mid-1980s. At that time, it offered just two databases: CAS ONLINE, an implementation of the CHEMICAL ABSTRACTS database designed for both bibliographic and chemical structure searching, and PHYSICS BRIEFS (PHYSIKALISCHE BERICHTE), which was produced by FIZ Karlsruhe. By the late 1990s, its online offerings had increased to more than 200 databases.

STN International's subject coverage, initially limited to the physical sciences and engineering, has broadened to include other scientific disciplines and selected non-scientific databases. It now encompasses biology, medicine, pharmaceuticals, agriculture, and food science, plus a limited selection of business and general reference databases. STN International's competitive position, however, is based on its superior coverage of chemistry and engineering. CAPLUS, STN's implementation of CHEMICAL ABSTRACTS, contains some abstracts omitted from that database, as well as preliminary citations for documents in the process of being indexed by Chemical Abstracts Service and references to articles cited in the table-of-contents pages of 1,300 journals. The CAOLD database, which is exclusive to STN International, contains bibliographic references for substances cited in the printed edition of *Chemical Abstracts* from 1957 through 1966. The REGISTRY database is the world's largest file of chemical substance information. It can be searched by chemical structures, partial structures, molecular formulas, and chemical dictionary terms. Chemical structure searching is also possible in other STN databases. In addition to bibliographic and chemical structure databases, STN International provides online access to the full texts of chemistry journals published by the American Chemical Society, AOAC International, Elsevier, the Royal Society of Chemistry, VCH Verlagsgesellschaft, John Wiley, and others. STN databases also provide excellent coverage of engineering specialties, materials science, and patent information. Some STN databases require a reading knowledge of German.

The FIZ Technik information service is operated by Fachinformationszentrum Technik, a not-for-profit organization sponsored by industrial research and development centers, industrial employers' organizations, and professional associations. Based in Frankfurt, Germany, FIZ Technik provides online access to over ninety databases, most of which deal with technology and such related topics as standardization, industrial management, and product manufacturing. While it offers several popular English-language databases, many of FIZ Technik's information resources are exclusive and require a reading knowledge of German, although some contain English-language subject headings or abstracts. Most of FIZ Technik's databases are produced in Europe, a number of them by FIZ Technik itself. About half of FIZ Technik's online offerings provide bibliographic coverage of engineering specialties, including the technology and manufacturing of plastics, rubber, textiles, glass, paper, lubricants, and wood products. Biology, chemistry, and physics information are presented in an applied science context. European industrial standards are covered by several databases. Without abandoning its technical emphasis, FIZ Technik has expanded its offerings to incorporate an impressive group of European company directories.

Of interest to scientific and biomedical researchers, several online services specialize in information about hazardous chemicals. The Toxnet on the Web service, operated by the National Library of Medicine, was mentioned above. Another example, the Chemical Information System (CIS), offers approximately thirty databases that cover technical, environmental, regulatory, and safety aspects of chemical substances, including pharmaceutical and commercial products. Originally known as the NIH/EPA Chemical Information System, the CIS online service was initially developed for the National Institutes of Health and the U.S. Environmental Protection Agency, but it was turned over to the private sector in 1984. Some CIS databases are produced by government agencies, such as the Environmental Protection Agency or the U.S. Coast Guard; others are obtained from commercial producers. While several CIS databases contain bibliographic citations or the full text of scientific and technical publications, most are non-bibliographic; they contain numeric data or directory-type information about chemical substances. While a few CIS databases are offered by other online services, most are exclusive and highly specialized.

The CCINFOline service, operated by the Canadian Centre for Occupational Health and Safety (CCOHS), offers approximately fifty databases dealing with occupational safety and the characteristics of potentially hazardous substances. CCINFOline is notable for its comprehensive coverage of health and safety issues and its many exclusive information resources, including databases produced by CCOHS itself. Some CCINFOline databases provide useful information about workplace hazards and control measures, including full-text access to material safety data sheets prepared by manufacturers and suppliers of chemical products. Others contain technical information about the properties, toxicity, and environmental fate of chemical substances. An excellent selection of online directories provides information about organizations and research projects concerned with occupational safety and health. While some CCINFOline databases emphasize Canadian developments in occupational safety and health, others have broader geographical appeal.

Several sci-tech information services and database producers have established fee-based sites on the World Wide Web for end-user searching by scientists, researchers, engineers, and others. As an example, the CC Connect service, operated by the Institute for Scientific Information (ISI), provides online access to the CURRENT CONTENTS database. Ei Village, a Web site established by Engineering Information Incorporated, provides online access to EI COMPENDEX, the EI PAGE ONE current awareness service, and other information resources, including the ILI STANDARDS WEB database. The STN Easy service provides Web-based access to a subset of databases offered by STN International. DIALOG Select, a Web-based service mentioned briefly above, includes a number of scientific and technical databases.

Search services for computer-assisted legal research have been available for more than a decade. They are widely used by law firms, corporate legal departments, government agencies, law school students, public affairs organizations, and others who need timely access to laws, judicial opinions, legal publications, and other documents. While multidisciplinary search services offer databases of legal interest, LEXIS, the legal component of the LEXIS-NEXIS service operated by Reed Elsevier, and WESTLAW are the two best known services designed specifically for online retrieval of legal information.

LEXIS offers online access to the full texts of federal and state codes, court cases, constitutions, rules, and regulations; administrative decisions from selected government agencies; legal publications; and other materials of interest to legal researchers. Like their NEXIS counterparts described above, LEXIS databases are organized into libraries that are subdivided into files of related documents or other materials. The General Federal Library, for example, contains files for the U.S. Code and decisions of the U.S. Supreme Court, Courts of

Appeals, Circuit and District Courts, Claims Courts, and Court of International
Trade, plus the Federal Register, Code of Federal Regulations, Federal Court
Rules, Federal Sentencing Guidelines, Congressional Record, Comptroller General
decisions, and opinions of the U.S. Attorney General. The LEXIS state libraries
contain statutes, cases, opinions, administrative decisions, and public
records for individual states and the District of Columbia. Specialized LEXIS libraries
cover admiralty law, banking regulations, bankruptcy law, broadcasting
and telecommunication regulations, corporate law, employment law, environmental
law, estates and trusts, health law, immigration law, insurance law,
patents and trademarks, labor law, public health and welfare, tax and securities
law, domestic and international trade regulations, transportation laws and regulations,
and military justice. Other LEXIS libraries cover legislation, case law,
and tax law for Canada, the United Kingdom, Ireland, France, Germany, the
Netherlands, Australia, New Zealand, and elsewhere.

LEXIS provides full text access to hundreds of law reviews, legal periodicals,
and other legal publications. The Legal Reference Library includes legal
directories, usage guides, and indexes. The LEXPAT library contains the full
text of U.S. patents. LEXIS users also can access EDLINE and EMBASE plus a
General Medical Library that includes selected medical journals; the DRUGDEX,
Drug Information Full Text, and FDC Reports databases; the EMERGINDEX,
which contains disease and trauma information; the POISINDEX, which contains
treatment protocols for toxic substances, and the PDQ database from the
National Cancer Institute. To attract accounting firms, LEXIS has expanded its
coverage of financial and tax issues. The Accounting, Tax, and Financial Library
contains annual reports, regulatory filings, government agency materials, and
pertinent cases.

West Publishing Company, the originator of the WESTLAW online service,
was acquired in 1996 by Thomson Corporation, a publisher of news and legal
information. Before the acquisition, West was a privately held publisher of
widely used legal reference works, including the *National Reporter System,
American Digest System, Corpus Juris Secundum,* and *Annotated State Statutes.* The
contents of those works and other legal resources are available online through
WESTLAW, which offers the full texts of federal regulations, administrative
law decisions, and federal and state court decisions, accompanied by editorially
prepared headnotes and synopses.

WESTLAW's legal databases are grouped into categories such as Jurisdictional
Materials, which is subdivided into Federal Databases and State and Territory
Databases, Practice-Area Materials, Texts and Periodicals, and News and
Information. Federal materials include case law databases from the U.S.
Supreme Court, U.S. Courts of Appeals, U.S. District Courts, Federal Circuit
Courts, U.S. Court of Federal Claims, and other federal courts; federal government
statutes, rules, regulations, and orders, including the Code of Federal Regulations
and United States Code Annotated; administrative law and regulations,
including the Code of Federal Regulations, Federal Register, Federal Acquisition
Regulations, and U.S. Attorney General opinions; and such specialized materials
as General Accounting Office Reports, Jury Verdict and Settlement Summaries,
and opinions and papers of certain Supreme Court Justices.

The state-oriented databases include statutes and court rules from all fifty states, the District of Columbia, Puerto Rico, and the Virgin Islands. WESTLAW also provides online access to state case law, administrative regulations, and specialized materials, including Uniform Commercial Code cases and public utilities reports. Practice area materials support legal research requirements in such specialized subject areas as antitrust and trade regulation, bankruptcy, civil rights, commercial law and contracts, environmental law, estate planning and probate, family law, government contracting, health law, intellectual property, international law, labor law, military law, product liability, and taxation. For retrieval and verification of case law citations, WESTLAW provides INSTA-CITE, which covers federal cases since 1754 and state cases since 1879, and Shepard's Citations and Shepard's Preview, which cover federal and state cases and administrative decisions. WESTLAW's excellent selection of online legal publications includes textbooks, law reviews, state bar association journals, and specialized legal publications.

Public affairs search services are specifically designed for online legislative tracking and research by law firms, political scientists, issues management specialists, corporate public affairs offices, and government agencies. The Washington Alert Service is operated by Congressional Quarterly Incorporated, a publisher of political science books and periodicals. It provides online access to information about U.S. Congressional committee and floor activity to support legislative tracking and other political research. The BILLTRACK database, which is updated daily, contains comprehensive legislative chronologies for all bills and resolutions introduced in the U.S. Congress since 1983, the year the Washington Alert Service began operation. Online information includes bill numbers and titles, dates of introduction, committee referrals, cosponsors, legislative and presidential actions, and related bill and law numbers. BILLTRACK also provides summaries of bills and resolutions prepared by the Congressional Research Service of the Library of Congress.

While legislative tracking information is available through other online services, Washington Alert Service offers a number of exclusive information resources, some of which are updated several times a day. The VOTE database, for example, contains brief descriptions of Congressional roll-call votes with breakdowns by party affiliation and cross-references to related votes. The SCHEDULE database provides information about committee and subcommittee schedules, including chairpersons, agendas, and anticipated witnesses, while the COMMITTEES database covers committee and subcommittee hearings, actions, and votes. The TESTIMONY database contains the complete texts of submitted witness statements and member remarks for every Congressional committee and subcommittee, while the COMREPORTS database contains the complete texts of Congressional committee reports. The MEMBERS database is an online, updated version of the Congressional Quarterly publication entitled *Politics in America*. It contains political and personal information about all members of Congress since 1987. In addition to monitoring Congressional activity, Washington Alert Service offers the STATETRACK database, which provides summary and status information for bills, proposed regulations, and newsworthy events in fifty state legislatures.

The Legi-Slate search service, a subsidiary of the *Washington Post,* provides online retrieval of bills and resolutions by the names of sponsoring members, date of introduction, stage in the legislative process, words in the text, or subject terms assigned by Legi-Slate analysts. The complete texts of bills and resolutions are usually online on the same day that printed copies become available from the Government Printing Office. Legi-Slate also offers online access to committee and subcommittee schedules and witness lists, house and floor votes, and the complete text of the Federal Register. Press information includes text and indexing of the *Washington Post, National Journal,* and *Congressional Quarterly Weekly Report.*

Implementation Requirements and Costs

Libraries that utilize online search services will incur a variety of general and search-specific costs. General start-up and ongoing costs are fixed in amount and are incurred regardless of the volume and nature of searches performed. Examples include the purchase or rental cost of workstation hardware and, where required, software; the cost of site preparation, such as electrical modifications and telephone line installation; training and documentation costs, including charges for instructional manuals, thesauri, and other search aids; and sign-up fees or other special payments imposed by certain search services. Search-specific costs are variable costs that depend on search characteristics for their occurrence and amount. Examples include telecommunication charges, database access and connect-time charges, online display and offline printing charges, and the cost of professional labor.

Compared to other areas of library automation, online searching involves the simplest equipment requirements and the lowest initial capital investment. As time-shared computer facilities, online search services are accessed by retrieval workstations installed at customer sites. To more easily attract customers by minimizing inconvenient and potentially expensive equipment requirements, all online search services support appropriately configured microcomputers as retrieval workstations. Typically, such microcomputers must be equipped with modems and appropriate communication software. Some online search services support any general-purpose communication software package capable of conventional ASCII asynchronous communication. Others require special communication programs that they supply to new customers. Web-based services are compatible with specified Web browser programs.

Most online services impose initial fees—variously described as sign-up charges, registration fees, or membership fees—or periodic fixed payments for account numbers and passwords. For librarians who received their graduate degrees before the mid-1970s, online searching represents a new aspect of professional practice requiring additional training. Since the late 1970s, most ALA-accredited library schools have offered one or more courses in online searching, but such courses typically emphasize the major North American multidisciplinary services, particularly DIALOG. Although they may be familiar with online retrieval concepts, new library school graduates will often require additional training to search other services effectively; at a minimum, librarians must learn the commands associated with a particular search service.

Where formal training is required, vendor-sponsored courses typically provide the fastest way to learn search commands and procedures. Most online search services offer intensive, introductory courses of one or two days' duration. Such courses are typically taught in major metropolitan areas or at universities or similar research facilities in other locations. It is advisable and customary for a library to train at least two persons to provide uninterrupted searching capability during vacations, sick leave, and periods of high demand. Some online search services will conduct private training sessions at customer sites.

To function effectively, online searchers will require some printed support materials. At a minimum, the search area should be equipped with operator's manuals for all services utilized. Some search services also publish separate guides for specific databases. In addition to manuals and other documentation specific to a given online service, searchers may require thesauri, subject classification lists, and other reference tools published by database producers. While such search aids are sometimes available online, it may prove less expensive and more convenient to purchase printed copies of the most frequently used materials.

Telecommunication charges are an example of a cost that varies directly with the duration of an online search. Some online services can be reached by direct dialing through the public telephone network. The resulting local or long-distance charges will vary with the caller's geographic location and telephone company. Some online services also impose a surcharge on direct-dial communication. As a lower-cost telecommunication alternative, all online services can be reached through one or more of the so-called value-added carriers. As defined in chapter 3, such companies operate computer-controlled networks consisting of leased telephone lines that link geographically dispersed computers with access nodes in selected locations. Libraries in areas served by value-added carriers can reach their access nodes through a local telephone call. They are charged for the local call plus the ensuing long-distance communication. In most cases, the charges will prove significantly lower than those attainable through conventional long-distance facilities—assuming, of course, that a network access node is available. Because access nodes are typically limited to well-populated metropolitan areas or university towns, libraries in rural locations must often make a long-distance telephone call to reach an access node. In such cases, the resulting combination of long-distance and value-added carrier charges may prove higher than the cost of a direct-dialed long-distance call to a given online service. Recognizing this, some online services provide an inward-WATS number for customers in areas outside network access nodes.

As an alternative to value-added carriers, online services are increasingly accessible through the Internet. The customer establishes an Internet connection through an organizational or commercial service provider and enters the telnet address of the desired online service. Some online services impose charges for such Internet access, but their hourly rates are typically lower than their value-added carrier charges. In addition, the customer must pay whatever telecommunication charges or other fees are associated with the Internet connection. For many academic, government, and corporate libraries, such costs are fully absorbed by the library's parent organization. Web-based search services invariably require an Internet connection.

Since the mid-1970s, the majority of online search services have charged users for the amount of time they are connected to a given database, regardless of the complexity of the retrieval operations performed or the amount of system resources utilized by a given search. Such elapsed-time charges are incurred whether an operator is entering search commands, receiving printed output, or merely sitting at a retrieval workstation formulating a search strategy or reviewing displayed information.

While there has been much discussion of their appropriateness, connect-time charging plans are easily understood and, when coupled with other costs discussed below, allow the user to make a fairly accurate preliminary cost estimate for a given search. Connect-time costs are customarily expressed as an hourly rate, but the searcher is only charged for the fraction of an hour actually spent online. Recognizing that most online sessions are considerably shorter than one hour, some services quote connect-time charges on a cost-per-minute basis. Regardless of the measure used, connect-time charges begin immediately after the online connection to a given information service is established, and they end when the online session concludes.

A few online services impose a uniform connect-time charge for all or most of their databases. In most cases, however, connect-time charges vary from one database to another and, for a given database, from one online search service to another. Connect-time rates are a composite of the online service's operating charges plus any royalties that must be paid to database producers. In their price lists, however, most online services present their connect-time charges as a single cost item with no breakdown of individual components. Some online services offer discounted connect-time rates to designated user groups, to subscribers of printed indexes that correspond to specific databases, for searches performed during off-peak hours, or to customers that make specified prepayments or guarantee minimum annual billings.

As an alternative or supplement to connect-time rates, some online services charge customers for the system resources utilized during a particular search. Proponents of this charging methodology argue that it more accurately reflects the difficulty of a given search, does not penalize slow typists or modems, and eliminates charges attributable to telecommunication delays or degraded response time during periods of peak usage. Database producers and online service operators are also concerned about lost revenues resulting from search techniques that reduce connect-time charges without a corresponding reduction in computer usage. Examples of such techniques include the use of communication software to prepare search strategies offline and the use of lower-cost databases for the initial entry of search commands that will subsequently be applied to more expensive databases. As a significant complication for librarians who must provide their clients with a preliminary estimate of search costs, resource-based charges can prove difficult to conceptualize and even more difficult to predict.

Some online search services have eliminated or drastically reduced their connect-time rates in favor of an "information-based pricing" model that charges customers for information retrieved, regardless of the amount of time spent online or the complexity of search commands executed. The rationale for this approach is that customers will pay for results, not for the act of searching. Flat-rate pricing plans are an increasingly common alternative to connect-time charges for high-volume customers. While all flat-rate pricing plans provide unlimited online access for a stipulated fee, specific provisions and restrictions vary. The simplest flat-rate plans eliminate connect-time rates entirely, but some online services combine flat-rate pricing with modest connect-time charges. As another alternative to connect-time, some online services impose a flat fee per search, regardless of its length or complexity.

Online display charges are imposed for bibliographic citations, abstracts, or other information displayed or printed during an online session. Such charges usually vary from database to database and, for a given database, with the data elements selected for display or printing. In most cases, online display charges are unit costs imposed on a per-record basis. In their price lists, online search services typically indicate online display charges for full records—that is, the most complete information contained in database records, including the full text of documents when available. Lower charges usually apply when online display is limited to specific fields, such as the title or a bibliographic citation without an abstract. As an alternative to per-record pricing, some search services charge by the number of characters or lines of information displayed or printed during an online session. With a few online services, downloading charges are enumerated separately in price lists. In most cases, however, downloading charges are identical to charges for online display of full records. Because downloading is a local software function that captures incoming information, a search service's computer cannot distinguish it from online display activity.

While the immediate availability of needed information is one of the principal attractions of online searching, some online services offer offline printing of bibliographic citations or other search results. The offline prints are produced at the search service's computer facilities and mailed or otherwise delivered to the customer. As with online display charges, offline printing rates vary from database to database and with the amount of information printed.

The professional labor of a librarian or other trained information specialist is often overlooked as a cost component in online searching. Unlike the technical services for which the workstations used to access bibliographic utilities may be operated by clerical personnel, online searching often involves the direct participation of professional librarians. Unmediated searching by scientists, faculty members, students, or other end users can be successfully employed in applications with straightforward information retrieval requirements, and online services increasingly support and encourage such end-user searching with graphical user interfaces and Web-based access. Library literature and the experience of practicing professionals, however, continue to affirm the value of a trained intermediary who is conversant with the latest developments in database structure and retrieval techniques and who will conduct a thorough presearch interview, translate the expressed information needs of a researcher or other requester into a logical search strategy and commands appropriate to a particular search service, review search results for relevance, and suggest possible additional searches. As a broad guideline that will necessarily vary with the searcher's experience and the complexity of the search itself, two minutes of preparation and follow-up are required for each minute spent online. For an online search lasting fifteen to twenty minutes, the total professional labor requirement will likely range from forty-five to sixty minutes.

Alternatives to Online Services

Online search services provide convenient access to multiple databases that may be obtained from a variety of sources. Such services emerged during the 1970s as a simpler, more cost-effective alternative to the in-house implementation of computerized information retrieval systems based on the direct procurement of machine-readable databases from their producers. As previously discussed, such databases had become increasingly available, typically on magnetic tape, during the late 1960s and early 1970s. With their prewritten retrieval software and usage-based pricing, online search services facilitated the rapid implementation of computer-based information retrieval by libraries with limited computing experience. As an additional advantage, high capital investments for hardware procurement and software development were avoided; as noted above, start-up costs for online searching are typically modest.

Since the late 1980s, however, there has been a renewal of interest in in-house implementations of specific databases. Such in-house implementations are sometimes described as "local online" to distinguish them from the remote, time-shared access provided by the search services discussed in this report. Local online implementations involve the procurement of databases on magnetic tape or other media for installation on a library's own computer equipped with appropriate retrieval software. Some vendors of integrated library systems described in chapter 6 support such locally mounted databases, sometimes described as journal citation databases, as an optional component. Typically, the integrated system vendor supplies a list of databases that are compatible with local mounting. The library must acquire the desired databases from their publishers by annual subscriptions or other arrangements. The integrated system vendor supplies programs to load the database on the library's computer and make it accessible through the library's online public access catalog, using OPAC commands and retrieval procedures. With some integrated systems, citations from library-owned journals are identified by a special symbol and automatically linked to the library's holdings information. In most cases, the database subscription includes a site license that permits unlimited searching by a specified number of OPAC terminals or users in a given location. Remote access is typically controlled by passwords. If a library's OPAC is accessible to the general public through the Internet or other telecommunication arrangements, the locally mounted databases are limited to authorized users. As an alternative to OPAC integration, some vendors offer databases for local implementation on a library's network server or intranet. In the latter case, the databases are searchable by Web browsers.

Many of the databases offered by online search services are available as CD-ROM information products for stand-alone or network installations. The number of publicly available CD-ROM databases for library reference applications has increased steadily since the mid-1980s when the technology was introduced. CD-ROM databases are typically accompanied by information retrieval software that is intended for installation on a computer's hard drive. In most cases, the software and its associated CD-ROM database are intended for Windows-based microcomputers, although products for Macintosh and Unix systems are also available. Unlike online systems, which often require formal training for effective searching, most CD-ROM retrieval programs are designed for novice users who will receive little or no instruction. As such, they make extensive use of menus, dialog boxes, prompts, and help screens to simplify retrieval operations.

Depending on the implementation and product licensing arrangement, a CD-ROM database may operate on a single microcomputer. Alternatively, one or more CD-ROM databases may be installed on a file server for access by multiple workstations through a local area network, intranet, or other telecommunications arrangement. In the latter case, the file server is typically equipped with multiple CD-ROM drives or a CD-ROM autochanger. Increasingly, CD-ROM databases can be searched by Web browser programs, and some products are Z39.50-compliant, which facilitates integration with online public access catalogs and permits searching with OPAC commands and procedures.

CD-ROM producers include conventional publishers and database creators who are seeking additional outlets for their products and companies, such as SilverPlatter Information, that were formed specifically to develop and market CD-ROM versions of existing databases produced by government agencies and commercial firms. Some operators of online search services—including Dialog Corporation, Ovid Technologies, and H. W. Wilson Company—also offer certain databases on CD-ROM. Some well-known databases, such as MEDLINE, are available from multiple CD-ROM producers.

Economic comparisons of online search services and local implementations of specific databases, whether on CD-ROM or integrated with an OPAC or intranet, are of obvious importance for librarians responsible for planning and procuring computer-based information products and services. Such comparisons must begin with an explanation of the different roles of fixed and variable charges in online search services and local database implementations. As outlined above, fixed costs associated with online searching include the purchase of required equipment and communication software, the cost of site modifications, training and documentation expenses, and the payment of initial subscriber charges or other special fees where applicable. Such costs are principally incurred as start-up expenses, although some additional fixed costs—for such things as equipment maintenance and ongoing searcher training—may be incurred annually. The remaining and usually most significant costs of online searching are variable charges, which are incurred when individual searches are performed.

With local database implementations, by contrast, fixed start-up costs predominate. In a marked departure from the variable, usage-based charges associated with online search services, CD-ROM information products and locally mounted databases are usually sold by subscription. The customer pays a fixed annual fee that permits unlimited searching without additional charges for connect-time, display, printing, or other operations. Given this difference, the economic relationship of online search services and local implementations is clear: local implementations of a given database will prove less expensive than their online counterparts when, and if, the annual online search service charges for that database exceed the subscription price of the locally installed version. From the cost standpoint, CD-ROM and locally mounted databases are best suited to databases that will be searched frequently. Online information services remain the preferred approach for databases that are searched occasionally. The break-even point to justify a subscription to a CD-ROM or locally mounted database varies with search service rates, search characteristics, and other factors. It can be determined only in the context of specific applications. For some databases, CD-ROM or locally mounted databases can prove less expensive than online information services for databases that are searched just four or five times per month.

Cost considerations, while important for decision making, necessarily ignore non-economic characteristics that limit the utility of local implementations and argue for online search services as the preferred database access alternative in certain situations. In particular, local implementations of individual databases are updated by replacement or supplements at specified intervals, usually monthly or quarterly but occasionally semiannually or annually. In some cases, however, database producers issue new records at more frequent intervals. Online search services typically add such records to their databases shortly after receipt, but delays inherent in CD-ROM production prohibit such frequent updating. Since research projects, business decision making, and other activities often require information that is as current as possible, local implementations of individual databases cannot entirely supplant online search services, even where unlimited searching for a fixed annual subscription fee offers an economic advantage. Further, differences in the coverage and content of online and locally mounted databases may affect performance in specific applications. In particular, some CD-ROM editions of bibliographic databases contain a subset of information included in their online counterparts.

It should be noted that online search services and local implementations are not mutually exclusive options for database access. The two approaches can be successfully combined in cost-effective hybrid implementations. Databases offered by online services can be searched to retrieve current information, while a local implementation can be employed for retrospective searches. Alternatively, information retrieved from a locally implemented database can be updated by periodic online searches. Some online search services and CD-ROM publishers actively promote such hybrid retrieval approaches.

The Document Delivery Problem

Used in this context, document delivery denotes the process whereby libraries provide users with access to the books, articles, reports, and other documents cited in catalogs, bibliographies, indexing and abstracting journals, and other finding aids. The introduction of computer-based information resources, including online catalogs and machine-readable databases, is often accompanied by a significant increase in the demand for document delivery. Paradoxically,

computer-based information resources give librarians the ability to quickly retrieve large numbers of potentially relevant bibliographic citations, but rising
prices for books and periodicals, coupled with declining acquisitions budgets,
make it increasingly unlikely that a given library's collection will contain the
documents identified by a computer search, thereby prompting an increase in
interlibrary loan activity.

Even assuming that existing interlibrary loan staffs can accommodate such
increases within a given library, there is some question whether conventional interlibrary loan provides a sufficiently rapid response to satisfy users' document
delivery demands. The several weeks usually required to complete an interlibrary loan transaction can offset any speed advantage gained through an online
search. In addition, computer users are accustomed to obtaining information
quickly. They may be more conscious and thus less tolerant of the delays inherent
in conventional interlibrary loan procedures. In a typical time-consuming manual bibliographic search, as performed by a researcher or other library user, citations are retrieved gradually and interlibrary loan requests submitted in small
batches at regular intervals. While loan requests are being processed, the search
for additional citations continues. With the computer-based information resources, by contrast, bibliographic searches are completed quickly. If a substantial
number of retrieved citations must be obtained from other libraries, the user's
work will slow down or even stop. As an added complication, interlibrary loan
channels may be glutted by a large volume of requests submitted in short intervals, further increasing the time required to complete a given loan transaction.

Efforts to address this problem have been directed toward the development
of improved interlibrary loan processes and alternative document delivery
methodologies. There have, for example, been several successful attempts to
facilitate library resource sharing and increase the speed of interlibrary loan
processing through technological intervention. As discussed in preceding chapters, many individual libraries and multilibrary systems use bibliographic utilities or computer-based union catalogs to provide more convenient and timely
access to collection-related information of potential use in interlibrary loan processing. Most bibliographic utilities include libraries' holdings information in
their databases. That information can be quickly retrieved online. The bibliographic utilities likewise support interlibrary loan subsystems or other forms of
computer-based, subscriber-to-subscriber communication for interlibrary loan
purposes. Such systems automatically route interlibrary loan requests to appropriate holding libraries.

Interlibrary loan services offered by bibliographic utilities can expedite the
identification of source libraries and submission of loan requests, but they do
nothing to speed the delivery of requested materials by the lending libraries.
Addressing this requirement, many libraries have installed facsimile machines.
Previously tried and abandoned as unreliable and impractical by libraries in the
1960s, facsimile devices are now faster, more versatile, and more reliable than
their unsatisfactory predecessors. As an alternative to interlibrary loan, database
producers and other companies—typically working in conjunction with online
search services—have developed various fee-based document delivery services.
Once a deposit account with a given service has been established, orders can be

placed for specified documents retrieved during online searches. The ordered documents may be mailed or faxed to the requester. While such document delivery services are typically more expensive than conventional interlibrary loan methodologies, order fulfillment time is greatly reduced.

Some vendors offer prepackaged document collections for sale to libraries. Following a pattern established by ERIC and NTIS, several publishers support their machine-readable databases with document collections offered for sale, partially or completely, on microfilm or microfiche. To minimize document delivery requirements by enabling researchers and other users to make more knowledgeable assessments of the probable relevance of retrieved citations, many databases are enhanced by abstracts, which may be sufficiently detailed to satisfy some information requirements. Problems of document delivery are eliminated, however, where online search services or locally mounted databases include the full text or images of indexed documents. Over one-third of DIALOG's bibliographic databases contain the full text of cited items, and that percentage is likely to increase. A smaller but growing number of online databases incorporate electronic document images for non-textual information. Patent databases published by Derwent, for example, include electronic images of illustrations. STN International provides online access to page images of American Chemical Society journals. UMI's ProQuest Direct service, as previously noted, provides image versions of numerous documents.

SUMMARY

Computer-based handling of ready-reference questions, literature searches, and other reference activity depends on the availability of machine-readable reference sources. Since the late 1960s, many publishers of printed reference tools have offered machine-readable versions of their products for use by libraries and other organizations. Historically, such databases have been most widely encountered in scientific and technical disciplines, but offerings in business and, to a lesser extent, the social sciences and humanities have expanded in recent years. In addition to databases that correspond to printed publications, some bibliographic databases have been developed specifically for computer-based implementations and have no printed counterparts. While the earliest machine-readable databases developed to support the reference activity were bibliographic in character, non-bibliographic directory-type and numeric databases are now widely available.

During the late 1960s and early 1970s, some libraries purchased machine-readable bibliographic and non-bibliographic databases for implementation on in-house computers using custom-developed information retrieval software. Most libraries, however, lacked access to the hardware and software resources required to implement such systems. Through the early 1970s, libraries' retrieval requirements were addressed by fee-based search services operated by producers of machine-readable databases or other organizations. Such services, like their in-house counterparts, customarily operated in the batch processing mode. They were eventually replaced by online search services.

Such services can be divided into three broad groups: (1) multidisciplinary online services that offer databases on a variety of subjects for a diverse clientele; (2) news- and business-oriented online services that provide multidisciplinary subject coverage but emphasize news and business information of practical significance; and (3) specialized search services that limit database coverage to particular subject areas, such as science or engineering, or to professional disciplines or activities, such as medicine or law. While they differ in the number and type of databases offered and the specific retrieval capabilities supported, all three types of online services share a common operating methodology. They purchase or otherwise obtain bibliographic and non-bibliographic databases in machine-readable form from their producers, convert the databases to a form required for storage on their computers, and allow libraries or other customers to perform various retrieval operations using prewritten database management software. Some services also offer private file capabilities that allow libraries to establish their own databases. Like general-purpose database management systems, the software provided by most online services features a non-procedural query language that permits a user working at an online terminal to initiate literature searches or other information retrieval operations by entering specified commands. These query languages provide powerful retrieval functionality, but they require user training. For novice users, many services offer menu-driven interfaces or, increasingly, Web browser interfaces.

In most cases, libraries using online search services must be equipped with appropriately configured microcomputers, although some services can be searched with conventional computer terminals. For long-distance telecommunications, most libraries use one of the value-added carriers or the Internet. Web-based services require an Internet connection. Search costs vary. Some online services assess usage charges on the basis of connect-time, with varying rates for different databases. Additional charges are imposed for online display, downloading, or offline printing of retrieved information. As a possible alternative to online searching, an increasing number of databases are available as CD-ROM information products or on magnetic tape for local implementation on an integrated library system, network server, or intranet. Offered on a subscription basis, such local databases can prove less expensive than online searching for reference sources that are accessed frequently, although a lack of timeliness and other performance limitations may render them unsuitable for some applications.

Because they permit the rapid retrieval of potentially relevant bibliographic citations, automated reference services can result in significant increases in the demand for document delivery. Such demands are increasingly difficult to accommodate at a time of rising subscription rates and retrenched collection development, thus prompting an increase in interlibrary loan activity. Because existing interlibrary loan methodologies cannot usually handle this increased demand, considerable attention has been given to the development of alternative document delivery systems. Examples include facsimile transmission, electronic document ordering, the purchase of entire document collections on microforms or optical disks, and online availability of documents in full text or image formats.

8

Digital
Libraries

Broadly defined, a digital library is a collection of computer-processible information or a repository for such information. In non-library applications, the phrase has been widely applied to centralized repositories of computer programs or machine-readable data. Information management specialists, policy makers, and politicians increasingly view such repositories as important components of an emerging National Information Infrastructure (NII). Online databases and CD-ROM information products, particularly those with multimedia or interactive video components, are often characterized by their producers as digital libraries. Alternatively, the phrase "digital libraries" has been applied to the computer storage devices on which large machine-readable information repositories reside. Optical disk jukeboxes and magnetic tape autochangers, for example, are sometimes characterized as digital libraries by their manufacturers or users.

Definitions employed in library literature are comparably broad. Some publications equate digital libraries with computerized, networked library systems. The Library of Congress describes its National Digital Library Project as a set of distributed repositories of managed content and a set of interfaces to that content. Other organizations and authorities have used the phrase to describe databases, including library catalogs, and document repositories that are accessible through the Internet. Still others characterize certain CD-ROM information products, particularly those that contain the complete contents of books or other publications, as digital libraries. The Digital Libraries Initiative—a joint undertaking of the National Science Foundation, Defense Advanced Research Projects Agency, and National Aeronautics and Space Administration—views a digital library as an environment for bringing together collections, services, and people to support the creation, dissemination, use, and preservation of data, information, and knowledge. The Digital Library Federation, a consortium of large research repositories, describes digital libraries as organizations that provide resources to interpret, distribute, preserve the integrity of, and ensure the persistence over time of collections of digital works.

According to these broad definitions, digital library status does not depend on the amount or nature of computerized information; libraries with online catalogs or CD-ROM databases, for example, are considered digital libraries. The definitions do not differentiate digital libraries as collections of computer-processable information from digital libraries as organizations that maintain and provide such information. Further, they do not distinguish digital libraries from other providers of computer-processable information, such as bibliographic utilities, online search services, or CD-ROM publishers.

This chapter adopts a narrower definition of a digital library than those cited above. For purposes of this discussion, a digital library is a library that maintains all, or a substantial part, of its collection in computer-processable form as an alternative, supplement, or complement to the conventional printed and microfilm materials that currently dominate library collections. Used in this context, the term "collection" denotes the documents that a library acquires or maintains, as opposed to catalogs, indexes, or other finding aids that provide information about those documents. A library's collection may include published materials, such as books and periodicals, or unpublished documents, such as the proprietary research reports maintained by many technical libraries or the personal papers encountered in manuscript repositories. Computer-processable representations of library materials encompass character-coded text, electronic document images, or combinations of text and images. Regardless of representations, a digital library's collection can be accessed online by authorized persons through local or wide area computer networks. Once accessed, materials from a digital library's collection can be displayed, printed, downloaded, or otherwise manipulated to satisfy particular users' requirements.

While they imply a revolutionary approach to library management, digital library concepts and technologies are more accurately characterized as evolutionary developments. As discussed in previous chapters, libraries have been creating, maintaining, and using computer-processable information for decades. Since the 1970s, thousands of libraries have implemented online catalogs as replacements for manually produced card catalogs. Through online information services and bibliographic utilities, libraries routinely obtain time-shared access to huge compilations of bibliographic citations; machine-readable versions of encyclopedias, directories, and other reference works; and a diverse group of non-bibliographic databases. Through the Internet, libraries can retrieve information from computers operated by government agencies, professional associations, universities, corporations, and other organizations, including other libraries. Libraries of all types and sizes purchase bibliographic and non-bibliographic information products on magnetic tape, CD-ROM, or other media for installation and operation on their own computers.

Historically, however, library automation has emphasized the computerization of bibliographic tools—catalogs, indexes, and other finding aids—rather than storage and retrieval of the books, periodicals, and other documents contained in library collections. While a growing percentage of the machine-readable databases discussed in chapter 7 incorporate the complete contents of books, journal articles, technical reports, or other works, most libraries continue to maintain such materials in their own collections in paper form or on microfilm. Digital library concepts and technologies provide a completely computerized approach to the storage and retrieval of library materials. The finding aids that support library collections are increasingly computerized; computer-based management of the collections themselves is the logical next step in library automation.

The following sections examine the emergence of digital libraries by surveying the history of digital library concepts, presenting examples of digital library initiatives, and summarizing the anticipated benefits of digital library implementations. Later sections of this chapter will discuss technologies and procedures for creating digital libraries, along with issues and concerns for system planners and library administrators.

EMERGENCE OF DIGITAL LIBRARIES

The concept of a digital library as a computer-based repository of books, journals, and other information resources has been much discussed at professional meetings; among scholars, researchers, and other library users; and in a diverse group of publications, ranging from professional library journals to speculative fiction. "Roboticized" libraries are components of the highly computerized societies depicted by some science fiction novelists. Computer-based storage and retrieval of library materials are likewise common elements in futuristic scenarios envisioned by professional librarians and information specialists. Although the earliest discussions of digital libraries predated the commercial availability of computers and digital storage technologies, they nonetheless envisioned innovative systems that would provide rapid, convenient access to voluminous collections of books and other library materials.

History

In one of the most influential and frequently cited precursors of digital library concepts appearing in the July 1945 issue of *Atlantic Monthly*, Vannevar Bush complained that antiquated manual approaches to information storage and retrieval impeded access to published research. As an alternative, he proposed a "mechanized private file and library . . . [for] books, records, and communications." Bush termed this imaginary mechanized library the "Memex," which he conceptualized as a personal workstation with internal storage facilities and indexing capabilities. Bush suggested computer-like mechanisms for the entry of retrieval commands and search terms by Memex users. Rather than employing digital technology, however, the Memex would store books, periodicals, and other documents on microfilm, which might be purchased from publishers in a Memex-ready format. As a computer-based finding aid for documents stored on another medium, the Memex was the conceptual precursor of computer-assisted retrieval (CAR) systems rather than true digital libraries, which are completely computer-based. As described briefly in chapter 4, CAR systems combine computer and micrographics technologies. Given the primitive nature of computer storage technology in the mid-1940s, a completely digital library would have been impossible. Practical direct-access storage devices did not become commercially available until the 1950s, and capacities of the earliest models were much too low for the voluminous contents of library materials.

Following Bush's lead, computer-based indexing of microforms was proposed in futuristic library scenarios delineated by researchers, librarians, and others during the 1950s and 1960s. Library interest in that approach to document storage and retrieval culminated in Project Intrex, the name given to a series of information transfer experiments conducted at the Massachusetts Institute of Technology between 1965 and 1973. The Project Intrex database, which ultimately reached 20,000 scientific and technical articles, was stored on microfiche. It was supported by an online computer-stored catalog and index, which included abstracts. In the manner of Bush's Memex, the microfiche themselves were stored in a desktop automated retrieval device adjacent to the computer terminal used to search the online catalog.

The designers of Project Intrex viewed their hybrid combination of computers and microforms as a compromise necessitated by the prevailing capacity limitations and high cost of computer storage devices available in the early 1970s. Completely computerized systems, while acknowledged to be impractical for technical and economic reasons, were nonetheless preferred by some researchers. A 1965 study of libraries of the future, sponsored by the Council on Library Resources, outlined the advantages of digital storage technology for library collections, emphasizing the implementation of associative indexing and other innovative retrieval concepts permitted by computerization. During the mid- to late 1960s, several demonstration projects explored the potential of digital storage and full-text indexing for selected library materials. Those projects converted the textual content of journal articles, reports, and other documents to machine-readable, character-coded form for computer storage. Conceived as experimental rather than operational in nature, they involved small numbers of documents, narrowly circumscribed applications, and tightly controlled user groups.

The earliest practical applications of digital library concepts involved full-text storage and indexing of legal and scientific documents. Perhaps the most famous example, the Ohio Bar Automated Research (OBAR) System, was developed in the late 1960s by Mead for the Ohio State Bar Association. Providing online access to the full text of legal statutes, it was the precursor of the LEXIS search service described in chapter 7. Similarly, the Legal Information Thru Electronics (LITE) System, implemented during the same time period by the U.S. Air Force, stored and indexed the complete text of the U.S. Code, along with legal and judicial interpretations and information about the disbursement of public funds. Digital library implementations by other government agencies and national laboratories stored the complete text of technical documentation and patents.

These early library implementations of text storage and retrieval technology relied on customized programming. During the mid- to late 1970s, several computer manufacturers and software developers introduced prewritten programs for computer-based storage, indexing, and retrieval of documents in character-coded form. Initially intended for mainframe and larger minicomputer installations, such prewritten software greatly simplified the implementation of text storage and retrieval applications. The best known examples, such as the IBM Storage and Information Retrieval System (STAIRS) and the Battelle Automated Search Information System (BASIS), were employed by hundreds of libraries. By the late 1980s, text storage and retrieval programs were available from dozens of vendors for most major computing environments, including microcomputers and local area networks. Their characteristics are described in chapter 3. Most library installations of text storage and retrieval technology have been in special libraries, particularly technical libraries and law libraries in corporations and government agencies. In some cases, the library's parent organization acquires a mainframe- or minicomputer-based text storage and retrieval program as an enterprise-wide information resource for use in office as well as library applications.

Strictly defined, text storage and retrieval programs manage textual information only. They cannot be applied to charts, graphs, line art, photographs, and other non-textual components of library documents. Thus, the text of a scientific monograph or journal can be stored in character-coded form; supporting illustrations, which are widely encountered in such works, must be omitted or converted to computer-processible form in some other way. Electronic document imaging technology addresses this limitation by storing library materials in a pictorial format rather than as character-coded text. Because electronic images preserve the appearance of individual pages, source documents can contain textual and non-textual information. Electronic document imaging systems are also preferable to text storage and retrieval technology where the appearance of documents has informational or evidentiary value. This is sometimes the case with manuscripts or archival records.

In business applications, as discussed in chapter 4, electronic document imaging systems offer a completely computerized alternative, complement, or supplement to conventional paper filing methodologies and microfilm technology. In digital library implementations, electronic document imaging technology can replace books, journals, and other printed materials with computer-processible page-images. U.S. government libraries were among the technology's first implementers. The most widely publicized early example, the Optical Disk Pilot Project initiated by the Library of Congress in 1982, involved digitized images of books, journals, and other research materials. The images were generated by document scanners from items in the Library of Congress's collections and recorded on optical disks for online retrieval. The project was designed to explore the preservation and reference implications of electronic document imaging and optical storage technology. An earlier document imaging implementation by the Library of Congress Cataloging Distribution Service was designed to simplify printing of catalog cards for items not included in the LC MARC database. In the mid-1980s, the Library of Congress also experimented with read-only videodiscs to store pictorial materials from its collections. During the same time period, library-related imaging systems were implemented by other government agencies, including the National Library of Medicine, the National Archives and Records Administration, the U.S. Patent and Trademark Office, and the National Air and Space Museum.

Digital Library Projects

Since the early 1990s, a number of libraries and related information agencies, such as archives and manuscript repositories, have initiated digital library implementations based on character-coded text or electronic document imaging technologies. Many of these implementations are conceived as pilot projects, proof-of-concept demonstrations, research projects, or other experimental endeavors that examine the feasibility and potential of digital library concepts and technologies. Others are highly focused implementations designed to facilitate specific research activities or library operations.

While digital library implementations vary in purpose and scope, some generalizations are possible. Academic libraries have initiated digital library projects to obtain a wider audience for archives, manuscripts, special collections, and other unique research materials. They have also used digital library implementations to facilitate access to items in high demand, such as reserve room materials or core collections of required readings that support specific curricula or instructional programs, such as distance learning programs. Public libraries have emphasized local history materials and other documents of interest to their user populations. Government library implementations provide on-line access to government publications and public records. Corporate libraries have targeted proprietary materials, such as technical reports, that support specific research activities. While a comprehensive survey of current digital library projects is beyond the scope of this book, some widely publicized examples are described below.

As previously noted, the Library of Congress has been implementing electronic document imaging systems for various experimental and operational purposes since the early 1980s. In 1994, it announced plans to create a National Digital Library by applying electronic document imaging, text storage and retrieval, and other technologies to selected print and non-print materials from its collections. The materials are being converted to machine-readable form by various devices and methodologies, including key-entry of textual information, document scanning, digital photography, and digitization of video and audio information. To avoid copyright protection issues, the initial implementation has emphasized research materials that are in the public domain. The Library of Congress views its National Digital Library Program as a critical component of the emerging National Information Infrastructure. It further envisions the National Digital Library as a collaborative effort that will ultimately encompass the collections of other libraries.

A number of university-based digital library projects have been funded by federal government agencies, scientific organizations, educational foundations, and private corporations. In 1994, the National Science Foundation, the National Aeronautics and Space Administration, and the Defense Advanced Research Projects Agency announced a joint initiative to support digital library projects and related research activities at six academic institutions. Some of the projects have obtained additional funding or other support from corporate or institutional sponsors. Among the funding recipients, the Stanford Digital Libraries Project at Stanford University is developing a uniform method of accessing computer-based information resources and services, including library catalogs, research databases, and personal information. Using a collection of computer literature as a test bed, the project is experimenting with a variety of user interfaces and retrieval methodologies, including information agents, to automate certain retrieval operations. It is also exploring economic and legal aspects of digital library implementations, including questions of copyright and intellectual property rights.

A digital library project at the University of California at Berkeley provides online access to technical reports, maps, video segments, computer models, and other documents and information about the California environment. A digital library infrastructure project at the University of Illinois will provide online access to engineering journals and other scientific publications. The University of Michigan Digital Libraries Research Project provides online access to multimedia information about earth and space sciences. The Alexandria Library Project at the University of California at Santa Barbara is developing a comprehensive range of digital library services for collections of spatially indexed and graphical information, such as digitized maps and air photos. The Informedia Project at Carnegie Mellon University is exploring retrieval methods for digital video collections dealing with science and mathematics. Project Mercury, an earlier digital library initiative at Carnegie Mellon, was designed to develop a campus-wide infrastructure for the electronic delivery of full-text and image documents to desktop computers installed in the library, in faculty offices, and in other locations.

Among other university-based projects, Columbia University has undertaken a variety of digital library initiatives, including online access to readings and art images that support undergraduate humanities courses. Also at Columbia, Project Janus was initiated in 1993 to provide online access to legal publications. At the University of Michigan, the JSTOR project is developing an online archive of scholarly journals. Project Open Book at the Yale University Library is converting selected microform collections to digitized images. The Networked Computer Science Technical Reports Library at Cornell University provides online access to documents produced by computer science departments and corporate and government research laboratories. An earlier Cornell project, the Chemistry Online Retrieval Experiment (CORE), created an online document collection derived from important scientific journals published by the American Chemical Society. The Perseus Project at Tufts University focuses on texts and images pertaining to ancient Greece. Since the late 1980s, Case Western Reserve University has been collaborating with IBM to define system requirements and management characteristics for a digital library to support the varied teaching and research activities of a large academic institution. Projects have involved the conversion of musical scores, medical reference works, engineering textbooks, radiographic materials, and art works. With funding from the Luce Foundation, Emory University has initiated a multiyear project to develop a prototype digital library and explore issues of cost, technology, user education, and governance.

As examples of the growing number of digital library initiatives and implementations outside the United States, the Centre for Experimental and Constructive Mathematics at Simon Fraser University in British Columbia provides online access to mathematics journals and related publications. The British Library's Electronic Beowulf Project provides digitized images of the Beowulf manuscript plus related manuscripts and other documents. The Corpus of Electronic Texts (CELT) program at the University College of Cork includes materials pertaining to Irish history and culture. In Switzerland, the RYHINER Project at the University Library of Berne has digitized manuscript maps and related documents from the Public Records Office in the Canton of Berne. The New Zealand Digital Library, operated by the University of Waikato, provides online access to computer science reports and bibliographies, as well as selected documents in other subject areas.

A number of professional organizations have been formed to address digital library issues and to develop strategies and procedures for digital library implementations. Examples include the previously mentioned Digital Library Federation, a consortium of large research libraries; the Center for the Study of Digital Libraries at Texas A&M University; the Task Force on Digital Libraries, established by the IEEE Computer Society; the Canadian Initiative on Digital Libraries, a consortium headed by the National Library of Canada; Nordinfo, which coordinates digital library activities among several Norwegian organizations; and the Digital Library Network, operated by the University of Library and Information Science in Japan.

Motives Underlying Digital Libraries

Digital library concepts and technologies offer significant potential for the improvement of library services while addressing certain problems traditionally associated with the management of library collections. Improved information retrieval and enhanced document delivery capabilities are widely encountered objectives of computer-based information systems in general and of digital library implementations in particular.

In conventional libraries, physical proximity to documents is a precondition for access and use. While online catalogs and other bibliographic databases can often be accessed from remote workstations located in offices, classrooms, or homes, users must visit the library to obtain required documents or arrange for physical delivery via mail or courier service. Addressing this limitation, digital library implementations provide online access to books, journal articles, and other library materials. When a search of an online catalog or reference database confirms the availability of a desired book or other publication, character-coded text or electronic page-images can be transmitted to remote workstations for display, printing, or other purposes. Software permitting, documents might also be routed to requesters by electronic mail.

Assuming the existence of appropriate local or wide area networking facilities, the physical location of materials in digital library collections is irrelevant. The online availability of character-coded text or electronic image representations of documents has been cited as a potentially important component of so-called virtual library implementations. Broadly defined, a virtual library relies on computer and communication technologies to provide rapid access to bibliographic citations as well as to the complete contents of books, journals, and other library materials. Virtual library users employ computer terminals or microcomputer-based workstations to request information that may be stored by a computer operated by the library to which the users are directly connected. In most cases, this will be an academic, public, school, or special library with which the user is associated through residence in a particular community, enrollment in a particular educational institution, or employment by a particular government agency, corporation, or other organization. If the required information is not available from the user's host computer, systems operated by other libraries or by other organizations, such as commercial information services, can be searched. This may be done automatically, in a manner that is transparent to the user, or interactively with the user's direct involvement. In the latter case, the user selects one or more computer systems from a displayed list, and a program launches searches based on the selections.

The virtual library concept is not new; transparent access to multiple library collections was proposed during the 1950s and 1960s, but available technology did not permit such arrangements. Prospects for practical implementations have improved, however, with the recent proliferation of data communication facilities and computer networks, particularly the Internet. In addition to providing online access and improving document delivery, digital library implementations provide useful retrieval capabilities that are impractical or impossible in conventional library environments. Through their database management components, text storage and retrieval systems and electronic document imaging systems can search database records for field values that contain specified character strings, either as complete words or as substrings within words. Term truncation, wildcard characters in search strings, and Boolean operations are widely supported. As a potentially attractive enhancement, text storage and retrieval technology can be implemented with full-text indexing, which permits retrieval of books, journals, or other library materials that contain designated words or portions of words. A user specifies a character string to be searched, and the text storage and retrieval system identifies documents that contain that character string.

Proximity commands can locate documents that contain two words within a specified number of words of one another. Depending on the system, users may be able to specify the sequence as well as the proximity of search terms. Some text storage and retrieval programs can locate two or more words that appear in the same sentence, paragraph, page, or other portion of a document. Hypertext capabilities may link interrelated documents, allowing words in previously retrieved text segments to be conveniently utilized as search terms. Users can request the display or printing of complete documents or of the specific text segments or pages in which search terms appear. With most text storage and retrieval systems, the search terms are highlighted—in bold characters, color, or reverse video—within displayed text. Some text storage and retrieval programs can rank documents for relevance based on the frequency of occurrence of search terms and their locations within documents.

A number of studies have examined the impact of full-text indexing on two widely utilized measures of retrieval effectiveness: recall (the ability to retrieve the maximum number of relevant documents) and precision (the ability to screen out irrelevant documents). These studies have generally concluded that searches based on the full texts of documents offer higher recall rates when compared to searches based on conventional subject headings. In particular, full-text searches can retrieve documents that cannot be retrieved by other methods, although some studies have observed a degradation of precision in applications that employ full-text indexing.

Retrieval advantages aside, digital library technologies can simplify the day-to-day maintenance and control of library collections. Since the 1960s, as discussed in chapter 6, libraries have used computer-based systems to keep track of materials in circulation; but such systems, while expensive to acquire and operate, cannot guarantee the timely return of circulating items. Books or other materials removed from the library may be misplaced, damaged by accident or through malicious intent, returned late, or simply never returned by borrowers. In a digital library, books and other materials do not circulate. Character-coded text or images of individual pages are transmitted electronically to retrieval workstations for display or printing. The integrity of library collections is maintained. Because digital library systems permit simultaneous access to information by multiple users, contention for library materials is eliminated and the continuous availability of documents is guaranteed. This is an important consideration for library materials in high demand, such as popular reference works or course-related readings maintained in an academic library's reserve room.

Among other advantages, certain labor-intensive housekeeping tasks, such as shelving newly acquired publications and reshelving items following their return from circulation, are eliminated in digital library implementations. Computer-processable versions of library materials are unaffected by reference activity. Unlike books or other paper documents, character-coded text and electronic document images cannot be damaged by frequent use or careless handling. Digital library technologies, particularly electronic document imaging, have consequently attracted considerable attention as alternatives to microfilming and conventional photocopying for document protection and preservation.

For many libraries, storage space is a scarce and expensive resource. Digital library implementations can dramatically reduce floor space requirements when compared to conventional shelf-type storage of books, journals, and other paper documents. Text storage and retrieval systems, in particular, have an unmatched ability to store large numbers of documents with impressive compactness. A six-by-nine-inch book page, for example, contains approximately 3,500 characters. Stored in character-coded form, that page will require 3,500 bytes of computer storage without full-text indexing or approximately 8,750 bytes with full-text indexing. A 300-page book will require approximately 1 megabyte of computer storage without full-text indexing or 2.5 megabytes with full-text indexing. One gigabyte (1 billion bytes) of computer storage can contain about 1,000 books (300,000 pages) without full-text indexing or 400 books (120,000 pages) with full-text indexing. Stored in paper form, 400 books will require approximately 50 linear feet of shelving, which will occupy about nine square feet of floor space. One thousand books will require approximately 125 linear feet of shelving, which will occupy about 22 square feet of floor space. For large document collections, significant reductions in floor space requirements are possible with high-capacity mass storage devices, such as magnetic disk arrays or optical disk autochangers (jukeboxes). The compaction offered by digital library implementations compares very favorably with microfilm recording, the traditional library technology of choice for space reduction.

CREATING DIGITAL LIBRARIES

The availability of books, journals, or other documents in machine-readable, computer-processible form is a precondition for digital library implementations. Some digital library initiatives have concentrated on information that is "born digitally"—that is, created originally and exclusively in computer-processible form. Examples include statistical data files, mapping data generated by geographical information systems, and machine-readable data generated by remote sensing devices, medical diagnostic equipment, and other scientific instrumentation. In many cases, "born digital" resources have no printed counterparts. Consequently, digital libraries that emphasize such information cannot be compared to conventional library collections.

Some digital library projects give users online access to character-coded text files or image databases that correspond to books, periodicals, and other library materials but are acquired in machine-readable form from publishers or other external sources. Examples include the UMLibText project at the University of Michigan; the Electronic Text Center, a collection of character-coded research materials at the University of Virginia; and the Center for Electronic Texts in the Humanities, a joint undertaking of Princeton University and Rutgers University. With the proliferation of word processing and computer-based typesetting systems since the 1970s, most publications are converted to character-coded form at some point in their production cycles. Few publishers, however, currently offer such computer-processible versions for sale to libraries. The full texts of journal articles, reports, and many other documents are contained in databases offered by online search services and CD-ROM publishers, but downloading of such materials in large quantities for use in digital library implementations is typically prohibited by copyright restrictions or user license agreements.

Unpublished research materials maintained by certain libraries are more likely to be readily obtainable in machine-readable form. Corporate or government libraries, for example, may be able to obtain word-processed versions of proprietary technical reports from the departments or other organizational units that created them. Similarly, university libraries can require doctoral degree recipients to submit word-processed versions of their dissertations for digital library implementations. Archives and manuscript repositories may be able to obtain word-processed versions of outgoing correspondence or other documents contained in office files or personal papers, but computer-processible versions are rarely available for documents that a person or organization receives from external sources. Even where such versions exist, format incompatibilities or damaged media may render them unusable for digital library implementations. As a significant additional complication, most libraries contain substantial backfiles of older publications and unpublished documents that predate computer technology. These materials, which exist only in human-readable form, must be converted to character-coded text or electronic images for computer storage and retrieval. Such conversion, which can involve formidable effort and high cost, is the most significant obstacle to digital library implementations.

Text-Based Implementations

In text-based digital library implementations, individual characters—letters of the alphabet, numeric digits, punctuation marks, and other symbols encountered in books, periodicals, or other library documents—are represented by distinctive, predetermined combinations of bits. In most cases, the American Standard Code for Information Interchange—the so-called ASCII code—defines the specific bit patterns that represent individual characters. Less commonly, the Extended Binary Coded Decimal Interchange Code (EBCDIC) may be utilized. As previously described, text-based implementations typically rely on prewritten text storage and retrieval programs, which are available from various vendors for many types of computers. Usually, computer hardware and text storage and retrieval software are purchased from different sources. Turnkey text storage and retrieval systems, consisting of preconfigured combinations of hardware and software, were available in the 1980s, but they are rarely encountered today. In many cases, a library already owns some or all of the hardware components required for text storage and retrieval implementations. Some of the integrated library systems discussed in chapter 6 offer text storage and retrieval components as optional application modules.

As with other aspects of library automation, the conversion of library materials to character-coded text involves a combination of fixed and variable costs. The purchase, lease, or rental of data entry equipment and, where required, software are the principal fixed cost components in document conversion operations. Depending on the system configuration, terminals or microcomputers may be used as data entry devices. As described in chapter 1, a terminal or microcomputer may be connected to a mainframe, minicomputer, or network server for direct key-entry in the online mode. Most text storage and retrieval programs permit such direct key-entry. Alternatively and more appropriately for books and other long documents, the entered information may be stored temporarily on a microcomputer's hard drive for batch transfer to a remote computer when an entire work has been converted or at predetermined intervals.

In any case, the conversion of library materials to character-coded text is a time-consuming, labor-intensive activity. Labor-based variable costs are associated with the following document conversion tasks:

1. Books, journals, or other documents to be converted to character-coded form must be removed from library shelves or other storage containers and transported to the data entry area. Depending on the application, documents may need to be checked for completeness or specific editions. When the data entry operations described below are completed, the documents must be returned to their original locations, transported to other storage areas, or discarded.

2. As discussed in chapter 1, data entry encompasses the following subtasks: (a) conversion of library documents to character-coded form by typing or other methods; (b) verification of the converted text to detect data entry errors;

and (c) correction of the detected errors, usually by overtyping them with the correct characters. Taken together, these subtasks are the most time-consuming and labor-intensive aspect of document conversion.

3. Supervisory labor is required for work scheduling, performance monitoring, problem resolution, and other control procedures.

As discussed in chapter 1, key-entry methodologies have dominated data entry operations since the inception of computing. To create character-coded text for use in digital library implementations, the contents of books, journals, and other library materials can be typed at a terminal or microcomputer. Operator skill, data entry procedures, source document characteristics, and other factors will affect input rates and, as a result, the time and cost of document conversion.

As outlined above, data entry work steps include verification and error correction as well as the initial typing of text. The purpose of verification is to detect errors committed during initial data entry. As explained in chapter 1, the most accurate approach to verification is double-keying, in which all information is entered twice and the second entry is compared to the first to detect discrepancies. While most often associated with the entry of field-oriented database records, double-keying is compatible with any type of information, including the complete text of books, journal articles, and other library documents. As previously discussed, however, double-keying will increase data entry time and labor requirement by a factor of about 2.3 when compared to single typing of information. As an alternative, proofreading of entered text requires less time. It will increase data entry labor requirements by a factor of about 1.6 when compared to single typing of information, but proofreading demands a high level of operator attentiveness and often leaves errors undetected.

To illustrate the extraordinary data entry time and labor requirements associated with text-based digital library implementations, assume that a university library wants to provide online access to 1,000 doctoral dissertations that are currently stored as typewritten copies in a special collections department. The full text of dissertations will be linked to bibliographic records in the library's online public access catalog. When the cataloging record for a given dissertation is retrieved during an OPAC search, the user will be given the option of viewing, downloading, or printing the dissertation itself. Dissertations average 300 double-spaced, typewritten pages in length, for a total of 300,000 pages to be converted. Assuming that pages contain 1,600 characters on average, initial conversion of the dissertations to character-coded text will require 480 million keystrokes. When double-keying and error correction are included, the total data entry workload rises to approximately 1.1 billion keystrokes. If data entry workers average 10,000 keystrokes per hour, the approximate conversion time will be 110,000 hours, the equivalent of 55 person-years. The conversion effort can be completed within five calendar years with a two-shift data entry operation employing six workers per eight-hour shift. If data entry operators are paid $10 per hour, the estimated labor cost for data entry, including verification and error correction, is $1.1 million or $1,100 per dissertation.

Taking another example, assume that a special library in a pharmaceutical company has a collection of 10,000 technical reports that contain proprietary information about the company's drug research and product development activities. The library wants to make the reports available through a corporate intranet to scientists and managers in offices and laboratories. The reports average 35 single-spaced, typewritten pages each for a total of 350,000 pages. Each page contains 3,200 characters on average. Initial conversion of the reports to character-coded text will require approximately 1.12 billion keystrokes. When double-keying and error correction are included, the total data entry workload rises to 2.58 billion keystrokes. If data entry workers average 10,000 keystrokes per hour, the required conversion time will be 258,000 hours (129 person-years). The conversion effort can be completed within five years with a two-shift data entry operation employing thirteen workers per eight-hour shift. At $10 per hour, the approximate labor cost for data entry, including verification and error correction, will be $2.58 million or $258 per report.

As a final example, assume that a liberal arts college wants to create a full-text digital library from a collection of 150,000 books. The full-text versions will be linked to bibliographic citations in the library's online public access catalog and will be retrievable through OPAC searches. The books average 300 pages each with 3,300 characters per six-by-nine-inch page. Initial conversion of the books to character-coded text will require approximately 149 billion keystrokes. When keystroke verification and error correction are included, the total data entry workload rises to approximately 343 billion keystrokes. To complete the conversion effort within five years will require a two-shift data entry operation with 1,715 workers per eight-hour shift. If data entry personnel average 10,000 keystrokes per hour, the required conversion time will be 34.3 million hours (17,150 person-years). If data entry operators are paid $10 per hour, the estimated labor cost for data entry, including verification and error correction, will be $343 million or $2,285 per book.

The labor costs estimated in the above examples can be reduced by replacing double-keying with proofreading, which may be performed more quickly than typing. Verification costs can be further controlled by strictly limiting the proofreading time per page. For a book page with 3,300 characters, for example, proofreading time might be limited to five minutes, which requires a sustained reading rate of 110 words per minute or 11 characters per second. At a typing rate of 10,000 keystrokes per hour, approximately twenty minutes would be required to type the same page. At these rates, substitution of proofreading for double-keying will reduce verification time and labor costs by 75 percent. Because initial key-entry and error correction work steps are unaffected by the verification method, however, total data entry time and labor costs will fall by about 35 percent. While that reduction is substantial, it will not necessarily make the document conversion effort more feasible; even with proofreading, the labor to convert 150,000 books to character-coded text will still exceed 22 million hours, which is equivalent to 11,000 person-years. Labor requirements aside, libraries contemplating proofreading as an alternative to double-keying must consider the potential for retrieval failures or other adverse consequences resulting from less effective error detection in converted documents, particularly where full-text indexing is employed.

The labor estimates presented above assume a straightforward conversion of documents to ASCII-coded form suitable for use with text storage and retrieval software. They do not include the time required to insert markup language codes that will format the converted text for Internet or intranet implementations. In such cases, additional labor will be required to enter markup codes and verify that text is correctly formatted.

As an alternative to in-house data entry for digital library implementations, books, journals, or other documents can be sent to a commercial service bureau for conversion to text. Such service bureaus are located in every North American city as well as in many less urbanized areas. One group of data entry service bureaus operates in countries—such as Mexico, China, the Philippines, Singapore, and Caribbean nations—where data entry workers are highly skilled and productive but wages are much lower than in North America. Such service bureaus are said to perform data entry "offshore," although they typically have a North American office that deals directly with customers. Regardless of location, most commercial service bureaus quote a data entry cost per 1,000 characters. That cost typically includes initial key-entry, verification of entered text by double-keying, and error correction. Shipping charges and the cost of recording media are usually additional. The converted documents are recorded as ASCII text files on magnetic tapes, diskettes, or other media specified by the customer. Some service bureaus can also perform HTML coding for Internet and intranet implementations.

To obtain a price quote for a specific application, a library can mail or fax copies of typical source documents to one or more service bureaus. Assuming that books, journals, or other documents can be sent away from the library for a period of time, commercial service bureaus can prove less expensive than in-house data entry. If source documents must be photocopied for shipment to the data entry service bureau, the cost savings will be reduced but not necessarily negated. As an additional advantage, use of a data entry service bureau can simplify logistics and reduce supervisory requirements for digital library projects.

Optical character recognition (OCR) is often cited as a labor saving alternative to key-entry for text-based digital library implementations. As defined in chapter 1, OCR is a computer input methodology that uses scanning technology and image analysis to identify or "read" characters contained in typewritten or printed documents. The recognized characters are converted to digitally coded text as if they had been key-entered. In digital library implementations, OCR operations begin with the preparation of documents for scanning. As described above, books, journals, and other library materials must be removed from shelves or other storage containers, transported to a scanning area, and, if necessary, checked for completeness or specific editions. Bound volumes often require special handling. For best results, they should be unbound or photocopied for scanning as individual pages. This increases preparation time, labor requirements, and cost when compared to preparation of library materials for key-entry.

Scanning speed ranges from less than one second per page to more than fifteen seconds per page, depending on document characteristics and the type of scanners and OCR software employed. Character recognition rates likewise vary. Some OCR products can process 7,000 or more letter-size, double-spaced pages per hour, which is about 1,000 times faster than key-entry by a full-time, experienced operator. With microcomputer-based OCR programs, recognition speed is partly determined by the microcomputer's hardware characteristics. With a high-speed microprocessor and ample random-access memory, recognition rates can exceed 100,000 characters per hour, the equivalent of 30 book pages per hour; that is more than 10 times faster than the average key-entry rate for a full-time, experienced operator.

Optical character recognition can reduce the time and labor required to convert books, journals, and other library materials to character-coded form, but OCR operations are not labor-free. The scanning and recognition rates cited above do not include the time required for preparatory and follow-up tasks. Pages must be loaded into or positioned on the scanner and removed when scanning is completed. While scanners can be equipped with automatic page feeders, they must be refilled periodically. Sheetfed scanners must be monitored for misfeeding of pages, jamming, and other equipment malfunctions. Improper page alignment, inadequate exposure, pages scanned upside down, or other problems will necessitate rescanning, which further degrades throughput. Assuming a scanning speed of six seconds per page, including time for page placement and removal, plus a recognition rate of 100,000 characters per hour (28 characters per second), an OCR system will require approximately 1.1 minutes to process a double-spaced, typewritten page. For the collection of 1,000 dissertations cited in the above example, the processing time for initial data entry will be 5,500 hours (2.75 person-years) as compared to 48,000 hours (24 person-years) for key-entry at 10,000 keystrokes per hour.

Comparable reductions in initial data entry time are attainable for other library materials. For single-spaced, typewritten documents, the combination of scanning time plus recognition time equals two minutes per page. For a collection of 10,000 technical reports averaging 35 pages each, the processing time for initial data entry by optical character recognition will be 10,000 hours (5 person-years) as compared to 112,000 hours (56 person-years) for key-entry at 10,000 keystrokes per hour. Assuming that pages are unbound or photocopied, the required OCR processing time for six-by-nine-inch book pages, including scanning and recognition, equals 2.1 minutes per page. For a collection of 150,000 books maintained by a college library, the processing time for initial data entry by optical character recognition will be 1.58 million hours (790 person-years) as compared to 14.85 million hours (7,425 person-years) for key-entry at 10,000 keystrokes per hour.

While conversion times for initial data entry via OCR are much lower than for key-entry, they are still formidable; even with OCR, initial data entry for a relatively small library collection can require many person-years to complete. In addition, the character-coded text produced by OCR programs must be verified and corrected. While the best OCR programs have impressive accuracy rates—99 percent or greater when recognizing books and journals, for example—accuracy must be confirmed through proofreading of recognized text. For that purpose, most OCR programs display text on a video monitor for operator examination and error correction. Unrecognizable or suspect characters are highlighted in color or marked with special symbols. A limited repertoire of word processing commands permits the correction of recognition errors through deletion, overtyping, and insertion of characters. While highlighted characters draw the operator's attention to possible errors, the entire content of each document must be verified for recognition accuracy. Because error correction is time-consuming and labor-intensive, OCR's cost advantage over other document conversion methodologies depends on high recognition accuracy, which is determined by document characteristics among other factors.

Image-Based Implementations

For digital library implementations, electronic document imaging technology can be acquired in several ways. Preconfigured electronic document imaging systems include all computer hardware and software components required for document imaging implementations. Such systems, which may be purchased or leased, include computer and peripheral devices as well as document imaging, indexing, and retrieval software. Available configurations range from single-workstation, microcomputer-based systems that are suitable for low-volume applications or demonstration projects to multiworkstation, networked systems that can satisfy complex, high-volume document management requirements. Alternatively, libraries can purchase prewritten document imaging software for use with separately purchased or leased computers and peripheral devices, some of which may already be owned by the library. Such software is offered by dozens of companies for many types of computers. The imaging software vendor specifies computer configuration requirements and provides a list of compatible imaging peripherals, such as document scanners, optical storage devices, and video monitors. Libraries can purchase the required hardware components at the best available price from the source of their choice.

As a variant approach to software-based implementation, electronic document imaging capabilities can be added as an enhancement to an existing computer application. As noted in chapter 4, the enhanced application is said to be "image-enabled." As an example, electronic document imaging capabilities might be added to an online public access catalog by linking page-images of books, journals, reports, or other library materials to bibliographic records that describe and index them. When OPAC users retrieve specific bibliographic records, they have the option of viewing or printing the document images. Some of the integrated library systems discussed in chapter 6 offer document imaging capabilities as an optional application module. Depending on the implementation method, electronic document images may be incorporated within an existing computer application; some database management systems, for example, can store document images as binary objects in fields of unlimited length. More commonly, database records and document images can be stored in separate computer files or by separate computer systems that are interlinked for retrieval purposes.

As part of their computer hardware configurations, electronic document imaging systems include special peripheral components for input, output, and storage of document images. Scanning workstations are the principal input devices in electronic document imaging implementations. The typical scanning workstation includes a document scanner with adapter boards and cables, a video monitor suitable for image inspection and index data entry, and software to support input tasks. Retrieval workstations must include bit-mapped video monitors with appropriate document display capabilities. Certain high-resolution bit-mapped monitors are specifically intended for electronic document imaging

A letter from George Washington to Thomas Jefferson stored as an image (a) and as character-coded text (b). The LC American Memory project makes versions available on the World Wide Web.

Letter George Washington to Thomas Jefferson, November 28, 1789

IMAGES

The Writings of George Washington from the Original Manuscript Sources, 1745-1799. John C. Fitzpatrick, Editor.--vol. 30

New York, November 30, 1789.

Dear Sir: You will perceive by the enclosed letter (which was left for you at the office of Foreign affairs when I made a journey to the Eastern States) the motives on which I acted with regard to yourself, and the occasion of my explaining them at that early period. Having now reason to hope, from Mr. Trumbulls report, that you will be arrived at Norfolk before this time (on which event I would most cordially congratulate you) and having a safe conveyance by Mr. Griffin, I forward your Commission to Virginia; with a request to be made acquainted with your sentiments as soon as you shall find it convenient to communicate them to me. With sentiments of very great esteem &c.[40]

[Note 40: From the original in the Jefferson Papers in the Library of Congress. (See note to Washington's letter to Thomas Jefferson, Oct. 13, 1789, ante.)]

applications. Configured with screens that measure 19 to 21 inches diagonally, they can legibly display a letter-size page in its entirety. Lower-resolution bit-mapped devices, such as VGA and SuperVGA monitors, are more widely available and much less expensive than high-resolution models, but they cannot legibly display a complete letter-size page. With low-resolution monitors, pages are displayed in a reduced-size format that is recognizable but not necessarily readable; that is, paragraphs and other formatting characters are detectable, but individual characters may not be legible. For character legibility, document images must be displayed in an enlarged partial-page format. In that mode, panning and scrolling commands are used to view specific page segments. While digital library implementations are designed to replace printed books with on-line access to computer-processible information, many users will require paper copies for reference or other purposes. Laser printers are typically used for hard copy output.

Electronic document images are usually stored on magnetic or optical disks. The latter may reside in jukebox units for unattended access. Compared to character-coded text, electronic document images will require much more storage space per page. Storage capacity requirements associated with specific library applications depend on several factors, including the linear dimensions of the documents from which electronic images are produced, the scanning resolution and scanning mode employed, and the effectiveness of compression algorithms in reducing the amount of information to be stored about each image. Typical storage requirements range from 50,000 to 60,000 bytes per single-spaced, letter-size page, which is fifteen to twenty times the amount of space required to store the same page in character-coded form. Storage requirements for images of large book pages can approach 100,000 bytes. Because they are densely printed, many library documents have limited compression potential; book pages, for example, are rarely double-spaced, and professional journal pages are often printed in two columns with narrow margins. Electronic images produced from library documents will typically require more storage space than images generated from office records.

As previously explained, books, journals, and other library materials are converted to computer-processable digitized images by document scanners. As computer input peripherals, most document scanners are designed for business applications. Their features and capabilities are well suited to digitization of the most commonly encountered office records: unbound letter-size pages containing dark, usually black, text or line art that is handwritten, typewritten, or printed on a light, usually white, background on one side of the page only. Compared to office files, library collections exhibit a greater variety of document characteristics.

While many office records are created internally, most library materials are acquired from publishers or other external sources. Libraries have no control over the physical and typographic attributes of such documents. Library materials may be smaller or larger than letter-size, and documents of different sizes are routinely intermixed within a library collection. A library's holdings may include leaflets, books, periodicals, newspapers, and maps. Regardless of document size, information may be printed on one or both sides of each page. Library documents may contain textual information in a variety of type fonts, sizes, and styles; within the same page of a scholarly book or journal, for example, section headings may be printed in a 14-point boldface style while footnotes appear as italicized text in 6-point type. Compound documents, which contain both text and graphics, are commonly encountered. Their graphic components may include bitonal line art, grayscale images, or color illustrations and photographs.

Photocopying and microfilming specialists have long recognized the special reprographic challenges posed by library materials. Books, journals, and other bound volumes dominate many library collections. Document conversion from bound volumes typically requires much greater time and effort than scanning of unbound documents. As a potentially significant constraint, flatbed scanners must be used. As described in chapter 1, a flatbed scanner features a flat exposure surface on which pages are individually positioned for scanning. Most flatbed scanners resemble desktop photocopiers in size, appearance, and operation. Pages are positioned facedown on a glass platen for digitization by optical and photosensitive components located beneath the glass.

While flatbed scanners can accommodate bound volumes, they are rarely optimized for that purpose. Decades of experience with photocopying of library materials have confirmed the cumbersome, time-consuming handling procedures associated with reproduction of bound pages. Bound volumes must be carefully and accurately positioned on the flatbed scanner's exposure surface in a manner that makes an entire page visible to the device's optical and photosensitive components. Few models have edge-mounted platens. As is the case with many photocopiers, bound volumes must be coerced into a flat position against the platen's glass surface so that information printed near the inner margins of pages can be exposed without distortion. Heavy or thick volumes, such as reference books or the bound annual volumes of scientific journals, can prove particularly awkward to align. Repeated exposures may be required to obtain satisfactory images. Unless two facing pages can be scanned in their entirety in a single exposure, time-consuming editing of digitized images will be required to remove portions of adjacent pages that were captured during the scanning process.

These complications can be avoided by unbinding books and other library materials for scanning as individual pages. As its principal advantage, unbinding simplifies and speeds document handling and page positioning. It also permits the use of sheetfed document scanners, which are often faster than flatbed models. Removal of bindings is unacceptable, however, where books, journals, and other documents must be returned to library shelves or otherwise retained in their original paper formats following scanning. As a less destructive alternative, bound materials can be photocopied to create unbound pages for scanning purposes. In some cases, a modest amount of photoreduction will permit the reproduction of two facing pages from a book or journal on a single letter-size sheet, thereby reducing the number of pages to be scanned. As its most obvious disadvantage, photocopying of library materials prior to scanning adds a time-consuming, labor-intensive work step to the document conversion process. Depending on the equipment employed, photocopying bound volumes can prove as cumbersome as scanning them. As a further constraint, the quality of photocopies may be inferior to the original pages, thus making it difficult to obtain usable digitized images.

Photocopying of library materials prior to scanning offers an additional, potentially significant advantage: It converts double-sided pages into single-sided ones. Most document scanners are simplex devices that digitize one side of a page at a time. They are intended for business applications where single-sided pages predominate. In library applications, however, two-sided pages are commonplace. With simplex scanners, two-sided pages must be turned over and repositioned to capture information contained on the reverse side. This procedure is time-consuming; it also prevents the use of automatic document feeders.

If photocopying of pages is not done prior to scanning, digital library implementations must address the problem of image capture from books, journals, and other two-sided documents. Vendors of electronic document imaging products provide several solutions. Some systems employ software-based techniques to simplify scanning of two-sided pages by simplex devices. The top sides of a stack of double-sided pages are scanned in sequence. The stack is then removed from the scanner, turned over, and the opposite sides scanned in reverse order. Software automatically links the related sides. Alternatively, duplex scanners can digitize both sides of a page in a single pass. Such devices employ sheetfed designs. They feature two sets of optical and photosensitive components located on opposite sides of the paper path. As their primary disadvantages, duplex scanners are more expensive than simplex models and they cannot scan bound volumes.

All scanners impose restrictions on the maximum size of input documents. With flatbed models, input size is constrained by the dimensions of the glass platen or other exposure surface on which documents are positioned for scanning. With the least expensive flatbed scanners, the glass platen measures approximately 9 by 12 inches, which is large enough to accommodate many but not all library materials. Flatbed scanners with larger exposure surfaces are available, but they are more expensive than letter-size models. Sheetfed scanners can usually accommodate larger pages than flatbed devices. Models capable of accepting A3-size pages (approximately 11 by 17 inches) are routinely available. They can accommodate many different types of library documents. The most commonly encountered book pages measure 7 by 10 inches or smaller. With the exception of certain art books, bound volumes rarely exceed A3-size. To digitize larger documents, libraries will require special equipment. Large-format sheetfed scanners are designed principally for engineering applications. They can accept drawings, maps, charts, and other documents measuring up to the international A0-size (approximately 36 by 48 inches).

The ability to obtain consistently legible results when scanning documents with highly varied typographic characteristics is an obvious concern for digital library implementations. A cursory examination of library materials will reveal a much broader range of type fonts, sizes, and styles than is likely to be encountered in office files. Scholarly journals and other research materials often contain text in small type sizes. In some cases, significant information is recorded in type sizes as small as 0.5 millimeter high. Although the total percentage of such characters in a given collection of library documents may be quite low, their legible reproduction is often essential.

The legibility of individual characters within electronic document images is directly affected by the scanning resolution employed in a particular implementation. As applied to electronic document imaging, resolution denotes the specific pattern and number of dots or pixels sampled during scanning of a given page. Resolution is typically expressed as the number of dots or pixels per inch within a scanned page. While scanning resolution is measured both horizontally and vertically, it is often identical in both directions. In such cases, one resolution measurement is stated and it is assumed to apply to both the horizontal and vertical dimensions of a scanned page.

As the scanning resolution is increased for a given page, the number of dots per square inch is correspondingly increased, while the size of each dot is decreased. A scanning pattern with small dots can capture finer details than a scanning pattern with large dots. Scanning resolution consequently determines the amount of detail in, and resulting sharpness of, electronic document images. Resolutions supported by available document scanners range from less than 100 dots per inch to more than 1,000 dots per inch, but that broad range is not supported by every device nor is it appropriate for every electronic document imaging application. In business applications, 200 dots per inch is generally considered the minimum scanning resolution compatible with consistently legible digitization of typewritten office documents and much printed material. For digital library implementations, however, a scanning resolution of 300 dots per inch or higher may be required for legible reproduction of footnotes or other small characters contained in certain research materials. Some image-based digital library projects employ scanning resolutions as high as 600 dots per inch. The suitability of a given resolution for a particular digital library implementation can be determined only by scanning a representative selection of library documents and examining displayed and printed representations of the resulting images.

While they offer increased image quality, high scanning resolutions pose several complications for digital library implementations. Scanning time is increased at higher resolutions. With most devices, a given page will require 50 percent longer to scan at 300 dots per inch than at 200 dots per inch. Labor requirements for the scanning portion of document conversion will increase correspondingly. Because higher scanning resolutions generate a greater number of dots per image, storage requirements and costs for digital library implementations will rise. If the scanning resolution is increased from 200 to 300 dots per inch, for example, the storage requirement for a given page will increase by a factor of at least 2.25, and the image recording capacity of a given storage medium will be reduced by at least 44 percent.

Many electronic document imaging implementations employ binary-mode scanning, in which a single bit encodes each pixel within a page. A pixel that reflects light in excess of a predetermined threshold amount is considered white and is encoded as a 0 bit. Where light reflectance values and their associated voltages are lower than a predetermined threshold value, the corresponding pixels are considered black and are each encoded as a 1 bit. With most documents, white pixels constitute the background areas of a page, while black pixels represent the information-bearing areas. Binary-mode scanning is appropriate for bitonal documents that contain textual information and line art, such as bar charts, graphs, scientific plots, and pen-and-ink illustrations. Most business documents, including office records and engineering drawings, are bitonal. Many library materials, however, contain photographs and illustrations that are printed in gray tones or colors. This is particularly the case with books, journals, and other publications in science, medicine, and the fine arts where narrative presentations are routinely supplemented by visual materials. Photographs and color illustrations are likewise commonplace in encyclopedias and other reference books.

With binary-mode scanners, grayscale or color pixels are encoded as either black or white, depending on their relative lightness or darkness. Where photographs or other gray areas within library documents convey essential information, some binary-mode scanners can operate in a halftone mode. Such devices employ a technique called "dithering" to simulate shades of gray by combining adjacent black and white pixels into blocks. Within each block, individual pixels are rendered in various combinations of black and white to give the appearance of gray areas. If the pixels within a given block are evenly divided between black and white, a medium shade of gray is simulated. Lighter or darker gray tones can be represented by adjusting the percentages of black and white pixels. Dithering will render color pixels as simulated gray tones. Color information is not encoded.

Dithering may yield usable images of library documents that contain occasional photographs or other grayscale representations. In such situations, a recognizable reproduction of broad features within a photograph is often acceptable. Where a more accurate reproduction of gray tones is required, true grayscale scanners utilize multiple bits to represent gray pixels. The number of gray shades that a given scanner can reproduce depends on the number of bits used to encode each pixel. Most grayscale devices operate in the 8-bit mode, which can encode 256 gray tones. For maximum flexibility, most grayscale scanners can also operate in the binary mode. The desired scanning mode is selected by the operator as page characteristics warrant. Some grayscale models also support dithering.

Grayscale scanners encode specific colors as shades of gray, depending on their tonality. Color-mode scanners can recognize and encode color information. Most models utilize 24 bits to represent colored pixels. Such devices can theoretically recognize and encode almost 16.8 million different colors, although the display devices and printers employed in electronic document imaging configurations cannot reproduce that variety of colors within a single image. Most color-mode scanners can also operate in the binary and grayscale modes. Once limited to expensive devices intended for sophisticated graphic arts applications, grayscale and color scanning capabilities are now widely available and highly affordable. Since the early 1990s, most manufacturers of binary-mode scanners have added one or more grayscale or color models to their product lines. The desktop publishing market, in particular, has stimulated sales volume for such devices.

While grayscale and color scanning can capture information that would be lost in the binary mode, they can have an adverse impact on other aspects of a digital library implementation. Electronic document images based on multibit grayscale or color coding schemes are larger and require more storage space than binary-mode images. All other things being equal, an 8-bit grayscale image will require eight times more storage space than an image of the same page scanned in the binary mode. Color mode images will require twenty-four times more storage space than an image of the same page scanned in the binary mode and three times more space than a grayscale image. As a further complication, grayscale and color scanning are usually much slower than binary-mode scanning.

As with the text-based digital library implementations discussed above, the conversion of books, journals, and other library materials to electronic document images involves a combination of fixed and variable costs. The purchase, lease, or rental of image capture equipment and related software are the principal fixed cost components in document conversion operations. Image capture requires scanning, image inspection, and data entry capabilities. Depending on the volume of documents to be converted and the procedures employed in a given digital library implementation, these image capture capabilities may be combined in a single workstation or embodied in separate devices. Labor-based variable costs are associated with the following document conversion tasks:

1. Books, journals, or other library materials to be converted to electronic document images must be removed from shelves or other storage containers and transported to a document conversion area. Depending on the application, documents may need to be checked for completeness or specific editions. In some cases, documents will be unbound or photocopied prior to scanning. When document conversion is completed, the documents will be returned to their original locations, transported to other storage areas, or discarded.

2. Image capture encompasses three subtasks: conversion of library documents to electronic images by scanning them; inspection of the resulting images, with rescanning as necessary; and entry of database records that contain index information for the converted documents. As discussed above, the data entry subtask encompasses initial entry of database records, which is typically performed by key-entry; verification of the entered information through double-keying or proofreading; and error correction.

3. Supervisory labor is required for work scheduling, performance monitoring, problem resolution, and other control procedures.

Of the variable cost components outlined above, the three image capture subtasks—scanning, inspection, and data entry—are the most time-consuming and labor-intensive. Scanning times attainable in a particular digital library implementation will depend on several factors, including equipment characteristics, the sizes of pages to be scanned, and the scanning resolution and digitization mode employed. Compared to flatbed scanners, sheetfed devices are usually faster and yield higher labor productivity. Pages can be inserted into a sheetfed scanner's transport mechanism at a much faster rate than they can be positioned on a flatbed scanner's glass platen. Positioning of bound volumes on a flatbed scanner can prove particularly time-consuming.

A scanner's rated speed is the elapsed time required to convert one page to an electronic document image, from the moment the page is positioned for scanning until digitization is completed. Rated speed is determined by a scanner's mechanical characteristics. In technical specification sheets or other descriptive documentation, manufacturers of document scanners cite rated speeds in seconds per page or pages per minute. In most cases, the indicated speeds assume a letter-size page digitized in the binary mode at a scanning resolution of 200 dots per inch. Because they have greater surface areas, large pages take longer to scan than small ones. As previously noted, binary mode digitization is faster than grayscale or color scanning. Because more pixels must be sampled, scanning time varies directly with the resolution applied to a given page.

Rated speeds of available scanners range from less than one second per page for high-volume models designed for centralized imaging departments and other production-intensive installations to more than ten seconds per page for low-volume devices intended for desktop publishing and other office applications with occasional scanning requirements. Mid-range scanners, with rated speeds of two to three seconds per page, are suitable for many digital library implementations. A scanner's rated speed, as defined above, measures just one part of the scanning process—the time required to sample pixels within a page. Scanning throughput, a more meaningful measure of scanning speed, is the time required to produce a serviceable digitized image from a scanned page. As a computer peripheral device, a document scanner is one component of a scanning workstation that also includes a computer, an image processing board, and software. The document scanner generates unformatted electronic images. The image processing board, or image processing software executed by the workstation's computer, performs digital coding, compression, enhancement, and other image manipulations required by a particular application. Scanning software formats electronic images for recording on designated magnetic or optical storage media. Operations performed by these workstations' components will have a significant impact on scanning throughput, which is invariably slower than a scanner's rated speed. Thus, a digital library implementation that employs a mid-range scanner with a rated speed of two to three seconds per page can expect scanning throughput of perhaps six to nine seconds per page. Several additional seconds will be required to position pages for scanning and remove them when scanning is completed.

Electronic document images may be inspected immediately after scanning or at a later time. In the former case, the scanning workstation's host computer displays successive images on a video monitor for operator examination. If the images are skewed, illegible, or otherwise unacceptable, the pages can be rescanned at once. As images are approved, they are recorded on magnetic or optical media. Alternatively, document scanning and image inspection may be performed at different times by separate workstations. Images are scanned in batches and stored in temporary files, pending inspection. Rejected images are deleted and the pages rescanned, either immediately or in subsequent batches.

In some digital library implementations, all electronic document images are individually examined. In other cases, inspection is applied to a predetermined percentage of images, selected randomly or according to predefined procedures. Regardless of methodology, the inspection time per page will depend on operator skill, the library's quality control expectations, and the characteristics, uniformity, and importance of the documents being scanned. Inspection personnel must determine that pages were scanned in the right reading position, that documents passed through the scanner without skewing or folding of edges or corners, and that no portions of the resulting images are obscured. Inspection personnel must also examine the displayed images for legibility. They must confirm that small typefaces are clearly resolved and that potentially troublesome information, such as faded text or light pencil marks, is adequately reproduced. If a displayed image does not satisfy the quality requirements defined for a given application, the page from which it was generated must be rescanned until satisfactory image quality is obtained or the page is judged to be unscannable.

The entry of index information for document images can be integrated with image inspection. When inspection is completed, the operator creates a database record that contains specified field values for the converted document. Key-entry is the most widely employed data entry methodology. Verification may be based on double-keying or proofreading, as previously discussed. Compared to text-based digital library implementations, electronic document imaging technology involves much less data entry. Where images of books, reports, or other documents are linked to bibliographic records in a library's catalog or another existing database, data entry is limited to a single field value, such as a document accession number, barcode number, or other unique identifier. In other cases, lengthier database records—including author, title, subject headings, and other bibliographic information—must be entered for each document.

In image-based digital library implementations, any aspect of document conversion—including document scanning, image inspection, and entry of index information—can be performed by the library itself or by a commercial service bureau. In the latter case, digitized images are produced from customer-supplied materials. The service bureau records the images and related index information on magnetic or optical media in a format compatible with the customer's electronic document imaging system. Service bureau charges depend on document characteristics, the volume of work to be performed, and other factors. Shipping charges and recording media costs may be embedded in per-page charges or quoted separately.

Conversion of library materials to electronic document images requires less labor, and will prove less costly, than conversion of the same materials to character-coded text. Image digitization is faster than key-entry or optical character recognition. Image inspection is faster than text verification. It obviously requires less labor to type and verify a small quantity of index information than to key-enter complete documents. To convert a collection of 1,000 dissertations totaling 300,000 pages to electronic document images will require about 700 hours for scanning, 2,500 hours for image inspection and any required rescanning, and 100 hours for key-entry, verification, and correction of index information, assuming that each dissertation is indexed with a 300-character database record that contains essential bibliographic information. At $10 per hour, the estimated labor cost would be $32,100 or $32.10 per dissertation. Assuming single-shift operation with two scanning workstations, the conversion can be completed within one year. As previously estimated, conversion of the same documents to character-coded text would require five years with double-shift operation and six data-entry workers per shift at a labor cost exceeding $1 million.

While less expensive than text-based implementations, image-based digital library conversions can prove time-consuming and costly in applications that involve large quantities of documents. Conversion of a library with 150,000 books totalling 15 million pages, for example, would require 100,000 hours for scanning, 375,000 hours for image inspection, and 450 hours for entry, verification, and correction of index information, assuming that data entry is limited to unique identifiers sufficient to link digitized images to bibliographic records in a library's online catalog. At $10 per hour, the estimated labor cost will exceed $4.75 million. With forty scanning stations and two-shift operation, the conversion will require two years to complete.

ISSUES AND CONCERNS

As an emerging area of library automation, digital library concepts and technologies offer excellent prospects for significant benefits for both library operations and library users, but they also raise serious issues and concerns. Foremost among these are issues of affordability and cost justification. As the preceding discussion indicates, digital library concepts and technologies can prove costly to implement. Ambitious digital library initiatives can require multimillion-dollar budgets, and that has been the case with some widely publicized projects. While required computer hardware and software components can be expensive, the high cost to convert library materials to the machine-readable form required for computer storage and online retrieval is a particular concern.

As with other aspects of library automation, economic concerns are often ignored by technology enthusiasts and early adopters. Cost calculation, affordability issues, and justification parameters are rarely examined at professional conferences or in publications dealing with digital library concepts and technologies. Many of the digital library initiatives and implementations described earlier in this chapter were conceived as demonstration projects. As such, they seldom address cost issues. Typically funded by government grants, educational foundations, corporate sponsors, or other external sources, rather than by library operating budgets, they are at least partially insulated from cost justification concerns. Adopting a research orientation, such projects are designed to examine the technical and logistic requirements for digital library implementations, along with the implications of digital library concepts for such non-technical issues as copyright protection, intellectual property rights, and equitable access by specific clienteles.

In any case, most of the digital library implementations undertaken to date are much too limited in scope to replace conventional library operations. They typically involve a relatively small collection of documents and serve narrowly defined user groups, such as faculty members in one university department or students enrolled in specific courses. Some implementations involve digital materials, such as computer databases or graphic files, that have no printed counterparts in library collections. While a number of industrial, government, and academic libraries have implemented text storage and retrieval systems and, more recently, electronic document imaging capabilities for operational applications, published descriptions of such implementations contain little, if any, information about costs. For library administrators, systems analysts, and others responsible for selecting and planning digital library implementations, however, reliable cost estimates are essential for budget preparation and cost-effectiveness analysis.

The high cost estimates presented in the preceding sections suggest that, for the foreseeable future, digital library implementations will require external funding or special appropriations. The annual operating budgets of most libraries have little, if any, excess funds that can be directed toward such costly projects. Digital library costs can be offset by savings, but the previously discussed benefits of digital library implementations include improved retrieval functionality and other considerations that are difficult to quantify for cost-justification purposes. It is unlikely that the substantial cost to convert library materials to machine-readable text or images can be quickly recovered through the elimination of circulation control or savings in floor space or library housekeeping operations. Such cost recovery, while possible in well-selected applications, can be realized only through accumulated savings over multiple years. As a further constraint, some digital library implementations coexist with conventional library collections, which must continue to be maintained and serviced for users who are unable or unwilling to access the machine-readable versions. To eliminate circulation control and reduce floor space requirements and housekeeping costs, digital library implementations must replace, rather than complement or supplement, existing library operations. Following conversion to text or images, library materials must be discarded or stored in less costly warehouse locations.

To reduce conversion costs, libraries should acquire digital library resources whenever possible, rather than creating them from their own collections. As previously discussed, libraries can obtain word processing versions of dissertations and proprietary research reports. A growing number of publishers offer digital text or image versions of journal articles indexed in popular databases. Such materials can be accessed through online services or CD-ROM information products. Full-text and image databases can also be acquired on magnetic tapes for implementation on an integrated library system or other local computer system. For the most part, however, such digital library resources emphasize recent issues of journals. Journal backfiles are seldom available for purchase in machine-readable form, nor are must books, reports, and other monographs in library collections. To convert such items to machine-readable form, libraries should consider cooperative projects that will spread the formidable effort and high cost of conversion among multiple institutions.

Further, libraries should concentrate on high-impact applications when planning and selecting materials for digital library implementations. Conversion of entire library collections is prohibitively expensive and has limited value; printed works and microforms remain appropriate for many reference and research requirements. In business, text storage and retrieval and electronic document imaging technologies are usually applied to office records and other documents that are referenced frequently to support important operations. By contrast, many digital library implementations involve archival documents, manuscripts, photograph collections, and other specialized research materials that are important but have limited audiences. Other applications might benefit a broader user community. In an academic library, for example, a digital library implementation can make reserve room materials conveniently accessible to commuting students, who may work full time and have limited opportunity to visit the library. Increasingly, the integrated library systems discussed in chapter 6 offer such "electronic reserve room" capability as an optional application module. Similarly, digital library implementations can provide library support for off-campus courses, which may be taught in secondary schools, hotels, military bases, or other locations that lack appropriate library collections. They can also support the growing number of interactive courses offered by academic institutions. Special libraries in business, government, and other organizations can use digital library implementations to deliver essential reference and research materials to users' desktops. In a pharmaceutical company, as previously noted, scientists can have online access to text or image versions of proprietary research reports required to support drug discovery, development, or testing. In a hospital, physicians and nurses can have online access to reference materials that contain diagnostic information or treatment protocols. In a manufacturing company, engineers and managers can have online access to project reports, standard operating procedures, and other technical documents.

Cost aside, digital library implementations raise questions and concerns about copyright and intellectual property. Conversion of certain publications to machine-readable form will require permission from copyright holders. Where large numbers of publications are involved, such permissions can require considerable time and effort to obtain. Copyright holders may be reluctant to make their publications accessible over computer networks, where use is difficult to control and prohibitions on local copying or downloading are difficult or impossible to enforce. Digital library implementations also pose problems for bibliographic instruction. While graphical user interfaces simplify retrieval operations, some user orientation and training will be required to describe available information resources and explain retrieval procedures. This can be accomplished through instructional sessions, written materials, or help screens.

SUMMARY

While some publications equate digital libraries with networked computer systems and online databases, a narrower focus defines a digital library as a library that maintains all, or a substantial part, of its collection in computer-processible form as an alternative, supplement, or complement to the conventional printed and microfilm materials that currently dominate library collections. A digital library can be accessed online by authorized persons through local or wide area computer networks. Once accessed, materials from a digital library's collection can be displayed, printed, downloaded, or otherwise manipulated to satisfy particular users' requirements. While they imply a revolutionary approach to library management, digital library concepts and technologies are more accurately characterized as evolutionary developments. Libraries have been creating, maintaining, and using computer-processible information for decades. The finding aids that support library collections are increasingly computerized. Computer-based management of the collections themselves is the logical next step in library automation.

The concept of a digital library has a long history in library literature and professional practice. Early experiments with computer-based indexing of microforms were eventually supplanted by completely computerized systems that stored library materials as character-coded text or electronic document images. Practical implementations of text-based and image-based digital libraries date from the 1970s and 1980s. Since the early 1990s, a number of libraries and related information agencies in the United States and elsewhere have initiated digital library projects. Academic libraries have implemented digital libraries to obtain a wider audience for unique research materials, such as archives and manuscripts, and to facilitate access to items in high demand, such as reserve room materials or core collections of required readings that support specific curricula or instructional programs. Public library projects have emphasized local history materials. Government library implementations provide online access to government publications and public records. Corporate libraries have targeted proprietary materials, such as technical reports, that support specific research activities. A number of professional organizations have been formed to address digital library issues and develop strategies and procedures for digital library implementations.

Digital library concepts and technologies offer significant potential for the improvement of library services while addressing certain problems traditionally associated with the management of library collections. Digital libraries provide online access to books, journal articles, and other library materials. When a search of an online catalog or reference database confirms the availability of a desired book or other publication, character-coded text or electronic page-images can be transmitted to remote workstations for display, printing, or other purposes. Assuming the existence of appropriate local or wide area networking facilities, the physical locations of materials in digital library collections are irrelevant. Digital library concepts also support virtual library implementations, which provide transparent access to multiple library collections. Among their other advantages, digital libraries support a variety of advanced retrieval capabilities. They can also simplify the day-to-day maintenance and control of library collections, reducing costs in the process.

The availability of books, journals, or other documents in machine-readable, computer-processable form is a precondition for digital library implementations. Some digital library initiatives have concentrated on information that is "born digitally"—that is, created originally and exclusively in computer-processable form. Others give users online access to digital versions of books, periodicals, and other library materials that are acquired in machine-readable form from publishers or other external sources. In many cases, however, libraries must convert books, periodicals, or other materials from their collections to character-coded text or electronic images for computer storage and retrieval. Such conversion, which can involve formidable effort and high cost, is the most significant obstacle to digital library implementations.

In text-based digital library implementations, books, periodicals, and other materials can be converted by key-entry or optical character recognition. In image-based implementations, documents are digitized by scanners. In both text-based and image-based implementations, documents are linked to bibliographic records in a library's online catalog or other database. When database records are retrieved, users are given the option of viewing or printing their associated documents.

As an emerging area of library automation, digital library concepts and technologies offer excellent prospects for significant benefits for both library operations and library users, but they also raise serious issues and concerns. Foremost among these are issues of affordability and cost justification. Digital library concepts and technologies can prove costly to implement. Most digital library projects are consequently funded by grants or special appropriations. To reduce conversion costs, libraries should acquire digital library resources whenever possible, rather than creating them from their own collections. Further, libraries should concentrate on high-impact applications when planning and selecting materials for digital library implementations. In addition to cost issues, digital library implementations raise questions and concerns about copyright, intellectual property, and user training requirements.

Index

William Saffady is a Professor in the Palmer School of Library and Information Science, Long Island University, where he teaches courses in various aspects of information management, including library automation. He previously held faculty positions at the State University of New York at Albany, Vanderbilt University, Pratt Institute, and Wayne State University. Professor Saffady is the author of over three dozen books and many articles on information management topics. In addition to teaching and writing, he serves as a consultant, providing training and analytical services to corporations, government agencies, and other organizations.